Bigelow's Printer
Troubleshooting
Pocket Reference

Bigelow's Printer Troubleshooting Pocket Reference

Stephen J. Bigelow

McGraw-Hill

New York   San Francisco   Washington, D.C.   Auckland   Bogotá
Caracas   Lisbon   London   Madrid   Mexico City   Milan
Montreal   New Delhi   San Juan   Singapore
Sydney   Tokyo   Toronto

Library of Congress Cataloging-in-Publication Data

Bigelow, Stephen J.
   Bigelow's printer troubleshooting pocket reference / Stephen J.
Bigelow.
      p.   cm.
   Includes index.
   ISBN 0-07-135420-4
   1. Computer printers—Maintenance and repair handbooks,
manuals, etc.   2. Computer printers handbooks, manuals, etc.
I. Title.
TK7887.7.B53797   2000
004.7'7—dc21   99-27803
                                     CIP

McGraw-Hill

*A Division of The **McGraw·Hill** Companies*

ISBN 0-07-135420-4

*The sponsoring editor for this book was Michael Sprague, the edit-
ing supervisor was Curt Berkowitz, and the production supervisor
was Claire Stanley. This book was set in Century Schoolbook by
Priscilla Beer of McGraw-Hill's Professional Book Group composi-
tion unit, in cooperation with Spring Point Publishing Services.*

Printed and bound by R. R. Donnelley & Sons Company.

This book is printed on recycled, acid-free paper containing a minimum of 50% recycled, de-inked fiber.

Disclaimer and Cautions

It is *IMPORTANT* that you read and understand the following information. Please read it carefully!

Personal Risk and Limits of Liability

The repair of personal computers and their peripherals involves some amount of personal risk. Use *extreme* caution when working with ac and high-voltage power sources. Every reasonable effort has been made to identify and reduce areas of personal risk. You are instructed to read this book carefully *before* attempting the procedures discussed. If you are uncomfortable following the procedures that are outlined in this book, *do not attempt them*—refer your service to qualified service personnel.

NEITHER THE AUTHOR, THE PUBLISHER, NOR ANYONE DIRECTLY OR INDIRECTLY CONNECTED WITH THE PUBLICATION OF THIS BOOK SHALL MAKE ANY WARRANTY, EITHER EXPRESSED OR IMPLIED, WITH REGARD TO THIS MATERIAL INCLUDING, BUT NOT LIMITED TO, THE IMPLIED WARRANTIES OF QUALITY, MERCHANTABILITY, AND FITNESS FOR ANY PARTICULAR PURPOSE. Further, neither the author, publisher, nor anyone directly or indirectly connected with the publication of this book shall be liable for errors or omissions contained herein, or for incidental or consequential damages, injuries, or financial or material losses resulting from the use, or inability to use, the material contained herein. This material is provided AS IS, and the reader bears all responsibilities and risks connected with its use.

Contents

List of Symptoms

Printers under Windows

Windows 3.1x Symptoms

Impact Printer Troubleshooting

Head/ribbon Symptoms

Ink-jet Printer Troubleshooting

Laser Printer Troubleshooting

Application-related Symptoms

Setup and Configuration

Printers are some of the hardiest and most reliable peripherals available for a personal computer. Unfortunately, they are hardly as foolproof as they used to be. Years ago, using a printer was simply a matter of making one simple connection to the PC, then powering the system on—the DOS-based applications themselves managed your fonts, graphic characters, and so on. With the proliferation of powerful, high-resolution printers under Windows 98, users are now faced with many more factors to consider: resolutions and page speeds are increasing; color (in both ink-jet and laser) printers now play an important role in offices; and Windows drivers can vastly affect your overall printing performance, and so on. As printers have become more complicated, so have the issues involved in selecting, connecting, and configuring a typical printer.

Selecting a Printer

Most new printers are still considered to be reasonably inexpensive, but selecting the *right* printer for your particular needs is often more difficult than it seems. Specifications are usually confusing and frequently misunderstood. There's a lot to consider when shopping for a new or used printer (besides just the price) but the most important issues are outlined below:

Resolution.   A printer's *resolution* is generally given as "dots per inch" (dpi). This specification denotes just how complex your image can be. Higher resolutions result in finer, more detailed images (but each page takes longer to print and requires far more printer memory). An inexpensive laser printer can achieve 600×600 dpi, resulting in excellent images. More sophisticated printers can reach 1200×1200 dpi, but these printers command a premium price. Ink-jet printers often use "uneven" resolutions such as 720×360 dpi or higher. The highest-resolution color printers can produce images that are indistinguishable from glossy photographs. If you typically use a printer for basic text and bitmap graphics, you can usually save some money and opt for a lower resolution. If you plan on producing high-quality graphics (i.e., Corel images), invest the money and select a high-resolution model.

Memory.   Image data sent to the printer are stored in a printer's *memory* until they can be processed into a printed image. Since impact and ink-jet printers form their images one line at a time, they require relatively little onboard memory (even for high resolutions). But laser printers form their images a whole page at a time, so there must be enough memory in the printer to hold every "dot" on a given page. Since higher resolutions provide substantially more "dots," a high-resolution laser printer may need as much as 64 MB (sometimes even more) to hold a complete image. If there is not enough memory to hold an image, a "memory overrun" error is generated. In actual practice, you'd need to add memory, scale the image size down, or reduce the printer's resolution in order to print the image. If you plan on basic text and images, you should be fine with 4–12 MB. If you're doing medium-quality graphics work (around 600 dpi), select a laser printer with at least 24 MB. For high-end images or "pre-press" work (1200 dpi), go with a minimum of 48 MB.

Throughput. Page speed defines the number of "pages per minute" (ppm) generated by a printer. Moving-carriage printers (such as impact or ink-jet) generally produce slower page rates (i.e., 2–6 ppm) because the print head moves back and forth. Laser printers typically run faster (6–15 ppm) since the entire page is printed at the same time. Color printers tend to run slower than monochrome printers. Printers used in an office environment—especially network printers—should have a faster throughput. Small-office and home printers with lighter printing demands can often accept slower, less-expensive printers.

Color. Printers are available in color and monochrome models. Monochrome printers are fine for all types of text and most graphics—even color separations for commercial printing. Color printers allow high-quality graphics and photographs that can easily be integrated into reports, sales presentations, and other materials. Color printers are typically slower and more expensive to operate than monochrome, so you should print in color *only* when necessary (keep the printer in "black/monochrome only" mode when printing text).

Media handling. Current printers handle more than just paper—transparencies, photo paper, envelopes, and index media are just a few of the media types that your printer might handle. If you plan on using specialized media, make sure that your printer will accept them.

Operating cost. Every printer costs a certain amount of money to operate. For example, the EP/toner cartridge for a Lexmark Optra R costs about $200 (US), but lasts for 4000 pages—this translates to about $0.05 per page. By contrast, a color ink-jet cartridge for a Brother color printer runs about $39 (US), but lasts for only about 100 pages—this is about $0.39 per page. Printing volume will have an effect on operating costs, so the more you run your printer, the more expensive it will be. You should also make sure that the media (i.e., toner or ink cartridge) for your printer is readily available.

Drivers. Printer performance is closely related to the quality of the drivers, so it's important that you have the latest driver versions for Windows 95/98. If you cannot locate current drivers on the printer maker's Web site, it may be difficult to keep the printer at peak performance when upgrading the operating system. Older printers may have difficulty after upgrading from Windows 3.1x.

Making It Work

Once you select a printer, the challenge is to make it work. The process generally involves unpacking the printer, connecting it to the PC, installing drivers, then testing the unit. If you've worked with printers before, these steps will probably look quite familiar, but you may find some interesting guidance in the steps below:

Get an adequate printer cable. Most current printers utilize an IEEE-1284 parallel port, and this means the PC's LPT port should be configured for ECP (or EPP) operation. You should also be sure to use a high-quality shielded printer cable less than 6' (slightly less than 2 meters) in length. It's fine to use an IEEE-1284 cable even if the printer port is set for an older "standard" or "bidirectional" mode.

Use a properly wired electrical outlet. Printers require adequate and "clean" power, so make sure that the location where you plan to use the printer is not overloaded with high-energy electrical devices (such as motors or air conditioners). The ac outlet should also be properly wired and grounded for safety.

Plan the location carefully. A printer typically requires several inches of clearance on each side once it's on the desk—this is necessary to ensure proper ventilation. Crowding the printer with other devices may result in overheating, and eventually cause the printer to malfunction. Of course, the printer should always be situated on a flat and stable surface.

Save your packaging. Unpack the printer carefully and be sure to set the packaging materials aside. If you need to return the printer for service, transport it to another location, or store it later, you can reuse that packaging. Once the printer is out of its packaging, you should remove any protective inserts, guards, or straps. Set them aside also. If there are clear plastic films covering your control panel and display, you should remove and discard them now.

Install your media. When the printer is in place, carefully install the toner or ink cartridge, then insert the paper, transparencies, labels, or other materials. Remember that the media must be appropriate for your particular printer.

Run a printer self-test. Before you connect the printer to the host computer, run a self-test to verify that the printer itself is in proper working condition. If there are problems in the self-test, you'll know that the problem is localized to the printer rather than the PC.

Connect the printer. Once you've tested the printer, power down the printer (and PC), then connect the

printer cable between the printer and the host computer. Power up the printer, then boot the computer. If
the printer is compatible with Plug-and-Play (PnP)
technology, Windows will detect the printer and allow
you to install the printer drivers from the printer's
software diskette(s). If Windows does not detect the
printer, you can add the printer manually using the
Add Printer wizard.

Switchbox Guidelines

The mechanical parallel port "switchbox" remains a
very popular tool for sharing several printers with the
same host computer, or allowing multiple parallel port
devices to share the same system. However, today's
intelligent parallel port devices place special demands
on the computer's parallel port since each device usually expects certain "initialization" data from the computer. Improper switchbox use frequently results in
data corruption to one or more parallel devices. Many
mechanical switchboxes can also prevent a parallel
port device from sending vital data back to the computer. If you're using a mechanical switchbox, be sure
to follow these guidelines:

- Never switch the box while your printer is spooling
  or receiving data. Always wait for the devices to be
  idle before switching.

- Never switch a parallel port device to a host computer that is off, then turn the computer on. A PC
  that's off can appear to send data (because of "float-
  ing" logic levels in the parallel port). Turn the computer on *before* turning on the parallel port
  device(s).

- Use a surge protector on each parallel port device.
  This prevents any power anomalies from passing
  from the parallel port device to the PC.

- Install driver software *only* for each particular device. Avoid the use of bidirectional utilities such as status monitors, remote controls, or status windows. These utilities expect regular communication with their respective parallel port device, and may report errors incorrectly if the switchbox is set to a different device.

- If you require full bidirectional capability from your parallel port devices, you might consider a new printer sharing device that fully supports bidirectional communication, or configure devices where the printer daisy-chains to a device providing a "passthrough" printer port.

- Finally, you can ensure that your parallel port device is working properly by removing the switchbox and connecting it directly to the PC. If the problem persists, replace the parallel port cable.

Fixing garbled print

Although switchboxes are generally regarded as simple and straightforward devices, they are hardly foolproof. Many printers and parallel port devices do not operate properly through a switchbox, and this often manifests itself as some form of "garbled print." If you are unable to print through the switchbox (or you're getting garbled print), try the following steps to help isolate the problem:

- *Check your cables*. Unplug both ends of the parallel cable between the PC and the switchbox, then carefully plug them back in. Do the same thing with the cable between the switchbox and the printer.

- *Try different cables*. If a direct connection doesn't work either, try a different cable.

- *Consider cable length*. Parallel cables should never be longer than 6 meters (approximately 20 feet) or

10 meters (approximately 33 feet) if you buy high-quality IEEE-1284 cables. If the cables are long, try using shorter ones.

■ *Check for data.* Try printing to LPT1.DOS to see that data are actually being sent.

■ *Tweak the document.* Reduce the complexity of the document or lower the printer resolution through the printer driver.

■ *Consider your driver.* Check the settings in your printer driver and adjust them if necessary, or try another compatible printer driver (i.e., an "emulation" driver) for your particular printer.

■ *Consider the switchbox.* Call the manufacturer of the switchbox for further help, or try another switching device.

> **NOTE:** Remember that damage to the printer's parallel port that is caused by a switching device is usually *not* covered under the printer's warranty.

Switchbox alternatives

On occasion a switchbox simply will *not* work. It may be that the switchbox doesn't support the bidirectional communications needed by the device, or that more than one device needs to initialize at boot time, but the switchbox can support only one at a time. In either case, you generally have three alternatives:

1. Try an electronic "printer sharing device" in place of the switchbox. This is a more expensive option than the switchbox, but usually prevents having to mess with the PC.

2. In cases where two PCs currently share one printer, utilize the second (alternate) port(s) on the printer—if the printer is so equipped.

3. In cases where one PC shares two printers (or par-

allel port devices), install another parallel port on the PC. But be careful: the IRQ used by LPT2 (IRQ5) is typically used by the sound card also.

Managing Printer Drivers

You'll certainly want to get the best possible performance from your printer once it's up and running, and this normally means managing your *printer drivers*. New printers need the correct drivers (or an acceptable emulation driver). Existing printers may need driver updates as bugs and compatibility issues are worked out. This part of the section guides you through the proper procedures for checking, installing, and updating your printer drivers under Windows 95/98.

Check the printer "Properties"

Printer property settings define the way in which your printer is configured and used by printing applications (such as Microsoft Word or Lotus 1-2-3). As a consequence, incorrect printer property settings can cause poor or incomplete output, or may cause your printer not to print at all. Check your printer properties as shown below:

- Click *Start*, select *Settings*, then click *Printers*.

- Right-click the printer you want to check, and then click *Properties*.

- Review the *Properties* dialog (Figure 1.1) and verify that the printer properties (such as printer memory and paper size) are correct.

- Once you're confident that the printer is configured properly, you can print a test page using the *Test Page* button, or simply click *Cancel* to close the dialog.

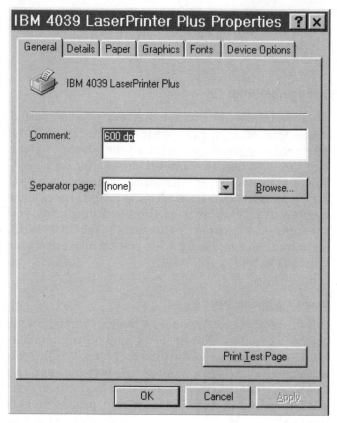

Figure 1.1 A typical printer *Properties* dialog.

Installing a new printer driver

Although the newest generation of printers are PnP-compatible and can be identified automatically, most "traditional" printers must be specified manually under Windows 95/98. You may also need to reinstall printers that you've removed previously, or replace printer drivers after a system crash. To install a new printer, follow these steps:

■ Click *Start*, select *Settings*, and then click *Printers*.

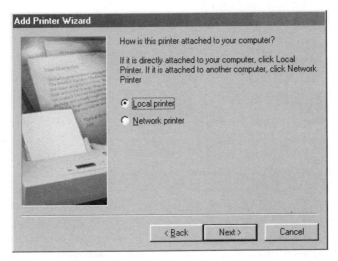

Figure 1.2 Choosing the printer type.

- Double-click the *Add Printer* icon, and then click *Next*.

- Click *Local Printer* or *Network Printer* as appropriate (Figure 1.2), and then click *Next*.

- If you click *Network Printer*, you are prompted for the network path for the printer. If you do not know the correct path, click *Browse*, or check with your network administrator. Click either *Yes* or *No* in response to *Do you print from MS-DOS-based programs?,* and then click *Next*.

- Click the appropriate manufacturer and model for your printer (Figure 1.3). If you have specific drivers (or new/upgraded drivers) for your printer, click the *Have Disk* button and specify the path to those new drivers; otherwise, click *Next*.

- If you chose to install a local printer, click the correct port (Figure 1.4). If you need to configure the printer port, click the *Configure Port* button. Then click *Next*.

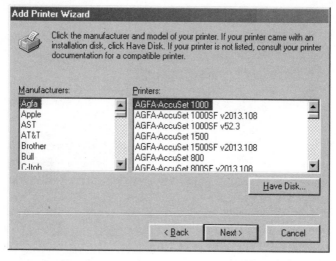

Figure 1.3   Selecting printer make and model.

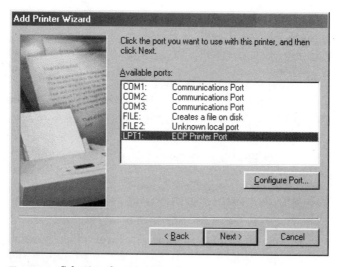

Figure 1.4   Selecting the printer port.

- Type a name for the printer (or accept the default name), and then click either *Yes* or *No* when asked *Do you want your Windows-based programs to use this printer as the default printer?* Click *Next*.

- To print a test page, click *Yes*, then click *Finish*. If the test page prints correctly, you can be certain that the printer should be ready to operate under Windows.

Updating printer drivers

From time to time, a printer's manufacturer (or even a third-party company like Microsoft) may release a printer driver that fixes certain bugs, improves printer performance, or addresses hardware compatibility issues. When new drivers become available, you'll need to download those drivers from the Internet and update the printer driver(s) currently on your system. To install an updated printer driver, follow these steps:

- Click *Start*, select *Settings*, and then open the *Control Panel*.

- Double-click the *Add New Hardware* icon.

- In Windows 95, click *Next*, click *No*, and then click *Next*.

- In Windows 98, click *Next*, and then click *Next* again to search for Plug-and-Play devices. If the device you are installing is not found, click *No, the device isn't in the list*, click *Next*, click *No, I want to select the hardware from a list*, and then click *Next*.

   NOTE: If Windows 98 finds your hardware when it searches for Plug-and-Play devices, click *Yes, the device is in the list*, click the device in the list, click *Next*, and then click *Finish*.

- Click the type of hardware for which you are installing the driver, click *Next*, then click *Have Disk*.

- Type the path for your new driver and click *OK*, click *Browse*, and locate the driver. Type the path for (or locate) the OEMSETUP.INF file from the manufacturer.

- In the dialog box displaying the .INF file, click *OK*, then click *OK* to continue.

- Click the correct driver and click *OK*, then click *Finish*.

- If the new hardware is Plug-and-Play compatible, you'll need to click *Next* and then click *Finish*.

Changing the printer's emulation

Most printers have one or more "emulation modes" that allow you to print with a different printer driver. For example, a Lexmark laser printer may emulate a Hewlett-Packard LaserJet, so you'd be able to use an HP LaserJet driver if a current Lexmark driver was not available (refer to the printer's documentation or manufacturer's Web site to learn which emulation modes are available for your particular printer). Remember that you may also need to adjust a setting on the printer's control panel in order to set its emulation mode. You can install the emulation driver with the *Add Printer* wizard (as if you were *Installing a new printer driver* as shown earlier). In many cases, you may be forced to use an emulation driver for older printers where a current (i.e., Windows 98) printer driver is not yet available from the manufacturer, or when the manufacturer's driver causes compatibility problems.

Try reinstalling the printer driver

If the printing problem seems to be corrected by using a different printer driver (i.e., using the printer in an "emulation mode"), you can try removing and reinstalling the currently available printer driver:

- Click *Start*, select *Settings*, then click *Printers*.

- Right-click the printer you want to remove, then click *Delete*.

- If you are prompted to remove all the files associated with the printer, click *Yes*.

- Again click *Start*, select *Settings*, then click *Printers*.

- Double-click the *Add Printer* icon, then follow the instructions in the *Add Printer* wizard to reinstall the Windows 95/98 printer driver from scratch.

Try the generic/text driver

When you have problems printing in Windows 95/98, but you don't have a newer/alternate driver available, try the Generic/Text Only printer driver in order to confirm the printer's operation:

- Click *Start*, select *Settings*, then click *Printers*.

- Double-click the *Add Printer* icon, and follow the instructions in the *Add Printer* wizard to install the Generic/Text Only printer driver.

- Try to print from your application with this driver.

Remember that a generic driver will *seriously* curtail your printer's features, so if the generic driver works, you should consider obtaining a new or suitable alternate driver for the printer, or replace the printer with a different model as soon as possible.

Try an alternate LPT.VXD file for Windows 95

Windows 95 may experience printing problems because of an older LPT.VXD file left over from Windows 3.1. Typical problems may take one of three forms:

1. You cannot print (or you receive timeout error messages) on recent Compaq computers when you print to any bidirectional printer.

2. You experience problems printing to any bidirectional printer on a computer with a PS/2-style LPT port (symptoms include an extra page being printed or PCL commands appearing on the printout).

3. You cannot use *Device Manager* to set an ECP port to run in standard LPT mode.

There is an alternate LPT.VXD file for Windows 95 that may resolve such problems. The alternate LPT.VXD file is located in the `\Drivers\Printer\Lpt` folder on the Windows 95 CD. To install the alternate LPT.VXD file, use Windows Explorer to rename the LPT.VXD file in the `\Windows\System` folder to LPT.OLD. Next, copy the LPT.VXD file from the `\Drivers\Printer\Lpt` folder on the Windows 95 CD to the `\Windows\System` folder on the hard disk. Now restart Windows 95 so that the new LPT file will take effect.

> **NOTE:** The alternate LPT.VXD file has the same file size and date as the original file. The version number of the alternate LPT.VXD file is 4.00.503 or 4.00.951 (you can determine the version number by right-clicking the LPT.VXD file and then clicking *Properties*).

Tips for printing .PRN and .PS files

You may find yourself faced with printing files that contain raw printer data (generally termed .PRN or .PS) files under Windows. This can be a handy trick when you need to print raw printer data. In most cases, these raw data files are created using programs using a PCL or PostScript driver. The .PRN files are typically created using a PCL printer driver, whereas .PS files are normally created using a PostScript printer driver. To print from a DOS command prompt, type the following line (where <x> is the correct LPT port number such as LPT1):

```
copy <path><filename.ext> LPT<x> /B
```

To enable "Drag and Drop" printing for .PRN or .PS files, try these steps:

- Use any text editor (such as Notepad) to create a file called PRINTER.BAT, and add the following line (where <x> is the correct LPT port number such as LPT1):

```
copy %1 lpt<x> /b
```

- Save the file in the Windows folder.

- Start Windows Explorer, and then click *Options* on the *View* menu.

- On the *File Types* tab, click *New Type*.

- In the *Description Of Type* box, type `Printer`.

- In the *Associated Extension* box, type `PRN` or `PS` (whichever is appropriate for your printer driver).

- Click *New*.

- In the *Action* box, type `print`.

- In the *Application Used To Perform Action* box, type:

```
c:\windows\printer.bat
```

- Click *OK*, then click *Set Default*.

- Using Windows Explorer, locate the PRINTER.BAT file in the Windows folder.

- Use the right mouse button to click the file, and then click *Properties* on the menu that appears.

- Click the *Program* tab, and then click the *Close On Exit* check box to select it. Click *OK*.

- Using the right mouse button, drag the PRINTER.BAT file to the desktop, and then click *Create Shortcut Here* on the menu that appears.

After you follow the preceding steps, you can print .PRN or .PS files by dragging a file onto a printer icon, dragging a file onto the PRINTER.BAT shortcut on the desktop, using the right mouse button to click a file (then clicking *Print*), or by double-clicking the file.

> **NOTE:** Remember that you must send a file created with a PCL printer driver to a PCL printer, and a file created with a PostScript printer driver must be sent to a PostScript printer.

Adjusting printer speed

Printing speed in Windows 95/98 is measured in one of two ways: "Return to application" (RTA) speed—defined as the length of time from when you click *Print* to when you regain control of the system; and "Printer page drop" speed—defined as the length of time from when you click *Print* to when the print job is finished. You can adjust each of these times by changing the printer's spool settings. To change spool settings:

■ Click *Start*, select *Settings*, then click *Printers*.

■ Right-click the printer you want to use, and then click *Properties*.

■ Click the *Details* tab, and then click the *Spool Settings* button.

For faster RTA:

■ Click *Start printing after first page is spooled*.

■ In most cases, choose .EMF as the spool data format (remember that PostScript printers support only the .RAW spool data format).

For faster printer page drop:

■ Click *Print directly to the printer*. If the local printer is being shared, the *Print directly to the printer* option is unavailable. To correct this, stop sharing the printer.

or

- Click *Start printing after last page is spooled*. In some cases, this option prevents laser printer engines from turning on and off during a print job.

Trouble Printing Through Windows

This is where you should start if you have trouble printing from Windows 95/98. The first step should be to verify that the printer itself is operating correctly, and that you can communicate with the printer through DOS:

- Verify that the printer is turned *on*, and see that it's *online*.

- Perform a printer *self-test* (the exact self-test method is different for each printer, so check your printer's documentation for specific instructions).

- If the self-test fails, the *printer* is defective, so it will require service.

- Now set up the printer on your local computer, and verify that no printer sharing devices or daisy-chained devices (such as SCSI CD-ROMs or Zip drives) are between the computer and printer.

- Restart your computer and press <F8> when you see the *Starting Windows 95/98* message, then choose the *Safe Mode Command Prompt Only* from the Startup Menu.

- Type the following line and then press <Enter>:

```
copy c:\autoexec.bat lpt1
```

For a laser printer, type:

```
copy c:\autoexec.bat lpt1 /b
```

For a PostScript printer (Windows 95 only), type:

```
copy c:\<path>\testps.txt lpt1
```

where `<path>` is the location of the `\Windows\ System` folder. If your printer is not connected to LPT1, substitute the correct port name in the preceding lines.

These commands copy a file to the printer. If the file is not printed (or you receive a Write Fault error), there may be a problem with the LPT port, the printer cable, or the printer itself. Try using a different printer cable or a different printer. When you copy a file to some ink-jet or laser printers, you may need to press the *Form Feed* or *Resume* key after the printer has received the job.

Delete .TMP and .SPL files

Since Windows prints in a graphical format, it relies heavily on hard drive space to store data that are being sent to the printer. There must be adequate drive space, or you may encounter *insufficient disk space* or other storage-related errors when trying to print. You can often free drive space by deleting temporary (.TMP) and spooler (.SPL) files:

- Start the computer at the *Safe Mode Command Prompt* from the Startup Menu.

- Type `SET` and press `<Enter>`, then note the location of the TEMP variable.

- Change to the temporary folder noted in the last step such as:

```
cd\windows\temp
```

- Now delete any temporary files (with a .TMP extension) in this folder such as:

```
del *.tmp
```

NOTE: As a rule, you'd prefer *not* to delete .TMP files from within Windows because Windows-based applications may use certain .TMP files. Deleting through DOS ensures that those files are *not* in use.

- Switch to the printer's spool folder such as:

```
cd\windows\spool\printers
```

- Finally, delete any spool files (with a .SPL extension) in this folder.

```
del *.spl
```

Once you've cleaned these files off the hard drive, run ScanDisk to check for damaged or cross-linked files, then run Defrag to defragment the drive.

Check/adjust the spool settings

When you can print from a DOS command prompt, but not from any Windows-based application, there may be a problem with the spool settings or bidirectional communication under Windows. You should try disabling the print spooler and/or bidirectional support to see if that clears things up:

- Click *Start*, select *Settings*, and then click the *Printers* icon.

- Right-click the printer that you're trying to print to, and then click *Properties* from the menu.

- Click the *Details* tab, click *Spool Settings*, then click the *Print directly to the printer* entry. If the local printer is being shared, you'll find that the *Print directly to the printer* option is unavailable. To correct this, stop sharing the printer.

- Bidirectional printing relies on the IEEE-1284 specification. If your printer and/or cable do not conform to this specification, bidirectional printing will not work in Windows 95/98. If your printer supports bidirectional communication, click *Disable bidirectional support for this printer*.

- Click the *OK*, and then click *OK* again to close the *Print Properties* dialog box.

- Now try to print from Notepad or WordPad.

If you can print now, try different combinations of spool settings and bidirectional support until you find a combination that works (i.e., disable bidirectional support with .RAW and .EMF spool data format settings, or try bidirectional support with the .RAW spool data format).

Trouble with Printer Port Hardware

There may be trouble with your printer port settings. Try printing from Windows (use Notepad or Word Pad). If you still have trouble printing, verify that the LPT port is set up correctly in *Device Manager*—for example, see that there are no conflicts, and that the port's resources are set correctly.

- Click *Start*, select *Settings*, and then click *Control Panel*.

- Double-click the *System* icon and click the *Device Manager* tab.

- Double-click *Ports (COM & LPT)*, then double-click the appropriate port for your printer [that is, *Printer Port (LPT1)*].

- Click the *Resources* tab and verify that the settings are correct for your printer port. For example, the I/O range for a standard LPT1 port is 0378h–037Ah. Also verify that the conflicting devices list reads *No conflicts*.

Try disabling the ECP mode

There are some hardware issues with certain IEEE-1284 "Enhanced Capabilities Port" (ECP) platforms and Windows. If you have problems printing (or experience garbled printout) using the printer port's ECP mode, try disabling the mode.

Windows 95:

- Click *Start*, select *Settings*, click *Control Panel*, and then double-click the *System* icon.
- On the *Device Manager* tab, double-click the *Ports (COM & LPT)* entry, then double-click the *ECP port*.
- On the *Driver* tab, click *Change Driver*, and then click *Show All Devices*.
- In the *Manufacturers* box, click *Standard Port Types*. In the *Models* box, click *Printer Port*, and then click *OK* until you return to *Control Panel*.
- Install the alternate LPT.VXD file as outlined in the previous section.

> **NOTE:** The alternate LPT.VXD file does not work on some Compaq computers, and you cannot disable the ECP port on these computers. If you cannot print to an ink-jet, dot-matrix, or laser printer from a Compaq computer because of problems with the ECP port, the alternate LPT.VXD file will *not* fix the problem. Obtain the SP1516.EXE file from Compaq. This file contains a driver that is loaded in the AUTOEXEC.BAT file that will disable the ECP port.

Windows 98:

- Click *Start*, select *Settings*, click *Control Panel*, and then double-click the *System* icon.
- On the *Device Manager* tab, double-click the *Ports (COM & LPT)* entry, then double-click the *ECP port*.
- On the *Driver* tab, click *Update Driver*. When the *Update Device Driver* wizard appears, click *Next*.

- Click *Display a list of all the device drivers in a specific location, so you can select the driver you want,* and then click *Next.*

- Click *Show All Hardware.*

- In the *Manufacturers* box, click *Standard Port Types.* In the *Models* box, click *Printer Port,* and then click *Next.*

- When the *Update Driver Warning* dialog box appears, click *Yes.*

- Click *Finish* and then click *Yes* to restart your computer.

  > **NOTE:** If the ECP port is redetected after you restart your computer, you may also need to change the port-related settings in your computer's CMOS Setup utility to disable the ECP. After you disable the ECP in the CMOS, repeat the preceding steps.

Try reinstalling/checking the printer port

If you note a hardware conflict with the printer port, or the port's settings are incorrect, you can use *Device Manager* to remove and reinstall the port.

- Click *Start,* select *Settings,* click *Control Panel,* and then double-click the *System* icon.

- On the *Device Manager* tab, double-click the *Ports (COM & LPT)* entry, then click the port your printer (that is, *Printer Port (LPT1)).*

- Click *Remove* to delete the port, and then restart your computer.

- Reopen the *Control Panel,* double-click the *Add New Hardware* wizard, then let Windows detect the hardware in your computer. This should reinstall the printer port.

You can use the Debug utility in your \Windows\

`Command` folder to verify the port settings. From the DOS command line type:

```
C:\WINDOWS\COMMAND\> debug        <Enter>

C:\WINDOWS\COMMAND\> d 40:0       <Enter>
```

This will return a string of numbers such as:

```
F8 03 F8 02 00 00 00 00-78 03 00 00 00 00 00 f7 01
```

which represent COM port and LPT port addresses. `F8  03` (03F8h) is COM1, `F8  02` (02F8h) is COM2, and `78  03` (0378h) is LPT1 (the `00  00` entries indicate no ports). Be sure that these addresses match the I/O address assignments in *Device Manager*. Finally, type `q` and press `<Enter>` to quit Debug.

Understanding Laser Printer Languages

Every printer receives commands from the host computer, and those commands tell the printer how to format the document being printed (that is, commands define typestyle, sizes, graphics characteristics, margins, and so on). These commands are the basis of a printer's *language*. Early printers used relatively simple command sets, but as printer technology advanced, printer languages have grown larger and more complex. Today, there are several important printer languages that you should be aware of—some of which are specific to individual printer manufacturers, and a few that are used throughout the computer industry (and have become de facto standards). This part of the section is intended to highlight some of the more popular printer languages.

The HP PCL family

HP PCL stands for *Hewlett-Packard Printer Command Language*. Hewlett-Packard introduced its first desktop laser printer in the early 1980s, and this printer soon became a leader in office printers. HP PCL (or simply PCL) is an "Escape Code" language, which means a command starts with the ASCII <Esc> character, followed by one or more other characters that comprise the specific command. Since PCL was originally devised for HP's earlier line of impact and ink-jet printers, it was already well defined by the time HP's first desktop laser printer (the 8-ppm LaserJet) was launched using the *PCL 3* language. As HP's family of laser printers has evolved, the PCL language has evolved with it, and most non-HP laser printers will emulate some level of PCL.

PCL 3. As one of the earliest desktop laser printer languages, the capabilities of PCL 3 were *very* limited—allowing relatively few, small bitmap fonts, and small bitmap graphics. The LaserJet was superseded by the LaserJet Plus (which still used PCL 3), but since the LaserJet Plus had more memory, it could manage more fonts and larger graphics within the limited PCL 3 framework. PCL 3 soon emerged as a standard that was widely copied by other desktop printer manufacturers, and is commonly referred to today as *LaserJet Plus emulation*. PCL 3 provided the commands and features needed for simple word-processing and data/graphic printing, and PCL 3 printers were primarily used as fast, quiet replacements for letter-quality daisywheel printers. Today, PCL 3 is considered obsolete.

PCL 4. The LaserJet Plus printer was superseded by the LaserJet II Series (also an 8-ppm printer), which included the LaserJet IIP (a 4-ppm personal printer), and the LaserJet IID (a duplex version of the LaserJet II). The LaserJet II introduced the PCL 4 language, which built upon PCL 3 by adding the ability to use more, larger bitmap fonts, and more bitmap graphics. The standard LaserJet II could manage just over half a page of bitmap graphics, but with additional onboard RAM, this could be expanded to a whole page.

PCL 4 is backward compatible with PCL 3 (that is, PCL 3 jobs would print perfectly well under PCL 4), but its additional features took PCL 4 well beyond the bounds of word-processing and allowed it to be used for charts, graphics, and simple desktop publishing tasks. The version of PCL 4 used on the LaserJet IIP was slightly enhanced over the version used on the standard LaserJet, and provided a compression method for bitmap graphics to reduce the amount of data required from the printer. While PCL 4 has been superseded by later PCL versions in office printers, it is still found in low-end personal printers because it requires relatively little processing power compared to later versions of the PCL language.

PCL 5.   Eventually, the LaserJet II was replaced by the 300-dpi HP LaserJet III family, which incorporated the PCL 5 language. The LaserJet III family included the standard 8-ppm office printer, along with the LaserJet IIID (8-ppm duplex), the LaserJet IIIP (4-ppm) personal printer, and the high-speed LaserJet IIISi (17-ppm duplex). PCL 5 represents an important advance over previous PCL versions: although it is still an "Escape Code" language, it offers most of the capabilities typically associated with a Page Description Language (or PDL). The primary features added for PCL 5 were outline fonts and vector graphics. This is an extremely powerful combination, and using these two features, it is possible to define almost any imaginable feature on a printed page. The vector graphics commands were provided by adding a version of HPGL (the Hewlett-Packard Graphics Language—the language used by Hewlett-Packard pen plotters) to the PCL 5 command set.

PCL 5 is designed to support complex documents, and works very well with desktop publishing, graphical design, and presentation software. In addition to

PCL 5, the HP LaserJet III series introduced a technique referred to as *Resolution Enhancement*, in which small dots are automatically placed at the edges of lines and characters to reduce the ragged edge (a.k.a. jaggies) sometimes visible on 300-dpi printers. Although the PCL 5 command set is largely backward compatible with PCL 4, the change from bitmap to outline fonts created some small incompatibilities (not all PCL 4 print jobs will appear properly on every PCL5 printer).

PCL 5e. The LaserJet III series was later replaced by the HP LaserJet 4. The LaserJet 4 introduced a higher printing resolution of 600 dpi; it added a fast bidirectional Centronics-type parallel port (called Bi-Tronics) that allowed the printer to give more status information to the computer; and it added a selection of fonts dedicated for use with Windows 95/98 application software. There are a few minor enhancements to PCL 5, resulting in the PCL 5e (enhanced) language. In most cases, these improvements allow the printer to "talk" to the computer in order to report status messages, errors, and so on (though the enhancements in PCL 5e do not have any significant effect on the page description functionality).

The LaserJet 4 series of printers includes the standard LaserJet 4 (600 dpi at 8 ppm), the LaserJet 4L personal printer (300 dpi at 4 ppm), the LaserJet 4P small-office printer (600 dpi at 4 ppm) and the LaserJet 4Si (600 dpi at 16 ppm). In addition to the basic range of models, the LaserJet 4 family is available with the Adobe PostScript Level 2 Page Description Language *in addition* to PCL 5e—these Adobe-enhanced models are designated by the letter "M" after the number (i.e., 4M, 4ML, 4MP, or 4SiMX).

PCL 5c. There is also a version of PCL 5 known as PCL 5c. This command set is used on HP color ink-jet printers, and the HP ColorJet color desktop laser printer. PCL 5c is fully backward compatible with PCL 5, but PCL 5c adds the command set needed to support color printing.

PCL emulation notes.   Although PCL was originally developed by Hewlett-Packard, the PCL format has been widely copied by other printer manufacturers who provide printers that "emulate" one or more HP models. Other manufacturers may describe their own printer models as "LaserJet IIP compatible," or "PCL 5 compatible," and so on. The majority of these printer emulations are very good, and offer the same facilities as the original HP printers (with even a few extra features added in), but you should remember that those printers use emulations (a.k.a. clones) of HP PCL. There may be small differences in the way those printers construct a page, and those differences can result in subtle distortions when compared with a print from a native HP printer.

The majority of application developers use HP printers when testing the ability of their driver software to produce PCL, and although the clone emulations are tested with most major software applications, there are a few applications that use obscure features of the PCL language that have not been properly tested by the clone manufacturers (and may not print correctly). When you encounter printing problems with a printer in "emulation" mode, try switching the printer to an older emulation mode, or switch to the manufacturer's specific driver.

The Adobe PostScript family

PostScript is a Page Description Language (PDL) developed by Adobe Corporation. Adobe was formed by people who left Xerox Corporation to set up their own company after creating Xerox Interpress—the proprietary PDL used by Xerox. Although Adobe does not manufacture laser printers, it licenses its PostScript

language to other manufacturers, and helps manufacturers design the printer controllers for PostScript
printers.

PostScript Level 1. The original version of PostScript
(dubbed *Level 1*) was first implemented by Apple
Computer Corporation on the Apple LaserWriter
printer (a 6-ppm desktop office printer), intended for
use with Apple Lisa and Macintosh computers.
PostScript offered a number of radical new features not
available on any other small laser printers at the time,
including outline fonts and vector graphics. The basic
structure of the PostScript language is very similar to a
conventional computer programming language. This
means the advanced features offered by a PDL could be
used in a very versatile and creative manner to create
complex images and designs. The Apple LaserWriter
was an instant success with users involved in desktop
publishing and graphic design, and PostScript became
the industry standard for complex printing applications
almost immediately. Apple's LaserWriter was soon
joined by the Apple LaserWriter Plus which offered
more memory, many more outline fonts, and a few
small enhancements to the PostScript language.

A large number of printer companies recognized the
value of PostScript, and formed alliances with Adobe
to produce PostScript printers of their own, but the
standard has always been set by the Apple printers—
successively introducing new features and refine-
ments into the PostScript language. The Apple
LaserWriter Plus was followed by the LaserWriter II,
LaserWriter IINT, and the LaserWriter IINTX, all of
which were 8-ppm, 300-dpi printers, but each of which
provided more processing power than the previous
model. Similar printers were available from other
manufacturers (some offering more features than the
Apple printers).

The rapid acceptance of PostScript by publishing
and graphics arts professionals led to the introduction

of phototypesetters based on the PostScript language. This meant that a PostScript job could be created on a computer, proof-printed on a desktop PostScript printer, and when completed, camera-ready masters could be printed out on a PostScript phototypesetter at very high resolution without any change in format. This development consolidated the position of PostScript in the publishing industry, and is now the universally accepted process for typesetting books, magazines, and other complex publications.

PostScript Level 2.   The disadvantage of PostScript was its speed—PostScript Level 1 required an enormous amount of processing power and was often *very* slow. There were also numerous compatibility issues since Level 1 was tweaked and enhanced as each new printer was equipped with PostScript. This meant that extensions to PostScript were created to cope with color, patterns, printers with multiple paper trays, duplex printers, and so on. To resolve these issues, Adobe released the first major enhancement to PostScript, *PostScript Level 2*.

PostScript Level 2 incorporates all the enhancements made to the original PostScript, setting a new baseline for the printer language. It also includes several new features and significant design changes that allow Level 2 to run much more efficiently and print more quickly. PostScript Level 2 is entirely backward compatible with the original PostScript, and will produce the same image for a job as you'd see in a PostScript Level 1 printer.

Other PostScript devices.   PostScript is not limited to use in printers. It is a device-independent language, and can be used by any device that creates an image as an array of dots. PostScript has been used to drive computer screens (on the NeXT range of workstations) and many phototypesetters. Computer screens normally have a resolution of around 80 dpi, whereas phototypesetters typically work at around 1200 dpi and 2400 dpi. PostScript may also be used to communicate documents between computers. Finally, Adobe has defined standards that will allow PostScript to be used for the transfer of pages between fax machines.

PostScript emulation clones.   Adobe Corporation does not sell printers. Rather, it receives revenue from licensing the PostScript language to printer manufacturers (who pay a fee to Adobe for each PostScript printer they sell). The license fees charged by Adobe were initially quite high, so some manufacturers tried to emulate the PostScript language. These PostScript emulations (or clones) vary considerably in quality and efficiency—some clones work well, others do not, but all PostScript clones have *some* problems since the PostScript language is very complex and difficult to imitate. There are no PostScript emulations that can be guaranteed to give *precisely* the same printed output as a printer using genuine Adobe PostScript. Adobe has reduced its license fees over the years, and most of the clone manufacturers have moved to genuine PostScript rather than attempt to emulate PostScript Level 2.

Microsoft Windows GDI

Windows is a very sophisticated operating system. It requires a high-performance computer with a fast processor, a lot of memory, and plenty of hard disk storage—these are also the features of a good printer controller. As a result, Windows is often used to prepare (or spool) a page for printing before sending it to the printer. This reduces the need for a separate dedicated high-performance printer controller.

Most Windows software applications describe a document in their own internal language, and then convert the document to a printer language such as PCL or PostScript before sending it to the printer. The printer then converts the printer language into an array of dots for printing. Since all software packages using the Windows environment *must* use the same language for describing documents, it is practical to make a printer that uses the Windows native language to describe a document (rather than convert to PCL or PostScript first). This language is called the Windows *Graphical Device Interface* (GDI), and is used by Windows to describe a document regardless of whether the image is to be displayed on the screen, sent to a printer, or transmitted by a fax machine.

For a printer that uses the Windows GDI language, a step is removed from the document preparation process. Instead of an application converting a document from its own language to a printer language, and the printer then converting the printer language to a bitmap, the document is simply sent to the printer in Windows GDI form *without* any conversion. The printer then needs only to convert the Windows GDI language directly into a bitmap for printing. This greatly reduces the amount of processing required by the computer to prepare a document for printing.

An alternative approach is to convert the Windows GDI language directly into a bitmap on the computer and send the bitmap to the printer. This approach requires the personal computer running Windows to be *very* powerful, but it allows the printer to be very simple and cheap (since all the printer has to do is receive and print the bitmap without any formatting). Many bitmaps are very large, and they are sent to the printer in a compressed form, which reduces the amount of time taken to transmit a page from the computer to the printer. Still, the communications process takes time, and it is not currently practical to send more than four to six pages per minute to a Windows GDI bitmap printer. This limits the use of Windows GDI bitmap printing to personal (home) printers, but such personal printers can be very cheap because the controller is so simple.

Windows GDI printers are available using both of the techniques described earlier, but the second method is generally the most common. Personal computers are becoming more powerful each year, and a low-cost PC based on the Intel Pentium II processor family (i.e., a Pentium II Celeron) is able to create bitmaps from the Windows GDI quite rapidly, and it is much easier to update the Windows GDI printing software in a personal computer than to change the software in a printer.

Manufacturer-specific languages

In addition to the standard languages for laser printers, there are several proprietary languages used by individual printer manufacturers. In some cases, the manufacturers provide their own language in addition to a standard language. In other cases, the manufacturer's language is the only one offered. Although every printer manufacturer wants to have its language adopted as the "industry standard," the fact that these languages have not become widely accepted does not detract from their usefulness—each language meets specific printing requirements, and many of these languages are used by programmers employed by companies to create in-house printing applications based on the unique features of a given language.

Kyocera PreScribe.   *Kyocera PreScribe* is used (along with PCL emulation) on Kyocera's family of office and workgroup printers. PreScribe is an easy language for programmers to use, and is particularly good at handling outline fonts. In actual practice, PreScribe is often used for custom minicomputer applications and applications using forms and barcodes, but it is poorly supported by most personal computer software. This means most Kyocera printers are employed in a PCL or PostScript emulation mode.

Canon CaPSYL. *CaPSYL* is Canon's proprietary language used with its family of office and workgroup printers. Canon is primarily a manufacturer of EP print engines (it supplies Hewlett-Packard and other manufacturers with print engines). Canon manufactures its own family of printers, but because of its strong relationship with Hewlett-Packard, Canon refrained from emulating HP printers for many years. CaPSYL is an advanced language capable of using outline fonts and sophisticated graphics and can be used for the most demanding printing applications. With the presence and popularity of PostScript, however, CaPSYL has not become popular and is not widely supported.

Xerox XES. Xerox designed and produced the world's first laser printers—and also introduced some of the first laser printer languages. The *Xerox Escape Sequences* (XES) were used with Xerox personal, office, and workgroup printers, and had been in use for many years. At its heart, XES is an old and simple escape code language. Although XES does not provide sophisticated features such as outline fonts, it does have good form support and bitmap graphics capabilities, as well as basic vector graphics. It is relatively easy for programmers to use, and was commonly used in large corporations by programmers creating custom in-house applications.

When office laser printers were a new phenomenon, XES was well supported by software vendors. But as new standards have emerged through the years, that support has dwindled. Today, most Xerox personal, office, and workgroup printers offer PCL and PostScript emulation (as either a standard feature or an option). Xerox supplies a few XES software drivers for the most common personal computer applications. Xerox also supplied mainframe software and communications interfaces that made XES printers a popular choice for decentralized mainframe printing.

Xerox JDL and Metacode.   The first laser printers produced by Xerox were large production printers for use
with mainframe computers (Xerox is still a market
leader in this type of printer). Xerox's *Job Description
Language* (JDL) is the language normally used to
communicate between mainframe computers and
Xerox production printers. JDL is designed to make
the mainframe do as little work as possible, leaving
the printer to do most of the formatting. Xerox supplied a wide range of software products for IBM mainframe computers, which enabled JDL to be used easily. The print job is formatted and converted from JDL
to Metacode inside a Xerox production printer, though
some mainframe and specialized publishing applications output Metacode directly (avoiding the JDL
stage). Since the use of JDL and Metacode is concen-
trated primarily in mainframe computer installations,
Xerox generally does not provide emulations of any
other manufacturers' languages on its production
printers.

Xerox Interpress.   *Interpress* is an early page description language, developed at Xerox by the people who
later left to form Adobe. Interpress was primarily
developed to communicate complex documents quickly
and efficiently between Xerox publishing workstations
and Xerox production printers via Xerox Ethernet networks (Xerox is one of the three companies that origi-
nated Ethernet). Interpress is a proprietary page
description language that is optimized for efficient communications and processing on Xerox printers, but it is
a difficult language for which to create software drivers. Interpress is integrated into Xerox production
printers and Xerox publishing workstations, and is not
uncommon in production publishing environments.
However, Interpress is not used outside of Xerox equipment and is not available on the smaller Xerox printers. Interpress is now an old language that is largely
considered obsolete, and Xerox is starting to make

PostScript available on its new printers (either built-in, or as separate PostScript-to-Interpress converters).

Océ FOL. Océ is one of the few European-based laser printer manufacturers. It provides a full range of office, workgroup, and low-speed production printers that support the Océ *Forms Overlay Language* (FOL) in addition to industry standard emulations (usually PCL or PostScript). FOL is exclusively designed for mainframe and minicomputers for the simple creation of forms and print jobs that use forms in a data-processing environment. As a consequence, FOL is not suitable for describing complex documents, but it is very easy for programmers to use to create invoices, account statements, and other common high-volume business documents.

IBM 3812. The *IBM 3812* was one of the first office laser printers produced by IBM, and is consequently supported by many IBM mainframe and minicomputer applications. The 3812 was not very sophisticated—like PCL 3 printers, it was best suited to word-processing and data-processing applications. But as many mainframe printing requirements are not terribly complex, the 3812 was adequate for most users' needs. The IBM 3812 is commonly emulated by other manufacturers who supply printers for IBM mainframes and minicomputers.

IBM IPDS. As other computer printers became more sophisticated, IBM mainframe users started demanding more printing features from IBM. IBM responded by developing a series of software products and printers offering *Advanced Function Printing* (or AFP). AFP is a way in which complex documents can be described on IBM mainframe and minicomputers, and converted to a print language by the operating system on the computer. The print language used by IBM mainframes and minicomputers for complex print jobs

is called *Intelligent Printer Data Stream* (IPDS), and
is basically an IBM proprietary page description language. IBM does not supply printer drivers for other
manufacturers' printers, and the IBM mainframe and
minicomputer operating systems are difficult to modify, so most printer manufacturers who supply printers for use on IBM systems using AFP *must* emulate
IPDS (the exception to this is Xerox, which produces
software that converts AFP to JDL). Each IBM IPDS
printer is slightly different, so most manufacturers
produce an emulation of a specific IBM printer (such
as the 3816).

DEC LN03 (DEC ANSI/Sixel).   Digital Equipment
Corporation (DEC) supplied a wide range of laser
printers for use with its minicomputer systems. DEC
was one of the first computer manufacturers to recognize the value of PostScript and incorporate it into its
high-end printers, but its entry-level laser printers
and dot-matrix printers use an escape code language
called *DEC ANSI/Sixel*, which uses ANSI (American
National Standards Institute) escape codes for the
positioning of text, selection of fonts, and so on (many
personal computers and computer terminals also use
ANSI escape sequences for positioning text on the
screen).

Since ANSI escape codes are primarily designed for
the manipulation of text, an additional mechanism is
required to manage graphics. Bitmap graphics are
supported, but are encoded in a special format, called
Sixels, designed to simplify communication across a
serial port. DEC ANSI/Sixel was initially used on dot-
matrix printers, but Digital's first desktop office laser
printer (the DEC LN03) also used DEC ANSI/Sixel.
The LN03 was supported by a wide range of applications on DEC minicomputers, so printer manufacturers who supply laser printers for DEC minicomputers
often provide an LN03 emulation. The LN03 was suitable for use with word-processing and data-processing

applications, and was suitable for simple graphics when expanded with extra memory (called the *LN03+*). More sophisticated applications on DEC minicomputers normally use PostScript printers.

Non-laser languages on laser printers

In addition to the many laser printer languages developed by printer manufacturers, a few classic laser printers provide emulations of other printer types (such as common dot-matrix and daisywheel printers). Although such emulations do not utilize a laser printer to its optimum capabilities, such support can be important when using old application software written before laser printers were common.

Epson FX. For many years, the *Epson FX* family of dot-matrix printers were the most popular dot-matrix printers in the world, and they are still supported by almost all software packages. Dot-matrix (impact) printers are generally low-resolution printers (typically no more than 180 dpi) that offer a small selection of fonts and typestyles. Laser printer emulations normally substitute these with high-quality 300-dpi fonts, so text quality on a laser printer is significantly better than the dot-matrix printer being emulated. Dot-matrix printers can print bitmap graphics (also at a low resolution). However, since it is difficult to scale bitmap graphics to higher resolutions, they do not usually look any better on a high-quality laser printer than on the original dot-matrix printer. Some laser printers emulate the old Epson FX-80 printer, others emulate the more recent FX-800 (a model compatible with the FX-80, but offering more features and a higher speed).

Xerox Diablo 630. In the formative years of personal computers, the *Xerox Diablo* 630 daisywheel printer was the industry standard letter-quality printer for business correspondence, and was widely emulated by other printer manufacturers. As a daisywheel printer, the Diablo 630 could not print graphics, and had few font selection capabilities (this required replacing the print wheel), but it is a useful emulation on laser printers that may be used with very old word-processing software.

IBM ProPrinter.   The *IBM ProPrinter* family of dot-matrix printers had the same general capabilities as the Epson FX printers, but used a character set that included all the characters available on an IBM-compatible personal computer display (including the special symbols for drawing lines and boxes). The ProPrinter family also worked with the graphics "screen dump" feature provided by IBM-compatible personal computers—this made the ProPrinter particularly useful for printing out graphics displays. As with the Epson FX emulations, text printed on a laser printer is significantly better quality, but graphics are not improved at all.

HPGL.   The *Hewlett-Packard Graphics Language* (known as HPGL) is widely used by pen plotters to produce engineering drawings. HPGL has been widely emulated by other plotter manufacturers, and is the de facto standard language for almost all pen plotters. A pen plotter is a slow device—a complex drawing can easily take half an hour to plot—and plotters are often noisy and difficult to set up. For these reasons, many laser printers offer an HPGL emulation—normally copying the HP7475A desktop plotter—which can be used for draft prints of drawings. Since most laser printers do not print in color, and cannot print on the very large paper sizes used by plotters, they are normally used only for draft prints. But in a few situations (such as printed circuit board design), laser printers are used in preference to plotters. HPGL version 2 has been incorporated into the PCL 5 language by Hewlett-Packard to provide PCL with vector graphics capabilities.

Emulation switching

Since many printers have several emulation modes, printers often have the ability to detect which emulation a print job is intended for, then automatically switch to that emulation. This feature is called *automatic emulation switching* (or AES), and is supported by many high-end office and workgroup printers. AES works by examining the commands in a print job, and determining which print language they belong to.

Some languages are very similar, and this frequently causes problems with AES. For example, the commands used by Epson FX printers and IBM ProPrinters are almost identical, so it is not possible for the AES software to determine which is the correct emulation. Other problems occur when a software driver has not followed normal conventions. In PostScript, the commands look like normal text—they don't contain escape codes—so unless the PostScript print job contains a header (normally something like: "%!PS-Adobe-2.0"), the emulation switching software will assume it is an unformatted text print job, and print it using an ordinary escape code language.

AES is not always reliable, but it usually works. As an alternative, some printers provide commands that will switch between emulations. By inserting the switching command immediately *before* the print job, the emulation can be selected by the computer. These emulation switching commands are unique to each printer manufacturer, so the computer will not know about them (or use them) unless it is equipped with a software driver for that specific brand and model of printer.

There is one other method of switching emulations: *communications port switching*. Printers that have more than one communications port are often able to have several computers attached, and switch between ports automatically. The most sophisticated of these printers may also allow each port to be assigned to a specific emulation. For example, the printer can be configured so that communications port A works in PostScript emulation mode and port B works in PCL.

Understanding the Media

One of the main advantages of modern printers is their versatility—the ability to print fine text and complex graphics on a wide range of media. Although paper is certainly the most common media, there are many other forms of media that you should be familiar with. This part of the section highlights many of the media types used with a typical ink-jet or laser printer.

> **NOTE:** Some printers can be *very* picky about the type of media they use. Using media that is not suitable for your printer may result in paper jams or poor image quality.

Paper

The most common type of printer media is *paper*. Paper can vary dramatically in its characteristics, although the best paper for general-purpose use in laser printers is high-quality 20-lb bond xerography-grade paper (this is also a fair choice for many ink-jet printers). Paper may be white, but colored papers may also be used. In order to ensure proper feeding, the paper should be cleanly and accurately cut. You may find that some cheap papers are inaccurately cut, and may deviate by 2–3 mm from the size claimed on the package. Also, cheap photocopying paper may be very dusty, and this should be avoided.

Paper weight. Remember that paper must traverse a difficult paper path, so paper that is too light or too heavy may simply refuse to feed properly. As a result, light or heavy paper is generally not suitable for most printers, and will usually cause frequent paper jams. Most laser and ink-jet printers are designed to work best with paper weights of around 80–90 gsm (grams per square meter), or 20–24 lbs in U.S. units. A few laser printers will use paper as light as 60 gsm (or 16 pounds), but this is usually the exception rather than the rule.

Paper condition. All papers must be kept dry—damp paper does not feed well and may skew or crease in the paper path. Print quality is usually poor on damp paper. On ink-jet printers, ink may tend to run or dry improperly in damp patches. On laser printers, damp patches may appear light (or not appear at all). In all cases, paper should be free of dust and dirt, which will contaminate the printer mechanism. Always use *fresh* paper (especially if the printer has been idle for a long time).

Paper surface and curl. All paper has a natural tendency to curl slightly, since it is stored in large rolls prior to being cut. The curl direction (opposite of the preferred printing surface) is normally marked on the paper's packaging, usually by an arrow. Most laser and ink-jet printers require paper to be loaded *curl upwards* (printing side *down*) to reduce misfeeds and paper jams.

Drilled paper. This is sometimes called *punched paper*. There is normally no problem in using drilled paper (ready for use in ring binders) with laser or ink-jet printers, but a little thought is required when loading drilled paper so that the holes are in the correct position relative to the text. Particular care is needed when loading drilled paper into a duplex printer, since the pages will be in the wrong order in the binder if the paper is loaded in the wrong orientation. Also ensure that the drilled paper is free of any small circular discs of paper (the holes) *before* loading (try fanning the paper first to weed out any little paper fragments).

Coated paper. Coated papers are generally not suitable for use in laser printers because the smooth surface of most coated papers causes inaccurate feeding and may cause jams. Toner does not bond well with most coated papers. There are a few semicoated papers designed for use with laser printers (such as Xerox ColorTech). If coated paper must be used, make sure that it is designed for use in laser printers, and be aware that it may not work perfectly in your particular laser printer. By comparison, ink-jet printers frequently use coated papers for "glossy photo" reproductions (you can see a detailed comparison of ink-jet papers in Section 4).

Laid, hammered, and woven papers. The terms *laid, hammered,* and *woven* all refer to textured papers. Most paper is "woven," and finely woven papers tend to work well in ink-jet and laser printers. However, many businesses use "laid" papers for their business correspondence for the very high quality image they present. Most laid papers are not suitable for use in laser or ink-jet printers because the pronounced texturing often interferes with the placement of toner or ink—this prevents an even and consistent print quality. Laid papers often misfeed or jam. There are a few laid papers (such as "Arjo Wiggins Conqueror Laser Laid 90gsm") which are designed for use in laser or ink-jet printers. If laid paper *must* be used, verify that it is designed for use in laser or ink-jet printers. Hammered papers typically carry some sort of embossed surface, and are not suitable for laser or ink-jet printers at all.

Plasticized paper. It is occasionally necessary to use paper outdoors (where it may get wet, and is generally exposed to the elements). When ordinary paper is used outside to display a notice or sign, it soon tears and blows away. There are papers that have a plastic coating to make them weatherproof and tear resistant. Most of these papers are not suitable for use in laser or ink jet printers. The plastic coating is too smooth for reliable feeding; toner or ink may not stick to the plastic surface; and the plastic may even melt under the high temperatures used by laser printer fusers. A few plasticized papers and adhesive labels have been designed for use with laser and ink-jet printers, but they are normally special-order items.

Recycled paper. Recycled paper is available for use in laser printers, ink-jet printers, and photocopiers. In general, recycled paper works adequately in most printers, but it does not always feed as reliably as new paper in *some* printer designs—this is usually because most recycled papers have an inferior surface quality when compared to new paper. Recycled paper is usually not white, but can be spotted by its off-white or buff colored appearance.

Pre-printed materials

Almost all businesses need to print on pre-printed stationery such as letterhead, or business forms like invoices. Using pre-printed stationery in laser printers imposes some special requirements that must be considered when ordering pre-printed materials. The fuser mechanism in a laser printer operates at a high temperature, and is capable of removing some inks from pre-printed paper (ruining the pre-printed stationery and contaminating the fuser rollers in the laser printer). High-temperature printing inks are available that are not affected by laser printers, and this should be specified to the printers when ordering pre-printed materials. Embossed papers (papers with logos or type that are raised to stand proud of the paper) do not feed very well, and the embossed effect is likely to be spoiled by the heat and pressure applied by the fuser.

Card stock

There are two considerations in printing on card stock: the stiffness of the card and its thickness. The stiffer a sheet of card stock is, the more likely it is to resist the bends in the paper path and cause a jam. Also, the thicker the card stock, the more difficult it is for the transfer corona to attract the toner from the EP drum and onto the card. The majority of laser and ink-jet printers will print on *light* card stock without problems, but for heavier card stock, you'll need to verify that the printer can handle that particular card thickness.

Small printers tend to have *very* tight bends in the paper path, whereas larger printers have more gentle bends, so card stock is more likely to jam in small printers than in large ones. To avoid jams with card stock, it is normally best to use the manual-feed feature on your printer (in conjunction with a "face-up" output tray if you have one) to obtain the straightest possible paper path. Most personal and office printers claim to accept card weights up to 30 lb (120 gsm), but with careful handling, most high-end printers will comfortably manage 40 lbs (160 gsm), and some will even feed 50-lb (200-gsm) card stock.

A few printers have a Thick Paper Mode (or Paper Thickness Adjustment) that can be selected from the printer's control panel. This does not adjust the printer's ability to feed heavy card stock, but increases the voltage through the transfer corona to help ensure good print quality on card. When a printer does offer a Thick Paper Mode, this feature should be used only when printing on card stock or other thick material, and should be turned *off* for normal printing—higher voltage in the transfer corona causes extra ozone generation, and may reduce the life of the corona.

Envelopes

Most laser and ink-jet printers will print on envelopes, although the manual-feed slot or a dedicated envelope feeder must be used. Problems arise in a laser printer when the envelope reaches the fuser: if the envelope curls (due to the heat and pressure) while passing through the fuser, or the edges of the envelope are not exactly square, the two sides (faces) of the envelope will not leave the fuser at exactly the same time. When this happens, a crease is formed on one face of the envelope, which is "ironed" in by the fuser.

Some brands of envelope are simply better than others in a given printer, so you should check the printer manual to determine the recommended type(s). Most printers require envelopes to be fed in a specific orientation (i.e., the "long" way with the flap to the left or the right). If your laser printer manual does not give specific guidance on the type of envelope to use, experiment with different types to determine which brands work best.

Labels

Self-adhesive labels are available for use with laser and ink-jet printers, but only labels that are designed for use with your particular printer type should be used. For example, labels that are not designed for use with a laser printer are likely to separate from their backing sheet in the printer mechanism, and wrap around one of the rollers (normally in the fuser), resulting in expensive repair bills. Labels not for use in an ink-jet printer may allow the ink to smudge or run. There are a number of label suppliers who supply sheets of labels designed for laser and ink-jet printers (such as Avery). Several leading word-processing and desktop publishing packages provide support for Avery labels within their mail-merge features, and some allow the user to define custom label formats.

Transparencies

Transparencies (overhead projection sheets) are typically very smooth, and may need to be fed through the printer manually (rather than being picked up from a paper tray). The main problem with transparencies is that it can be difficult to attract toner or dry ink on them. The surface textures and coatings of transparencies vary considerably between brands, and different brands work best with different models of printer. Laser printer and ink-jet printer manufacturers normally recommend a particular brand of transparency for use with their printers, though it's unlikely that a transparency suited to a laser printer would work as well in an ink-jet printer.

2

Printer Maintenance and Testing

Printers are some of the most reliable and hardy peripherals available for the personal computer, but they are hardly foolproof—printers *do* periodically require routine maintenance in order to ensure their proper operation. Maintenance certainly isn't difficult, but it *is* important. This section outlines the procedures needed to properly maintain impact, ink-jet, and laser printers, then covers the use of the PRINTERS utility.

Impact Printer Maintenance

Impact printers offer rugged, basic performance that is ideal for simple text and multipart forms. To help keep your impact printer in the best possible condition, there are several simple maintenance steps you should perform on your printer. Impact printer maintenance should be performed every 6 months (or whenever print quality deteriorates).

> **NOTE:** Check your printer's documentation for specific cautions or warnings before performing any of the steps outlined below. If your documentation warns against a

particular step (or suggests an alternate procedure), the documentation should take precedence.

Basic impact maintenance

1. *Power down the printer*. Before attempting any kind of cleaning, be sure to power off and unplug the printer, and disconnect the signal cable from the host computer. If the printer has been running, allow at least 15 minutes for the print head to cool before opening the printer.

2. *Open the printer*. Remove any plastic shrouds to expose the inside of the printer, and set the shrouds aside.

3. *Remove the paper*. Open the tractor clips and remove the paper supply. If the paper is old, wet, dirty, or otherwise damaged, it should be discarded and replaced.

4. *Move the print head back*. Take note of the print head spacing lever, then move the lever all the way back to put the maximum amount of space between the print head and the platen.

5. *Remove the ribbon cartridge*. Take the ribbon out of the printer and set it aside. If the print is faded or old, discard the ribbon cartridge and replace it with a fresh one.

6. *Clean the outside of the printer*. When cleaning the printer, use only mild solvents such as glass cleaner or isopropyl alcohol on a clean, lint-free towel. Never spray cleaner onto or into the printer—spray cleaner onto the towel, then wipe down the printer. Dry the outer covers carefully.

7. *Clean the inside of the printer*. Use a can of compressed air or vacuum cleaner to remove any accumulations of dust and debris from inside the printer's mechanisms.

8. *Clean the print head*. If there's an accumulation

of dried ink and "gunk" on the print head, it may be necessary for you to clean the print head. Use a screwdriver to remove the print head, then clean the print wires using a clean swab dipped in isopropyl alcohol. Gently secure the print head back into place. Remove any dust from the print head's cooling fins.

9. *Check the platen rollers*. Rotate the platen and check the rollers for any signs of damage or paper fragments. Clean the platen rollers and gently remove any paper fragments from the paper feed path.

10. *Check the carriage belt*. A thin motorized belt pulls the print head carriage back and forth along a thin rail. Check that the belt is reasonably tight—it should have no more than a quarter inch of play. If you notice that the belt is damaged or frayed, you should replace the belt as soon as possible.

11. *Check the carriage mounting*. Ensure that the carriage itself is seated securely to its rail. If either the belt or carriage shows too much play, you may see problems in the print head's side-to-side positioning. Wipe down the guide rail with a clean, dry paper towel.

12. *Install a new ribbon cartridge*. Reattach the ribbon cartridge—if the cartridge is worn out, install a new cartridge. Make sure that the ribbon passes around the front of the print head, then tighten up the ribbon to remove any slack.

13. *Install new paper*. Make sure that the paper is installed securely and close the tractor clips. If the paper has a "printing" side, make sure that the "printing" side is positioned facing the print head. Check that the paper feed lever is set in the correct mode for your paper's installation.

14. *Move the print head forward*. Readjust the print head back to its original position (if you want a

darker image, try edging the print head a notch or two closer). Use the platen knob to advance the paper to the next page separation.

15. *Reattach the cables.* Reconnect the ac line cord and reattach the parallel port cable to the host computer. Make sure that the printer power switch is still off.

16. *Run a self-test.* You'll want to run a printer self-test to check the printer's operation. Let the self-test run—it shouldn't take too long to complete a cycle. Review the self-test carefully, and see that the print is clear and crisp. If you're satisfied with the self-test results, return the impact printer to service.

NOTE: Use printer covers to keep dust, pet hair, and other foreign matter out of the printer—there are standard-sized plastic covers that will fit most printer models (towels will work well if you cannot find an adequate cover). Remember *not* to run the printer while it's covered—otherwise, the heat emitted by the printer can eventually damage the printer's circuits.

Impact quick checks

If your printer is printing poorly (or with the wrong format), there are several possible culprits to consider:

- *Printer won't communicate.* Verify that the printer is connected to a working port at the host computer, and that the printer cable is intact.

- *Print is light.* If print is too light, the problem is probably an exhausted ribbon. Turn off the printer (allow several minutes for the print head to cool) and replace the ribbon with a fresh one. Make sure that the ribbon passes in *front* of the print head.

- *Text is garbled (but otherwise clear).* Make sure that the correct printer is selected through the printing application. If there is no entry for your particular printer, install the latest driver version.

- *Text is in the wrong position (but otherwise clear).* Make sure that your paper is installed in the printer correctly (and see that the continuous-feed page separation is positioned properly).

- *Output is sloppy.* The print head may be dirty. Try cleaning the print head manually and see that there are no paper fragments or other obstructions.

Tackling major impact problems

In most cases, routine maintenance can be accomplished in a matter of 15 to 30 minutes, and there are no "ill-effects" to the printer—but this doesn't always happen. There are a few common issues that *do* crop up during maintenance:

- *Power.* If the printer doesn't turn on, check the ac line cord at both the wall and the printer, and then check the printer's power switch (it may sound silly, but it really is a common oversight).

- *Check the online status.* If the printer's online status indicator is not lit, check the printer's setup. Verify that the paper and ribbon are both installed properly. Also check that the signal cable is securely attached between the printer and the host computer. If the signal cable uses clips or screws to attach the cable to the PC or printer, see that those clips/screws are employed. You might also wish to try a signal cable that you know is good.

- *Check cable length.* If the printer still refuses to go online when connected to the computer (or just prints garbage), the signal cable may indeed be defective. Printer signal cables should be high-quality, shielded, and not exceed 6 feet in total length between the printer and host computer. If there is another parallel port device or switch box between the printer and computer, try connecting the printer and PC directly.

- *Check the paper feed.* If you find that your continuous-feed paper is crumpling or jamming when it's fed through the printer, chances are that the tractor feed mode lever is set improperly (i.e., tractor "push" instead of tractor "pull"). If you're loading single-sheet paper, the feed lever should be set to "friction feed."

- *Excessive heating.* If the printer cuts out during seemingly normal operation, the print head may be cutting out from excessive heating. This is usually a normal mechanism to protect the print head, but frequent halts may suggest inadequate cooling—make sure that the print head's cooling fins have been cooled adequately.

- *Check the driver.* Make sure that the printing application has selected the correct printer. Also verify that the printer driver is the latest version (you can download the very latest version from the printer manufacturer's Web site). If you find that there are no printers listed, you'll need to install the drivers for your particular printer.

Ink-Jet Printer Maintenance

Ink-jet printers are one of the best values in color printing. Now available for less than $150, ink-jet printers have revolutionized the home printer market by making high-quality, high-resolution printing available to everyone. Ink-jet printers have even made color printing economical. But no printer retains its quality unless it's well maintained. There are several simple maintenance steps you should regularly perform on your printer—ink-jet printer maintenance should be performed every 4 months (or whenever print quality deteriorates).

NOTE: Check your printer's documentation for specific cautions or warnings before performing any of the steps outlined below. If your documentation warns against a particular step (or suggests an alternate procedure), the documentation should take precedence.

Basic ink-jet maintenance

1. *Power-down the printer.* Before attempting any kind of cleaning, be sure to power off and unplug the printer, and disconnect the signal cable from the host computer. If the printer has been running, allow at least 10 minutes for the power supply to discharge before opening the printer.

2. *Open the printer.* Remove any plastic shrouds to expose the inside of the printer, and set the shrouds aside.

3. *Remove the paper.* Open the paper tray and remove the paper supply. If the paper is old, wet, dirty, or otherwise damaged, it should be discarded and replaced. Take a moment and wipe out the paper tray.

4. *Move the print head back.* If your particular ink-jet printer has a space adjustment, take note of the print head spacing lever, then move the lever all the way back to put the maximum amount of space between the print head and the platen.

5. *Remove the ink cartridge(s).* Take the black ink cartridge (and color cartridges) out of the printer and set them aside. If the print is faded or old, discard the ink cartridge(s) and replace them with fresh ones.

6. *Clean the outside of the printer.* When cleaning the printer, use only mild solvents such as glass cleaner or isopropyl alcohol on a clean, lint-free towel. Never spray cleaner onto or into the

printer—spray cleaner onto the towel, then wipe down the printer. Dry the outer covers carefully.

7. *Clean the inside of the printer.* Use a can of compressed air or vacuum cleaner to remove any accumulations of dust and debris from inside the printer's mechanisms.

8. *Clean the ink head(s)/cartridge(s).* If there's an accumulation of dried ink and "gunk" on the ink head/cartridge, it may be necessary for you to clean the ink cartridge. Clean the face of the ink cartridge using a clean swab dipped in isopropyl alcohol. Keep the ink cartridge(s) aside until you're ready to reinstall them.

9. *Check the platen.* Check the platen surface and paper handling rollers for any signs of damage or paper fragments. Clean the platen roller and gently remove any paper fragments from the paper feed path.

10. *Check the carriage belt.* A thin motorized belt pulls the print head carriage back and forth along a thin rail. Check that the belt is reasonably tight—it should have no more than a quarter inch of play. If you notice that the belt is damaged or frayed, you should replace the belt as soon as possible.

11. *Check the carriage mounting.* Ensure that the carriage itself is seated securely to its rail. If either the belt or carriage shows too much play, you may see problems in the print head's side-to-side positioning. Wipe down the guide rail with a clean, dry paper towel.

12. *Install the new ink head(s)/cartridge(s).* Reattach the ink head(s)/cartridge(s)—if the cartridge is worn out, install a new cartridge. Make sure that the electrical contacts are clean and connected securely.

13. *Install new paper.* Make sure that the paper is installed securely and evenly in the paper tray. If

the paper has a "printing" side, make sure that the "printing" side is positioned to feed through facing the ink cartridge.

14. *Move the print head forward.* If the ink-jet printer has a head position adjustment, readjust the print head back to its original position.

15. *Reattach the cables.* Reconnect the ac line cord and reattach the parallel port cable to the host computer. Make sure that the printer power switch is still off.

16. *Run a self-test.* You'll want to run a printer self-test to check the printer's operation. Let the self-test run—it shouldn't take too long to complete a cycle. Review the self-test carefully, and see that the print is clear and crisp. If you're satisfied with the self-test results, return the ink-jet printer to service.

> **NOTE:** Use printer covers to keep dust, pet hair, and other foreign matter out of the printer—there are standard-sized plastic covers that will fit most printer models (towels will work well if you cannot find an adequate cover). Remember *not* to run the printer while it's covered—otherwise, the heat emitted by the printer can eventually damage the printer's circuits.

Ink cartridge tips

- *Keep the cartridge in its packaging.* Do not remove the ink cartridge from its packaging until you're ready to install it. Do not use ink that has expired. Do not use ink cartridges that have been damaged, that are leaking, or that have had protective devices removed.

- *Remove the tape.* Before installing a new ink cartridge, make sure that you remove the protective tape covering the ink nozzles.

- *Store idle cartridges carefully.* If you have a printer that requires you to change cartridges to switch between printing colors and black, make sure you store your idle cartridges in the storage containers that came with your printer. If you don't have those containers, use a zip-up plastic bag.

NOTE: After you're done changing cartridges, you might have to notify your printer's device driver since many drivers monitor the ink level in the cartridge— you might need to adjust its settings when the cartridge is replaced.

Ink-jet quick checks

If your printer is printing poorly (or with the wrong format), there are several possible culprits to consider that might get you started again:

- *Printer won't communicate.* Verify that the printer is connected to a working port at the host computer, and that the printer cable is intact.

- *Print is light.* If print is too light, the problem is probably an exhausted ink cartridge. Turn off the printer and replace the ink cartridge with a fresh one. Make sure that the cartridge is installed securely, and see that the electrical contacts are clean.

- *Text is garbled (but otherwise clear).* Make sure that the correct printer is selected through the printing application. If there is no entry for your particular printer, install the latest driver version.

- *Text is in the wrong position (but otherwise clear).* Make sure that the appropriate paper type is installed in the printer correctly.

- *Output is sloppy.* The ink cartridge/nozzles may be dirty. Try purging the ink cartridge (or cleaning the nozzles manually) and see that there are no paper fragments or other obstructions preventing the proper flow of ink.

Tackling major ink-jet problems

- *Power*. If the printer doesn't turn on, check the ac line cord at both the wall and the printer, and then check the printer's power switch (it may sound silly, but it really is a common oversight).

- *Ink buildup*. When the printer is having problems with ink buildup (i.e., streaks on printed pages or faulty type), the problem could be with the ink cartridge or print head. If it's the print head, there is probably a buildup of ink in the nozzles. Try cleaning or purging the ink cartridge.

- *Careful for grinding noises*. If you hear unusual grinding noises, your print carriage might be stuck. Turn off and unplug the printer, then take a look at the carriage system. If the carriage is stuck, you'll see it will not move smoothly across the printer.

- *Check the online status*. If the printer's online status indicator is not lit, check the printer's setup. Verify that the paper and ink cartridge are both installed properly. Also check that the signal cable is securely attached between the printer and the host computer. If the signal cable uses clips or screws to attach the cable to the PC or printer, see that those clips/screws are employed. You might also wish to try a signal cable that you know is good.

- *Check cable length*. If the printer still refuses to go online when connected to the computer (or just prints garbage), the signal cable may indeed be defective. Printer signal cables should be high-quality, shielded, and not exceed 6 feet in total length between the printer and host computer. If there is another parallel port device or switch box between the printer and computer, try connecting the printer and PC directly.

- *Check the paper feed*. If you find that your sheet feed paper is crumpling or jamming when it's fed through the printer, chances are that there is an obstruction in the paper path.

- *Check the driver.* Make sure that the printing application has selected the correct printer. Also verify that the printer driver is the latest version (you can download the very latest version from the printer manufacturer's Web site). If you find that there are no printers listed, you'll need to install the drivers for your particular printer.

Laser Printer Maintenance

Laser printers generally produce the fastest and highest-quality print of any printing technology available today. Whereas "traditional" laser printers produce only black and white output, later models offer four-color (CMYK) printing for high-speed "photo-quality" output. Many laser printers are falling in price, and are now affordable for small offices and home users. But for all the convenience and power supplied by a laser printer, they are extremely delicate devices, and image quality will quickly degrade without regular maintenance. You should perform laser printer maintenance every 3 months under regular use, whenever the printing appears distorted, or whenever you replace the toner cartridge.

> **NOTE:** Laser printers use high-voltage power supplies and heat as an integral part of the image formation system. If the printer has been running, be sure to allow at least 15 minutes for the high-voltage supply to discharge and the fusing system to cool before opening the printer for maintenance.

> **NOTE:** The steps offered in this section are appropriate for many types of printers, but you should refer to the documentation for your particular printer before attempting any service. In all cases, your printer's documentation should take precedence over the steps outlined below.

Basic laser printer maintenance

1. *Power-down the printer*. Before attempting any kind of maintenance, be sure to power off and unplug the printer, and disconnect the signal cable from the host computer. If the printer has been running, allow at least 15 minutes for the high-voltage power supply to discharge and fusing unit to cool before opening the printer.

2. *Remove the paper*. Open the paper tray and remove the paper supply. If the paper is old, wet, dirty, or otherwise damaged, it should be discarded and replaced with ordinary 20-lb xerography-grade paper. Take a moment and wipe out the paper tray.

3. *Clean the outside of the printer*. When cleaning the printer, use only mild solvents such as glass cleaner or isopropyl alcohol on a clean, lint-free towel. Never spray cleaner onto or into the printer—spray cleaner onto the towel, then wipe down the printer. Dry the outer covers carefully.

4. *Remove the EP engine/toner cartridge*. Open the laser printer's case to expose the EP engine/toner cartridge inside. You'll need to remove the EP engine/toner cartridge now (be sure that the printer is off, and wait at least 15 minutes before opening the printer). Gently remove the EP engine/toner cartridge from inside the printer, then set it aside in a safe place. Keep the cartridge cool and dry, and do not expose it to direct sunlight.

5. *Clean toner from the printer*. Remove any accumulations of toner, paper fragments, or other debris from inside the printer's mechanisms. *Never* use an ordinary vacuum to remove toner from the printer. Toner uses microfine powder, which is far too fine for the vacuum's bag—the toner will just "blow through" the bag and cause a

real mess. Instead, use a tack-cloth or a clean cloth with just a little cold water to wipe out paper dust and toner sitting along the ribs of the printer's paper path.

6. *Clean the transfer corona area.* Now gently clean off the plastic cover guarding the transfer corona, and wipe off the sawtooth-shaped paper discharge guide.

7. *Clean the fusing rollers/cleaning pad.* Fusing rollers are normally wiped down by a thin cleaning pad—this keeps residual toner from building up and appearing on subsequent pages. You should replace the cleaning pad whenever you replace the EP engine/toner cartridge (but you may replace the cleaning pad by itself if it's extremely dirty). Insert the new cleaning pad into its slot and clip it into place if necessary.

8. *Check the primary corona.* If the printer uses a primary corona (i.e., an older SX-type EP engine), you should clean the corona periodically to prevent buildups of dust and debris from fouling the wire and causing long black streaks on your pages. Take the cleaning tab and move it back and forth across the corona wire several times.

9. *Clean the optical deck.* You may also need to clean the light source aperture. Use a cleaning swab and a little isopropyl alcohol to wipe down the lens, then dry the lens with a fresh swab.

10. *Check/replace the ozone filter.* The high voltages used in laser printers generate a lot of ozone gas that can cause respiratory irritation if you breathe it for too long. Ozone filters can easily be replaced by removing the filter cover, replacing the filter, and reinstalling the cover.

11. *Reinstall the EP engine/toner cartridge.* When replacing the original EP engine/toner cartridge, "even out" the toner by gently shaking the car-

tridge back and forth. Reinsert the toner cartridge into the printer and be sure that it's seated evenly, then close the printer cover so that it locks into place.

12. *Install new paper*. Make sure that the paper is installed securely and evenly in the paper tray. If the paper has a "printing" side, make sure that the "printing" side is positioned to feed through facing the drum (usually printing side "down" in the tray).

13. *Reattach the cables*. Reconnect the AC line cord and reattach the parallel port cable to the host computer. Make sure that the printer power switch is still off.

14. *Run a self-test*. You'll want to run a printer self-test to check the printer's operation. Let the self-test run—it shouldn't take too long to complete a cycle. Review the self-test carefully, and see that the print is clear and crisp. If you're satisfied with the self-test results, return the laser printer to service.

NOTE: There may be specialized cleaning utilities available for your particular printer (they may be available for download directly from the manufacturer's Web site). These special programs send instructions to your printer that burn off toner particles that may be clogging your printer.

NOTE: Use printer covers to keep dust, pet hair, and other foreign matter out of the printer—there are standard-sized plastic covers that will fit most printer models (towels will work well if you cannot find an adequate cover). Remember *not* to run the printer while it's covered—otherwise, the heat developed by the printer can eventually damage the printer's circuits.

Toner cartridge tips

■ *Store the toner carefully*. Toner is very sensitive to changes in temperature, humidity, and so on. Keep the toner cartridge in its original packaging, and store the toner in a cool, dry place.

■ *Avoid expired toner*. Toner cartridges all have expiration dates. Before installing a new toner cartridge, be sure that the cartridge is fresh.

■ *Remove the tape*. Most toner cartridges use one or more strips of tape to protect the cartridge. Be sure to remove any strips of tape before installing the new toner cartridge.

■ *Recycle the old cartridge*. Most exhausted toner cartridges can be recycled by returning the cartridge to the manufacturer (often in the new toner's original box).

■ *Update the printer driver*. You might have to notify your printer's driver software after you're done changing toner cartridges because some printer drivers monitor the toner level in the cartridge, and must adjust their settings when the cartridge is replaced.

Laser printer quick checks

■ *Printer won't communicate*. Verify that the printer is connected to a working port at the host computer, and that the printer cable is intact.

■ *Print is light or blotchy*. If print is too light, the problem is probably an exhausted toner cartridge. Try redistributing the toner and adjusting the print density dial. Turn off the printer and replace the toner cartridge with a fresh one. Make sure that the cartridge is installed securely. Do not use an expired toner cartridge.

■ *Text is garbled (but otherwise clear)*. Make sure that the correct printer is selected through the printing application. If there is no entry for your particular printer, install the latest driver version.

■ *Paper won't feed*. Check to see that the paper tray is

installed properly, and verify that the tray is not overloaded, or packed with different types of media at the same time.

- *Paper jams frequently*. This may be due to incompatible, old, damaged, or overloaded media (or different types of media in the paper tray simultaneously). If problems persist, check for obstructions in the paper path.

Tackling major laser problems

- *Power*. If the printer doesn't turn on, check the ac line cord at both the wall and the printer, and then check the printer's power switch (it may sound silly, but it really is a common oversight). Some newer printers don't have power switches because they are on continuously (though most of the time they are in power-saving mode). If you have one of these printers, there should be a printer reset button that you can use to see if your printer's power is on.

- *Check the online status*. If the printer's online status indicator is not lit, check the printer's setup. Verify that the paper, EP engine, and toner cartridge are both installed properly. Also check that the signal cable is securely attached between the printer and the host computer. If the signal cable uses clips or screws to attach the cable to the PC or printer, see that those clips/screws are employed. You might also wish to try a signal cable that you know is good.

- *Check cable length*. If the printer still refuses to go online when connected to the computer (or just prints garbage), the signal cable may indeed be defective. Printer signal cables should be high-quality, shielded, and not exceed 6 feet in total length between the printer and host computer. If there is another parallel port device or switch box between the printer and computer, try connecting the printer and PC directly.

- *Check the paper feed*. If you find that your sheet feed paper is crumpling or jamming when it's fed through the printer, chances are that there is an obstruction in the paper path. Open the printer and check for bits of paper or labels that might be interfering with the paper jam.

- *Check the driver*. Make sure that the printing application has selected the correct printer. Also verify that the printer driver is the latest version (you can download the very latest version from the printer manufacturer's Web site). If you find that there are no printers listed, you'll need to install the drivers for your particular printer.

Printer performance tips

- *Reduce printing resolution*. Try reducing the resolution from 600 dpi to 300 dpi—decreasing the printer's resolution allows the printer to output much more easily. Under Windows you usually can set your printer's resolution by altering its driver settings. Click *Start* and highlight *Printers* from the *Settings* menu. Right-click your printer's icon and select *Properties*. Click through the tabs to find the resolution controls and set your printer's resolution to a lower figure (if possible) then click *OK*.

- *Check the printer driver*. Older or buggy printer drivers can often impair printer performance. If the printer isn't performing at its peak, try downloading and installing the latest printer drivers directly from the printer manufacturer (try to avoid generic or third-party printer drivers). If the system are using printer utility software (such as print managers), try disabling or uninstalling that software.

- *Check disk space*. Since the PC usually spools a print job to a temporary file on the disk, check that there is at least 50 MB of free space on the disk. If your virtual memory settings are fixed, try allowing Windows to manage the virtual memory automatically.

- *Add printer memory.* In order to print large, high-resolution images, the printer may require additional memory. Try adding RAM to the printer. If there is no space to add more memory, you may need to replace the existing memory modules with larger ones.

Using PRINTERS

One of the major limitations of printer troubleshooting has been *testing*. Traditionally, a technician was limited to the self-test of each unique printer, or printing simple documents from a text editor or other basic application. There are two problems with this haphazard approach. First, self-tests and simple printouts do not always test every feature of the printer in a clear fashion. Second, such testing is hardly ever uniform—the quality and range of testing can vary radically from printer to printer. Dynamic Learning Systems has addressed this problem by developing *PRINTERS*—a PC-based utility designed to provide you with a suite of standardized printer tests. You will learn how to get your own copy of PRINTERS, install it on your PC, and use it productively in a matter of minutes. PRINTERS not only exercises a printer's main functions (i.e., carriage, line feed, print head, and so on), but it also allows you to test printer-specific functions through the use of escape sequences. You will find PRINTERS to be an inexpensive and handy addition to your toolbox.

All about PRINTERS

PRINTERS is a stand-alone DOS utility designed to drive virtually any commercial impact, ink-jet, or Laser/LED (EP) printer through a series of exercises and test patterns specially tailored to reveal faults in the printer's major subassemblies. By reviewing the printed results, you will be able to estimate the source of a printer's problems with a high degree of confidence. Online help and tutorial modes provide additional information about each test, and help you to understand the printed results. A variety of options allow you configure PRINTERS for over 220 unique printers, and tailor performance for speed and print quality. A handy Manual Code section allows you to enter Escape Code Sequences and text that can test specific functions of *any* printer.

Obtaining your copy of PRINTERS

You can buy a copy of PRINTERS directly from Dynamic Learning Systems. Feel free to photocopy the order form at the end of the book, and fill out the requested information carefully (please remember that all purchases must be made in US dollars). When you fill out the order form, you can select the companion disk alone, a one-year subscription to our premier newsletter *The PC Toolbox*, or take advantage of a very special rate for the disk *and* subscription. The disk is provided in 3.5″ high-density format.

Installing and starting from the floppy drive

Your first task should be to make a backup copy of PRINTERS on a blank floppy disk. You can use the DOS DISKCOPY function to make your backup. For example, the command line:

```
C:\> diskcopy a: a:    <ENTER>
```

will copy the original disk. Keep in mind that you will have to do a bit of disk swapping with this command. If you wish to use a floppy drive besides A:, you should substitute the corresponding letter for that drive. If you are uncomfortable with the DISKCOPY command, refer to your DOS manual for additional information. PRINTERS is designed to be run directly from the floppy disk, so you can keep the original disk locked away while you run from the copy. This allows you to take the disk from machine to machine so that you will not clutter your hard drive, or violate the licensee agreement by loading the software onto more than one machine simultaneously:

1. To start PRINTERS from the floppy drive, insert the floppy into the drive and type the letter of that drive at the command prompt and press <ENTER>. The new drive letter should now be visible. For example, you can switch to the A: drive by typing:

   ```
   C:\> a:    <ENTER>
   ```

   the system will respond with the new drive letter:

   ```
   A:\>_
   ```

2. Then, type the name of the executable file:

   ```
   A:\> printers   <ENTER>
   ```

3. If you are using a floppy drive other than A:, you should substitute that drive letter (such as B:) in place of the A:. PRINTERS will start in a few moments and you will see the title screen and disclaimer. Press any key to pass the title screen and disclaimer, and you will then see the main menu.

Installing and starting from the hard drive

If you'll only be using one PC and you have an extra 1.0 MB or so, you should still go ahead and make a backup copy of the PRINTERS disk as described in the previous section, but it would probably be more convenient to install the utilities to your hard drive.

There is no automated installation procedure to do this, but the steps are very straightforward:

1. Boot your PC from the hard drive and when you see the command prompt, switch to the root directory by typing the `cd\` command:

```
C:\> cd\    <ENTER>
```

the system should respond with the root command prompt:

```
C:\>_
```

2. Use the DOS `md` command to create a new subdirectory that will contain the companion disk's files. One suggestion is to use the name PRINTERS such as:

```
C:\> md printers    <ENTER>
```

then switch to the new subdirectory using the `cd\` command:

```
C:\> cd\printers    <ENTER>
```

The system should respond with the new subdirectory label such as:

```
C:\PRINTERS>_
```

You may also use any DOS-valid name for the subdirectory, or nest the directory under other directories if you wish. If you are working with a hard drive other than C:, substitute that drive label for C:.

3. Insert the backup floppy disk into the floppy drive. Use the DOS `copy` command to copy all of the floppy disk files to the hard drive such as:

```
C:\PRINTERS> copy a:*.* c:    <ENTER>
```

This instructs the system to copy all files from the A: drive to the current directory of the C: drive. Since PRINTERS is not distributed in compressed form, decompression (or "unzipping") is not needed.

4. After all files have been copied, remove the floppy disk and store it in a safe place. Then, type the name of the utility you wish to use such as:

```
C:\> printers    <ENTER>
```

The title screen and disclaimer for PRINTERS should appear almost immediately. Press any key to pass the title screen and disclaimer, and you will then see the main menu.

The work screen

After you pass the title screen and disclaimer, you will see the *work screen* as illustrated in Figure 2.1. The top of the work screen contains the title bar and main menu bar. The bottom of the work screen contains the message bar and copyright bar. Most of the work screen is empty now. There are six entries in the main menu bar—these are the essential areas that you will be concerned with while using PRINTERS:

- *Configure*: allows you to select the program's operating parameters
- *Impact*: allows you to run a selection of tests for Impact printers
- *Ink Jet*: allows you to run a selection of tests for Ink-Jet printers
- *Laser/LED*: allows you to run a selection of tests for EP printers
- *About*: shows you more information about PRINTERS
- *Quit*: leave PRINTERS and return to DOS

Configuring the program

To configure the various options available in PRINT-ERS, click on *Configure* in the main menu bar (or press <C>). The CONFIGURE menu will appear as shown in Figure 2.2. You can return to the work

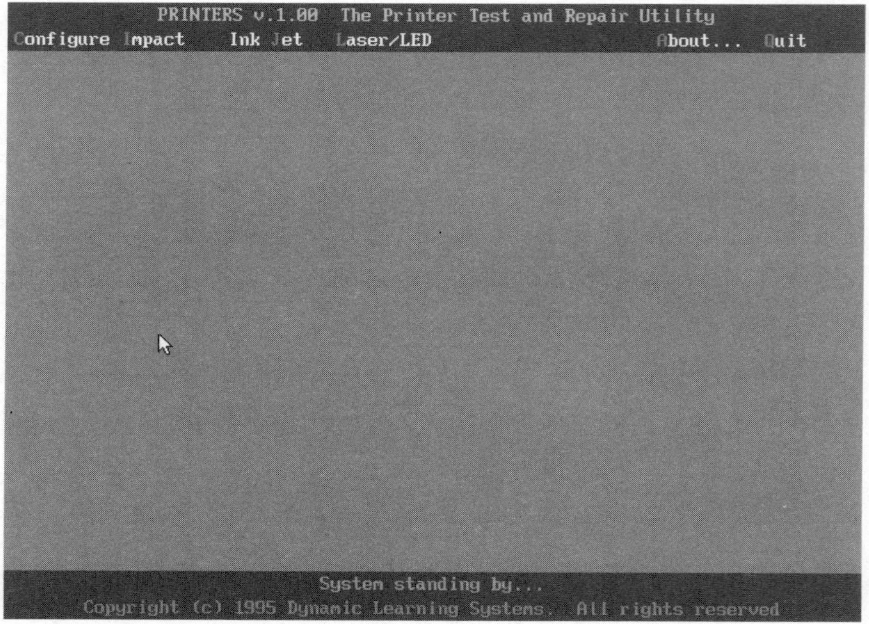

Figure 2.1 The PRINTERS work screen.

The screen contents:

PRINTERS v.1.00 The Printer Test and Repair Utility

Configure Impact Ink Jet Laser/LED About... Quit

System standing by...
Copyright (c) 1995 Dynamic Learning Systems. All rights reserved

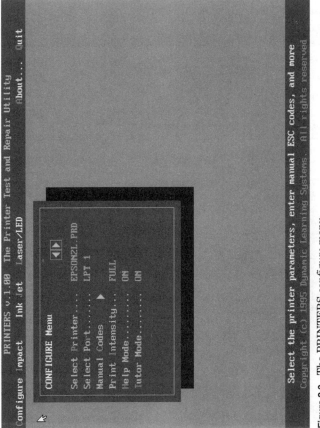

Figure 2.2 The PRINTERS *configure* menu.

screen at any time by pressing the <ESC> key or right-clicking anywhere in the display.

Select printer.   PRINTERS is compatible with the vast majority of Epson and Hewlett-Packard compatible printers now in the market, but the utility provides an extensive library of over 220 specific printer drivers. These drivers allow PRINTERS to produce the detailed graphic test patterns used in the program. Table 2.1 shows a comprehensive listing of supported

TABLE 2.1   PRINTERS Driver Index

Manufacture/ Printer model	Definition	Resolution	B&W/ COL
Adobe PostScript— All models	PS.PRD	300×300	B&W
Color PostScript— All models	PSC.PRD	300×300	COL
	Alps		
ALPS DMX800	EPSON9L.PRD	60×72	B&W
ALPS DMX800	EPSON9M.PRD	120×72	B&W
ALPS DMX800	EPSON9H.PRD	120×216	B&W
ALPS DMX800	EPSON9VH.PRD	240×216	B&W
LSX 1600	HPLSRL.PRD	75×75	B&W
LSX 1600	HPLSRM.PRD	100×100	B&W
LSX 1600	HPLSRH.PRD	150×150	B&W
LSX 1600	HPLSRVH.PRD	300×300	B&W
	AMT		
Accel, Office Printer	AMTVL.PRD	60×60	B&W
Accel, Office Printer	AMTL.PRD	120×60	B&W
Accel, Office Printer	AMTM.PRD	120×120	B&W
Accel, Office Printer	AMTH.PRD	240×120	B&W
Accel, Office Printer	AMTVH.PRD	240×240	B&W

Manufacture/ Printer model	Definition	Resolution	B&W/ COL
	AMT		
Accel, Office Printer	AMTVVH.PRD	480×240	B&W
Accel, Office Printer	AMTCVL.PRD	60×60	COL
Accel, Office Printer	AMTCL.PRD	120×60	COL
Accel, Office Printer	AMTCM.PRD	120×120	COL
Accel, Office Printer	AMTCH.PRD	240×120	COL
Accel, Office Printer	AMTCVH.PRD	240×240	COL
Accel, Office Printer	AMTCVVH.PRD	480×240	COL
TracJet	HPLSRL.PRD	75×75	B&W
TracJet	HPLSRM.PRD	100×100	B&W
TracJet	HPLSRH.PRD	150×150	B&W
TracJet	HPLSRVH.PRD	300×300	B&W
	Anadex		
DP Series	ANDXDPL.PRD	72×72	B&W
DP Series	ANDXDPH.PRD	144×144	B&W
WP Series	ANDXWPL.PRD	72×72	B&W
WP Series	ANDXWPH.PRD	144×144	B&W
WP Series	ANDXWPCL.PRD	72×72	COL
WP Series	ANDXWPCH.PRD	144×144	COL
	Anatex Data Systems		
ADS 2000	EPSON9L.PRD	60×72	B&W
ADS 2000	EPSON9M.PRD	120×72	B&W
ADS 2000	EPSON9H.PRD	120×216	B&W
ADS 2000	EPSON9VH.PRD	240×216	B&W
	Apple		
Imagewriter II	APPLECL.PRD	60×72	COL
Imagewriter II	APPLECM.PRD	120×72	COL
Imagewriter II	APPLEL.PRD	60×72	B&W
Imagewriter II	APPLEM.PRD	120×72	B&W
Laserwriter, IIf, IIg, Personal	PS.PRD	300×300	B&W

Manufacture/ Printer model	Definition	Resolution	B&W/ COL
	AT&T		
Model 475	CITOHVL.PRD	80×72	B&W
Model 475	CITOHL.PRD	96×72	B&W
Model 475	CITOHM.PRD	136×72	B&W
Model 475	CITOHH.PRD	160×72	B&W
Model 475	CITOHVH.PRD	160×144	B&W
Model 570	EPSON9L.PRD	60×72	B&W
Model 570	EPSON9M.PRD	120×72	B&W
Model 570	EPSON9H.PRD	120×216	B&W
Model 570	EPSON9VH.PRD	240×216	B&W
Model 583	EPSON2L.PRD	60×60	B&W
Model 583	EPSON2M.PRD	120×60	B&W
Model 583	EPSON2H.PRD	180×180	B&W
	Axonix		
LiteWrite, MilWrite	EPSON9L.PRD	60×72	B&W
LiteWrite, MilWrite	EPSON9M.PRD	120×72	B&W
LiteWrite, MilWrite	EPSON9H.PRD	120×216	B&W
LiteWrite, MilWrite	EPSON9VH.PRD	240×216	B&W
	Bezier		
BP4040	PS.PRD	300×300	B&W
	Blue Chip		
M 200	EPSON9L.PRD	60×72	B&W
M 200	EPSON9M.PRD	120×72	B&W
M 200	EPSON9H.PRD	120×216	B&W
M 200	EPSON9VH.PRD	240×216	B&W
	Brother		
1824L, 2024L	BRO24H.PRD	180×180	B&W
1550, 1809, HL-8e	BRO9L.PRD	60×72	B&W
1550, 1809, HL-8e	BRO9M.PRD	120×72	B&W
1550, 1809, HL-8e	BRO9H.PRD	120×216	B&W

Manufacture/ Printer model	Definition	Resolution	B&W/ COL
	Brother		
1550, 1809, HL-8e	BRO9VH.PRD	240 × 216	B&W
Twinriter 5 WP mode	BROTWNL.PRD	60 × 72	B&W
Twinriter 5 WP mode	BROTWNM.PRD	120 × 72	B&W
Twinriter 5 WP mode	BROTWNH.PRD	120 × 216	B&W
Twinriter 5 WP mode	BROTWNVH.PRD	240 × 216	B&W
M-4309A	EPSON9L.PRD	60 × 72	B&W
M-4309A	EPSON9M.PRD	120 × 72	B&W
M-4309A	EPSON9H.PRD	120 × 216	B&W
M-4309A	EPSON9VH.PRD	240 × 216	B&W
HL-8V, -10V, -4Ve	HPLSRL.PRD	75 × 75	B&W
HL-8V, -10V, -4Ve	HPLSRM.PRD	100 × 100	B&W
HL-8V, -10V, -4Ve	HPLSRH.PRD	150 × 150	B&W
HL-8V, -10V, -4Ve	HPLSRVH.PRD	300 × 300	B&W
HL-4PS, HL-8PS	PS.PRD	300 × 300	B&W
HT-500PS	PSC.PRD	300 × 300	COL
	Bull HN Information Systems		
Compuprint 970	EPSON9L.PRD	60 × 72	B&W
Compuprint 970	EPSON9M.PRD	120 × 72	B&W
Compuprint 970	EPSON9H.PRD	120 × 216	B&W
Compuprint 970	EPSON9VH.PRD	240 × 216	B&W
	Camintonn		
TurboLaser PS-Plus 3	PS.PRD	300 × 300	B&W
	CAL-ABCO		
Legend 1385, CP-VII	EPSON9L.PRD	60 × 72	B&W
Legend 1385, CP-VII	EPSON9M.PRD	120 × 72	B&W
Legend 1385, CP-VII	EPSON9H.PRD	120 × 216	B&W
Legend 1385, CP-VII	EPSON9VH.PRD	240 × 216	B&W

Manufacture/ Printer model	Definition	Resolution	B&W/ COL
	CalComp		
ColorMaster Plus	PSC.PRD	300×300	COL
	Canon		
BJ 130 Inkjet	CANONBJH.PRD	180×180	B&W
BJ 130 Inkjet	CANONBJV.PRD	360×360	B&W
LBP-8	CANONLL.PRD	75×75	B&W
LBP-8	CANONLM.PRD	100×100	B&W
LBP-8	CANONLH.PRD	150×150	B&W
LBP-8	CANONLVH.PRD	300×300	B&W
PW-1156A	EPSON9L.PRD	60×72	B&W
PW-1156A	EPSON9M.PRD	120×72	B&W
PW-1156A	EPSON9H.PRD	120×216	B&W
PW-1156A	EPSON9VH.PRD	240×216	B&W
BJ-800, BJ-830, BJ-20	EPSON2L.PRD	60×60	B&W
BJ-800, BJ-830, BJ-20	EPSON2M.PRD	120×60	B&W
BJ-800, BJ-830, BJ-20	EPSON2H.PRD	180×180	B&W
BJC-800, BJC-830	EPSON2CH.PRD	180×180	COL
BJC-800, BJC-830	EPSON2CV.PRD	360×360	COL
PJ1080A Inkjet	CANONPJ.PRD	84×84	COL
	Centronics		
All Models	CENTRONL.PRD	60×60	B&W
	CIE		
CI-250, CI-500	EPSON9L.PRD	60×72	B&W
CI-250, CI-500	EPSON9M.PRD	120×72	B&W
CI-250, CI-500	EPSON9H.PRD	120×216	B&W
CI-250, CI-500	EPSON9VH.PRD	240×216	B&W
	Citizen		
MSP-10/25, 200GX	CITZN9L.PRD	60×72	B&W
MSP-10/25, 200GX	CITZN9M.PRD	120×72	B&W
MSP-10/25, 200GX	CITZN9H.PRD	120×216	B&W
MSP-10/25, 200GX	CITZN9VH.PRD	240×216	B&W
MSP-10/25, 200GX	CITZN9CL.PRD	60×72	COL
MSP-10/25, 200GX	CITZN9CM.PRD	120×72	COL
MSP-10/25, 200GX	CITZN9CH.PRD	120×216	COL

Manufacture/ Printer model	Definition	Resolution	B&W/ COL
	Citizen		
MSP-10/25, 200GX	CITZN9CV.PRD	240 × 216	COL
GSX-140/130/145/ 240, PN48	CITZN24L.PRD	60 × 60	B&W
GSX-140/130/145/ 240, PN48	CITZN24M.PRD	120 × 60	B&W
GSX-140/130/ 145/240, PN48	CITZN24H.PRD	180 × 180	B&W
GSX-140/130/145/ 240, PN48	CITZN24V.PRD	360 × 360	B&W
GSX-140/130/ 145/240, PN48	CITZ24CH.PRD	180 × 180	COL
GSX-140/130/ 145/240, PN48	CITZ24CV.PRD	360 × 360	COL
	Compaq		
PageMarq 15/20	HPLSRL.PRD	75 × 75	B&W
PageMarq 15/20	HPLSRM.PRD	100 × 100	B&W
PageMarq 15/20	HPLSRH.PRD	150 × 150	B&W
PageMarq 15/20	HPLSRVH.PRD	300 × 300	B&W
	C.Itoh		
8510, 8600, Prowriter	CITOHVL.PRD	80 × 72	B&W
8510, 8600, Prowriter	CITOHL.PRD	96 × 72	B&W
8510, 8600, Prowriter	CITOHM.PRD	136 × 72	B&W
8510, 8600, Prowriter	CITOHH.PRD	160 × 72	B&W
8510, 8600, Prowriter	CITOHVH.PRD	160 × 144	B&W
C-310, 5000	EPSON9L.PRD	60 × 72	B&W
C-310, 5000	EPSON9M.PRD	120 × 72	B&W
C-310, 5000	EPSON9H.PRD	120 × 216	B&W
C-310, 5000	EPSON9VH.PRD	240 × 216	B&W
C-610, C-610II, Prowriter	EPSON2L.PRD	60 × 60	B&W
C-610 C-610II, Prowriter	EPSON2M.PRD	120 × 60	B&W
C-610 C-610II, Prowriter	EPSON2H.PRD	180 × 180	B&W

Manufacture/ Printer model	Definition	Resolution	B&W/ COL
	C.Itoh		
ProWriter CI-4/CI-8/CI-8e	HPLSRL.PRD	75 × 75	B&W
ProWriter CI-4/CI-8/CI-8e	HPLSRM.PRD	100 × 100	B&W
ProWriter CI-4/CI-8/CI-8e	HPLSRH.PRD	150 × 150	B&W
ProWriter CI-4/CI-8/CI-8e	HPLSRVH.PRD	300 × 300	B&W
	Dataproducts		
8050/8070	DATAPM.PRD	168 × 84	B&W
8050/8070	DATAPCM.PRD	168 × 84	COL
8052C	IBMCLRL.PRD	60 × 72	B&W
8052C	IBMCLRM.PRD	120 × 72	B&W
LX-455	EPSON9L.PRD	60 × 72	B&W
LX-455	EPSON9M.PRD	120 × 72	B&W
LX-455	EPSON9H.PRD	120 × 216	B&W
LX-455	EPSON9VH.PRD	240 × 216	B&W
LZR 1555/1560	HPLSRL.PRD	75 × 75	B&W
LZR 1555/1560	HPLSRM.PRD	100 × 100	B&W
LZR 1555/1560	HPLSRH.PRD	150 × 150	B&W
LZR 1555/1560	HPLSRVH.PRD	300 × 300	B&W
LZR-960	PS.PRD	300 × 300	B&W
	Datasouth		
All Models	DATASL.PRD	72 × 72	B&W
All Models	DATASH.PRD	144 × 144	B&W
XL-300	EPSON9L.PRD	60 × 72	B&W
XL-300	EPSON9M.PRD	120 × 72	B&W
XL-300	EPSON9H.PRD	120 × 216	B&W
XL-300	EPSON9VH.PRD	240 × 216	B&W
	DEC		
LA50, LA100, LN03, DECwriter	DECLAL.PRD	144 × 72	B&W
LA50, LA100, LN03, DECwriter	DECLAH.PRD	180 × 72	B&W
LA75+, LA424	IBMGRL.PRD	60 × 72	B&W
LA75+, LA424	IBMGRM.PRD	120 × 72	B&W
LA75+, LA424	IBMGRH.PRD	120 × 216	B&W
LA75+, LA424	IBMGRVH.PRD	240 × 216	B&W

Manufacture/ Printer model	Definition	Resolution	B&W/ COL
	DEC		
multiJET 2000	HPLSRL.PRD	75 × 75	B&W
multiJET 2000	HPLSRM.PRD	100 × 100	B&W
multiJET 2000	HPLSRH.PRD	150 × 150	B&W
multiJET 2000	HPLSRVH.PRD	300 × 300	B&W
DECLaser 1150/ 2150/2250/3250	PS.PRD	300 × 300	B&W
	Desktop		
Laser Beam	HPLSRL.PRD	75 × 75	B&W
Laser Beam	HPLSRM.PRD	100 × 100	B&W
Laser Beam	HPLSRH.PRD	150 × 150	B&W
Laser Beam	HPLSRVH.PRD	300 × 300	B&W
	Diablo		
S32	DIABLSL.PRD	70 × 70	B&W
C-150 Inkjet	DIABLCCM.PRD	120 × 120	COL
P Series, 34LQ	EPSON9L.PRD	60 × 72	B&W
P Series, 34LQ	EPSON9M.PRD	120 × 72	B&W
P Series, 34LQ	EPSON9H.PRD	120 × 216	B&W
P Series, 34LQ	EPSON9VH.PRD	240 × 216	B&W
	Diconix		
150	EPSON9L.PRD	60 × 72	B&W
150	EPSON9M.PRD	120 × 72	B&W
150	EPSON9H.PRD	120 × 216	B&W
150	EPSON9VH.PRD	240 × 216	B&W
	Dynax-Fortis		
DM20, DH45	BROTWNL.PRD	60 × 72	B&W
DM20, DH45	BROTWNM.PRD	120 × 72	B&W
DM20, DH45	BROTWNH.PRD	120 × 216	B&W
DM20, DH45	BROTWNVH.PRD	240 × 216	B&W
	Epson		
LQ, SQ, or Action Printer Models	EPSON2L.PRD	60 × 60	B&W
LQ, SQ, or Action Printer Models	EPSON2M.PRD	120 3 60	B&W

Manufacture/ Printer model	Definition	Resolution	B&W/ COL
	Epson		
LQ, SQ, or Action Printer Models	EPSON2H.PRD	180 × 180	B&W
LQ, SQ, or Action Printer Models	EPSON2VH.PRD	360 × 360	B&W
LQ, SQ, or Action Printer Models	EPSON2CH.PRD	180 × 180	COL
LQ, SQ, or Action Printer Models	EPSON2CV.PRD	360 × 360	COL
EPL-6000/7000/ 7500	EPSON6L.PRD	75 × 75	B&W
EPL-6000/7000/ 7500	EPSON6M.PRD	100 × 100	B&W
EPL-6000/7000/ 7500	EPSON6H.PRD	150 × 150	B&W
EPL-6000/7000/ 7500	EPSON6VH.PRD	300 × 300	B&W
MX, FX, RX, JX, LX, and DFX	EPSON9L.PRD	60 × 72	B&W
MX, FX, RX, JX, LX, and DFX	EPSON9M.PRD	120 × 72	B&W
FX, RX, JX, LX, and DFX	EPSON9H.PRD	120 × 216	B&W
FX, RX, JX, LX, and DFX	EPSON9VH.PRD	240 × 216	B&W
MX, FX, RX, JX, LX, and DFX	EPSON9CL.PRD	60 × 72	COL
MX, FX, RX, JX, LX, and DFX	EPSON9CM.PRD	120 × 72	COL
FX, RX, JX, LX, and DFX	EPSON9CH.PRD	120 × 216	COL
FX, RX, JX, LX, and DFX	EPSON9CV.PRD	240 × 216	COL
GQ 3500 Native Mode	EPSONGQH.PRD	300 × 300	B&W
ActionLaser II/ EPL-8000	HPLSRL.PRD	75 × 75	B&W
ActionLaser II/EPL-8000	HPLSRM.PRD	100 × 100	B&W
ActionLaser II/ EPL-8000	HPLSRH.PRD	150 × 150	B&W
ActionLaser II/ EPL-8000	HPLSRVH.PRD	300 × 300	B&W

Manufacture/ Printer model	Definition	Resolution	B&W/ COL
	Everex		
Laser Script LX	HPLSRL.PRD	75×75	B&W
Laser Script LX	HPLSRM.PRD	100×100	B&W
Laser Script LX	HPLSRH.PRD	150×150	B&W
Laser Script LX	HPLSRVH.PRD	300×300	B&W
Laser Script LX	PS.PRD	300×300	B&W
	Facit		
4528	FAC4528L.PRD	60×60	B&W
4542, 4544	FAC4542L.PRD	70×70	B&W
B2400	EPSON2L.PRD	60×60	B&W
B2400	EPSON2M.PRD	120×60	B&W
B2400	EPSON2H.PRD	180×180	B&W
B3550C	EPSON9L.PRD	60×72	B&W
B3550C	EPSON9M.PRD	120×72	B&W
B3550C	EPSON9H.PRD	120×216	B&W
B3550C	EPSON9VH.PRD	240×216	B&W
	Fortis		
DP600S	HPLSRL.PRD	75×75	B&W
DP600S	HPLSRM.PRD	100×100	B&W
DP600S	HPLSRH.PRD	150×150	B&W
DP600S	HPLSRVH.PRD	300×300	B&W
DH45	BROTWNL.PRD	60×72	B&W
DH45	BROTWNM.PRD	120×72	B&W
DH45	BROTWNH.PRD	120×216	B&W
DH45	BROTWNVH.PRD	240×216	B&W
DM2210, DM2215	EPSON9L.PRD	60×72	B&W
DM2210, DM2215	EPSON9M.PRD	120×72	B&W
DM2210, DM2215	EPSON9H.PRD	120×216	B&W
DM2210, DM2215	EPSON9VH.PRD	240×216	B&W
DQ 4110, 4210, 4215	EPSON2L.PRD	60×60	B&W
DQ 4110, 4210, 4215	EPSON2M.PRD	120×60	B&W
DQ 4110, 4210, 4215	EPSON2H.PRD	180×180	B&W
DP600P	PS.PRD	300×300	B&W
	Fujitsu		
24C	FUJI24CH.PRD	180×180	B&W

Manufacture/ Printer model	Definition	Resolution	B&W/ COL
	Fujitsu		
24C	FUJI24CV.PRD	360 × 180	B&W
24C	FUJ24CCH.PRD	180 × 180	COL
24C	FUJ24CCV.PRD	360 × 180	COL
24D	FUJI24DL.PRD	60 × 60	B&W
24D	FUJI24DM.PRD	90 × 90	B&W
24D	FUJI24DH.PRD	180 × 180	B&W
DL 1200/3600/ 4400/4800/5800	EPSON2L.PRD	60 × 60	B&W
DL 1200/3600/ 4400/4800/5800	EPSON2M.PRD	120 × 60	B&W
DL 1200/3600/ 4400/4800/5800	EPSON2H.PRD	180 × 180	B&W
RX 7200/7300E, PrintPartner 10	HPLSRL.PRD	75 × 75	B&W
RX 7200/7300E, PrintPartner 10	HPLSRM.PRD	100 × 100	B&W
RX 7200/7300E, PrintPartner 10	HPLSRH.PRD	150 × 150	B&W
RX 7200/7300E, PrintPartner 10	HPLSRVH.PRD	300 × 300	B&W
RX 7100PS	PS.PRD	300 × 300	B&W
	GCC		
BLP II(S)	PS.PRD	300 × 300	B&W
	GENICOM		
3180-3404 Series	GENICOML.PRD	72 × 72	B&W
3410, 3820, 3840	EPSON9L.PRD	60 × 72	B&W
3410, 3820, 3840	EPSON9M.PRD	120 × 72	B&W
3410, 3820, 3840	EPSON9H.PRD	120 × 216	B&W
3410, 3820, 3840	EPSON9VH.PRD	240 × 216	B&W
1040	EPSON2L.PRD	60 × 60	B&W
1040	EPSON2M.PRD	120 × 60	B&W
1040	EPSON2H.PRD	180 × 180	B&W
4440 XT	IBMGRL.PRD	60 × 72	B&W
4440 XT	IBMGRM.PRD	120 × 72	B&W
4440 XT	IBMGRH.PRD	120 × 216	B&W
4440 XT	IBMGRVH.PRD	240 × 216	B&W
7170	HPLSRL.PRD	75 × 75	B&W
7170	HPLSRM.PRD	100 × 100	B&W
7170	HPLSRH.PRD	150 × 150	B&W
7170	HPLSRVH.PRD	300 × 300	B&W

Manufacture/ Printer model	Definition	Resolution	B&W/ COL
	Gorilla		
Banana	GORILLAM.PRD	60 × 63	B&W
	Hermes		
Printer I	EPSON9L.PRD	60 × 72	B&W
Printer I	EPSON9M.PRD	120 × 72	B&W
	Hewlett-Packard		
7600 Model 355, DesignJet	HP7600M.PRD	102 × 102	B&W
7600 Model 355, DesignJet	HP7600H.PRD	406 × 406	B&W
7600 Model 355	HP7600CM.PRD	102 × 102	COL
7600 Model 355	HP7600CH.PRD	406 × 406	COL
LaserJet/DeskJet— All Models	HPLSRL.PRD	75 × 75	B&W
LaserJet/DeskJet— All Models	HPLSRM.PRD	100 × 100	B&W
LaserJet/DeskJet— All Models	HPLSRH.PRD	150 × 150	B&W
LaserJet/DeskJet— All Models	HPLSRVH.PRD	300 × 300	B&W
LaserJet 4	HPLSRVVH.PRD	600 × 600	B&W
DeskJet 500C/ 550C, PaintJet XL300	HPDSKCL.PRD	75 × 75	COL
DeskJet 500C/ 550C, PaintJet XL300	HPDSKCM.PRD	100 × 100	COL
DeskJet 500C/ 550C, PaintJet XL300	HPDSKCH.PRD	150 × 150	COL
DeskJet 500C/ 550C, PaintJet XL300	HPDSKCVH.PRD	300 × 300	COL
PaintJet— All Models	90 × 90 HPPNTM.PRD	B&W	
PaintJet— All Models	HPPNTH.PRD	180 × 180	B&W
PaintJet— All Models	HPPNTCM.PRD	90 × 90	COL
PaintJet— All Models	HPPNTCMT.PRD	90 × 90	COL

Manufacture/ Printer model	Definition	Resolution	B&W/ COL
	Hewlett-Packard		
PaintJet— All Models	HPPNTCH.PRD	180 × 180	COL
QuietJet	HPQJTEL.PRD	96 × 96	B&W
QuietJet	HPQJTEM.PRD	192 × 96	B&W
QuietJet	HPQJTEH.PRD	192 × 192	B&W
QuietJet	HPQJTL.PRD	96 × 96	B&W
QuietJet	HPQJTM.PRD	192 × 96	B&W
QuietJet	HPQJTH.PRD	192 × 192	B&W
ThinkJet	HPTNKEM.PRD	192 × 96	B&W
ThinkJet	HPTNKM.PRD	192 × 96	B&W
LaserJet 4 (with PostScript)	PS.PRD	300 × 300	B&W
	Hyundai		
HDP-910/920	EPSON9L.PRD	60 × 72	B&W
HDP-910/920	EPSON9M.PRD	120 × 72	B&W
	IBM		
3852-1 84 × 84	Color Inkjet COL	IBM381CM.PRD	
3852-2 100 × 96	Color Inkjet COL	IBM382CM.PRD	
3852 Color Inkjet	IBM38M.PRD	84 × 63	B&W
Color Printer	IBMCLRL.PRD	60 × 72	B&W
Color Printer	IBMCLRM.PRD	120 × 72	B&W
Graphics, Proprinter, 2380 series	IBMGRL.PRD	60 × 72	B&W
Graphics, Proprinter, 2380 series	IBMGRM.PRD	120 × 72	B&W
Graphics, Proprinter, 2380 series	IBMGRH.PRD	120 × 216	B&W
Graphics, Proprinter, 2380 series	IBMGRVH.PRD	120 × 216	B&W
Personal Printer 2390, ExecJet	EPSON2L.PRD	60 × 60	B&W
Personal Printer 2390, ExecJet	EPSON2M.PRD	120 × 60	B&W

Manufacture/ Printer model	Definition	Resolution	B&W/ COL
IBM			
Personal Printer 2390, ExecJet	EPSON2H.PRD	180×180	B&W
LaserPrinter 6p/10p	HPLSRL.PRD	75×75	B&W
LaserPrinter 6p/10p	HPLSRM.PRD	100×100	B&W
LaserPrinter 6p/10p	HPLSRH.PRD	150×150	B&W
LaserPrinter 6p/10p	HPLSRVH.PRD	300×300	B&W
IDS			
440	IDS440L.PRD	64×64	B&W
Prism, 560, 480, P132, P80	IDSM.PRD	84×84	B&W
Prism, 560, 480, P132, P80	IDSCM.PRD	84×84	COL
Integrex			
Colour Jet 132	INTE132L.PRD	60×60	B&W
JDL			
750	JDL750L.PRD	60×60	B&W
750	JDL750M.PRD	90×90	B&W
750	JDL750H.PRD	180×180	B&W
750	JDL750CL.PRD	60×60	COL
750	JDL750CM.PRD	90×90	COL
750	JDL750CH.PRD	180×180	COL
Kentek			
K30D	HPLSRL.PRD	75×75	B&W
K30D	HPLSRM.PRD	100×100	B&W
K30D	HPLSRH.PRD	150×150	B&W
K30D	HPLSRVH.PRD	300×300	B&W
Kodak Diconix			
150	EPSON9L.PRD	60×72	B&W
150	EPSON9M.PRD	120×72	B&W

Manufacture/ Printer model	Definition	Resolution	B&W/ COL
	Kodak Diconix		
150	EPSON9H.PRD	120×216	B&W
150	EPSON9VH.PRD	240×216	B&W
Ektaplus 7008	HPLSRL.PRD	75×75	B&W
Ektaplus 7008	HPLSRM.PRD	100×100	B&W
Ektaplus 7008	HPLSRH.PRD	150×150	B&W
Ektaplus 7008	HPLSRVH.PRD	300×300	B&W
Color 4	HPPNTM.PRD	90×90	B&W
Color 4	HPPNTH.PRD	180×180	B&W
Color 4	HPPNTCM.PRD	90×90	COL
Color 4	HPPNTCMT.PRD	90×90	COL
Color 4	HPPNTCH.PRD	180×180	COL
	Kyocera		
Ecosys a-Si FS-1500A	HPLSRL.PRD	75×75	B&W
Ecosys a-Si FS-1500A	HPLSRM.PRD	100×100	B&W
Ecosys a-Si FS-1500A	HPLSRH.PRD	150×150	B&W
Ecosys a-Si FS-1500A	HPLSRVH.PRD	300×300	B&W
	Laser Computer		
190E, 240	EPSON9L.PRD	60×72	B&W
190E, 240	EPSON9M.PRD	120×72	B&W
190E, 240	EPSON9H.PRD	120×216	B&W
190E, 240	EPSON9VH.PRD	240×216	B&W
	Laser Master		
Unity 1000/1200XL, WinPrinter 800	HPLSRL.PRD	75×75	B&W
Unity 1000/1200XL, WinPrinter 800	HPLSRM.PRD	100×100	B&W
Unity 1000/1200XL, WinPrinter 800	HPLSRH.PRD	150×150	B&W
Unity 1000/1200XL, WinPrinter 800	HPLSRVH.PRD	300×300	B&W
TrueTech 800/1000	PS.PRD	300×300	B&W

Manufacture/ Printer model	Definition	Resolution	B&W/ COL
	Malibu		
All Models	MALIBUL.PRD	60×60	B&W
	Mannesmann Tally		
160	MAN160L.PRD	50×64	B&W
160	MAN160M.PRD	100×64	B&W
160	MAN160H.PRD	133×64	B&W
420, 440	MAN420L.PRD	60×60	B&W
Spirit 80, 81	MANSPRTL.PRD	80×72	B&W
Spirit 80, 81	MANSPRTM.PRD	160×72	B&W
Spirit 80, 81	MANSPRTH.PRD	160×216	B&W
905, 908, 910, 661, 735	HPLSRL.PRD	75×75	B&W
905, 908, 910, 661, 735	HPLSRM.PRD	100×100	B&W
905, 908, 910, 661, 735	HPLSRH.PRD	150×150	B&W
905, 908, 910, 661, 735	HPLSRVH.PRD	300×300	B&W
MT150/9,MT151/9	EPSON9L.PRD	60×72	B&W
MT150/9,MT151/9	EPSON9M.PRD	120×72	B&W
MT150/9,MT151/9	EPSON9H.PRD	120×216	B&W
MT150/9,MT151/9	EPSON9VH.PRD	240×216	B&W
MT150/24,151/24, 82	EPSON2L.PRD	60×60	B&W
MT150/24,151/24, 82	EPSON2M.PRD	120×60	B&W
MT150/24,151/24, 82	EPSON2H.PRD	180×180	B&W
All PostScript models	PS.PRD	300×300	B&W
	Microtek		
TrueLaser	PS.PRD	300×300	B&W
	Mitsubishi		
DiamondColor Print 300PS	PSC.PRD	300×300	COL
CHC-S446i ColorStream/DS	PSC.PRD	300×300	COL

Manufacture/ Printer model	Definition	Resolution	B&W/ COL
MPI			
All Models	MPIL.PRD	60 × 72	B&W
All Models	MPIM.PRD	120 × 72	B&W
All Models	MPIH.PRD	120 × 144	B&W
NEC			
P2200/3200/3300/ 5300/9300 models	NEC24L.PRD	60 × 60	B&W
P2200/3200/3300/ 5300/9300 models	NEC24M.PRD	120 × 60	B&W
P2200/3200/3300/ 5300/9300 models	NEC24H.PRD	180 × 180	B&W
P2200/3200/3300/ 5300/9300 models	NEC24VH.PRD	360 × 360	B&W
P2200, P5300, 24 pin models	NEC24CH.PRD	180 × 180	COL
P2200, P5300, 24 pin models	NEC24CVH.PRD	360 × 360	COL
8023	NEC8023L.PRD	72 × 72	B&W
8027A	NEC8027L.PRD	80 × 72	B&W
P2, P3, CP2, CP3, 9 pin models	NEC9L.PRD	60 × 60	B&W
P2, P3, CP2, CP3, 9 pin models	NEC9M.PRD	120 × 60	B&W
P2, P3, CP2, CP3, 9 pin models	NEC9H.PRD	120 × 120	B&W
P2, P3, CP2, CP3, 9 pin models	NEC9VH.PRD	240 × 240	B&W
P2, P3, CP2, CP3, 9 pin models	NEC9CL.PRD	60 × 60	COL
P2, P3, CP2, CP3, 9 pin models	NEC9CM.PRD	120 × 60	COL
P2, P3, CP2, CP3, 9 pin models	NEC9CH.PRD	120 × 120	COL
P2, P3, CP2, CP3, 9 pin models	NEC9CVH.PRD	240 × 240	COL
LC 890XL, SilentWriter 95	HPLSRL.PRD	75 × 75	B&W
LC 890XL, SilentWriter 95	HPLSRM.PRD	100 × 100	B&W
LC 890XL, SilentWriter 95	HPLSRH.PRD	150 × 150	B&W
LC 890XL, SilentWriter 95	HPLSRVH.PRD	300 × 300	B&W

Manufacture/ Printer model	Definition	Resolution	B&W/ COL
NEC			
All PostScript models	PS.PRD	300×300	B&W
NewGen			
TurboPS/400p/ 630En/660/ 840e/880	HPLSRL.PRD	75×75	B&W
TurboPS/400p/ 630En/660/ 840e/880	HPLSRM.PRD	100×100	B&W
TurboPS/400p/ 630En/660/ 840e/880	HPLSRH.PRD	150×150	B&W
TurboPS/400p/ 630En/660/ 840e/880	HPLSRVH.PRD	300×300	B&W
TurboPS/1200T	HPLSRL.PRD	75×75	B&W
TurboPS/1200T	HPLSRM.PRD	100×100	B&W
TurboPS/1200T	HPLSRH.PRD	150×150	B&W
TurboPS/1200T	HPLSRVH.PRD	300×300	B&W
North Atlantic Quantex			
All Models	NORTHL.PRD	72×72	B&W
All Models	NORTHM.PRD	120×72	B&W
All Models	NORTHH.PRD	144×72	B&W
Okidata			
Okimate 20	OKI20L.PRD	60×72	COL
2410, 2350	OKI2410L.PRD	72×72	B&W
2410, 2350, 24 pin models	OKI24L.PRD	60×60	B&W
2410, 2350, 24 pin models	OKI24M.PRD	120×60	B&W
2410, 2350, 24 pin models	OKI24H.PRD	180×180	B&W
2410, 2350, 24 pin models	OKI24VH.PRD	363×363	B&W
2410, 2350, 24 pin models	OKI24CH.PRD	180×180	COL
ML-92, ML-93, ML-82, ML-83 (w/o P&P)	OKI9L.PRD	72×72	B&W

Manufacture/ Printer model	Definition	Resolution	B&W/ COL
	Okidata		
ML-92, ML-93, ML-82, ML-83 (w/o P&P)	OKI9M.PRD	144 × 72	B&W
ML-92, ML-93, ML-82, ML-83 (w/o P&P)	OKI9H.PRD	144 × 144	B&W
Preceding models (w/Plug & Play)	EPSON9L.PRD	60 × 72	B&W
Preceding models (w/Plug & Play)	EPSON9M.PRD	120 × 72	B&W
Preceding models (w/Plug & Play)	EPSON9H.PRD	120 × 216	B&W
Preceding models (w/Plug & Play)	EPSON9VH.PRD	240 × 216	B&W
Laserline (HP)	HPLSRL.PRD	75 × 75	B&W
Laserline (HP)	HPLSRM.PRD	100 × 100	B&W
Laserline (HP)	HPLSRH.PRD	150 × 150	B&W
Laserline (HP)	HPLSRVH.PRD	300 × 300	B&W
Pacemark 3410	EPSON9L.PRD	60 × 72	B&W
Pacemark 3410	EPSON9M.PRD	120 × 72	B&W
Pacemark 3410	EPSON9H.PRD	120 × 216	B&W
Pacemark 3410	EPSON9VH.PRD	240 × 216	B&W
Microline 184 Turbo	IBMGRL.PRD	60 × 72	B&W
Microline 184 Turbo	IBMGRM.PRD	120 × 72	B&W
Microline 184 Turbo	IBMGRH.PRD	120 × 216	B&W
Microline 184 Turbo	IBMGRVH.PRD	240 × 216	B&W
OL 810 LED	HPLSRL.PRD	75 × 75	B&W
OL 810 LED	HPLSRM.PRD	100 × 100	B&W
OL 810 LED	HPLSRH.PRD	150 × 150	B&W
OL 810 LED	HPLSRVH.PRD	300 × 300	B&W
OL 830	PS.PRD	300 × 300	B&W
	Olympia		
NP	EPSON9L.PRD	60 × 72	B&W
NP	EPSON9M.PRD	120 × 72	B&W
NP	EPSON9H.PRD	120 × 216	B&W
NP	EPSON9VH.PRD	240 × 216	B&W

Manufacture/ Printer model	Definition	Resolution	B&W/ COL
	Output Technology		
All models	EPSON9L.PRD	60×72	B&W
All models	EPSON9M.PRD	120×72	B&W
All models	EPSON9H.PRD	120×216	B&W
All models	EPSON9VH.PRD	240×216	B&W
LaserMatrix 1000 Model 5	HPLSRL.PRD	75×75	B&W
LaserMatrix 1000 Model 5	HPLSRM.PRD	100×100	B&W
LaserMatrix 1000 Model 5	HPLSRH.PRD	150×150	B&W
LaserMatrix 1000 Model 5	HPLSRVH.PRD	300×300	B&W
	PMC		
DMP-85	NEC8027L.PRD	80×72	B&W
	Panasonic		
All Models (9-pin printers)	PANASL.PRD	60×72	B&W
All Models (9-pin printers)	PANASM.PRD	120×72	B&W
All Models (9-pin printers)	PANASH.PRD	120×216	B&W
All Models (9-pin printers)	PANASVH.PRD	240×216	B&W
All Models (24-pin printers)	EPSON2L.PRD	60×60	B&W
All Models (24-pin printers)	EPSON2M.PRD	120×60	B&W
All Models (24-pin printers)	EPSON2H.PRD	180×180	B&W
KX-P4410/4430	HPLSRL.PRD	75×75	B&W
KX-P4410/4430	HPLSRM.PRD	100×100	B&W
KX-P4410/4430	HPLSRH.PRD	150×150	B&W
KX-P4410/4430	HPLSRVH.PRD	300×300	B&W
All PostScript models	PS.PRD	300×300	B&W
	PostScript		
All models	PS.PRD	300×300	B&W

Manufacture/ Printer model	Definition	Resolution	B&W/ COL
	Printronix		
L2324	HPLSRL.PRD	75×75	B&W
L2324	HPLSRM.PRD	100×100	B&W
L2324	HPLSRH.PRD	150×150	B&W
L2324	HPLSRVH.PRD	300×300	B&W
	QMS		
All PostScript models	PS.PRD	300×300	B&W
	Quadram		
Quadjet	QUADRL.PRD	80×80	B&W
Quadjet	QUADRCL.PRD	70×72	COL
	Qume		
All PostScript models	PS.PRD	300×300	B&W
	Raster Devices		
All PostScript models	PS.PRD	300×300	B&W
	Ricoh		
All PostScript models	PS.PRD	300×300	B&W
	Riteman		
All models	EPSON9L.PRD	60×72	B&W
All models	EPSON9M.PRD	120×72	B&W
All models	EPSON9H.PRD	120×216	B&W
All models	EPSON9VH.PRD	240×216	B&W
	Royal		
CJP 450	HPLSRL.PRD	75×75	B&W
CJP 450	HPLSRM.PRD	100×100	B&W
CJP 450	HPLSRH.PRD	150×150	B&W
CJP 450	HPLSRVH.PRD	300×300	B&W

Manufacture/ Printer model	Definition	Resolution	B&W/ COL
	Samsung		
Finalé 8000	HPLSRL.PRD	75×75	B&W
Finalé 8000	HPLSRM.PRD	100×100	B&W
Finalé 8000	HPLSRH.PRD	150×150	B&W
Finalé 8000	HPLSRVH.PRD	300×300	B&W
	Seikosha		
GP-100A	SEIKOL.PRD	60×63	B&W
SP-180AI/1600AI/ 2400/2415, BP-5460	EPSON9L.PRD	60×72	B&W
SP-180AI/1600AI/ 2400/2415, BP-5460	EPSON9M.PRD	120×72	B&W
SP-180AI/1600AI/ 2400/2415, BP-5460	EPSON9H.PRD	120×216	B&W
SP-180AI/1600AI/ 2400/2415, BP-5460	EPSON9VH.PRD	240×216	B&W
SL-230AI, LT-20	EPSON2L.PRD	60×60	B&W
SL-230AI, LT-20	EPSON2M.PRD	120×60	B&W
SL-230AI, LT-20	EPSON2H.PRD	180×180	B&W
	Sharp		
JX 720	SHARPCM.PRD	60×63	B&W
JX-9500H	HPLSRL.PRD	75×75	B&W
JX-9500H	HPLSRM.PRD	100×100	B&W
JX-9500H	HPLSRH.PRD	150×150	B&W
JX-9500H	HPLSRVH.PRD	300×300	B&W
JX-9500PS	PS.PRD	300×300	B&W
	Siemens		
PT90, PT88S	EPSON9L.PRD	60×72	B&W
PT90, PT88S	EPSON9M.PRD	120×72	B&W
PT90, PT88S	EPSON9H.PRD	120×216	B&W
PT90, PT88S	EPSON9VH.PRD	240×216	B&W
	Smith-Corona		
D-200, D-300	EPSON9L.PRD	60×72	B&W

Manufacture/ Printer model	Definition	Resolution	B&W/ COL
	Smith-Corona		
D-200, D-300	EPSON9M.PRD	120 × 72	B&W
D-200, D-300	EPSON9H.PRD	120 × 216	B&W
D-200, D-300	EPSON9VH.PRD	240 × 216	B&W
	Star Micronics		
Delta, Radix, Gemini, SD, SR, NX, XR	STAR9L.PRD	60 × 72	B&W
Delta, Radix, Gemini, SD, SR, NX, XR	STAR9M.PRD	120 × 72	B&W
NX, and XR Series	STAR9H.PRD	120 × 144	B&W
NX, and XR Series	STAR9VH.PRD	240 × 144	B&W
SB-10	STAR24H.PRD	180 × 240	B&W
NB24-15, XB24-10/ 15, SJ-48, NX-2430	EPSON2L.PRD	60 × 60	B&W
NB24-15, XB24-10/ 15, SJ-48, NX-2430	EPSON2M.PRD	120 × 60	B&W
NB24-15, XB24-10/ 15, SJ-48, NX-2430	EPSON2H.PRD	180 × 180	B&W
LaserPrinter 4	HPLSRL.PRD	75 × 75	B&W
LaserPrinter 4	HPLSRM.PRD	100 × 100	B&W
LaserPrinter 4	HPLSRH.PRD	150 × 150	B&W
LaserPrinter 4	HPLSRVH.PRD	300 × 300	B&W
LaserPrinter 4 Star Script	PS.PRD	300 × 300	B&W
	Synergystex		
CF1000	HPLSRL.PRD	75 × 75	B&W
CF1000	HPLSRM.PRD	100 × 100	B&W
CF1000	HPLSRH.PRD	150 × 150	B&W
CF1000	HPLSRVH.PRD	300 × 300	B&W
	Talaris		
1590-T Printstation	HPLSRL.PRD	75 × 75	B&W
1590-T Printstation	HPLSRM.PRD	100 × 100	B&W
1590-T Printstation	HPLSRH.PRD	150 × 150	B&W
1590-T Printstation	HPLSRVH.PRD	300 × 300	B&W
	Tandy (Radio Shack)		
2100 Series	TAN2100L.PRD	60 × 60	B&W

Manufacture/ Printer model	Definition	Resolution	B&W/ COL
	Tandy (Radio Shack)		
2100 Series	TAN2100H.PRD	180×180	B&W
DMP-430/440	TAN430M.PRD	120×144	B&W
CGP-220	TANCGPCL.PRD	70×72	COL
CGP-220	TANCGPL.PRD	80×80	B&W
Most Tandy Printers	TANDYL.PRD	60×72	B&W
Most Tandy Printers	TANDYM.PRD	60×144	B&W
IBM Emulation	TANIBML.PRD	60×72	B&W
IBM Emulation	TANIBMM.PRD	120×72	B&W
IBM Emulation	TANIBMH.PRD	120×216	B&W
IBM Emulation	TANIBMVH.PRD	240×216	B&W
DMP-310	EPSON9L.PRD	60×72	B&W
DMP-310	EPSON9M.PRD	120×72	B&W
DMP-310	EPSON9H.PRD	120×216	B&W
DMP-310	EPSON9VH.PRD	240×216	B&W
LP 950	HPLSRL.PRD	75×75	B&W
LP 950	HPLSRM.PRD	100×100	B&W
LP 950	HPLSRH.PRD	150×150	B&W
LP 950	HPLSRVH.PRD	300×300	B&W
	Tektronix		
PhaserII PXe/ IIsd/III PXi	PSC.PRD	300×300	COL
	Texas Instruments		
855/857/865	TI855CL.PRD	60×72	COL
855/857/865	TI855CM.PRD	120×72	COL
855/857/865	TI855CH.PRD	120×144	COL
855/857/865	TI855CVH.PRD	120×144	COL
855/857/865	TI855L.PRD	60×72	B&W
855/857/865	TI855M.PRD	120×72	B&W
855/857/865	TI855H.PRD	120×144	B&W
855/857/865	TI855VH.PRD	144×144	B&W
850	EPSON9L.PRD	60×72	B&W
850	EPSON9M.PRD	120×72	B&W
TI MicroLaser Turbo/XL Turbo	HPLSRL.PRD	75×75	B&W
TI MicroLaser Turbo/XL Turbo	HPLSRM.PRD	100×100	B&W
TI MicroLaser Turbo/XL Turbo	HPLSRH.PRD	150×150	B&W

Manufacture/ Printer model	Definition	Resolution	B&W/ COL
	Texas Instruments		
TI MicroLaser Turbo/XL Turbo	HPLSRVH.PRD	300×300	B&W
	Toshiba		
1350	TOSH1350.PRD	180×180	B&W
24-Pin Models	TOSH24CE.PRD	360×360	COL
24-Pin Models	TOSH24CH.PRD	180×180	COL
24-Pin Models	TOSH24CV.PRD	360×180	COL
24-Pin Models	TOSH24H.PRD	180×180	B&W
24-Pin Models	TOSH24VH.PRD	360×180	B&W
24-Pin Models	TOSH24EH.PRD	360×360	B&W
Express Writer 301/311	EPSON2L.PRD	60×60	B&W
Express Writer 301/311	EPSON2M.PRD	120×60	B&W
Express Writer 301/311	EPSON2H.PRD	180×180	B&W
PageLaser GX200/ GSX400	HPLSRL.PRD	75×75	B&W
PageLaser GX200/ GSX400	HPLSRM.PRD	100×100	B&W
PageLaser GX200/ GSX400	HPLSRH.PRD	150×150	B&W
PageLaser GX200/ GSX400	HPLSRVH.PRD	300×300	B&W
	Unisys		
AP 1327/9 Mod5, 1371, 115, 37	EPSON9L.PRD	60×72	B&W
AP 1327/9 Mod5, 1371, 115, 37	EPSON9M.PRD	120×72	B&W
AP 1327/9 Mod5, 1371, 115, 37	EPSON9H.PRD	120×216	B&W
AP 1327/9 Mod5, 1371, 115, 37	EPSON9VH.PRD	240×216	B&W
AP 1234	EPSON2L.PRD	60×60	B&W
AP 1234	EPSON2M.PRD	120×60	B&W
AP 1234	EPSON2H.PRD	180×180	B&W
AP 92/94 Mod 37 (HP)	HPLSRL.PRD	75×75	B&W
AP 92/94 Mod 37 (HP)	HPLSRM.PRD	100×100	B&W

Manufacture/ Printer model	Definition	Resolution	B&W/ COL
	Unisys		
AP 92/94 Mod 37 (HP)	HPLSRH.PRD	150 × 150	B&W
AP 92/94 Mod 37 (HP)	HPLSRVH.PRD	300 × 300	B&W
AP 94 (PostScript)	PS.PRD	300 × 300	B&W
	Xante		
Accel-a-Writer 8000	HPLSRL.PRD	75 × 75	B&W
Accel-a-Writer 8000	HPLSRM.PRD	100 × 100	B&W
Accel-a-Writer 8000	HPLSRH.PRD	150 × 150	B&W
Accel-a-Writer 8000	HPLSRVH.PRD	300 × 300	B&W
	Xerox		
2700/4045	XER2700L.PRD	77 × 77	B&W
2700/4045	XER2700H.PRD	154 × 154	B&W
4020 Inkjet	XER4020C.PRD	120 3 120	COL

printers and their corresponding driver entries. By default, PRINTERS is set to use the EPSON2L.DRV driver (a generic Epson 24-pin impact printer driver). Refer to Table 2.1 to select the appropriate driver, then scroll through the available printer drivers by left-clicking on *Select Printer* (or press <p>). As you scroll through each driver, you can see details about each driver in the message bar.

> **SPECIAL NOTE:** If you accidentally pass the desired driver, you can scroll backward through the driver list by pressing <SHIFT> and <p> simultaneously (capital <P>).

Select port. PRINTERS is designed to operate a printer on LPT1 through LPT3, or COM1 or COM2. Left-click on *Select Port* (or press <r>) to scroll through available ports. Remember to connect your printer to the appropriate port before proceeding. By default, LPT1 is the selected port.

Manual codes.   Most printers provide a suite of printer-specific functions and features (i.e., bold print, underlining, double-width print, double-height print, and so on). Although it would be virtually impossible for any diagnostic to test each of these functions for every available printer, PRINTERS provides a means for you to test your printer's functions manually using printer codes (also referred to as *Escape Sequences* or *Escape Codes*). The Manual Codes feature provides a printer technician with almost unlimited versatility in checking and verifying the more subtle features of a printer's operation.

> **INFORMATION ALERT:** In order to enter an Escape Code, you will need the User's Manual for your particular printer. The diskette's documentation lists Escape Codes for several popular printer models, but to test printer-specific functions, you will need printer-specific documentation.

To enter an Escape Code, left-click on *Manual Codes* (or press <C>) in the CONFIGURE menu. A text entry window will appear below the CONFIGURE menu as in Figure 2.3. You may enter up to 50 characters per line. Pressing the <TAB> key or right-clicking anywhere on the display will abort the text entry routine. If you make a mistake in typing, simply backspace past the error and correct the mistake.

Example 1: Setting the Panasonic KX-P1124 to "Underline" mode.   With the text entry routine running, reset the printer (by turning it off and on), then enter the following text, then press <ENTER>:

```
This is a test of default text
```

Your printer should print this text string in its default font and pitch. Now let's set the printer to its *underline mode* using the code <ESC>-1 (from the PRINTERS documentation). Type the three keystrokes and press <ENTER>. Keep in mind that when you press the

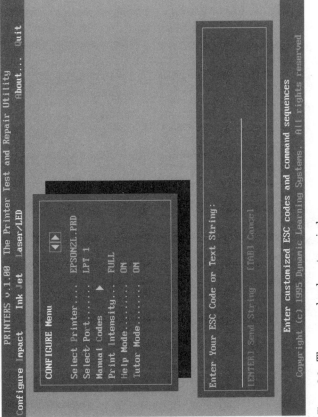

Figure 2.3 The manual code entry window.

<ESC> key, a backspace arrow will appear in that space:

```
<ESC>-1
```

The printer should now be in *underline mode,* so type the following text and press <ENTER>:

```
This is the printer's underline mode
```

The printer should produce this text "underlined." To turn the underline mode off, enter the code <ESC>-0 (from PRINTERS documentation). Type the three keystrokes and press <ENTER>. Keep in mind that when you press the <ESC> key, a backspace arrow will appear in that space:

```
<ESC>-0
```

Now type the following text and press <ENTER>:

```
The underline mode is off
```

The type should no longer be underlined. To leave the text entry routine, press <TAB> or right click anywhere on the display.

Example 2: Setting the Panasonic KX-P1124 to "Letter Quality" (LQ) Mode. With the text entry routine running, reset the printer (by turning it off and on), then enter the following text, then press <ENTER>:

```
This is the printer's default text
```

Your printer should print this text string in its default font and pitch. Now let's set the printer to its LQ mode using the code <ESC>x1 (from PRINTERS documentation). Type the three keystrokes and press <ENTER>. Keep in mind that when you press the <ESC> key, a backspace arrow will appear in that space:

```
<ESC>x1
```

The printer should now be in letter-quality mode, so type the following text and press <ENTER>:

```
This is the printer's LQ mode
```

The printer should produce this text in higher quality than the default. To turn the LQ mode off, enter the code <ESC>x0 (from PRINTERS documentation). Type the three keystrokes and press <ENTER>. Keep in mind that when you press the <ESC> key, a backspace arrow will appear in that space:

```
<ESC>x0
```

Now type the following text and press <ENTER>:

```
The letter quality mode is off
```

The type should be back in its draft form. To leave the text entry routine, press <TAB> or right-click anywhere on the display.

Print intensity. The *print intensity* setting allows you to set the overall darkness and lightness (i.e., contrast) of your test images. There are two choices: HALF and FULL. By default, all images are printed at FULL intensity (maximum contrast). At HALF intensity, the shading is lightened to reduce the image's contrast. You can toggle between FULL and HALF intensity by clicking on *Print Intensity* (or pressing <I>).

For low-resolution devices (i.e., impact printers at 75 dpi or less), FULL intensity will typically yield superior results. For medium-to-high resolution devices (i.e., ink-jet and almost all EP printers), HALF intensity is often better. Of course, you may experiment to find the best settings for your particular printer.

Help mode.   PRINTERS is designed with two online documentation sources that are intended to provide instruction and guidance before and after a test is conducted. The HELP screens appear before the selected test starts, and will give insights into the purpose and objectives of the selected test. You may toggle the HELP mode on or off by left-clicking on *Help Mode* (or pressing <H>). By default, the HELP mode is on. If you turn the HELP mode off, the selected test will start immediately.

Tutor mode.   PRINTERS is designed with two online documentation sources that are intended to provide instruction and guidance before and after a test is conducted. The TUTOR screens appear after the selected test is complete, and will give advice on how to interpret the printed results. You may toggle the TUTOR mode on or off by left-clicking on *Tutor Mode* (or pressing <T>). By default, the TUTOR mode is on. If you turn the TUTOR mode off, there will be no instruction provided when the test is finished.

Running the impact tests

The impact tests allow you to check the operations of almost any impact dot-matrix printer (and any 9-pin or 24-pin printer capable of Epson emulation). From the main menu bar, left-click on *Impact* (or press <I>). The IMPACT DMP Test Menu will appear as shown in Figure 2.4. You can return to the main menu at any time by pressing the <ESC> key or right-clicking anywhere in the display. There are seven functions available from the IMPACT DMP test menu:

- *Preliminary Setup Information*: supplies initial information to help you set up and operate the printer safely

- *Carriage Transport Test*: allows you to test the Impact DMP carriage transport system

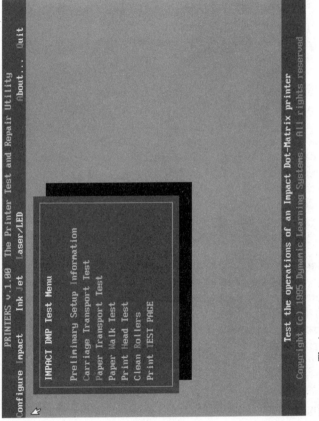

Figure 2.4 The impact test menu.

- *Paper Transport Test*: allows you to test the Impact DMP paper transport system

- *Paper Walk Test*: allows you to check friction feed paper transport systems in Impact DMPs

- *Print Head Test*: allows you to test the Impact DMP print head assembly

- *Clean Rollers*: allows you to check and clean the paper handling rollers

- *Print TEST PAGE*: provides a uniform test pattern for initial or final printer inspection

Preliminary setup information. You may access the preliminary setup information screen by left-clicking on *Preliminary Setup Information* (or press <I>). This is not a test per se, but an information screen intended to provide helpful setup information. Novice troubleshooters will find it helpful to review this information before attempting any of the test sequences below. Experienced troubleshooters may find this to be a handy reminder. To leave the information screen, press <ESC> or right-click anywhere in the display.

Carriage transport test. Impact printers are "moving carriage" devices—that is, the print head is carried left and right across the page surface. This movement is handled by the carriage transport mechanism. Proper printing of text and graphics demands that the print head be positioned precisely in both its left-to-right and right-to-left movement. The *Carriage Transport Test* is designed to test carriage alignment by generating a series of vertical lines as shown in Figure 2.5. The print head sweeps from left to right, producing a series of vertical tick marks—then reverses direction and produces a right-to-left series of tick marks. Similarly, each line of tick marks is the result of two independent passes. Using this approach, we can check carriage alignment not just between lines, but within the same line.

PRINTERS: The Printer Test and Alignment Utility V.1.00
IMPACT CARRIAGE REGISTRATION Test Pattern

Figure 2.5   Printout of the carriage transport test.

If the tick marks are not aligned precisely, there may be some mechanical slop in the carriage mechanics. Badly or erratically placed tick marks may indicate a fault in the carriage motor driver circuitry, or in the carriage home sensor. If marks within the same line are aligned precisely at the edges (but not elsewhere in the line), there may be wiring problems in the print head or print head cable. You may start this test by left-clicking on *Carriage Transport Test* (or press `<C>`).

Paper transport test.   There are two traditional means of moving paper through a printer: *pull* the paper (with a tractor feed), or *push* the paper (with a friction feed). Regardless of the means used, paper must be carried through a printer evenly and consistently—otherwise, print will overlap and cause distortion. The *Paper Transport Test* is designed to check the paper transport system's operation. Although the Paper Transport Test will work with any transport type, it is intended primarily for tractor feed systems that pull the paper through. The test pattern counts off a number of marked passes. You must check each pass to see that they are spaced evenly apart. If not, there may be a problem with the transport mechanics, motor, or driving circuitry. You may start this test by left-clicking on *Paper Transport Test* (or press `<P>`).

Paper walk test.   Like the last test, the *Paper Walk Test* is designed to check the paper transport system's operation. Whereas the Paper Transport Test is best utilized with tractor feed paper transports, the Paper Walk Test is intended primarily for friction feed systems that push the paper through. The test pattern generates a series of evenly spaced horizontal lines. You must check each pass to see that they are spaced evenly apart. If not, there may be a problem with the transport mechanics, motor, or driving circuitry.

Another problem particular to friction feed paper transports is the tendency to "walk the page." Proper friction feed operation depends on roller pressure applied *evenly* across the entire page surface. Any damage, obstructions, or wear may cause excessive roller pressure that can allow the page to spin clockwise or counterclockwise. If you notice lines closer together on the left or right side of the image, the roller assembly may need adjustment or replacement, or there may be an obstruction in the paper path. You may start this test by left-clicking on *Paper Walk Test* (or press <W>).

Print head test. Ideally, every pin on the print head should fire reliably. In actual practice, however, age, lack of routine maintenance, and heat buildup can affect firing reliability. This often results in horizontal white lines in the text where the corresponding print wires fail. The best way to stress-test an impact print head and detect problems is by printing a dense graphic. The impact print head test produces a large black rectangle as shown in Figure 2.6—this demands the proper operation of all print wires, and will often reveal any age, damage, or heat- and maintenance-related issues. You can adjust the speed and density of printing by adjusting print intensity and driver resolution under the CONFIGURE menu.

PRINTERS: The Printer Test and Alignment Utility V.1.00
IMPACT PRINT HEAD Test Pattern

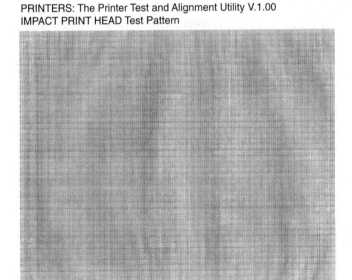

Figure 2.6 Printout of the impact print head test.

Examine the black rectangle for horizontal white lines. Consistent white lines indicate that a print wire is not firing. Check and clean the face of the print head to remove any accumulations of debris that may be jamming the print wire(s). If the problem persists, there may be a fault in the print head or print wire driver circuitry. If white lines appear only briefly or intermittently, there may be wiring problems with the print head cable, or within the print head itself. There may also be an intermittent problem in the corresponding print wire driver circuit. Finally, print intensity should be relatively consistent throughout each pass. Light (faded) printing may indicate trouble with print head wear or spacing, ribbon quality, or the power supply. You may start this test by left-clicking on *Print Head Test* (or press <H>).

Clean rollers.   To combat the dust and debris that naturally accumulate in the printer's mechanics, it is customary to periodically clean the main rollers that handle paper—usually the platen and other major rollers. This is especially important for friction feed paper transports where age and any foreign matter on the rollers can interfere with the paper path and "walk" the page. While it is possible (and sometimes more convenient) to rotate the rollers by hand using the platen knob, the Clean Rollers function provides a paper advance that allows you to streamline the routine cleaning/rejuvenation of roller assemblies. Note that paper *must* be present in the printer to use this function.

The typical cleaning procedure involves rotating the rollers while wiping them gently with a clean cloth lightly dampened with water. You may use a bit of very mild household detergent to remove "gunk" that resists water alone, but avoid using detergent regularly since chemicals applied to rubber and other synthetic roller materials can reduce their pliability. *Never use harsh detergents or solvents—ever*! If you choose to try rejuvenating the rollers with a roller cleaning solvent, use *extreme* caution. First, work in a well-ventilated area (solvent fumes are dangerous). Second, it is impossible to predict how cleaning solvents will affect every possible roller material, so always try the solvent on a small edge patch of the roller in advance. You may start this procedure by left-clicking on *Clean Rollers* (or press <R>). A single cycle will advance the paper transport by two pages.

Print TEST PAGE.   The *TEST PAGE* is typically the first and last test to be run on any printer. Initially, the test page will reveal problems with the print head, paper transport, or carriage transport. You can then proceed with more detailed tests to further isolate and correct the problem(s). When the repair is complete, the TEST PAGE is proof of the printer's operation that you may keep for your records or provide to your customer. The moving-head TEST PAGE pattern is illustrated in Figure 2.7. You may start this test by left-clicking on *Print TEST PAGE* (or press <T>).

Running the ink-jet tests

The ink-jet tests allow you to check the operations of almost any ink-jet dot-matrix printer (and any printer capable of HP DeskJet emulation). From the main menu bar, left-click on *Ink Jet* (or press <J>). The INK JET DMP Test Menu will appear as shown in Figure 2.8. You can return to the main menu at any time by pressing the <ESC> key or right-clicking anywhere in the display. There are seven functions available from the INK JET DMP test menu:

- *Preliminary Setup Information*: supplies initial information to help you set up and operate the ink-jet printer safely

- *Carriage Transport Test*: allows you to test the Ink Jet DMP carriage transport system

PRINTERS: The Printer Test and Alignment Utility V.1.00
IMPACT TEST PAGE Pattern

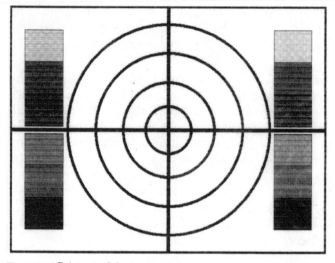

Figure 2.7 Printout of the impact test page.

- *Paper Transport Test*: allows you to test the Ink Jet DMP paper transport system
- *Paper Walk Test*: allows you to check friction feed paper transport systems in Ink Jet DMPs
- *Print Head Test*: allows you to test the Ink Jet DMP print head assembly
- *Clean Rollers*: allows you to check and clean the paper handling rollers
- *Print TEST PAGE*: provides a uniform test pattern for initial or final printer inspection

Preliminary setup information. You may access the preliminary setup information screen by left-clicking on

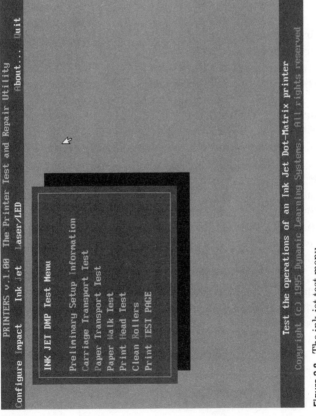

Figure 2.8 The ink-jet test menu.

Preliminary Setup Information (or press <I>). This is not a test per se, but an information screen intended to provide helpful setup information. Novice troubleshooters will find it helpful to review this information before attempting any of the ink-jet test sequences below. Experienced troubleshooters may find this to be a handy reminder. To leave the information screen, press <ESC> or right-click anywhere in the display.

Carriage transport test. Like impact printers, ink-jet printers are "moving carriage" devices—that is, the print head is carried left and right across the page surface. This movement is handled by the carriage transport mechanism. Proper printing of text and graphics demands that the print head be positioned precisely in both its left-to-right and right-to-left movement. The *Carriage Transport Test* is designed to test carriage alignment by generating a series of vertical lines (similar to Fig. 2.5). The print head sweeps from left to right producing a series of vertical tick marks—then reverses direction and produces a right-to-left series of tick marks. Similarly, each line of tick marks is the result of two independent passes. Using this approach, we can check carriage alignment not just between lines, but within the same line.

If the tick marks are not aligned precisely, there may be some mechanical slop in the carriage mechanics. Badly or erratically placed tick marks may indicate a fault in the carriage motor driver circuitry, the mechanical home sensor, or the optical position encoder. If marks within the same line are aligned precisely at the edges (but not elsewhere in the line), there may be wiring problems in the ink-jet print cartridge or print head cable. You may start this test by left-clicking on *Carriage Transport Test* (or press <C>).

Paper transport test. There are two traditional means of moving paper through a printer: *pull* the paper (with a tractor feed), or *push* the paper (with a friction feed). Regardless of the means used, paper must be carried through a printer evenly and consistently—otherwise, print will overlap and cause distortion. The *Paper Transport Test* is designed to check the paper transport system's operation. Whereas the Paper Transport Test will work with any transport type, it is intended primarily for tractor feed systems that pull the paper through. The test pattern counts off a number of marked passes. You must check each pass to see that they are spaced evenly apart. If not, there may be a problem with the transport mechanics, motor, or driving circuitry. You may start this test by left-clicking on *Paper Transport Test* (or press <P>).

Paper walk test. Like the last test, the *Paper Walk Test* is designed to check the paper transport system's operation. Whereas the Paper Transport Test is best utilized with tractor feed paper transports, the Paper Walk Test is intended primarily for friction feed systems that push the paper through. Today's ink-jet printers utilize friction feed systems almost entirely. The test pattern generates a series of evenly spaced horizontal lines. You must check each pass to see that they are spaced evenly apart. If not, there may be a problem with the transport mechanics, motor, or driving circuitry.

Another problem particular to friction feed paper transports is the tendency to "walk the page." Proper friction feed operation depends on roller pressure applied evenly across the entire page surface. Any damage, obstructions, or wear may cause excessive roller pressure that can allow the page to spin clockwise or counterclockwise. This is especially evident in inexpensive ink-jet systems. If you notice lines closer together on the left or right side of the image, the roller assembly may need adjustment or replacement, or there may be an obstruction in the paper path. You may start this test by left-clicking on *Paper Walk Test* (or press <W>).

Print head test. Ideally, every nozzle on the ink cartridge should fire reliably. In actual practice, factors such as cartridge age, lack of routine maintenance, low ink levels, and circuit defects can affect firing reliability. This often results in horizontal white lines in the text where the corresponding print nozzles fail. The best way to stress-test an ink-jet print head and detect problems is by printing a dense graphic. The ink-jet print head test produces a large black rectangle (similar to Figure 2.6)—this demands the proper operation of all print nozzles, and will often reveal any age, damage, or maintenance-related issues. You can adjust the speed and density of printing by adjusting print intensity and driver resolution under the CONFIGURE menu. Remember that this is a very dark image that will require a substantial amount of ink to form. If the current ink cartridge is marginal, you may need to install a new ink cartridge before proceeding.

Examine the black rectangle for horizontal white lines. Consistent white lines indicate that a print nozzle is not firing. Check and clean the face of the print cartridge to remove any accumulations of dried ink or debris that may be jamming the print nozzle(s). If the problem persists, there may be a fault in the print cartridge or print nozzle driver circuitry. If white lines appear only briefly or intermittently, there may be wiring problems with the print head cable, or within the print cartridge itself. There may also be an intermittent problem in the corresponding print nozzle driver circuit. Finally, print intensity should be relatively consistent throughout each pass. Light (faded) printing may indicate poor paper selection, low ink levels, or trouble with the print nozzle power supply. You may start this test by left-clicking on *Print Head Test* (or press <H>).

Clean rollers. To combat the dust and debris that naturally accumulate in the printer's mechanics, it is customary to periodically clean the main rollers that handle paper—usually the platen and other major rollers. This is especially important for friction feed paper transports where age and any foreign matter on the rollers can interfere with the paper path and "walk" the page. Few contemporary ink-jet designs allow you to rotate the rollers by hand (using a platen knob), so the Clean Rollers function provides a paper advance that allows you to streamline the routine cleaning/rejuvenation of roller assemblies. Note that paper *must* be present in the printer to use this function.

The typical cleaning procedure involves rotating the rollers while wiping them gently with a clean cloth lightly dampened with water. You may use a bit of very mild household detergent to remove "gunk" that resists water alone, but avoid using detergent regularly since chemicals applied to rubber and other synthetic roller materials can reduce their pliability. *Never use harsh detergents or solvents—ever*! You may start this procedure by left-clicking on *Clean Rollers* (or press <R>). A single cycle will advance the paper transport by two pages.

Print TEST PAGE. The TEST PAGE (such as the one shown in Figure 2.7) is typically the first and last test to be run on any printer. Initially, the test page will reveal problems with the print cartridge, paper transport, or carriage transport. You can then proceed with more detailed tests to further isolate and correct the problem(s). When the repair is complete, the TEST PAGE is proof of the printer's operation that you may keep for your records or provide to your customer. You may start this test by left-clicking on *Print TEST PAGE* (or press <T>).

Running the laser/LED tests

The *Laser / LED (EP) tests* allow you to check the operations of almost any electrophotographic (EP) printer (any printer capable of HP LaserJet emulation). From the main menu bar, left-click on *Laser/LED* (or press <L>). The Laser/LED Test Menu will appear as shown in Figure 2.9. You can return to the main menu at any time by pressing the <ESC> key or right-clicking anywhere in the display. There are seven functions available from the INK JET DMP test menu:

- *Preliminary Setup Information*: supplies initial information to help you set up and operate the EP printer safely

- *Toner Test*: allows you to check the effects of low/expired toner or poor toner distribution

- *Corona Test*: allows you to quickly identify the location of fouling on the Primary or Transfer corona wires

- *Drum and Roller Test*: allows you to identify the source of repetitive defects in the printer

- *Fuser Test*: allows you to check for low or inconsistent fusing

- *Paper Transport Test*: allows you to quickly and conveniently check the paper transport without wasting time or toner

- *Print TEST PAGE*: provides a uniform test pattern for initial or final printer inspection

Preliminary setup information.   You may access the preliminary setup information screen by left-clicking on *Preliminary Setup Information* (or press <I>). This is not a test per se, but an information screen intended to provide helpful setup information for EP testing. Novice troubleshooters will find it helpful to review this information before attempting any of the test sequences below. Experienced troubleshooters may find this to be a handy reminder. To leave the information screen, press <ESC> or right-click anywhere in the display.

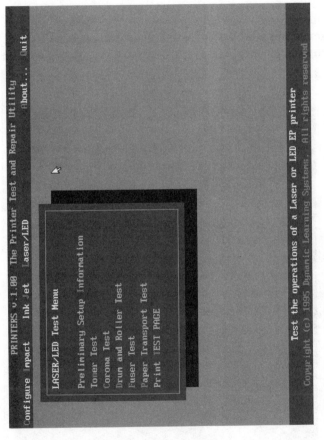

PRINTERS v.1.00 The Printer Test and Repair Utility

Configure Impact Ink Jet Laser/LED   About... Quit

LASER/LED Test Menu

Preliminary Setup Information
Toner Test
Corona Test
Drum and Roller Test
Fuser Test
Paper Transport Test
Print TEST PAGE

Test the operations of a Laser or LED EP printer
Copyright (c) 1995 Dynamic Learning Systems. All rights reserved

Figure 2.9 The laser/LED test menu.

Toner test. *Toner* is the raw material (the medium) that is used to form printed images—the "ink" of the EP printer. As a consequence, low, expired, poor-quality, or poorly distributed toner will have an impact on print quality. The *Toner Test* is designed to test toner condition by printing a full-page black graphic as shown in Figure 2.10. Light streaks appearing vertically along the page (usually on either side of the image) are typical of a low-toner cartridge. A light image may be compensated for by increasing the print intensity wheel (on the printer itself), but it may also

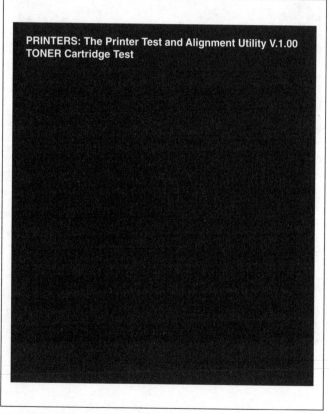

Figure 2.10   Printout of the laser toner test.

suggest a poor-quality toner cartridge or expired toner. If a fresh toner cartridge fails to correct the problem and print intensity is already set high, the fault may be in the printer's high-voltage power supply. Remember that EP printing technology is heavily dependent on paper type and quality. Light splotches may be the result of damp or coated paper. Try a supply of fresh, dry 20-lb xerography-grade paper. You may start this test by left-clicking on *Toner Test* (or press <n>).

Corona test. EP technology relies on high voltage to produce the electrostatic fields that charge the EP drum, and attract toner off the drum to the page. These fields are established by a primary corona and a transfer corona, respectively. A *corona* is really nothing more than a length of thin wire, but it has a critical impact on the evenness of the electric field it produces. Later EP engines replace corona wires with charge rollers, but the effect is the same as corona wires. The *Corona Test* pattern shown in Figure 2.11 is designed to highlight corona problems.

The dust and paper particles in the air tend to be attracted to high-voltage sources such as corona wires. Over time, an accumulation of foreign matter will weaken the field distribution and affect the resulting image. Fouling at one or more points on the primary corona will always cause toner to be attracted to those corresponding points on the drum—this results in black vertical streaks that can be seen against a white background. Conversely, fouling at one or more points on the transfer corona will prevent toner at those corresponding points from being attracted off the drum and onto the page—this results in white vertical streaks that can be seen against a black background. You may start this test by left-clicking on *Corona Test* (or press <C>).

Drum and roller test. In spite of the high level of refinement in today's EP printers, image formation is

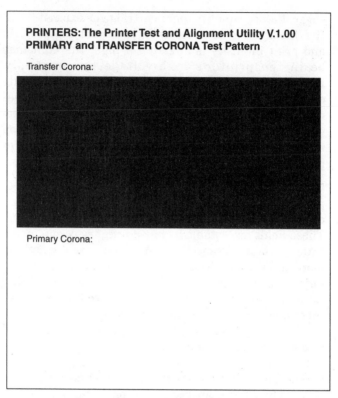

Figure 2.11 Printout of the laser corona test.

still a delicate physical process. Paper must traverse a torturous course through a series of roller assemblies in order to acquire a final, permanent image. With age, wear, and accidental damage, the various rotating elements of an EP printer can succumb to marks or other slight damage. Whereas such damage is incidental, the results can be seen in the printed output.

Consider the EP drum itself. It has a circumference of about 3.75″. This means that any one point on the drum will approach every page surface at least twice. If a nick were to occur on the drum surface, it would appear in the final page at least twice, separated by about 3.75″. Since each of the major roller assemblies has a slightly different circumference, it is possible to quickly identify the source of a repetitive defect simply by measuring the distance between instances. The *Drum and Roller Test* pattern shown in Figure 2.12 is designed to help you correlate measured distances to problem areas. For example, a defect that occurs every 3.75″ can be traced to the EP drum, an error that occurs every 3″ or so can be traced to the fusing rollers, and a defect that occurs every 2″ can often be related to the development roller. You may start this

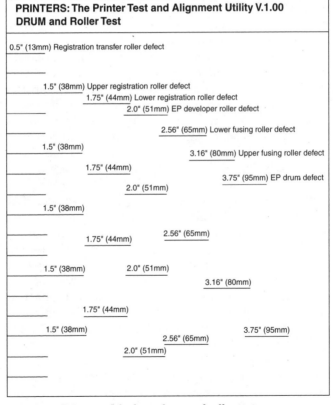

Figure 2.12   Printout of the laser drum and roller test.

test by left-clicking on *Drum and Roller Test* (or press
<D>).

Fuser test.   Fusing is a vital part of the image formation process—it uses heat and pressure to literally
melt toner into the paper fibers. To ensure proper fusing, the upper fusing roller must reach and maintain
a fairly narrow range of temperatures. When temperature is marginally low, fusing may not be complete.
The *Fuser Test* is intended to check the stability of a
fusing system's temperature control by running a
series of full-page test graphics. You can then run your
thumb briskly over each page. Low or inadequate fusing will result in toner smudging (you can see toner on
your thumb). You can then take the appropriate steps
to optimize fusing temperature.

   This test is intended to detect *marginal* or inconsistent fusing performance. It will not catch a serious or
complete fusing system failure because the printer
will generate an error message and halt if the fusing
assembly fails to reach proper fusing temperature in
90 seconds or so, or falls below a minimum temperature for a prolonged amount of time. You may start
this test by left-clicking on *Fuser Test* (or press <F>).

Paper transport test.   The paper transport system of an
EP printer is a highly modified friction feed system
designed to carry paper through the entire image formation system. There are also a series of time-sensi-
tive sensors intended to track each page as it passes
(and detect jam conditions). When you work on any
aspect of the printer's mechanics, you are affecting
paper transport. The *Paper Transport Test* is intended
to eject five sheets of blank paper (saving toner and
printing time). You can use this test to help you troubleshoot problems in the paper path, or verify that
any repairs you may have made do not obstruct the
paper path. Once a repair is complete, it is recommended that you verify the paper path before running

test patterns. You may start this test by left-clicking on *Paper Transport Test* (or press <P>).

Print TEST PAGE. The TEST PAGE is typically the first and last test to be run on any Laser/LED printer. Initially, the Laser/LED test page (shown in Figure 2.13) will reveal problems with the toner cartridge, paper transport, fusing system, coronas, or writing mechanism. You can then proceed with more detailed tests to further isolate and correct the problem(s).

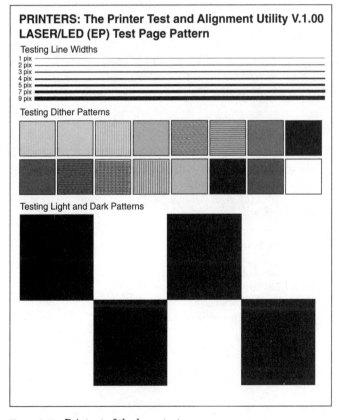

Figure 2.13 Printout of the laser test page.

When the repair is complete, the TEST PAGE is proof of the printer's operation that you may keep for your records or provide to your customer. You may start this test by left-clicking on *Print TEST PAGE* (or press <T>).

About PRINTERS

To learn about the PRINTERS program, click on *About* in the main menu bar (or press <A>). An information box will appear in the middle of the display. To clear the information box, press the <ESC> key or click the right mouse button anywhere in the display.

Quitting PRINTERS

To quit the PRINTERS program and return to DOS, click on *Quit* in the main menu bar (or press <Q>). After a moment, the DOS prompt will appear.

Making PRINTERS better

Dynamic Learning Systems is dedicated to providing high-quality, low-cost diagnostic utilities—we are always interested in ways to improve the quality and performance of our products. We welcome your comments, questions, or criticisms:

Dynamic Learning Systems
PO Box 282
Jefferson, MA 01522-0282
Fax: 508-829-6819
E-mail: *sbigelow@cerfnet.com*
Web: *http://www.dlspubs.com*

Printers under Windows

In the days of DOS, printing functions were incorporated into the DOS application itself. This often meant that the application supported few printers, or the printer would need to be used in a suitable "emulation" mode. As the PC world has moved from DOS to Windows, printer support was shifted from the application to the operating system. And with broader support for more printers, any Windows application could take advantage of any installed printer using a "universal" set of printer drivers.

Unfortunately, the use of such global printer support has added a new level of problems for PC users and technicians alike—it's no longer enough to just "fix the printer." Today's technicians should also be able to recognize print quality and performance issues that arise *outside* of the printer as a result of driver problems. This chapter is intended to provide you with a comprehensive set of symptoms and solutions for printer problems that are normally related to Windows 3.1, Windows 95, and Windows 98.

> **NOTE:** Although this chapter discusses Windows-related issues, it is not intended to cover Windows architecture or design concepts. For detailed technical information on Windows, refer to the "Resource Kit" for your particular Windows version (usually available from your local computer store or bookstore).

Printing Tips for Windows 98

Windows 98 provides extensive support for a wide variety of printers, but there are some limitations that you should be aware of. The following section outlines many of the font, driver, and printer-specific issues that you'll face under Windows 98. These issues are listed alphabetically for quick reference.

Canon Color Ink-Jet

When working with a Canon color bubble-jet (BJC), there are some driver differences between Windows 3.1/95 and Windows 98. Be sure to upgrade the Canon BJC-70, BJC-600, BJC-600e, BJC-800, or BJC-4000 drivers when upgrading to Windows 98.

Fargo Primera/Fargo Primera Pro

Some older driver versions for the Fargo Primera and Primera Pro printers do not operate correctly under Windows 98. The Fargo Primera requires version 4.3 or later, and the Primera Pro requires version 2.7 or later.

HP DeskJet 340, 1000C, 1100C, and 1120C

These HP DeskJet printers require the very latest drivers for optimum performance. Windows 3.1 and older Windows 95 drivers may result in poor/limited functionality when used under Windows 98. You can use the Windows 98 native driver included with the Windows 98 CD, or download and install the latest HP drivers from *www.hp.com*.

HP DeskJet 400, 500, 600, 700, and 800 series

If you upgraded to Windows 98 from Windows 3.1, your HP DeskJet printer will not run properly. Delete your HP DeskJet printer driver after upgrading to Windows 98:

- Click *Start*, point to *Settings*, and then click *Printers*.

- Click on your printer to select it, then press *Delete*.

- Follow the instructions on your screen.

- Download the latest HP printer driver at *www.hp.com*, then install the new driver using the SETUP.EXE utility.

If you notice a loss of functionality using the native Windows 98 drivers, download the latest driver from HP. Note that drivers for the HP DeskJet 660C, 68XC, 69XC, 850C, 855C, and 870C are available on your Windows 98 CD in the \Drivers\Printers folder.

HP DeskJet Portable 310/320

The recommended drivers for these printers are already included as a standard part of the Windows 98 operating system. Follow the standard Windows 98 printer installation process for these HP printers (through the *Add Printer* wizard), using the drivers that came with your Windows 98 CD. If you'd prefer to use HP-specific drivers, download and install them from HP at *www.hp.com*.

HP LaserJet printers

When adding an HP LaserJet or HP Color LaserJet printer to your Windows 98 system, you can get optimized printing performance by following the guidelines below. To obtain the latest HP printer drivers, check the Hewlett-Packard Web site at *www.hp.com/cposupport/eschome.html*.

- *HP LaserJet 4 Printer (PCL support)*. For optimum performance, download and install the latest Windows 98 drivers from Hewlett-Packard.

- *HP LaserJet 4Si, 4L, 4P, 4 Plus, 4V, 5, and 5P Printers (PCL support)*. You'll need the HP TrueType screen fonts to match your internal printer fonts. Insert "Disk 1" of the *HP LaserJet Printing System* disk set into a floppy drive. Click *Start* and *Run*. In the *Run* dialog box, type: A:\Setup. Click *Custom* installation, and then click the appropriate HP LaserJet printer. Click *HP TrueType Screen* fonts. Click the *Printer Driver*, *Status Window*, and the *Travel Guide* check boxes to clear them. Click *OK*, and then follow the instructions on your screen.

- *HP LaserJet 5L, 5MP, 6L, 6P, and 6MP Printers*. You'll need the HP TrueType screen fonts to match your internal printer fonts. Locate the disks that came with your HP LaserJet printer. If you cannot find your software disks, download the latest drivers from the Hewlett-Packard Web site. Insert the "HP LaserJet Printing System Disk 1" into the appropriate drive. Click *Start*, and then click *Run*. Type A:\Setup. Select the *Typical* installation option, then follow the instructions on your screen.

- *HP Color LaserJet Printer*. You should have the very latest drivers for your printer. Locate the disks that came with your HP Color LaserJet printer. If you cannot find the disks, download the latest drivers from the Hewlett-Packard Web site. Insert the "HP Color LaserJet Printer" disk into the appropriate floppy disk drive. Click *Start*, select *Settings*, and then click *Printers*. Click *Add Printer*, and then follow the instructions presented by the *Add Printer* wizard. Click *Have Disk*. If you are prompted to replace or update the driver, click *Yes*.

> **NOTE:** To use Image Color Matching support in Windows 98, install the HP Color LaserJet driver that shipped with Windows 98.

HP OfficeJet 500 and 600

You should uninstall the HP OfficeJet (Series 500 and 600) *before* you upgrade to Windows 98—if you've already upgraded to Windows 98 from Windows 3.1, your HP OfficeJet will not run properly. To determine which software updates are available for the HP OfficeJet (Series 500 and 600) products, check out the HP Web site at *www.hp.com/go/all-in-one*.

HP OfficeJet Pro 1150C

If you've upgraded to Windows 98 from Windows 3.1, your HP OfficeJet Pro 1150C printer may not operate correctly. To fix this problem, select *Cancel* on the Plug-and-Play screen, then uninstall your HP OfficeJet Pro driver software. Install the Windows 95/98 driver that shipped with your HP OfficeJet Pro 1150C. If you install the default drivers accompanying Windows 98, you'll lose the scanning features on your OfficeJet Pro 1150C. Delete the "default" OfficeJet Pro 1150C printer driver from the \printers folder and install the Windows 95/98 driver that shipped with your OfficeJet Pro 1150C.

If you've upgraded to Windows 98 from Windows 95, the Scan Picture function of an HP OfficeJet Pro 1150C may not work with some applications. If you experience a problem, uninstall the HP OfficeJet Pro 1150C software, then reinstall the Windows 95 software that shipped with your HP OfficeJet Pro 1150C. Click *Start*, select *Settings*, click *Control Panel*, double-click *Printers*, click *Add Printer*, and then follow the instructions that guide you through the *Add Printer* wizard. Select *Have Disk* and point to your CD-ROM drive (or the path where you saved the downloaded driver). If you do not have the CD, you can download the latest driver from *www.hp.com/go/officejet-pro*.

HP PhotoSmart Photo printer

The PhotoSmart Photo printer does *not* support printing from Windows 3.1, so you *must* install the Windows 95/98 printer driver software from the original CD. You can also download the latest driver from Hewlett-Packard at *http://hpcc920.external.hp.com/cpossupport/indexes1/photprd.html*. Use the SETUP.EXE program to install the driver software either from the CD (or the downloaded file). Do *not* allow the printer to be autodetected through Plug-and-Play, and do not use the *Add Printer* wizard.

You may encounter several common error messages when installing the drivers. If you see a message such as *Error finding LST file*, click *Ignore* and complete the installation. This occurs because of changes to the Windows 98 file system, so you wouldn't be able to access the built-in multimedia presentation without getting the newest version of the driver from the Web. If you find a message that reads *The file or folder 'REMIND.EXE'...cannot be found*, click the *OK* button and complete the installation process. This file is used only for running the online registration, but you can start the online registration by running *C:\Program Files\HP PhotoSmart\Photo Printer\ IntQuest\ Iqrunner.exe*.

HP Printer/Scanner/Copier Series 300

Uninstall the HP Printer/Scanner/Copier 300 software *before* you upgrade to Windows 98—if you've already upgraded to Windows 98 from Windows 3.1, the HP 300 will not run properly. To determine what software updates are available for HP 300, check out the HP Web site at *www.hp.com/go/all-in-one*.

LaserMaster printers

The Windows 3.1 printer driver for LaserMaster printer products will *not* function under Windows 98. For tips on obtaining drivers that *are* compatible with Windows 98, contact LaserMaster Technical Support at the phone number listed in the documentation that came with your printer.

Lexmark Custom and MarkVision drivers

Some early versions of MarkVision and the Lexmark custom printer drivers are *incompatible* with Windows 98. To avoid system problems, Windows 98 disables these components when you upgrade from Windows 95 (if you're currently running LEXBCE 1.03 or earlier). If you have a version later than LEXBCE 1.03, Lexmark software works correctly on Windows 98. To determine which version of LEXBCE you have, use Windows Explorer. Go to your `\windows\system` subdirectory. Right-click LEXBCE.DLL, and then click *Properties*. Click the *Version* tab, and then locate the *File* version information. You can obtain the latest Lexmark driver from *www.lexmark.com*.

NEC SilentWriter SuperScript 610

The Windows 3.1 printer driver for NEC SilentWriter SuperScript printers will *not* function under Windows 98. Check out the NEC printer Web site in order to obtain the latest NEC drivers for SilentWriter SuperScript printers.

Panasonic KX-P6100, KX-P6300, and KX-P6500

Some versions of the printer installation software will *not* operate correctly under Windows 98. This will result in *Unknown Windows Version* error messages. If you experience this problem while trying to install the driver software for this printer, check with the Panasonic Web site to download the latest printer drivers.

QMS JetScript boards

To print with QMS JetScript boards under Windows 98, create a port called LPTx.DOS (where LPTx is LPT1, LPT2, or LPT3—depending on how the JetScript board is configured). If you do not have a printer driver installed, click *Start*, point to *Settings*, click *Printers*, double-click *Add Printer*, and then follow the instructions on your screen. To create a port called LPTx.DOS:

- Click *Start*, point to *Settings*, click *Printers*, right-click the icon for the *QMS JetScript* printer, and then click *Properties*.
- Click *Details*, and then click *Add Port*.
- Click *Other*, and then click *Local Port*.
- Click *OK*, and then enter the name of the port you want to add (i.e., LPT1.DOS).
- Click *OK*, and then click *OK* again to close the *Printer Properties* dialog box.

The printer should be ready to use.

TrueType fonts

As a rule, TrueType fonts are not available on ink-jet printers when used in low-resolution modes (i.e., 75 to 150 DPI). However, this limitation does not apply to laser and impact printers. Keep in mind that

TrueType fonts are *not* available when you use the Generic/Text Only printer driver.

Windows 3.1x

PC industry old-timers will probably recall that each DOS application printed with its own distinctive look and feel, and some were better than others. Windows designers envisioned a world where printing is a function performed *independently* of the particular Windows applications. This relieves the need to specify printers and ports for each application as you do under DOS—printers and ports need be selected only *once* through a single, centralized printing applet (i.e., the Windows 3.1 *Print Manager*). By loading specific printer drivers for each printer attached to the PC, it is possible to handle the detailed font and image data typically present under Windows. Ultimately, centralized Windows provides a uniform printing "engine" capable of producing high-quality text and graphics on a vast array of printers, yet it does not require Windows applications to drive the printers *directly*. When you encounter printing problems under Windows 3.1x, take a look at the symptoms below.

Windows 3.1x symptoms

Symptom 3.1: The printer does not work at all. Start by checking the printer itself—it should be plugged in and turned on, and the self-test should work properly.

- *Check the printer cable.* Check the cable between the printer and computer. A loose or faulty printer cable can wreak havoc on your printing.

- *Check under DOS.* Try leaving Windows and printing through a DOS application such as EDIT or another simple word processor. If you can get a DOS application to print, you know the printer, cable, and computer (the *hardware*) is working together, so the trouble lies in the Windows configuration.

■ *Check the hardware*. If a DOS application won't print, suspect a hardware fault. Examine the printer's particular DIP switch, jumper, and front panel control settings, or refer to the other troubleshooting tactics below.

■ *Check the Print Manager*. Open your *Print Manager* and take a look at the Printer control window. Make sure the correct printer is selected (you may have to install a new printer driver through the *Add* button) and connected to the proper printer port. If the wrong printer driver or port is active, your printer will probably not work at all. When your new printer comes with its own printer driver, you should install that driver instead of the original Windows equivalent because the driver accompanying the new printer is typically better than the native Windows version.

■ *Check serial connections (if any)*. If you are using a serial printer, check the serial parameters through the *Settings* function in the *Connect* window. Keep in mind that the *Settings* selection is active only after a COM port has been chosen for connection. If everything looks right so far, take a look at the printer *Setup* window.

■ *Check the other setup parameters*. If the paper size, resolution, or memory setting is invalid, the printer may hang up or fail to print. Double-check the installation of any memory or font cartridges in the printer (you should power down the printer before doing this), and make sure the correct memory and cartridge(s) are selected in the *Setup* window.

Symptom 3.2: The page prints, but the format is incorrect. Your printer hardware is probably set up properly, but one or more Windows selections are probably wrong.

- *Check the application.* Most applications (i.e., Microsoft Publisher) provide a comprehensive set of layout and format parameters that outline the formation of the printed page. If the application is setting up the page improperly, the page will *certainly* be printed incorrectly. Try printing through another Windows application if possible. If another application prints, the problem is likely in the original application and not in the *Print Manager* configuration. However, if the trouble persists in another Windows application, the trouble may be in the *Print Manager*.

- *Check the Print Manager.* Open the *Print Manager* and check the printer selection in the *Printer* control window. If the wrong printer is selected, the erroneous printer driver can upset your printing. Select the correct printer and try printing again. You may have to add the correct printer driver if it is not yet available. If your printer came with its own printer driver, you should install that driver instead of the original Windows equivalent because the driver is typically newer than the native Windows version.

- *Check the other setup parameters.* Examine the parameters in the printer *Setup* window. Paper size, graphics resolution, memory setting, and page orientation can all affect the page formatting. Bad settings here can also cause printing problems.

- *Check the hardware.* If you cannot find an error in the *Print Manager*, take a look at your printer itself. Refer to the printer's user manual and check any DIP switches, jumpers, or front panel controls that affect page formatting. If any font cartridges are installed, power down the printer and see that they are all installed correctly.

Symptom 3.3: Paper advances, but no print appears on the page. Chances are good that communication is taking place properly between the printer and computer, but there is a glitch in the Windows setup.

- *Check the Print Manager*. Check the selected printer in the *Printer* control window. If the wrong printer is currently selected, the printer command codes may not be recognized by the printer (except perhaps for the page feed). Select the correct printer and try printing again. If your printer came with its own printer driver, you should install that driver instead of the original Windows equivalent because the driver accompanying the printer typically provides better performance than the Windows version.

- *Check the other setup parameters*. Begin by checking the paper source specified in the *Setup* window. An incorrect paper source may allow paper to advance from an incorrect source, but no printing may be completed.

Symptom 3.4: Printing seems far too slow.   Since Windows prints *everything* in graphics mode (text as well as images), printing tends to be somewhat slower when compared to text printing under DOS. However, there are some tactics that you can use to boost printing speed.

- *Shut down unneeded applications*. You may also wish to shut down any unneeded applications running in the background before starting a new print job—this also frees time for Windows to concentrate on the print job.

- *Adjust print priority*. If you are using the Windows *Print Manager* (or another third-party print manager), try increasing the *priority* of the print job—higher priority increases the amount of time Windows allocates to the job.

- *Check file fragmentation.* When printing images and other graphics, Windows 3.1x produces *temporary files*—these files can sometimes be quite large. If your hard drive is heavily fragmented, the printer spool may be delayed by excessive hard drive seeks. Leave Windows 3.1x and try defragmenting your hard drive.

- *Try printer fonts.* For additional speed, try printing your documents using only printer fonts—these are the font names denoted with a printer symbol next to them rather than a "TT" (TrueType) symbol.

- *Try a lower resolution.* You might also consider lowering the resolution of your printer. For example, if you are printing at 600 × 600 resolution, try lowering the resolution to 300 × 300.

- *Check your printer drivers.* Make sure that you are using the correct printer driver for your specific printer, and check that the driver is the *latest* version. If drivers came bundled with your printer, try using them instead of native Windows 3.1x drivers since custom or manufacturer-specific drivers often provide better performance than native Windows drivers.

Symptom 3.5: PostScript graphics appear to print slowly from an LPT port. In some PC hardware and printer driver combinations, graphics may seem to print unusually slowly. Often, this is not a problem directly, but simply the result of your system's setup.

- *Try compressing bitmaps.* You can often speed printing under Windows 3.1x by disabling the *Compress Bitmaps* check box in the printer's *Advanced Options* dialog. Although this will speed printing, it will also increase the amount of time needed for an application to regain control (i.e., the hourglass symbol will remain longer). Also, do not disable the *Compress Bitmaps* check box if you are printing through a serial port (COM1 through COM4).

> **NOTE:** This tactic will affect only graphics printing—it will not affect the printing speed of text-only documents.

Symptom 3.6: You see an error message such as *Offending Command: MSTT #### Undefined* **when trying to print to a PostScript printer.** This is a problem that occurs frequently when the printer runs out of virtual memory. Since Windows transfers fonts to a PostScript printer using an MSTT #### numbering scheme (where #### is the four-digit number), the printer may drop fonts, and this typically causes an error when that font is needed in the printing process.

- *Adjust virtual memory.* Start your correction by checking that the virtual memory setting (in the *Advanced Options* dialog under the PostScript driver) is appropriate for the amount of memory in the printer. You can also reduce the amount of printer memory used by Windows 3.1x by disabling the *Clear Memory Per Page* box in the *Advanced Options* dialog. This may slow printing a bit, but will reduce the demands on printer memory.

Symptom 3.7: Your bidirectional impact or ink-jet printer is not printing in bidirectional mode under Windows 3.1x. This is not the fault of Windows, the driver, or the printer. Unidirectional printing is *necessary* because moving-carriage printers cannot achieve the precision necessary for high-resolution printing when operating in bidirectional mode, so Windows printer drivers are designed to be unidirectional. If you are using an unsupported printer that is set to operate in bidirectional mode, you may see lines and text appear "jaggey." Try setting the printer to unidirectional (or graphics) mode.

Symptom 3.8: After installing or upgrading an application, you encounter problems printing from one or more Windows 3.1x applications. You (or the installation program) may have accidentally inserted a space in the SET TEMP= line in AUTOEXEC.BAT. That extra space causes a problem when Windows 3.1x attempts to locate the TEMP directory, and this prevents temporary printing files from being produced—as a result, you cannot print. The same problem can occur when you forget to include a backslash character in the TEMP directory path (i.e., SET TEMP=C:TEMP).

- *Check the setup command line.* To correct this problem, use a text editor to edit your AUTOEXEC.BAT file. Locate the SET TEMP= line and be sure that it is entered correctly, and see that there are no extra spaces added after the line (i.e., SET TEMP=C:\TEMP). After you make your changes, save the corrected AUTOEXEC.BAT file and restart the system so that those changes can take effect.

Symptom 3.9: Some of the text (usually on an impact printer) may be cut off or missing in the printout. Often, this problem is related to an incompatibility between the video board (i.e., an ATI Mach 32 board) and the printer driver. Since many older Gateway 2000 systems were shipped with ATI video cards and drivers, there is a higher probability of this problem occurring on older Gateway systems. You might try an alternate or generic printer driver. If this is not acceptable, reducing the video mode to VGA or SVGA through the Windows Setup can sometimes alleviate this problem—at least temporarily. Ink-jet and laser jet printers are typically free of this problem.

Symptom 3.10: Fine lines (under ¼ pt) may appear randomly across the printed page. This occurs primarily with older HP LaserJet printers, and is often the result of a conflict between the printer driver and the

Orchid video driver (such as for the Orchid Fahrenheit 1280 video board). Orchid has addressed these problems with an upgraded video BIOS and video driver. Your best course is to contact the video board manufacturer for video driver/BIOS upgrade information. You might also try an alternate video card and driver.

Symptom 3.11: The printing is garbled or missing. Printing is taking place, but it is distorted or missing in areas. There are a number of potential problems that you should check for.

- *Check the cable.* Begin by inspecting the printer cable. Loose or damaged cables can cause serious data loss. Make sure the cable is intact and connected properly.

- *Try clearing the printer.* You can also try turning the printer off for a few moments to clear its internal memory (also remember to delete any jobs outstanding in the *Print Manager*). Restart the printer and try printing again.

- *Check the printer driver.* Open the printer control window and check the selected printer. An incorrect printer driver can result in all types of garbled or intermittent printing. Select the proper printer (*add* a printer if necessary) and try printing again. If your printer came with its own printer driver, you should install that driver instead of the original Windows equivalent because the driver accompanying the printer is typically superior to the native Windows version.

- *Check serial handshaking.* If you are using a serial printer, there may be a serious problem with your *handshaking* (the way data flow is controlled between computer and printer). There are two types of handshaking: XON/XOFF (or *software* handshaking), and CTS/RTS (or *hardware* handshaking). If handshaking is inoperative, a high baud rate can overflow the printer's buffer. Try reducing the baud rate to a slow crawl of about 300 and try printing again. If print is correct or greatly improved at a low baud rate, check the flow control (perhaps try a known-good cable). Make sure the printer's flow control method matches the Windows *Program Manager* settings.

Symptom 3.12: Only part of the page is printed correctly. The remainder of the page is either garbled or missing. This kind of behavior is almost always due to setup or memory issues.

- *Check the printer's setup characteristics*. Examine the paper size and page orientation settings. Faulty page information there can turn your printing in strange directions that confuse your desired format.

- *Check the printer's memory*. Make sure the memory selection is set properly for your particular printer. If memory is set properly but part of the printed image is still being lost, there simply may not be enough memory to hold the entire image (also known as a *buffer overflow*). Refer to your application and try condensing or resizing the print to a smaller area of the page.

- *Simplify the image*. You can try adding memory to the printer (be sure to update the memory setting in the *Setup* window), or consider reducing the printer's resolution (or simplifying the content of the image).

Symptom 3.13: After upgrading LaserMaster's WinPrint 1.0 to WinPrint 1.5, you receive an error message such as *Illegal Function Call*. The WinPrint utility is attempting to reference an earlier WinPrint font that may no longer be available. Unfortunately, you will need to remove the fonts from your system, then reinstall

WinPrint. Exit Windows and reboot the computer. Restart Windows and open the WinPrint program group. Under the program group, you will see the *Fontman* icon. Select *Fontman*, choose all installed fonts, then select *Remove*. This will remove the WinPrint fonts from your system. If you see fonts remaining, choose *Verify*, then select *no* when asked if you want to use those fonts under WinPrinter. Next, choose *yes* when asked if you want to delete references to these fonts for WinPrint and WinSpool. Exit Windows and then restart it. When Windows is running again, restart the WinPrint installation program. Once the reinstallation is complete, you can add fonts in the WinPrint Font Manager.

Symptom 3.14: The PC hangs when using SuperPrint 2.0 under Windows 3.1. There are basically two variations of this problem. First, the system may hang when SuperPrint 2.0 is installed. Second, you cannot print to an HP LaserJet printer once SuperPrint 2.0 is installed. In both cases, the reason for this trouble is that the Zenographics SuperPrint product requires version 2.2 in order to be fully compatible with Windows 3.1. Your best course is to contact Zenographics for an upgrade. If you must go ahead and install the older version, *do not perform a default setup*. Of course, if SuperPrint is already installed and there is difficulty printing to an HP LaserJet, disable the SuperQue (print spooler) under SuperPrint.

Symptom 3.15: When using the LaserMaster WinSpool or WinJet accelerators with a PostScript printer, you see an error message such as *This PostScript job is not supported by WinSpool*. This is a problem with the PostScript driver (versions 3.52 and 3.53). Try accepting the error message and continuing—in many cases, the printing will still occur properly. If problems persist, try reinstalling the LaserMaster driver on LPT2—this will also enable printing from LPT1. If LaserMaster is allowed to install on LPT1 during its default installation, there may be a conflict. As a more long-term fix, you should consider trying version 3.5 or 3.51 of the LaserMaster PostScript driver.

Symptom 3.16: When you switch from a LaserMaster WinJet 300 to a WinJet 800, you see an error message such as *WinPrint Manager Printer Error: VPD cannot register frame buffer.* This may then be followed by other system error messages. When you switch from a LaserMaster WinJet 300 to the WinJet 800, you need to edit the SYSTEM.INI file. If you fail to do this, errors will occur. When a WinJet 300 is installed, you will need to add the following lines to the [386Enh] section of SYSTEM.INI:

```
device=LMLPV.386   ;WinPrint
device=LMCAP.386 ;WinPrint
device=LMMI.386   ;WinPrint
```

When you install a WinJet 300 over a WinJet 800, you must remove the following line from the [386Enh] section of SYSTEM.INI such as:

```
device=LMLPV.386 ;WinPrint
device=LMHAROLD.386 ;WinPrint
device=LMCAP.386 ;WinPrint
device=LMMI.386 ;WinPrint
```

The WinJet 800 installation adds the following lines to the [386Enh] section of the SYSTEM.INI file:

```
device=LMHAROLD.386 ;WinPrint
device=LMCAP.386 ;WinPrint
device=LMMI.386 ;WinPrint
```

When you install a WinJet 800 over a WinJet 300, you must remove the following line from the [386Enh] section of SYSTEM.INI such as:

```
device=LMLPV.386 ;WinPrint

device=LMHAROLD.386 ;WinPrint

device=LMCAP.386 ;WinPrint

device=LMMI.386 ;WinPrint
```

Symptom 3.17: The printer does not utilize its resident font cartridge(s) or soft font(s). There are several possible issues that you should be familiar with.

- *Reseat your font cartridges.* When the printer uses one or more font cartridges, turn off the printer and reseat all cartridges to be sure they are installed correctly. Restart the printer and try printing again.

- *Check the printer's Setup.* Make sure that all appropriate font cartridges are selected. Windows 3.1x can support a maximum of two cartridge listings. If the font cartridge you are using is not shown in the cartridge selector list, you will probably have to identify the cartridge's fonts through the soft font installer.

- *Try a new .PCM file.* If you are using a new font cartridge that was developed after the printer driver was written, you may need a .PCM (printer cartridge metrics) file to tell Windows how to handle those "new" fonts. Install the .PCM file included with the font cartridge the same way you would install a soft font.

- *Check your soft fonts.* See that the desired fonts are listed in the HP Font Installer window. Reset the printer and try reloading the soft fonts to the printer.

- *Check the printer's memory.* Printer memory must hold the soft fonts, so a printer with limited memory may not have enough for soft fonts. Try loading only one or two soft fonts and attempt printing again. If a limited soft font download works, you may want to expand the printer's memory capacity.

Symptom 3.18: The Generic/Text-Only printer driver does not use the multiple paper trays and various paper sizes of a printer.   This is a direct limitation of the printer driver. The "generic" printer driver was designed to support a wide variety of different printers, but in order to be compatible across a wide range of printers, it is necessary to abandon particular features that one printer may have but another may not. If you cannot find a specific printer driver on the Windows 3.1x installation disks, contact the printer manufacturer to obtain the latest copy of the Windows printer driver(s)—this may be difficult today with the prevalence of Windows 95 and Windows 98. The alternative is to continue using the generic driver without the benefit of your printer's special features.

Symptom 3.19: You see an error message such as *Control Panel cannot perform the current operation because <filename> is not a valid printer-driver file.*   This error can often occur when choosing *Setup* from the *Printers* dialog under the *Control Panel*. In most cases, there are three cases that will cause this error: (1) the EXPAND.EXE or LZEXPAND.DLL files are corrupted or from a different version of Windows, (2) the printer driver is invalid or corrupted, or (3) you are installing a Windows 3.11 printer driver under Windows 3.1. When an invalid printer driver is specified, you may see the Print command of most Windows applications dimmed (grayed-out).

■ *Return to MS-DOS*. Check the file dates on EXPAND.EXE and LZEXPAND.DLL. Verify that their file dates are consistent with other Windows or WFWG files on your system. If not, you should manually expand the proper versions of these files from installation disks into their appropriate directories. A typical command to copy EXPAND.EXE and reinstall the LZEXPAND.DLL file from the installation disk might be:

```
copy a:\expand.exe c:\windows\expand.exe
```

then

```
expand a:\lzexpand.dl_ c:\windows\system\
 lzexpand.dll
```

- *Check the startup files*. Now that you have the correct versions of EXPAND.EXE and LZEXPAND. DLL on the system, rename the suspect printer driver file(s), and check the path statement in AUTOEXEC.BAT to be sure that the Windows directory is the first directory in the path.

- *Recheck the drivers*. Restart Windows and reinstall the suspect printer drivers by choosing the *Printers* icon from the *Control Panel*. You can then select the *Add* button, and *Install* the correct driver(s) again. You could also run the *Print Manager*, then choose *Printer Setup*, *Add*, then *Install*. Finally, if you have been installing Windows 3.11 drivers in Windows 3.1, install the proper drivers for the version of Windows you are using, or download the driver from the Microsoft Web site.

Symptom 3.20: When printing on an ink-jet printer (i.e., the HP DeskJet 500), you see garbage lines, blocks, and unwanted characters when printing using TrueType fonts. Chances are that the printer driver being used with the ink-jet printer is outdated or corrupt. Obtain the latest version of the Windows 3.1x driver from Microsoft or the printer's manufacturer. Until a new driver is installed, try using a similar driver or reducing the printer's resolution—in some cases, the unwanted printing will go away (at the expense of resolution).

Symptom 3.21: When printing on an impact printer (i.e., a Panasonic KX-P1124 or KX-P2123), you see garbled, missing, or misaligned text. Either the current printer driver is missing or corrupt, or the driver is incompatible with the printer's internal ROM.

■ *Check the printer driver*. Make sure that the latest driver version is installed correctly. If problems persist, consider upgrading the printer's internal ROM.

■ *Consider a similar driver*. Note that this symptom typically occurs only with older dot-matrix printers, and a new ROM is often not available for obsolete or discontinued products. When this situation develops, try an alternate compatible or generic printer driver.

Symptom 3.22: The printer always prints in the highest-quality mode available, even though a "draft"-quality mode has been selected. This is typically due to an error or oversight in the printer driver—especially prevalent in older drivers for impact and ink-jet printers. The preferred method of correcting this problem is to update the printer drivers with newer versions, or choose an alternate compatible or generic printer driver that does provide draft-mode printing.

Symptom 3.23: When printing a scaled TIFF image to an HP LaserJet III or IV, a vertical line prints on the left side of the image. The line may also appear on the right side of the image, or in a corner. This is due to problems with some HP printer drivers (such as HPPCL5A.DRV). If you are encountering this problem printing to an HP LaserJet III, obtain the newest printer driver from Microsoft or Hewlett-Packard. If you are encountering the problem with an HP LaserJet IV, get the latest driver from HP. Until a new driver can be obtained, try scaling the image to a different size—the problem seems to occur only at particular horizontal/vertical size ratios, so altering this ratio even slightly may circumvent the problem.

Symptom 3.24: When using a color ink-jet printer, the black output appears somewhat green.   This problem appears typically in HP ink-jet printers such as the HP 500C. When using the color ink cartridge with the print mode set to *All Color*, only the color cartridge is used to print. As a result, dark colors such as black are actually made up of yellow, magenta, and cyan. It is the printer driver that decides how to mix the colors, but an incorrectly tested printer driver may allow less-than-ideal mixing, resulting in a slightly "greenish" black. The way to correct this problem is to set the print mode to *Black and Color* rather than *All Color*. You can make this adjustment under the *Control Panel* function by selecting the *Printer* icon, choosing *Setup*, then changing the print mode. This feature will cause the ink cartridge to use true black ink when printing blacks. In all cases, you should be sure that you are using the latest driver for your ink-jet printer.

Symptom 3.25: You encounter GPF errors when attempting to print very small bitmap images.   This problem occurs most frequently with HP LaserJet II printers operating at low resolutions (i.e., 75 dpi), but it may occur on any EP printer using the UNIDRV.DLL driver. This is typically the result of a problem in older versions of the Microsoft Universal Printer driver UNIDRV.DLL. Your best course here is to update UNIDRV.DLL by downloading a new version from the Microsoft Web site, or download a suitable driver from the manufacturer's Web site.

Windows 95/98 Troubleshooting

As with earlier versions of Windows, the Windows 95 platform provides all of the printing resources needed by Windows applications. But the Windows 95 printing system makes some significant advances over older printing systems—incorporating a suite of new (and badly needed) features. A 32-bit printing engine and enhanced parallel port support promise to produce smoother printing, while returning control to the application sooner. Image color matching capabilities allow the screen image colors to better match the colors generated by a color printer. Usability features such as *point-and-print* support, deferred printing, and print services for NetWare try to streamline the printing process. Enhanced font support allows you to install an unlimited number of fonts, and use up to 100 fonts in a document.

Still, with all of these enhancements, printing under Windows 95 is not always as foolproof as users and technicians like to believe. Printer installation/ driver problems, network problems, and general printer errors can all occur. This part of the chapter is intended to illustrate some of the troubleshooting techniques used to identify and isolate printing problems, then explain the solutions for a selection of typical Windows 95 printing faults. First, there are some tactics you can use to help isolate problems.

The "Safe Mode"

Windows 95/98 can crash if an incorrect or corrupt driver is selected, or if there is a conflict between the two or more system drivers. There may also be problems if Windows 95/98 fails to detect the correct video board in the PC. The symptoms of such a fault may range from poor or erratic video performance to complete system failures. Under Windows 3.1x, you would probably address such problems by trying the PC in "standard VGA mode" (640 × 480 × 16), but this tactic required you to switch drivers in *Windows Setup*. Windows 95/98 provides you with a "safe mode" option that you can select during startup. Restart the computer. When you see *Starting Windows 95* or *Starting Windows 98* displayed on the screen, press the <F8> key. Choose the *Safe Mode* startup option to run the PC in VGA mode. If your problem disappears in VGA mode, you can safely suspect that the video driver is corrupt, outdated, incorrect, or conflicting with another driver.

Check and correct the printer driver

In order for the printer to run efficiently, a properly written 32-bit printer driver must be loaded under Windows 95/98. If the driver is outdated, incorrect, or "buggy," the printer will not run correctly (if at all). You can check your printer driver by double-clicking on the *My Computer* icon, then double-click on the *Printers* icon. You can then add a printer or select one of your currently installed printers. Right-click on the desired printer, then click on *Properties*. This will bring up the printer *Properties* dialog. Select the *Details* "page." The controls on this page allow you to adjust port settings, drivers, time-outs, and spool settings. Next, select the *Paper* "page," and click on the *About* button. This will tell you which driver version is in use. If this is not the latest version, try a newer driver.

Printing directly to the printer port

Often, it can be difficult to tell whether the source of trouble is in printer hardware or system software. Printing directly to the printer port is one way to verify the printer hardware without the clutter of Windows 95 or its applications. Exit Windows 95 to the DOS prompt, and use the following command to print a file:

```
copy /b filename lpt1:
```

This command takes the binary file *filename*, and sends that file directly to the selected port. If the printer responds and prints the file correctly, the printer's hardware is working fine, and your trouble is in Windows 95/98 or its application(s). If the printer does not run under DOS, the printer, the PC, or the communication cable may be defective.

Controlling bidirectional support

Windows 95/98 is designed to support EPP printer ports conforming to the IEEE-1284 standard. However, not all PCs, printers, and parallel cable assemblies are designed to accommodate the added demands of IEEE 1284, and printing problems can result. You can disable bidirectional support in the *Spool Settings* dialog. You can reach the *Spool Settings* dialog by clicking the *Spool Settings* button in the *Details* page you saw previously. If problems occur with bidirectional printing on, then disappear once bidirectional control is turned off, you should leave bidirectional printing off until you can arrange more compatible hardware.

Clearing spooler files

There are some instances when errors in the print spool can cause print faults. When this occurs, the spool will not always clear—causing the error to persist even when Windows 95/98 is restarted. Fortunately, it is not too difficult to clear the spool files. Leave Windows 95 to MS-DOS and switch to the \SYSYEM\SPOOL\PRINTERS directory, then delete all .SPL files. Next, switch to the \TEMP directory and erase any .TMP files. You should then shut down and restart the computer to finish cleaning up the .SPL files.

Windows 95/98 symptoms

Symptom 3.26: You cannot print to a printer (local or network). There are many possible causes for this kind of problem, so start with the basics.

- *Check your power and connections.* See that your printer is plugged in and turned on (this is a frequent oversight). Also see that the printer's communication cable is secure between the printer and host PC. Check the printer for adequate paper, and address any error messages that may be present.

- *Clear the printer.* If the printer is on, connected, and online, but no printing is taking place, turn the printer off and wait about 10 seconds before turning it on again. This clears the printer's internal buffer.

- *Print to a file.* If problems persist, try printing to a file (rather than to the printer). Then go to the MS-DOS prompt and print the file directly to the printer port as explained earlier. If this works, the problem is in the Windows 95/98 setup.

Symptom 3.27: You cannot print when using a Windows 3.1x printer driver. Printer drivers are essential to successful printer operation. If the wrong driver is installed (or if the correct driver is outdated or corrupt), the printer will simply not work properly (if at all). Under Windows 95/98, printer driver problems are most significant when an older 16-bit driver (i.e., from Windows 3.1x) must be used under Windows 95 because no 32-bit driver exists. This driver "mismatch" can often cause the printer to freeze or produce irregular print. Errors will also occur if the incorrect 32-bit driver is selected for a printer. Check the printer driver and see that it is a current 32-bit driver. If not, install an appropriate driver (you may need to download an updated driver from the printer manufacturer's Web site). If problems persist, try reinstalling the suspect driver.

Symptom 3.28: You cannot print due to an application problem. This is usually caused by an incorrect printer configuration or other setup issue.

- *Check the application's printer setup.* Make sure that the desired printer is selected, along with the correct tray, page orientation, resolution, and other printing parameters.

- *Close unneeded applications.* If problems persist, try saving and closing other applications that may be open—this means you will be printing from the only running application. If the problem disappears, you may have a conflict between one or more applications under Windows 95/98. Try restarting each of the closed applications individually, and try printing after each application is started. The point at which problems return will reveal the conflict.

- *Print from a different application.* If isolating the application does not correct the problem, try printing from a different application. When you are able to print successfully from a different application, your original application may be corrupt or contain a software bug. You may try reinstalling the suspect application, or contact the application's manufacturer for a workaround or software patch.

Symptom 3.29: You cannot print due to a print spooler problem. This problem occurs fairly infrequently, and may not be intuitively obvious from any outward symptoms. Try shutting down the print spooler (as described earlier) and printing directly to the printer port. If the problem disappears, you may have a printer spooler problem. Use ScanDisk to examine your disk space and integrity. Repair any disk problems that you may encounter, then try restoring the print spooler. If problems persist, switch *EMF spooling* to *RAW spooling* in the *Spool Settings* dialog, or leave spooling disabled.

Symptom 3.30: You cannot print with a bidirectional printer setup. Current PC designs and multi-I/O boards use the IEEE-1284–compliant advanced parallel ports (also known as ECP or EPP ports). When faced with printing problems—especially for a newly installed printer—try disabling bidirectional support through the computer's CMOS Setup. If the problem disappears, the PC's parallel port may not be IEEE-1284–compatible, or your printer cable may not support IEEE-1284 communication. In that case, you will need to leave bidirectional printing disabled until you have the hardware in place to support advanced printing (i.e., a new IEEE-1284–compatible LPT board). If you find that the ECP/EPP mode is currently disabled, try reenabling it.

Symptom 3.31: Graphic images are garbled or otherwise printed incorrectly. There are many reasons why a printer might not receive a graphic image correctly.

- *Check the printer's setup.* Check the printer configuration in the printing application to be sure that the tray, orientation, resolution, and other image-related parameters are set properly.

- *Check the memory.* Large images can require substantial amounts of printer memory. Check the printer to see that it has enough memory to support the graphic image size. Try adding more memory or replacing the existing memory.

- *Disable the print spooler.* If you are attempting to print a large document, or deal with a large number of documents over a network, try printing shorter or fewer jobs—the spooler may be overloaded. You may also try shutting the spooler off.

- *Check/replace the printer driver.* Start the computer in its "safe mode" and try printing again. If the problem disappears, there may be a printer driver problem or conflict. Try installing the latest driver for your printer.

Symptom 3.32: Only partial pages are printed. There are several reasons why a printer might not receive a complete page correctly, but most issues are related to the printer's configuration.

- *Check the printer's setup.* Setup issues should always be suspected first. Check the printer configuration in the printing application to be sure that the tray, orientation, resolution, and other image-related parameters are set properly.

- *Check the printer's memory.* Verify that the printer has enough memory to support the printed image size—complex page layouts typically require substantial amounts of memory, and incomplete pages are often the result of high complexity in the printed page.

- *Simplify the page.* Try simplifying the page layout or content (i.e., remove some objects). If the printed page is missing certain text styles, check that the corresponding font (or a suitable substitute) is installed. If problems persist, enable TrueType fonts as graphics.

Symptom 3.33: Printing is noticeably slower than normal. Slow printing under Windows 95/98 is typically the result of poor hardware performance, or a printer driver issue/conflict.

- *Check the free disk space.* Printing can be very demanding of disk space for temporary files, so a drive nearing maximum capacity may not have enough space to create the needed temporary files. If your drive is down to a few MB, you should free additional space by backing up and eliminating unneeded files.

- *Check for drive fragmentation.* Another printing speed factor is drive file fragmentation. Excessive fragmentation will make the drive work much harder when reading and writing files, so printing from highly fragmented files will be correspondingly slower. Run a disk defragmenter (such as Defrag) to examine and correct file fragmentation on the drive.

- *Check system resources.* Low resources can impair printing performance—especially if you are running several complex applications simultaneously. Shut down unneeded applications, and try rebooting the PC (if necessary) to free more memory.

- *Check the printer spooling.* Verify that print spooling is enabled, and that .EMF (Enhanced Metafile) spooling support is selected.

- *Check the printer driver.* See that the correct printer driver is selected for your printer. If problems persist to this point, try starting the system in its "safe mode" and try printing again. If this corrects the problem, there may be an application or driver conflict that you will need to isolate.

Symptom 3.34: The computer stalls during the printing process.   This can sometimes occur if there is a resource problem (i.e., insufficient disk space) to develop adequate temporary files.

- *Check the free disk space.* If fewer than 10 to 15 MB are available on your hard drive, free additional space if necessary.

- *Check the printer spooling.* Verify that print spooling is enabled, and that .EMF (Enhanced Metafile) spooling support is selected.

- *Check the printer driver.* See that the correct printer driver is selected for your printer. If problems persist to this point, try starting the system in its "safe mode" and try printing again. If this corrects the problem, there may be an application or driver conflict that you will need to isolate. Check and reinstall the printer driver. Even if you choose not to reinstall the drivers, check that they are all up to date.

Symptom 3.35: You cannot print through Windows 95/98.
There are many possible variations of this problem.
For example, you are unable to print from Windows-based programs, but you can print from DOS programs (i.e., EDIT.COM). When printing under Windows, you may see an error such as *The printer could not be found.* In other cases, the `Print` command on the *File* menu in Notepad may be unavailable. This behavior can occur if the WIN.INI file has a read-only attribute—this may occur after you upgrade to Windows 98. Remove the read-only attribute from the WIN.INI file, and then install the printer driver again to update the WIN.INI file:

- Click *Start*, point to *Find*, then click *Files or Folders*.

- In the *Named* box, type `win.ini`, then click *Find Now*.

- In the list of files, right-click the WIN.INI file, then click *Properties*.

- Click the *Read-Only* check box to clear it, then click *OK*.

- Quit the *Find* tool and restart your computer.

Install the printer driver using the steps below:

- Click *Start*, point to *Settings*, and then click *Printers*.

- Right-click your printer, and then click *Properties*.

- On the *Details* tab, click *New Driver*.

- In the *Manufacturers* box, click your printer's manufacturer, and then click the appropriate model in the *Models* box.

- Click *OK*, and then click *OK* again.

Symptom 3.36: After upgrading to Windows 95, you cannot print to an HP DeskJet printer. There are many possible variations of this problem that you should be familiar with. When printing to a DeskJet, you may see *Out of memory*, *Not enough memory*, or *Printer offline* errors. When trying to install the HP DeskJet printer drivers included with Windows 95, you see an error message stating that UNIDRV.DLL is already in use. Other errors may include *Cannot print to device LPT1* or *Could not start print job*. Your entire document may be printed as random or unintelligible characters, graphics may be printed but text is not, or text may be printed but graphics are not. These problems are usually caused because the Windows 3.1 drivers for the HP DeskJet printer were not successfully upgraded to the Windows 95 versions. You'll need to delete the old HP drivers and reinstall the proper ones:

- Double-click the *Printers* icon in *Control Panel*.

- Right-click the HP DeskJet printer, and then click *Delete* on the menu that appears. If there's more than one HP DeskJet printer in the `Printers` folder, repeat this for each DeskJet printer.

- Locate and remove the DESKJET.INI and DESKJETC.INI files in the `Windows` folder.

- Locate and remove the driver files in the `\Windows\System` folder listed in Table 3.1.

TABLE 3.1 List of HP DeskJet Files that Can Be Removed

DESKJETC.DRV	HPV660C.HPC	HPVQP.DLL
HPDSKJET.DRV	HPVBG.EXE	HPVRES.DLL
HPSETUP3.DLL	HPVCM.HPM	HPVTTPCL.DLL
HPV1284.DLL	HPVCNFIG.EXE	HPVUI.DLL
HPV500.HPC	HPVDOS.DLL	HPVWCPS.DLL
HPV500C.HPC	HPVDSM.EXE	HPVWIN.DLL
HPV510.HPC	HPVEXT24.DLL	SCONFIG.DLL
HPV520.HPC	HPVHT.DLL	TBKBASE.DLL
HPV540_A.HPC	HPVMLC.DLL	TBKCOMP.DLL
HPV540_B.HPC	HPVMLCH.EXE	TBKNET.EXE
HPV550C.HPC	HPVMON.DLL	TBKUTIL.DLL
HPV560C.HPC	HPVPML.DLL	TBOOK.EXE

- Rename all the OEM<n>.INF files in the \Windows\Inf folder (where <n> is an incremental number starting at 0). Do *not* use the OEM*.INF wildcard to rename files—doing this may cause the wrong files to be renamed.

- If the HP DeskJet "Status Monitor" is in the *Startup* group, remove it. Right-click the Taskbar, then click *Properties* on the menu. Click the *Start Menu Programs* tab, and then click *Remove*. Double-click the *Startup* branch to expand it. Click the HP DeskJet "Status Monitor" shortcut, then click *Remove*. Click *Close* and restart your computer.

- Use the *Add Printer* wizard to reinstall the HP DeskJet printer. Make sure to select the DeskJet driver included with Windows 95 (not the Windows 3.x HP printer driver). If the new DeskJet printer does not show up in the *Add New Hardware* list, remove the DRVIDX.BIN and DRVDATA.BIN files from the \Windows\Inf folder. This will update the *Add New Hardware* device database.

Symptom 3.37: There are blank pages when printing. This is a known issue with printers such as the Canon LBP-8IV—the first few pages print correctly, but the remaining pages are blank. This problem can occur if the Canon LBP-8IV (or similar) printer is attached to the computer with a parallel cable over 4 feet in length. The blank pages occur because the Canon LBP-8IV printer defaults to a 30-second time-out (this setting cannot be changed). To correct this problem, connect the printer and host PC using a parallel cable shorter than 4 feet—the recommended length specified in the Canon LBP-8IV printer documentation. If the cable length is correct, try a better-quality cable.

Symptom 3.38: You encounter SPOOL32 error messages when trying to print.   Error messages may include

SPOOL32 caused a General Protection Fault in module KERNEL32.DLL, SPOOL32 caused an Invalid Page Fault in module KERNEL32.DLL, or *SPOOL32 caused a Stack Fault in module KERNEL32.DLL.* SPOOL32.EXE is a 32-bit Windows 95/98 component that manages the spooling of print jobs. Spooling allows the PC to quickly process a print job by temporarily storing it on the hard disk before sending it to the printer. This allows the system to return control to the printing program much sooner, so SPOOL32 error messages can occur if something is preventing the print job from being spooled properly. Start by disabling all nonessential drivers and programs. Under Windows 95:

- Click *Start*, select *Find*, then click *Files or Folders*.
- Click the *Include Subfolders* check box to clear it.
- In the *Named* box, type `config.sys autoexec.bat`, then click *Find Now*.
- In the list of found files, right-click the AUTOEXEC.BAT file, click *Rename*, then type a new name for the AUTOEXEC.BAT file (i.e., AUTOEXEC.OLD).
- Repeat the process for your CONFIG.SYS file.
- Quit the *Find* tool and reboot the computer.

Use the following steps to "clean boot" to Windows 98:

- Click *Start*, select *Programs, Accessories, System Tools*, then click *System Information*.
- On the *Tools* menu, click the *System Configuration Utility*.
- On the *General* tab, click the following check boxes to clear them:

Process CONFIG.SYS File
Process AUTOEXEC.BAT File
Process WINSTART.BAT File

Process SYSTEM.INI File
Process WIN.INI File
Load Startup Group Items

- Click *OK*, quit the *System Information* tool, then restart your computer.

The clean-boot process eliminates the possibility that an antivirus program or other utility is causing the error message (it should also disable any third-party printing software such as Hewlett-Packard Port Monitor or Epson Spooler). Now change the spooling format from Enhanced Metafile (.EMF) to .RAW, and attempt to print *directly* to the printer instead of spooling the print job:

- Click *Start*, select *Settings*, then click *Printers*.

- Right-click the printer you are using, and then click *Properties*.

- On the *Details* tab, click *Spool Settings*.

- Click *Print Directly To The Printer*.

- In the *Spool Data Format* box, click *RAW*.

- Click *OK*, click *OK* again, and then close the *Printers* window.

Some printer drivers have coding errors that may cause one of these error messages to occur. To determine if this is the case, update or change the printer driver. There may also be a terminate-and-stay-resident (TSR) or other program that prevents SPOOL32.EXE from being run when Windows 95/98 starts. Using a text editor such as Notepad, add the following line to the [Windows] section of the WIN.INI file:

```
<drive>:\<windows>\system\spool32.exe
```

where <drive> is the hard drive where Windows 95/98 is installed, and <windows> is the folder where Windows 95/98 is installed.

Symptom 3.39: There are problems printing when third-party device drivers are installed. You may see an error such as *Error writing to LPTx for Printer <xxxx>*. There may be a problem with the Network (or the password is incorrect). In *Device Manager*, IRQ 7 may be listed as being used by an unknown device. These types of problems are typically caused by third-party device drivers being loaded in the [386Enh] section of the SYSTEM.INI file. The following device drivers are known to prevent programs from printing:

- Cis1284.386 by Canon Multipass
- Hpypeppy.386 by Hewlett-Packard
- Lex01.386 by Lexmark
- Lexsw2.386 by Lexmark
- Mpass.386 by Canon Multipass
- Okiport.386 by Okidata laser printers
- Sumovmi.386 by Panasonic KXP-6100 laser printers
- Vcpd.386
- Vecpd.386 by Netscape Navigator

Open the SYSTEM.INI file in Notepad, then remove or disable any of the following lines in the [386Enh] section (you can disable a command line by placing a semicolon at the beginning of the line):

```
DEVICE=<path>\Cis1284.386
DEVICE=<path>\Lex01.386
DEVICE=<path>\Okiport.386
DEVICE=<path>\Sumovmi.386
DEVICE=<path>\Vcpd.386
DEVICE=<path>\Vecpd.386
```

Save your changes, close Windows, then restart the system. If the problem persists, disable any lines in the [386Enh] section that list a driver with a .386 extension.

Symptom 3.40: You find that international fonts are printed as ASCII on PostScript printers.   This occurs with some international versions of Windows. High-byte symbols (non-ANSI symbols) are printed as ASCII characters instead of the appropriate international character, or some TrueType fonts (i.e., Arial, Times New Roman, or Courier) are printed as ASCII characters instead of Hebrew or Arabic. You'll probably find that TrueType font substitution is enabled, so you should configure your printer to use TrueType fonts exclusively:

- Click *Start*, select *Settings*, then click *Printers*.
- Right-click the PostScript printer, and then click *Properties*.
- On the *Fonts* tab, click the *Always Use TrueType Fonts* option button.
- Click *OK*.

Symptom 3.41: You cannot print reliably when a shared printer name contains spaces.   You find that you cannot print to a network printer (or printing is unreliable from some programs in Windows 95). There may be error messages such as *Cannot open printer driver* or *Cannot connect to printer—Check printer setup*. This problem can occur if the name of the shared printer you're using contains spaces. Some programs incorrectly parse the device lines for network printers in the WIN.INI file, so programs that use the device lines for network printers (instead of using COM-MDLG.DLL) incorrectly treat spaces in names as delimiters between share names.

One solution is to remove the spaces from the name of the print server or shared printer (perhaps replace the space with an underscore "_" character). Another solution is to capture a parallel port to the shared printer, then install the printer to that port:

- Click *Start*, and then click *Help*.

- Click the *Index* tab and type `capture`.

- Select the *capturing printer ports* topic, then click *Display*.

- Follow the instructions in the Help topic.

Symptom 3.42: You cannot print in "landscape" orienta-tion.   Landscape documents (including envelopes) are incorrectly printed in portrait orientation on the printer. This is a known problem on printers such as the Lexmark Medley printer using the Lexmark Medley Monochrome printer driver version 5.09.95. When you're using this printer driver, the landscape orientation option is unavailable in the *Page Setup* dialog.

The best workaround for this type of problem is to download and install the latest driver from Microsoft or the printer manufacturer. If there is no later driver available, try an emulation driver. For example, the Lexmark Medley printer is functionally identical to the Lexmark ExecJet 4076 IIc printer—you can install the IBM/Lexmark ExecJet 4076 II printer dri-ver included with Windows 95/98 to print mono-chrome documents in landscape orientation.

Symptom 3.43: You see a SPOOL32 error such as *SPOOL32 caused an invalid page fault in module.*   Also, when you try to print to a LANtastic network printer, you may receive a message such as *SPOOL32 caused an invalid page fault in module WNPP32.DLL*. This error can occur if the real-mode LANtastic drivers use the wrong syntax to capture a printer port (you may require an updated LANTNET.DRV file from Artisoft). Edit the STARTNET.BAT file in the `\lantasti` folder and disable the `net use LPTx` statement:

- Use any text editor (such as Notepad) to open the STARTNET.BAT file.

- Type REM at the beginning of the net use LPT1 statement.

- Save the STARTNET.BAT file and then close the editor.

- Restart your computer.

For a more permanent fix, you may be able to obtain the updated LANTNET.DRV file from Artisoft's Web site.

Symptom 3.44: There are missing TrueType fonts in WordPad or Word.   You may not be able to select TrueType fonts in applications like WordPad or Word, even though you can select TrueType fonts in Excel, and you can view TrueType fonts in your \fonts folder. This typically means that your default printer is one that does not support TrueType fonts (such as a Generic/Text Only printer). Try the following steps to work around this issue:

- Click *Start*, select *Settings*, then click *Printers*.

- If you already have another printer installed that supports TrueType fonts, use the right mouse button to click the printer, and then click *Set as default*.

- If you do *not* have another printer installed that supports TrueType fonts, double-click *Add New Printer* to install the driver for your printer. Follow the instructions on the screen to install the printer.

Symptom 3.45: A small amount of text is sent to the printer when you start Windows.   In most cases, what little text there is may appear garbled or unintelligible, and the printer may (or may not) eject the page after the text is printed. The printer may also display an error code (for example, on HP LaserJet printers, *Error 22* may appear). When you attempt to print, you may see a message that the printer is offline or out of paper.

This behavior generally occurs when the DRVWP-PQT.VXD virtual device driver is loaded. This file is typically installed by Seagate Backup software, and is typically located in the \Windows\System\Iosubsys folder as well as the \Arcada\System folder. This driver is also installed by Windows 98 Backup. The driver detects tape devices connected to a parallel port. During the detection process, a string of text is sent through the parallel port to be interpreted by tape devices. Some printers interpret this string as printable text (the output may also be sent to the printer during modem or port detection as well). This issue is also known to occur on the following printers:

Canon BJC-5000

Canon MultiPASS 5000

Canon BJC-4300

To prevent this driver from being loaded (don't try this if you have a tape backup device connected to a parallel [LPT] port on your computer):

- Click *Start*, select *Find*, and then click *Files or Folders*.

- In the *Named* box, type drvwppqt.vxd, and then click *Find Now*.

- Rename all instances of the file by changing the filename extension (you must change the extension to prevent the driver from being loaded).

Symptom 3.46: You cannot print a Device Manager report to a file.   When you attempt to print a *Device Manager* report to a file, the report may not be printed (but you may not receive an error message). This behavior can occur if Microsoft Fax is set as the default printer. Change the default printer to a printer *other* than

Microsoft Fax. Click *Start*, select *Settings*, and then click *Printers*. Right-click a printer (other than Microsoft Fax), and then click *Set As Default*.

> **NOTE:** If you don't have another printer configured to set as the default, install any suitable printer by clicking *Add Printer*, and then install a new printer using the *Add Printer* wizard.

Symptom 3.47: Color text and graphics may not print correctly. This happens most frequently with HP DeskJet 1200C or 1600C color printers—some text or graphics may not be printed with the exact color in which they appear on the screen (or they may not be printed at all). This behavior occurs because of issues with the UNIDRV.DLL file, as well as dithering limitations of the particular printer (i.e., HP DeskJet 1200C and 1600C). New/updated drivers are often the solution to this kind of trouble.

The HP DeskJet 1200C printer uses the HPPCL5MS.DRV printer driver included with Windows 95/98, which can cause this problem (other HP DeskJet color printers that use the HPPCL5MS.DRV printer driver do not exhibit this behavior). You can work around this problem by installing the Windows 3.1 printer driver included with the HP DeskJet 1200C printer.

The HP DeskJet 1600C often has dithering issues, so try disabling dithering. Click *Start*, select *Settings*, and then click *Printers*. Right-click your HP 1600C printer, and then click *Properties*. Click the *Graphics* tab. Under *Dithering*, click *None*, and then click *OK*.

Symptom 3.48: You get an error message when printing from Adobe Acrobat. This often happens when you try to print Adobe Acrobat (.PDF) documents from Acrobat reader version 3.01 in duplex—your printer may stop responding, and you may receive the following error message *79 SERVICE (0142)—TRAP:0D*

ADR:007D1588. This is a frequent problem with more recent printers such as the HP 5Si/5Si MX PS. To resolve this issue, you'll need to download and install the most current printer driver from HP.

Symptom 3.49: You cannot print multiple copies of a document. When you attempt to print multiple copies of a document, the *Number of Copies* box may be unavailable in the *Print* dialog box (the *Collate* check box may also be unavailable). This is known issue with Windows 98 and some HP printers such as the HP DeskJet 400. You can work around this problem at least temporarily by printing only one copy of the document at a time. A more permanent solution is to use a different printer driver:

- Click *Start*, select *Settings*, and then click *Printers*.

- Right-click your printer (i.e., the HP DeskJet 400), and then click *Properties*.

- On the *Details* tab, click *New Driver*, and then click *Yes* when you are prompted to continue.

- In the *Manufacturers* box, click a suitable manufacturer, then click a suitable model in the *Models* box (i.e., select an HP DeskJet 500).

- Click *OK*, and then click *OK* again.

   NOTE: When selecting a "similar" printer driver, some features specific to your particular printer may be lost.

Symptom 3.50: You receive an error message when printing a sample file included with "Astound" by Gold Disk. You generally receive a General Protection Fault (GPF) error such as *<Program> caused a general protection fault in module <xxxxxx> at <address range>*. This is a known problem with HP LaserJet 4 series and HP LaserJet III series printer drivers on an LPT port. To work around this issue, try printing the sample file(s) using a suitable emulation printer driver.

Symptom 3.51: The Plug-and-Play printer is detected as an "unknown device." If you install a PnP printer using the *Add New Hardware* wizard, and choose to install the printer as an unknown device (because Windows 98 doesn't provide a driver for your printer), the printer may not work correctly—it may also be missing from the `Printers` folder. In some cases, your printer may appear in *Device Manager* as an "unknown device." This issue typically occurs if Windows 98 doesn't have a driver for your printer. Windows 98 names a device "unknown" if it does not have a driver for the device. To correct this problem, install the printer driver for your particular printer.

Symptom 3.52: The printer cannot print in duplex mode. This is a known issue with some printers such as the HP 660C under Windows 98—even though the printer fully supports duplex functionality. This is often caused when using the Windows 95 driver under Windows 98, and you receive an error such as *Printer driver problem—Data needed by the printer driver cannot be found or has been corrupted. Restart Windows and try printing again.* This behavior occurs because the HP DeskJet 660C printer driver included with Windows 98 does *not* support duplex printing (and the driver version included with Windows 95 is incompatible with Windows 98). To fix this problem, you should download and install the updated Windows 98 driver for your printer.

Symptom 3.53: When using "Imaging for Windows," the document is printed in all black. When you print a black-and-white document (i.e., a fax or scanned image) using the "Imaging for Windows" environment, the document is printed in all black, or you receive an error message such as *Color management options are missing or unavailable.* This kind of error occurs when an Image Color Matching profile (an .ICM file) isn't associated with the printer (or if you are using an earlier printer driver).

- *Associate a .ICM profile.* One solution to this problem is to associate a .ICM profile with your particular printer. Click *Start*, select *Settings*, and then click *Printers*. Right-click your particular printer and click *Properties*, then click the *Color Management* tab. Click the *Add* button. In the *Add Profile Association* dialog box, click the appropriate .ICM file for your printer (to determine which profile to use, contact the printer's manufacturer). For example, most Canon color printers should use a profile that starts with "BJC," and most HP color printers should use the "Diamond Compatible 9300k G2.2" profile. When you've selected the right profile, click *Add*, and then click *OK*.

- *Update the printer driver.* Another solution to the problem is to update the printer's driver to the latest Windows 98 version.

Symptom 3.54: You receive a *SPOOL32 caused a General Protection Fault in module <unknown> at <address>*. Other errors may include *SPOOL32 caused an Invalid Page Fault in module <unknown> at <address>*, or *SPOOL32 caused a Stack Fault in module <unknown> at <address>*. This is a known issue when printing to Canon MultiPASS Multifunction printers, and these error messages can occur if the Exclusive Port Control check box is selected in Canon's MultiPASS Desktop Manager utility (we'll use this printer as an example). One solution is to clear the Exclusive Port Control check box:

- Click *Start*, select *Programs*, and then click *MultiPASS Desktop Manager*.

- On the *File* menu, click *Preferences*.

- Click the *Exclusive Port Control* check box to clear it, and then click *OK*.

- Now restart your computer.

Another alternative is to disable Enhanced Metafile (.EMF) spooling:

- Click *Start*, select *Settings*, and then click *Printers*.
- Right-click your Canon printer, and then click *Properties*.
- Click the *Details* tab, and then click *Spool Settings*.
- In the *Spool Data Settings* box, click *.RAW*.
- Click *OK*, and then click *OK* again.

Symptom 3.55: There are problems printing to an Epson Action Laser 1600 printer. When you send a print job from a Windows 98 system to an Epson Action Laser 1600, your computer may run slowly (your print job may not complete successfully). This problem is normally caused by using an older Epson printer driver. If you're using an older Epson printer driver, it *may* prevent the installation of a newer driver. To resolve this problem, rename the files in Table 3.2 to an .OLD file extension, restart your computer, and then install the printer driver from your Windows 98 CD (you may need to use the Find/Files or Folders feature in Windows Explorer to locate each file).

> **NOTE:** When you restart the computer, Windows 98 detects your printer and starts the *Add New Printer* wizard.

TABLE 3.2   List of Epson Action Laser 1600 Files to Be Renamed

EPHEW.PRD	SID2BRDW.DLL	SID2LIBW.DLL
EPHPW.DRV	SID2BRFW.DLL	SID2OVL.ISD
SID2BIDW.DLL	SID2CTLW.DLL	SID2OVL.ITD
SID2BMGW.DLL	SID2DATW.DLL	SID2SFMW.DLL
SID2BMGW.EXE	SID2DLGW.DLL	SID2WST1.ITD

Symptom 3.56: Your printer prints the "Euro" symbol incorrectly.   This is a known issue with the HP LaserJet 5Si and 5Si/5Si MX PS printers. When you print a document that contains a "Euro" symbol, the "Euro" symbol may be printed as a black dot or blank space. This behavior also occurs if TrueType fonts are *not* sent to the printer as bitmap soft fonts. Adjust the TrueType font configuration:

- Click *Start*, select *Settings*, and then click *Printers*.

- Right-click your printer (i.e., HP LaserJet 5Si or 5Si/5Si MX PS printer), and then click *Properties*.

- Click the *Fonts* tab.

- Click *Always Use TrueType Fonts*, click *Send Fonts As*, click *Bitmaps under TrueType Fonts*, click *OK*, and then click *OK* again.

- As an alternative, click *Download TrueType fonts as bitmap soft fonts* and then click *OK*.

Symptom 3.57: You encounter an error message when installing software for an Epson Stylus Color printer.   This is due to a printer software compatibility problem. When you attempt to install the "Easy Setup Software" (EASY500.EXE) for your Epson Stylus Color 500 printer, you may receive an error message such as *EPSIN500 caused a general protection fault in module EPSIN500.EXE at 0003:00000068*. To work around this problem, install version 2.2AE (or later) of the Epson Stylus Color 500 printer drivers and setup software.

Symptom 3.58: You find that white text on a black background does not print properly.   When you attempt to print an Adobe Acrobat (.PDF) document with white text on a black background (from any version of Acrobat reader to an HP printer), only the black background is printed. This occurs if your printer uses a "Printer Control Language" (PCL) driver. This is a limitation of many PCL drivers (this issue does not occur with PostScript drivers). The best solution is to download and install the latest PCL driver for your printer. In the meantime, you can switch to raster graphics:

- Click *Start*, select *Settings*, and then click *Printers*.
- Right-click your particular printer and then click *Properties*.
- On the *Graphics* tab, click *Use Raster Graphics*.
- Click *OK*, and then close the *Printers* folder.

Symptom 3.59: When printing a Web page with tables containing italic characters, some characters may be cut off. You notice that this happens on PCL printers. Some accented characters may have an "overhang adjustment" that is larger than the width of the character. This causes an unnecessary break in the printed text because the width is incorrectly calculated as a very large number. For example, the "overhang adjustment" for `width=30` could be 50 (which results in a fill width of -20). Instead of -20, the result is a large positive number. Contact the Microsoft support site for a patch at *http://support.microsoft.com/support/supportnet/default.asp*

Symptom 3.60: The printer outputs colored text in black and white. This is a known issue with printers like the Canon BJ-200EX printer where colored text is printed in black and white instead of gray shades. This is almost always a driver problem, and can usually be resolved by downloading and installing the latest driver for your printer.

Symptom 3.61: When you install Internet Explorer with an older Lexmark printer, you receive an error message. Typical errors include *Load error #35: Cannot access BCE server*, *Load error #5: Initialize failed*, *Load error*

#35: Couldn't register with BCE server, or *Load error #5: Initialize failed*. This is a known issue with older Lexmark printers under Windows 98 and Internet Explorer, and requires some changes to the Registry (be sure to back up the Registry and your "emergency disk" before proceeding). First obtain and install the most current printer driver for your printer from the manufacturer, then remove the values from the following registry keys (this example is for Lexmark):

```
HKEY_LOCAL_MACHINE\SOFTWARE\Microsoft\Windows\
CurrentVersion\Run\Lexstart.exe
```

```
HKEY_LOCAL_MACHINE\System\Currentcontrolset\
Control\Print\Monitors\Lexmarkprintmonitor\
Lexlmpm.dll
```

```
HKEY_LOCAL_MACHINE\SOFTWARE\Lexmark\Markvision
```

Symptom 3.62: There are missing TrueType fonts. You may notice that some TrueType fonts are not present in the Fonts folder, or you see an error message if you try to add a TrueType font such as *The <fontname> TrueType font is already installed*. You may also note that TrueType fonts are not listed in any program, or that previously created documents are printed differently (or the formatting is changed when you view the document). In other cases, custom desktop settings may have changed fonts. The problem is that the Registry key that lists TrueType fonts may be damaged or missing. Use the FONTREG.EXE tool that adds a registry key allowing the installation of TrueType fonts. To run FONTREG.EXE and install the fonts:

- Click *Start*, and then click *Run*.

- Type FONTREG in the *Open* box, and then click *OK*.

- In *Control Panel*, double-click *Fonts*.

- In the *File* menu, click *Install New Font*.

- In the *Folders* box, select the folder that contains the TrueType fonts (i.e., `\Windows\Fonts`).

- Click *Select All*, and then click *OK*.

> **NOTE:** If your documents are not printed the way you expect, remove and reinstall the appropriate printer driver.

> **NOTE:** Windows 95/98 has a limit of approximately 1000 fonts.

Symptom 3.63: Your impact printer seems to print slowly after upgrading Windows. In addition, the printer may print only unidirectionally rather than bidirectionally. This normally happens when your document contains TrueType fonts instead of printer fonts—since TrueType fonts are sent to an impact printer as graphics, they are printed in graphics mode (which is slow). If you were using printer fonts with your previous version of Windows, and you are using TrueType fonts with your current version of Windows, printing may often seem much slower. Also, if you're using Windows 95 or 98, it's probably configured to spool print jobs to your computer's hard disk until the printer is ready to print—this allows Windows 95/98 to return control to the program that you are printing from much faster, but it may cause overall printing speed to seem slower.

- *Try using printer fonts.* If the documents you're printing contain TrueType fonts instead of printer fonts, you should switch to printer fonts. Printer fonts appear in font lists with a printer icon next to the font name, whereas TrueType fonts appear in font lists with "TT" next to the font name. If printer fonts do not appear in font lists in programs that you print from, you may be using a Windows 95 printer driver that does *not* support printer fonts.

> **NOTE:** Some of the printer drivers included with Windows 95 do *not* support printer fonts. When you're using one of these drivers, TrueType fonts are used in place of printer fonts—this may cause your documents to print slowly.

- *Try reducing print quality.* If your printer is printing in only one direction, configure your printer to use a lower print resolution or print quality, or a lower-quality printer font. For example, if your printer is currently configured to print in letter-quality (LQ) mode, you may be able to work around this problem by configuring it to print in draft mode instead. Double-click the *Printers* icon in *Control Panel*, use the right mouse button to click the printer that you want to configure, click *Properties*, and then click the *Graphics* tab to modify the print resolution or the *Device Options* tab to modify the print quality.

- *Disable spooling.* If you're using Windows 95 or 98, configure it to print directly to the printer instead of spooling print jobs to your hard disk. Doing so may improve overall printing speed, but it may also increase the amount of time that it takes for Windows to return control to the program you are printing from. Click *Start*, select *Settings*, click *Control Panel*, and then double-click *Printers*. Right-click the printer that you want to configure, click *Properties*, and then click the *Details* tab. Click *Spool Settings*, click *Print directly to the printer*, click *OK*, and then click *OK* again.

Symptom 3.64: You encounter plotting problems under Windows. Plotters are very similar to ordinary printers, but there are unique plotter issues that you should be aware of when working under Windows 95/98. Reset and self-test the plotter. Turn off the plotter, wait a few seconds, then turn the plotter back on again—this should clear the plotter's memory.

Perform a self-test on the plotter (if the self-test fails, the plotter will require service). If possible, set up the plotter on your local computer, and verify that no plotter sharing devices or daisy-chained devices (such as a SCSI CD-ROM drive) are connected between the computer and plotter.

Try plotting from DOS. Restart your computer—when you see the *Starting Windows 95* message, press the <F8> key, choose *Step-By-Step Confirmation*, and then answer *No* to all questions. For Windows 98, press and hold down the <Ctrl> key after your computer completes the POST, and then choose *Step-By-Step Confirmation* from the Startup menu. Type the following line, and then press <Enter>:

```
edit testplot.bat
```

Type the following lines in the new file:

```
mode com1:9600,n,8,1,p
pause
echo IN:SP1:PD4000,4000;SP0: > COM1
```

> **NOTE:** If the plotter is not connected to COM1, substitute the correct port name in the preceding lines.

Save the new file and quit Edit, then type the following line and then press <Enter>:

```
testplot.bat
```

The MODE command should now set up the port, and you should see the entries below:

```
Resident portion of Mode loaded
COM1: 9600,N,8,1,P
Press any key to continue
```

Press <Enter>. If a diagonal line is *not* plotted, there may be a problem with the port, the cable, or the plotter. You may want to try using a different plotter cable, or try a different plotter. Try plotting to a different port. If plotting from COM1 doesn't work, reboot the PC and try configuring the printer to use COM2.

- Click *Start*, select *Settings*, then click *Printers*.
- Click the *Plotter* icon in the *Printers* folder.
- On the *File* menu, click *Properties*.
- Click the *Details* tab.
- In the *Print To The Following Port* box, click *COM2*.
- Click *OK*.
- Now start Notepad, type some text in Notepad, then try to plot the text.

If problems persist, try plotting to a file. If a file is created, copy the file to the port:

- Click *Start*, select *Settings*, then click *Printers*.
- Click the *Plotter* icon in the *Printers* folder.
- On the *File* menu, click *Properties*.
- Click the *Details* tab.
- In the *Print To The Following Port* box, click *FILE*: (creates file on disk).
- Click *OK*.

Now start Notepad, type in some text, and then try to plot the text. Name the output file TEST.PRN. If the plotter driver does not plot to the file, try the same procedure in Safe Mode. If you cannot plot to a file in Safe Mode (or if the output is poor), try removing the driver from the *Printers* folder and reinstall the driver. If the driver *does* plot to a file only in Safe Mode, some other software is conflicting with the driver, so try "clean booting" the system. Under Windows 95, rename the CONFIG.SYS file to CONFIG.OLD, and rename AUTOEXEC.BAT to AUTOEXEC.OLD.

Restart your computer. Under Windows 98, click *Start*, select *Programs*, *Accessories*, *System Tools*, and *System Information*. On the *Tools* menu, click *System Configuration Utility*. Clear the following check boxes:

Process CONFIG.SYS File

Process AUTOEXEC.BAT File

Process WINSTART.BAT File

Process SYSTEM.INI File

Process WIN.INI File

Load Startup Group Items

Click *OK*, quit *System Information*, then restart the computer.

> **NOTE:** This technique lets you isolate the specific file entry that is causing the problem—once the offending file entry is determined, you can edit the appropriate file or Registry entry to remove the reference and return the System Configuration Utility to normal.

> **NOTE:** Do not try plotting from WordPad or Paint. Paint prints raster data that plotters cannot use. Plotting from WordPad does not work because WordPad cannot wrap text correctly with the plotter driver.

Check your *Device Manager* settings. If you cannot plot from Notepad, verify that the port is set up correctly in *Device Manager* (for example, confirm that there are no conflicts between the port and other devices). To open *Device Manager*, use the right mouse button to click *My Computer*, and then click *Properties* on the menu that appears. Click the *Device Manager* tab, double-click *Ports (COM & LPT)*, and then double-click the appropriate port for the plotter. Now click the *Resources* tab and verify that the settings are correct for the plotter's communications port (for example, the standard I/O range for COM1 is 03F8-03FF and its IRQ is 4). Also verify that the *Conflicting Devices* list reads *No conflicts.*

If a conflict exists (or the port's settings are incorrect), use *Device Manager* to remove and reinstall the port. To open *Device Manager*, use the right mouse button to click *My Computer*, and then click *Properties* on the menu that appears. Click the *Device Manager* tab, double-click *Ports (COM & LPT)*, and then highlight the appropriate port for your plotter. Click *Remove*, and then restart your computer. In *Control Panel*, double-click the *Add New Hardware* icon, and then let the *Add New Hardware* wizard redetect the port hardware in your computer.

Try changing or reinstalling the plotter driver. A new driver can be used to improve performance, fix bugs, or expand plotter support. A newer plotter driver for use with Windows 95/98 may be available from Microsoft or from the plotter's manufacturer. If the problem seems to be corrected by using a different plotter driver, remove and reinstall the plotter driver (preferably with a newer version).

Make sure that there is enough hard disk space to handle plotter files. As a rule, there should be at least 3 MB of free space on the hard disk that contains the temporary folder. Remove temporary and spool files. Restart your computer to the DOS mode. Type SET and press <Enter>, then note the location pointed to by the TEMP variable. Change to the folder listed by the TEMP variable. For example, if TEMP is set to c:\windows\temp, type the following line and then press <Enter>:

```
cd\windows\temp
```

Delete any temporary files in the folder (temporary files normally have a .TMP extension). To delete these files, type:

```
del *.tmp
```

NOTE: You should not delete these files from within Windows because Windows (or a Windows-based program) may be using one of these files.

Change to the spool folder, type the following line, and press <Enter>:

```
cd\windows\spool\printers
```

Delete any spool files in the folder (spool files usually have a .SPL extension). To delete these files, type:

```
del *.spl
```

Now, restart your computer normally.

If the hard disk becomes fragmented, or there are cross-linked files on the hard disk, you can encounter plotting problems. To check for file problems, click *Start*, select *Programs*, *Accessories*, *System Tools*, and then click *ScanDisk*. Let ScanDisk run normally. When ScanDisk is finished, use Defrag to reorganize the disk files. Click *Start*, select *Programs*, *Accessories*, *System Tools*, and then click *Disk Defragmenter*. If problems persist, try plotting directly to the plotter port:

- Click *Start*, select *Settings*, and then click *Printers*.
- Click the *Plotter* icon in the *Printers* folder.
- On the *File* menu, click *Properties*, then click the *Details* tab.
- Click *Spool Settings*, then click *Print directly to the printer*.
- Click *OK*, and then click *OK* again.

Now type some text in Notepad, and then try to plot the text. Finally, if you're still having communication problems with the plotter, try changing the flow control setting:

- Click *Start*, select *Settings*, and then click *Printers*.
- Click the *Plotter* icon in the *Printers* folder.
- On the *File* menu, click *Properties*.
- Click the *Details* tab, then click *Port Settings*.
- In the *Flow Control* box, click *XON/XOFF* (or *Hardware*, or *None*).
- Click *OK*, and then click *OK* again.

Symptom 3.65: There are printing problems after installing the HP JetAdmin Service.   After you install the HP JetAdmin service, you may be unable to view the properties for *any* of your installed printers. If you right-click a printer icon in the Printers folder, you may also receive an error message such as; *Explorer caused an Invalid Page Fault in module KERNEL32.DLL at 015F:BFFABEA*. If you click *Close*, and then click *Properties*, you may encounter an error message similar to; *RUNDLL32 caused an Invalid Page Fault in module KERNEL32.DLL at 015F:BFF8ABEA*. If you click *Close*, you may then be able to view the properties for your printer. This type of problem occurs if you have installed the Windows 98 HP JetAdmin drivers (version 2.54) from the Windows 98 CD, and you *then* install the HP JetAdmin service. Uninstall the HP JetAdmin service and reinstall it:

- Click *Start*, select *Settings*, click *Control Panel*, and then double-click *Network*.
- Click *Add*, and then click *Service*.
- Click *Hewlett-Packard*, click *HP Jet Admin*, and then click *Cancel* while the files are being copied.
- Restart your computer.
- Click *Start*, select *Settings*, click *Control Panel*, and then double-click *Network*.
- Click *HP JetAdmin*, click *Remove*, and then restart your computer again.
- Now install the HP JetAdmin service from scratch.

Printer
Troubleshooting

Troubleshooting is an odd pursuit that falls somewhere between being an art and a science. Success takes a keen eye, a clear head, and a real understanding of the printer mechanism (not to mention a healthy dose of patience and persistence). In order to troubleshoot a printer successfully, you'll need to be able to *identify* the problem clearly, *isolate* the problem to some software or hardware fault, *correct* the suspected fault quickly and cost-effectively, then *retest* the printer to ensure that the fault has been corrected. If the problem persists, you'll need to start the cycle again from the beginning. This is a tried-and-true technique used by many professional technicians. Fortunately, you've got a great deal of hands-on troubleshooting help in this book—this section covers a wide range of impact, ink-jet, and laser symptoms that have been accumulated from countless hours of experience and research. Once you locate a symptom or issue that is similar to yours, just walk through the suggested solution(s). Remember to record your work so that you'll know what has and has *not* been done. Now it's time to roll up your sleeves and get started.

NOTE: As with all mechanical and electronic troubleshooting, there is a possibility of personal injury and/or damage to the device that you're trying to repair. If you are uncomfortable or unable to follow the procedure(s) suggested for your symptom, *do not* attempt them. Instead, refer the work to other more experienced technicians.

Guidelines for Safe and Effective Troubleshooting

The most important part of all troubleshooting is *your safety*. You must also be conscious of the value of the printer that you're trying to fix (especially if you're fixing it for someone else). The following guidelines offer some important suggestions that may help to ensure your personal safety, save valuable time, and improve your troubleshooting effectiveness:

- *Test and record*. Always try the printer first and examine its symptoms for yourself. Making repair decisions based on someone else's vague or partial description of a problem can send you running in circles.

- *Check the basics*. Printers need power and a proper connection to a working PC. Make sure that the printer powers on properly, and is using a known-good printer cable attached to a properly configured printer (a.k.a. LPT) port.

- *Check the consumables*. Proper printing relies on an adequate supply of acceptable paper and fresh media (i.e., toner, ink, ribbon, and so on). Many printing problems can be traced to odd paper (such as coated or embossed papers) or expired/exhausted media. Always verify that the printer is using a recommended paper and fresh media before assuming a more serious problem.

- *Check the drivers*. Many printer problems are caused by buggy or outdated printer drivers. Before you start troubleshooting, check online with the printer's manufacturer to see if there's a current recommended driver (or an acceptable "emulation" driver). Download the latest printer driver(s) and have them on-hand if necessary.

■ *Check the product manual.* A printer's user guide often contains helpful information regarding setup, recommended paper types, upgrade requirements, and so on. If you don't have access to the manual, check online with the printer's manufacturer to see if there's a product manual in Adobe Acrobat (.PDF) format that you can download and refer to.

■ *Keep it safe.* Whenever troubleshooting requires you to check a part or perform work inside a printer, always turn the printer off *and* unplug it from its ac outlet before working on it. This prevents the possibility of accidental electrocution.

■ *Let it cool first.* Impact print heads and laser fusing rollers can become *extremely* hot during normal operation. This presents a burn hazard for novice technicians. After turning off and unplugging the printer, be sure to wait at least 10 minutes for the print head or fusing unit to cool before opening the printer.

■ *No extra parts.* Pay careful attention to the screws, fittings, brackets, shrouds, or other assemblies removed from a printer. Each part should be replaced precisely, and there should be no extra screws or other items left over after a repair. You may need to make notes of exactly how the printer was disassembled.

■ *Never add lubricants.* Modern printers are designed with mechanisms that do not generally require lubrication. As a consequence, adding lubricant to a mechanism may actually interfere with a mechanism's normal operation. Do *not* add lubricant unless it is specifically suggested in the printer's user or service manual—and use only the minimum quantity or recommended lubricant.

- *Isolate carefully.* When troubleshooting, it is important that you change only one device, part, configuration setting, or driver at any one time—then retest. Changing more than one "thing" at a time makes it impossible to tell just which "thing" was at fault.

- *Retest thoroughly.* Once a printer is fixed and completely reassembled, be sure to test the printer thoroughly. Use the printer's self-test features, and try printing through a Windows application (such as Microsoft Word). Run and test the printer continuously for a period of time (a.k.a. "burn it in") before returning it to service.

Impact Printer Troubleshooting

The impact dot-matrix printer (or simply *impact printer*) is largely regarded as the workhorse of industrial printing (Figure 4.1). Individual metal print wires are assembled into a die cast metal *print head* housing. There may be 7, 9, or 24 print wires in the head depending on the sophistication of the particular printer. The print head is mounted on a *carriage* that is carried back and forth along a *rail* by a *belt* that is driven by a *motor*. The print head is connected to the *electronic control unit* (ECU) through a long, flat, flexible cable, called the *print head cable*.

When the host computer sends a character to be printed, a series of vertical dot patterns representing that character (in its selected font and size) are recalled from the printer's permanent memory. The ECU sends each dot pattern in turn through a series of print wire *driver circuits*. It is the driver circuits that amplify digital logic signals from main logic into the fast, high-energy pulses needed to fire a print wire. As a pulse reaches the firing solenoid, it creates

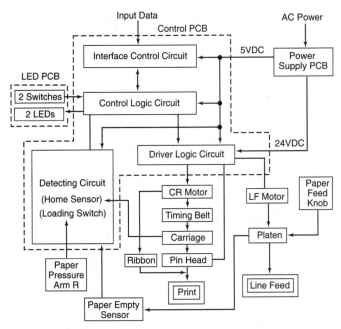

Figure 4.1 Block diagram of an impact dot-matrix printer. (*Courtesy of Tandy Corporation*)

an intense magnetic field that shoots its print wire forward against the page. After the pulse is complete, a spring pulls the print wire back to its rest position.

Impact heating problems

One of the major problems with impact printing is the eventual buildup of heat. The substantial amount of current needed to fire a solenoid is mostly converted into heat that must be dissipated by the print head housing. Under average use, the metal housing will dissipate heat quickly enough to prevent problems. But heavy use can cause heat to build faster than it dissipates. This happens most often when printing bit-image graphics where many print wires may fire continuously. Excessive or prolonged heating can cause unusual friction and wear in print wires. In extreme cases, uneven thermal expansion of hot pins within the housing may cause them to jam or bend.

To combat the buildup of heat, impact print heads are cast with a series of *heat sink fins*. If you look at a print head, you will see the heat sink fins. In order for heat sink fins to be effective, they must be exposed to the open air—buildup of dust, dirt, and paper debris will prevent heat from venting to the air. When inspecting an impact print head, always make sure that the heat sink fins are clear.

> **NOTE**: The *Basic Printer Maintenance* video covers impact cleaning and maintenance in detail. You can obtain this 40 minute video show from Dynamic Learning Systems using the order form at the back of the book.

Ribbon transport troubleshooting tips

As with an ordinary typewriter, the ribbon cartridge contains a length of inked ribbon that is pulled across the print head. Each time a character is printed, the ribbon is advanced. A *ribbon transport* mechanism is used to advance the ribbon. When trouble occurs with the ribbon transport, the ribbon no longer advances properly (if at all). Ink is quickly used up, and the printing becomes faded or indistinct. The following tips can help you to isolate ribbon transport problems:

- *Replace the ribbon cartridge first.* Before you actually begin to tinker with a ribbon transport mechanism, examine the ribbon cartridge as the printer operates. If the ribbon drive shaft advances, inspect the ribbon itself—it may simply be exhausted. Try replacing the ribbon cartridge and retest the printer. A ribbon cartridge that does not advance may be kinked or jammed within its cartridge. Install a fresh ribbon and retest. If normal operation returns, discard the defective ribbon cartridge.

■ *When the ribbon does not advance.* If the ribbon drive shaft does not turn (or a fresh ribbon does not correct your problem), examine the ribbon transport mechanics. The PRINTERS utility can produce a set of carriage returns that you can use to observe the ribbon transport. Unplug the printer and remove the ribbon cartridge. You will observe the long ribbon drive shaft that inserts into the ribbon cartridge. Grouped just below and behind the drive shaft, you will find a series of other small gears and friction rollers that make up the ribbon transport. The mechanism can be assembled on the carriage or on the printer's mechanical frame.

■ *Clean / replace the ribbon transport mechanics.* Although it is never desirable to operate a printer without its ribbon, it is usually safe to do for limited periods of time as long as paper is available to absorb print wire impact (*refer to your owner's manual for any specific warnings or cautions*). You may have to perform some minor disassembly to observe the entire ribbon transport. While the printer is running, watch the ribbon transport mechanism for any parts that may be loose, sticking, or jammed together. Dust and debris may have accumulated to jam the mechanism. Use a clean cotton swab to wipe away any foreign matter. If the transport mechanism is severely worn, it may have to be replaced entirely.

Head/ribbon symptoms

NOTE: An impact print head can become *extremely hot* during the printing process. Turn off and unplug the printer, and be sure to allow at least 10 minutes of idle time for the print head to cool before attempting any service.

NOTE: Use the PRINTERS utility to generate standard printer test patterns. You can obtain PRINTERS from Dynamic Learning Systems, using the order form at the back of the book.

Symptom 4.1: Print quality seems poor—dots appear faded or indistinct. All other operations appear normal. If you have the PRINTERS utility, run a Print Head Test. The pattern should yield a solid black rectangle. In normal operation, the graphic rectangle drawn by an impact print head will not be absolutely homogeneous—you will be able to discern slight tone differences in each pass—but the print should be sharp and the color tone should be consistent.

- *Check the ribbon*. If the print seems excessively light, or there are patches of light and dark areas, you should begin by carefully examining the *ribbon*. It should be reasonably fresh and it should advance normally while the carriage moves back and forth.

- *Check the ribbon advance mechanism*. A ribbon that is not advancing properly (if at all) may be caught or jammed internally, so install a fresh ribbon and retest the printer. If the ribbon still does not advance properly, troubleshoot the printer's ribbon advance mechanics.

- *Check the head spacing*. Most printers are designed with one or two small mechanical lever adjustments that can alter the distance between print head and platen by several thousandths of an inch. This adjustment allows print intensity to be optimized for various paper thickness. If the print head is too far away from the platen, the resulting print may appear light or faded. If spacing is already close (or nonadjustable), turn your attention to the print head itself.

- *Clean the print wires*. Turn off and unplug the printer, then check each print wire in the head assembly. Print wires should all be free to move, sliding in and out without restriction—except for mechanical tension from the return spring (keep in mind that you will probably have to remove the print head from its carriage assembly). If you find a tremendous buildup of foreign matter, wipe off each wire as gently as possible. Use a stiff cotton swab dipped lightly in alcohol or light-duty household oil. *Do not use harsh chemical solvents*! Finally, wipe down the front face of the print head with a soft, clean cloth. Once all wires are moving freely again (and any loosened gunk has been removed), replace the print head and retest the printer. If you *do* remove the print head for cleaning, be sure to read-just the head spacing lever(s) to keep the head parallel to the platen.

- *Check the print head cable*. Another possible problem area may be in the print head cable itself. If the cable (especially the ground) connections are loose or marginal, the increased resistance in the print wire circuits may lighten the print. Try reseating the print head cable one or more times. If this does not help, try replacing the print head cable. If problems continue (or the cable cannot be replaced without exchanging the print head), try a new print head assembly.

- *Check the print head electronics*. It is the print head driver circuitry that supplies energy necessary for print wire operation. There could be a loss of solenoid driving voltage or some other defect in your print head driver circuits. You may need to troubleshoot or replace the print head driver circuits.

Symptom 4.2: Print has one or more missing dots that resemble "white line(s)" across the page.   This also takes place during a self-test or Test Page. The "white line(s)" should be equally noticeable in text as well as graphics. Assuming that all other operations of the printer are correct, a loss of one or more dot rows suggests that the corresponding print wire(s) will not fire. In most cases, this is due to a fault in the print head, the print head cable, or the corresponding driver circuitry. However, you will need to explore each step in order to determine the point of failure.

- *Clean the print wires.* Turn off and unplug the printer, then check each print wire in the head assembly. Print wires should all be free to move, sliding in and out without restriction—except for mechanical tension from the return spring (keep in mind that you will probably have to remove the print head from its carriage assembly). If you find a tremendous buildup of foreign matter, wipe off each wire as gently as possible. Use a stiff cotton swab dipped lightly in alcohol or light-duty household oil. *Do not use harsh chemical solvents!* Finally, wipe down the front face of the print head with a soft, clean cloth. Once all wires are moving freely again (and any loosened gunk has been removed), replace the print head and retest the printer. If you *do* remove the print head for cleaning, be sure to readjust the head spacing lever(s) to keep the head parallel to the platen.

- *Replace the print head.* If cleaning does not free the print wire(s), the print head mechanism may be defective. Replace the print head mechanism (as well as the print head cable).

- *Replace the ECU.* As a rule, printer driver circuits rarely fail, but it can happen. If the problem persists after replacing the print head and print head cable, you'll need to troubleshoot or replace the printer's driver circuits (probably the entire ECU board).

Symptom 4.3: Print appears "smeared" or exceedingly dark.   All other operations appear normal. Smeared or

PRINTERS: The Printer Test and Alignment Utility V.1.00
IMPACT TEST PAGE Pattern

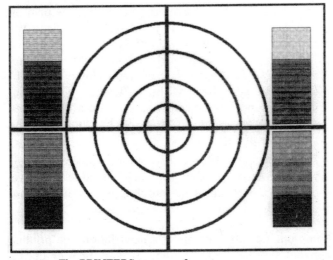

Figure 4.2 The PRINTERS test page format.

extremely dark print is best discovered with a textured graphic or text (such as the printer's self test or
the Print Test Page feature in PRINTERS), as shown
in Figure 4.2. However, smeared print is relatively
easy to correct.

- *Check the head spacing.* One of the most likely reasons for smeared print in an impact printer is that
  the print head is too close to the platen. When the
  head is too close, the print wires may not have
  enough time to retract before the carriage moves—
  thus smearing the print. Try retracting the print
  head a bit using the position adjustment lever.

- *Clean the print wires.* Another possible problem can occur when gunk accumulates on and in the print head. Foreign matter can affect the dimensions and stroke of the print wires. It can also jam the print wires in an extended position and prevent them from retracting before the carriage moves—again smearing the print. Turn off and unplug the printer. You can then remove the print head and clean the face and print wires. Use a stiff cotton swab dipped lightly in alcohol or light-duty household oil. *Do not use harsh chemical solvents!* Wipe down the front face of the print head with a soft, clean cloth. Once all wires are moving freely again (and any loosened gunk has been removed), replace the print head and retest the printer.

- *Replace the print head.* If problems continue at this point, chances are that your print head is defective, or fouled with gunk so badly that cleaning is not effective. Try replacing the print head.

Symptom 4.4: After installing a new ribbon, the printing appears smeared and streaked. If your printer uses a ribbon shield, this problem occurs when the ribbon shield is either loose or missing. Remove the ribbon cartridge and check the ribbon shield: if it's loose, secure it in place; if it's missing, find it and reinstall it. Also check that the print head position lever is not set too close to the platen.

Symptom 4.5: Printer does not print under computer control. You'll notice that operation probably appears correct in the self-test mode. This behavior is usually caused by communication problems between the printer and host computer.

- *Make sure the printer is "online."* Before you disassemble the printer, take a moment to check its *online* status. There is almost always an indicator on the control panel that is lit when the printer is selected. If the printer is not selected (online), then it will not receive information from the computer, even if everything is working correctly.

■ *Check your paper.* Paper may have run out, in which case you will have to reselect the printer manually after new paper is installed.

■ *Check your control panel options.* Even the simplest printers offer a variety of options that are selectable through the keyboard (i.e., font style, character pitch, line width, etc.). However, you must often go offline in order to manipulate those functions, then reselect the printer when done. You may have selected a function incorrectly, or forgotten to reselect the printer after changing modes.

■ *Check software settings.* Make sure that you have selected the correct printer in your software, and that you have the very latest printer driver installed.

■ *Check your communication interface cable.* The cable may have become loose or unattached at either the printer or computer end. If this is a new or untested cable, make sure that it is wired correctly for your particular interface. An interface cable that is prone to bending or flexing may have developed a faulty connection, so try another cable.

■ *Check the printer's internal setup.* Double-check the printer's dual inline package (DIP) switch settings or setup configuration. DIP switches are often included in older printers to select certain optional functions such as serial communication format, character sets, default character pitch, or automatic line feed. If you are installing a new printer, or you have changed the switches to alter an operating mode, it may be a faulty or invalid condition. DIP switches also tend to become unreliable after many switch cycles. If you suspect an intermittent DIP switch, rock it back and forth several times, then retest the printer.

■ *Replace the ECU*. When everything checks out, you will have to disassemble the printer and troubleshoot its interface circuits and main logic. In many cases, you'll need to replace the interface module (or the entire ECU) outright.

Symptom 4.6: Print head moves back and forth, but does not print (or prints only intermittently). This also frequently takes place during a self-test or test patterns when the printer is not communicating with the host computer.

■ *Check the ribbon*. If the print appears to gradually fade in and out, check your printer ribbon first. Make sure that it is installed and seated properly between the platen and print head. If the ribbon has dislodged from the head path or is totally exhausted, no ink will be deposited on paper. If the ribbon is in place, make sure that it advances properly as the carriage moves. A ribbon that does not advance properly may be caught or jammed internally, so install a fresh ribbon and retest the printer. If the ribbon still fails to advance, troubleshoot or replace the printer's ribbon advance mechanism.

■ *Check the print head cable*. If the print appears to cut in and out suddenly, suspect an intermittent connection—connection problems in the print head cable or within the print head itself can lead to highly erratic head operation. Replace any print head cable that appears defective.

■ *Check the printer's voltage levels*. Apply printer power and measure the print head driver voltage (usually +12 or +24 V dc). If driver voltage is low or nonexistent, the driver circuits will not produce enough energy to fire a print wire. Marginal supply outputs can result in intermittent operation. Check your circuit connections. If you find that the power supply voltage is low or erratic, troubleshoot or replace the printer's power supply. (If the power supply is integrated into the ECU and must be replaced, you will have to replace the entire ECU outright.)

■ *Check the print head.* Turn off and unplug the printer, then disengage the print head from its carriage. Use a general-purpose multimeter on a low-resistance scale to measure the resistance of each firing solenoid. If the head is completely inoperative, the common ("ground") lead may be intermittent or open. If you find any open or shorted firing solenoid, replace the print head mechanism. If you cannot test the print head as described here, try replacing it.

■ *Replace the ECU.* If your print head is still intermittent or totally inoperative, chances are that there is a serious problem in the printer's driver circuits—the print head logic/drivers are intermittent or have failed entirely. If you have an oscilloscope, you can troubleshoot the print head signals through the ECU (the point at which the signals disappear is the point of failure). If you do not have an oscilloscope handy, simply replace the driver circuits or entire ECU board outright.

Electronic/control symptoms

Symptom 4.7: A RAM error is indicated with a text message or blinking LED. Whereas an error message may be relatively easy to understand, blinking LEDs can be a bit more difficult to follow. Typically, the *Power LED* will blink on and off three times quickly, go dark for about 500 ms (half a second), then repeat (though your own printer may use a different error sequence).

■ *Replace the RAM.* A RAM error indicates that the printer's onboard memory has failed. With basic printers, you may simply be able to replace the RAM ICs on the ECU. For more sophisticated printers (i.e., laser printers), you may try systematically replacing the SIMM devices on the printer's ECU.

■ *Replace the CPU.* The printer's onboard microprocessor also frequently uses a small amount of internal RAM, so if the problem persists after replacing the printer's memory, you must try replacing the printer's microprocessor.

■ *Replace the ECU.* If problems still continue, or you'd prefer to avoid the component-level work involved in RAM or processor replacement, replace the ECU board entirely.

Symptom 4.8: A ROM checksum (or similar) error is reported. Permanent memory holds the instructions that run a printer, as well as any resident fonts. When the printer is first initialized, a checksum value for each ROM is calculated, then compared to the checksum stored in each ROM. If the calculated value matches the stored value, the ROM is considered good; otherwise, the ROM is assumed bad, and an error message is generated. For relatively simple printers, the firmware and font data can be stored on a single IC. For more complex printers, however, a number of permanent memory devices may be needed.

■ *Replace the ROM(s).* Typically, ROMs are DIP-type ICs that are inserted into sockets on the printer's main board (a.k.a. the ECU). This means that ROMs are often easy to replace—if you can find them. Unfortunately, replacement ROMs are not always easy to come by. You'll need to contact the printer's manufacturer for replacement ROM(s). The first ROMs to suspect are the "firmware" ROMs since they hold the instructions for your printer. A firmware failure will allow the printer to malfunction during operation. "Font" ROM problems are generally less catastrophic. At worse, certain font styles and sizes may appear distorted.

■ *Replace the ECU*. If you cannot locate replacement ROMs (or new ROMs have no effect), your only real alternative then is to replace the printer's ECU or main logic controller board.

Symptom 4.9: The control panel does not function at all. No keys or indicators respond, but the printer appears to operate normally under computer control.

■ *Check the control panel wiring*. Open your printer enclosure and expose the control panel circuit. Make sure that any connector(s) or wiring from the panel are installed properly and securely. If you have just finished reassembling the printer, perhaps you forgot to reconnect the control panel, or reconnected it improperly. Interconnecting wiring may have been crimped or broken during a previous repair.

■ *Replace the ECU for simple printers*. It is rare that a simple control panel (i.e., one using just LEDs and pushbuttons) will fail outright. When a total failure occurs in this case, the trouble is almost always in the ECU rather than the control panel (the microprocessor or controller IC that manages the control panel has probably failed). Try replacing the ECU.

■ *Replace the panel for sophisticated printers*. When problems occur with a sophisticated control panel (i.e., one that contains display or other active circuitry), it is more likely that the control panel's onboard controller IC that failed. It is the local controller IC that handles the LEDs, switches, and LCD panel (if included). Try replacing the local controller IC on the control panel. If this is not possible, replace the entire control panel module.

■ *Replace the ECU for sophisticated printers*. In most cases, a new control panel should solve your problem, but in the rare event that problems still persist, the fault will then almost certainly be in the ECU. Your best course now is simply to replace the main logic board or other module that drives the control panel.

Symptom 4.10: One or more keys is intermittent or defective. You probably find that excessive force or multiple attempts may be needed to operate the key(s), but the printer appears to operate normally otherwise. You will find this symptom most often in older, heavily used printers. In almost every instance, this symptom is simply the result of faulty keys. Switch contacts eventually wear out with age and use—you may see this as "stubborn" or "sticky" keys. Ideally, the preferred course would be to replace the questionable switches. Unfortunately, replacement switches are often not available. If you cannot replace the defective keys, you will have little choice but to replace the entire control panel module.

Symptom 4.11: One or more LED/LCD displays fail to function. The printer appears to operate normally otherwise. LEDs and LCDs are notoriously reliable devices, so it is unlikely that the display itself has failed. Rather, you should first suspect the circuit that drives the LED/LCD.

- *Check the control panel wiring.* Open your printer enclosure and expose the control panel circuit. Make sure that any connector(s) or wiring from the panel are installed properly and securely. If you have just finished reassembling the printer, perhaps you forgot to reconnect the control panel, or reconnected it improperly. Interconnecting wiring may have been crimped or broken during a previous repair.

- *Replace the ECU for simple printers.* It is rare that a simple control panel (i.e., one using just LEDs and pushbuttons) will fail outright. When a total failure occurs in this case, the trouble is almost always in the ECU rather than the control panel (the micro-processor or controller IC that manages the control panel has probably failed). Try replacing the ECU.

■ *Replace the panel for sophisticated printers.* When problems occur with a sophisticated control panel (i.e., one that contains display or other active cir-cuitry), it is more likely that the control panel's onboard controller IC has failed. It is the local con-troller IC that handles the LEDs, switches, and LCD panel (if included). Try replacing the local con-troller IC on the control panel. If this is not possible, replace the entire control panel module.

■ *Replace the ECU for sophisticated printers.* In most cases, a new control panel should solve your problem, but in the rare event that problems still persist, the fault will then almost certainly be in the ECU. Your best course now is simply to replace the main logic board or other module that drives the control panel.

Symptom 4.12: The LCD display is dark or displaying gib-berish. This symptom arises in high-end printers that employ LCDs in addition to (or instead of) LED indicators.

■ *Check the control panel wiring.* Start by checking the LCD module's connector to see that it is installed properly and completely—this is a fre-quent oversight when reassembling a printer from another repair.

■ *Replace the LCD module.* If the control panel is working otherwise, chances are that the LCD mod-ule is defective, so try replacing the LCD unit.

■ *Replace the control panel.* If the control panel has failed (i.e., switches not responding), the local con-troller IC in the control panel has probably failed. Replace the controller IC. If you cannot replace the controller IC, replace the control panel subassembly entirely.

Symptom 4.13: The printer does not initialize from a "cold start" turn-on. There may or may not be visible activity in the printer after power is turned on, but power indicators are lit. The printer's self-test does not work.

- *Check the printer's error code or message.* If a printer encounters an error during its initialization, there will be a visible or audible indication of the fault. Audible tones, flashing light sequences, or an alphanumeric error code are just some typical failure indicators (your user's manual will list any error codes and their meanings). If the error is "expected" (an error that is checked and handled by the printer's firmware), the printer will simply wait until the error is corrected. *Paper out* errors are a commonly "expected" error. However, "unexpected" errors can cause the printer to freeze or behave erratically for no apparent reason. ROM or microprocessor defects are considered unexpected failures—main logic has no way of dealing with such problems—so there is no way of knowing just how your printer will respond (if it works at all).

- *Check the power supply.* Use an ordinary multimeter to measure the logic supply voltage levels being provided by the power supply (usually +5 V dc). If this voltage is low or absent, logic devices will not function properly (if at all). A low or missing voltage output suggests a defective power supply. Troubleshoot the power supply or replace the supply assembly outright.

- *Check for RAM errors.* An initialization process can stall if the microprocessor detects a faulty RAM location. Some printers may display an error code indicating a RAM error. Replace the RAM chip(s) and retest the printer. If normal operation returns, you have isolated the defective component(s).

- *Replace the ECU.* If the problem persists, chances are that you've encountered a serious fault in the printer's main logic circuit. Replace the electronic control unit (ECU) outright.

Symptom 4.14: Printer operation freezes or becomes highly erratic during operation.   Typically, you must activate the printer from a "cold start" to restore operation. The self-test may work until the printer freezes.

■ *Check the power supply.* Use an ordinary multimeter to measure the logic supply voltage levels being provided by the power supply (usually +5 V dc). If this voltage is low, intermittent, or absent, logic devices will not function properly (if at all). A low or missing voltage output suggests a defective power supply. Troubleshoot the power supply or replace the supply assembly outright.

■ *Check the printer's firmware ROM(s).* The printer's onboard processor requires constant access to its firmware ROM in order to operate properly. Each instruction and data location must be correct, or the processor will become hopelessly misdirected. If you find that the printer operates only to some consistent point where it freezes or acts strangely, the ROM may be defective. Replace the firmware ROM(s) if possible and retest the printer thoroughly. If normal operation returns, you have probably isolated the problem.

■ *Replace the ECU.* If the problem persists, chances are that you've encountered a serious fault in the printer's main logic circuit. Replace the electronic control unit (ECU) outright.

Symptom 4.15: After power-on, you notice that the printer menus are incomplete, or certain settings are missing. This is a known problem with some impact printers such as the Okidata ML-390/1 Turbo, which prints out the printer's menu without such settings as the page width (i.e., Rear Feed). In virtually all cases, the printer had a false firmware reading during its power on initialization. Manually reset the printer. The exact reset sequence is a bit different for every printer (but for the Okidata ML-390/1 Turbo, you'd reset the printer by holding down the *Form Feed* and *Tear* buttons while turning on the printer).

Symptom 4.16: The print head halts in midpass, and the printer's "pause" light flashes. The printer may also beep. In most cases, the print head has overheated—the halt in printing is merely an automatic temperature "cutoff." Wait several minutes and see if the printer resumes normal operation. If so, there's no need to worry. If the printing does not resume, the printer's ECU may require replacement.

> **NOTE**: Dust filling the print head's cooling fins can impair normal cooling. Keep the cooling fins clear by brushing/blowing any accumulations of dust.

Symptom 4.17: There are five or more beeps when the printer is turned on. This is a known issue with printers such as the Epson ActionPrinter 5500, and is usually caused by problems with the print head's home position switch.

■ *Clear the home sensor(s).* Shut printer power off, then slide print head from left to right about 10 times (ensure that the print head touches each side of the carriage). Now center the print head and power the printer back on.

■ *Replace the home sensor(s).* If the error persists, the home sensor(s) may be defective. Try replacing the home sensor(s).

■ *Replace the ECU.* If the print head home sensor(s) appear to be working properly, the problem is most likely in the printer's ECU logic. Replace the home sensor interface module, or replace the entire ECU board outright.

Mechanical symptoms

Symptom 4.18: A paper or carriage advance does not function properly (if at all). The printer relies on motors to move paper and the print head. Problems with a paper or carriage advance can typically be traced to motor-related or electronic motor control faults.

■ *Check for mechanical damage.* Inspect the printer carefully for any signs of mechanical damage or obstructions (i.e., a stripped paper feed gear or broken carriage belt). Clear any obstructions of paper fragments or other foreign matter from the mechanics. Replace any damaged mechanical parts or subassemblies.

■ *Check the motor connections.* Turn off and unplug the printer, then check the cables to your suspect motor. Try reinstalling the motor connector at the ECU (where the motor driver circuits are located).

■ *Check the motor voltage.* Next, check the motor voltage by inspecting the +24 volt output from the power supply. If the motor voltage is low or absent, troubleshoot or replace the power supply.

■ *Replace the ECU.* If the motor voltage is present, the problem is likely in the motor driver circuits on the ECU. Try replacing the ECU outright.

■ *Replace the motor.* If problems still persist, the related motor (i.e., the carriage or paper advance motors) may be defective. Try replacing the particular motor—remember that this may require a substantial amount of mechanical disassembly and reassembly.

Symptom 4.19: The bottom feed tractor mechanism isn't working (usually after you install it). Paper will not feed from the bottom feed (push) tractor—only from the rear feed (pull) tractor. Check the installation of the bottom push tractor mechanism against the printer's manual and see that the mechanism is installed correctly. You may need to remove the mechanism, recheck the installation instructions, then try reinstalling the bottom feed tractor mechanism properly.

> **NOTE**: For certain printers, there is a partition in the bottom of the printer that will not allow the left pin feed mechanism to move flush left if it is not correctly positioned *before* the bottom feed unit is installed. This creates an error condition because paper does not cover the paper out sensor.

Symptom 4.20: Paper out alarm shows up on the control panel even though paper is available, or it does not trigger when paper is exhausted. In most cases, you'll find that the problem is related to the paper sensor itself, though the ECU logic may also have failed.

■ *Check and adjust the paper switch (mechanical).* If your paper sensor is a mechanical switch, place your multimeter across its leads and try actuating it by hand. You should see the voltage reading shift between a logic 1 and logic 0 as you trigger the switch. If you measure some voltage across the switch but it does not respond (or responds only intermittently) when actuated, replace the defective switch. If it responds as expected, check its contact with paper to be sure that it is actuated when paper is present. You may have to adjust the switch position or thread paper through again to achieve better contact.

■ *Check the paper switch (optical).* Test an optical paper sensor by placing your multimeter across the photosensitive output and try to actuate the sensor by hand—this may involve placing a piece of paper or cardboard in the gap between transmitter and receiver. You should see the phototransistor output shift between logic 1 and logic 0 as you trigger the optoisolator. If it does not respond, check for the presence of dust or debris that may block the light path. If excitation voltage is present, but the photo-transistor does not respond, it is probably defective. Replace the optoisolator.

■ *Replace the ECU.* If the problem persists, chances are that you've encountered a serious fault in the printer's main logic circuit that interprets paper sensor signals. Replace the electronic control unit (ECU) outright.

Symptom 4.21: The paper "feeds out" completely when you install new paper. With paper in the printer, the alarm indicator on the printer remains ON. In many cases with single-sheet paper transports, the paper completely "feeds out" of the printer when the paper is parked. Check the paper sensor. Your paper sensor may be stuck or not working correctly. The paper sensors are usually located below the platen, about 2 to 3 inches from the left and behind the platen on the left side (look for black plastic tab). If you notice that the switch is stuck, use a paper clip to wiggle the black plastic tab (the switch) to pop it free and allow it to move freely.

Symptom 4.22: Carriage does not find its home position. This may result in a frozen initialization or erratic print spacing, and is usually caused by sensor switch problems. As with paper sensors, the sensing element can be mechanical or optical.

■ *Check and adjust the paper switch (mechanical).* If the "home sensor" is a mechanical switch, place your multimeter across its contacts and try actuating the switch by hand. You should see a voltage reading switch between a logic 1 and logic 0 as the switch is actuated. If voltage is present but the switch does not respond (or responds only intermittently), replace the defective switch. If it does respond, check its contact with the carriage to be sure that it actuates when the carriage is in its home position. You may have to adjust the switch position to achieve a better contact.

- *Check the paper switch (optical).* An optical "home sensor" can be checked in much the same manner. Place your multimeter across the phototransistor output and try to actuate the sensor by hand by blocking the optical gap with a piece of paper or cardboard. You should see the output voltage shift between a logic 0 and logic 1 as the sensor is actuated. If the phototransistor does not respond, check for dust or debris that may be blocking the light path. If excitation voltage is present but the phototransistor does not respond, replace the defective optoisolator.

- *Replace the ECU.* If the problem persists, chances are that you've encountered a serious fault in the printer's main logic circuit that interprets home sensor signals. Replace the electronic control unit (ECU) outright.

Symptom 4.23: Carriage moves erratically or inconsistently. You notice a number of errors in print spacing across the page. This is generally due to a problem with the carriage motor, the carriage positioning sensor, or the ECU that interprets the carriage position signals.

- *Check for mechanical damage.* Inspect the printer carefully for any signs of mechanical damage or obstructions (i.e., a loose or broken carriage belt). Clear any obstructions of paper fragments or other foreign matter from the mechanics. Replace any damaged mechanical parts or subassemblies.

- *Check the motor connections.* Turn off and unplug the printer, then check the cables to your carriage motor. Try reinstalling the carriage motor connector at the ECU (where the motor driver circuits are located).

- *Check the motor voltage.* Next, check the carriage motor voltage by inspecting the +24 volt output from the power supply. If the motor voltage is low or absent, troubleshoot or replace the power supply as required.

- *Replace the ECU.* If the carriage motor voltage is present, the problem is likely in the motor driver circuits on the ECU. Try replacing the ECU outright.

- *Replace the motor.* If problems still persist, the carriage motor may be defective. Try replacing the carriage motor—remember that this may require a substantial amount of mechanical disassembly and reassembly.

    NOTE: Excessive or inappropriate lubrication along the carriage rail can sometimes cause carriage positioning problems.

Symptom 4.24: The paper advance does not function, or functions only intermittently. All other functions check properly. This kind of trouble is almost always due to mechanical failures, but can also be caused by paper advance motor or ECU problems.

- *Check the paper path and mechanics.* When a paper advance fails to work at all, begin by observing the paper feed drive train assembly. Check any pulleys or gears to ensure that all parts are meshed evenly and are able to move freely. You can watch this by turning the platen knob located outside of the printer. Remove any foreign objects or obstructions that may be jamming the drive train. *Never* try to force a drive train that does not turn freely! Realign any parts that appear to be slipping or incorrectly aligned.

- *Check the motor connections.* Turn off and unplug the printer, then check the cables to your paper advance motor. Try reinstalling the paper advance motor connector at the ECU (where the motor driver circuits are located).

- *Check the motor voltage.* Next, check the paper advance motor voltage by inspecting the +24 volt output from the power supply. If the motor voltage is low or absent, troubleshoot or replace the power supply as required.

- *Replace the ECU.* If the paper advance motor voltage is present, the problem is likely in the motor driver circuits on the ECU. Try replacing the ECU outright.

- *Replace the motor.* If problems still persist, the paper transport motor may be defective. Try replacing the paper transport motor—remember that this may require a substantial amount of mechanical disassembly and reassembly.

Symptom 4.25: Paper gathers or bunches up at the tractor-feed sprocket wheels.   This is a symptom relatively common to older printers (or printers that have had their tractor-feed mechanism serviced improperly). The platen and sprocket wheels must transfer paper at *exactly* the same rate to achieve smooth paper handling. If the sprocket wheels are moving a bit too slowly (relative to the platen) for any reason, the paper will eventually "bunch up" at the sprocket wheels.

- *Check the paper path and mechanics.* When you notice paper bunching up, observe the paper feed mechanics. Check any pulleys or gears to ensure that all parts are meshed evenly and are able to move freely. You can watch this by turning the platen knob located outside of the printer. Remove any foreign objects or obstructions that may be jamming the drive train. *Never* try to force a drive train that does not turn freely! Realign any parts that appear to be slipping or incorrectly aligned.

■ *Check the paper transport clutch*. Some printers add a clutch assembly that can engage and disengage the tractor-feed unit from the drive train. If there is a clutch mechanism present, see that it is engaged fully and properly. You may wish to "pop the clutch" in and out a few times to ensure positive contact. Inspect the drive train gears *very* carefully—especially the teeth on the tractor gear itself. If one or more teeth are missing, the tractor assembly will "skip" a bit, and may behave erratically. Replace any worn or damaged gears. You may need to replace this clutch assembly entirely.

Symptom 4.26: Paper slips or walks around the friction-fed transport. Friction-feed is an ideal system for "single sheet" printers, but friction depends on factors such as paper weight, coatings, and roller conditions.

■ *Check your paper*. Friction-feed paper transports are designed to work with only certain types of paper—brands within a certain range of thickness and weight. Very fine (light bond) paper or very heavy (card stock) paper will probably not advance properly. Slick or other unusual coatings can also upset a friction-feed system. Check the specifications for your particular printer to find its optimum paper type. If you find that you are using an unusual type of paper, try the printer using standard 20-lb bond xerography-grade paper.

■ *Check the paper path*. Inspect your paper path for any debris or obstructions that may be catching part of the paper sheet. A crumpled corner of paper jammed in the paper path or caught in the feed guide can easily interfere with subsequent sheets. Turn off and unplug the printer, and remove all obstructions (be very careful not to nick any of the rollers). A straightened paper clip can often get into spaces that your fingers and tools cannot. Use thin needle-nose pliers to put a small hook in the wire's end for grabbing and pulling the obstruction. *Do not disassemble the rollers unless absolutely necessary.*

■ *Clean the rollers.* Advance the paper feed knob manually (if possible) and take careful note of each roller condition. An even, consistent paper feed depends on firm roller pressure applied evenly across its entire length. Rollers that are very dirty, or old and dry, may no longer be applying force evenly. Clean your rollers with light glass cleaner. Do *not* use rubber rejuvenating compounds on those rollers since almost no rollers are made from rubber today—rejuvenating compound can damage the rollers.

■ *Replace the rollers.* If the rollers are old or damaged beyond cleaning, your best solution is to replace the entire paper feed/transport assembly.

Symptom 4.27: Paper wrinkles or tears as it passes through the printer. Tractor-feed paper transport systems are remarkably reliable, so it is very rare to encounter tearing problems using the tractor approach.

■ *Check the paper feed selection.* Many later-model impact printers offer a selection of paper feed paths. A mechanical lever is typically used to switch between tractor ("pull") and friction ("push") feed modes. If paper suddenly seems to wrinkle or tear along its perforations during printing, the first thing to check should be the paper feed selector lever.

■ *Check the paper path.* If your printer's paper feed mode is set correctly, check the paper path for any debris or obstructions that may be catching the paper. Fragments of torn paper caught in the feed guide can easily jam the paper path. Carefully remove all obstructions that you may find, but use extreme caution to prevent damage to your rollers or feed guide. *Do not disassemble the paper transport unless it is absolutely necessary.* If problems persist, you may have to replace the entire paper feed/transport assembly.

Application or setup symptoms

Symptom 4.28: The printer prints italic numbers instead of a shaded character. This is a common issue with impact printers like the Okidata 320/1 Turbo. The problem is almost always because the wrong character set is selected. Instead of printing in the "Epson" Upper ASCII Character Set II (where the italic characters 0, 1, and 2 print as shaded patterns), the printer is probably configured to use the "Epson" Upper ASCII Character Set I. Use the printer's control panel to change the character set from the default (usually character set "1") to character set "2." In most cases, changing the character set will work for any impact printer using an "Epson" emulation.

Symptom 4.29: Printing seems awfully slow when printing through Windows. This is not necessarily a problem. Since Windows sends everything to the printer as graphics images (even text), it will *not* send out the code for bidirectional or draft printing when using the standard Windows driver. This is done to ensure that each pass of the print head is aligned properly (as might happen if the head is allowed to move in both directions). By contrast, a printer usually prints in faster bidirectional mode under DOS because the data are not sent as graphics—it uses the internal fonts programmed in the printer.

- *Check the driver*. Make sure that you're using the latest manufacturer-specific driver for your printer (especially if the printer is compatible with a later language like ESC/P2, which can use the printer's internal scalable fonts for printing). Older or "emu-lation" drivers may not offer the performance you need.

■ *Reduce the resolution.* Since higher-resolution images require more bitmap data, reducing the image's resolution will reduce the amount of data that must be passed to the printer, and this can often speed printing. This tactic may be especially helpful if you're making test or "draft" prints.

Symptom 4.30: You notice that the print "runs over" into part of another page. This kind of problem almost always means that the printing software isn't config-ured properly.

■ *Check the printer page setup.* If you're using single sheets, you need to verify that the printing software is set up for either single sheet paper (or 61 lines per page); otherwise, it may print a few lines on a second page if the document is over 61 lines.

■ *Check the printing software.* Some older DOS print-ing software may not have those settings if it is designed to be used only with tractor-feed paper. For Windows software, make sure to select *Sheet Feeder Bin 1* for your paper source in the Printer setup. In a few cases, you may need to update your printing software (and perhaps the printer driver) for proper operation.

Symptom 4.31: You cannot set "landscape" orientation when printing through DOS. This is not necessarily a problem. DOS does not process files graphically. Most printers have no landscape fonts built-in, and there are no emulation/language codes to make them print in landscape format. Since landscape printing is processed as graphic data, it is normally only possible from the driver in a Windows (3.1, 95, 98, or NT) envi-ronment. The only real workaround is to use a third-party software utility for DOS such as *Sideways* or *Allways* that would make landscape printing possible from DOS.

Symptom 4.32: You cannot configure proper print layouts on labels, checks, postcards, and so on. This is usually because the printer's Windows driver doesn't properly recognize user-defined page sizes. You will need to use an emulation driver (i.e., the LQ-850 driver) instead and set it up for custom paper size. You can use the following steps to adjust the Windows 3.1 printer drivers:

- Open the *Main* group from the *Program Manager*.
- Open the *Control Panel*.
- Open *Printers*.
- Go to Setup for the *LQ-510* or *LQ-850* (or other appropriate emulation mode for your printer).
- Click the dropdown menu for the *Paper Size* and select *User Defined Size*.
- Select the *length* and *width* of the page, and then click *OK*.
- Open the printing application and verify the page setup of the program is set for the new driver.

You can use the following steps below to adjust the Windows 95/98 printer drivers:

- Click *Start* from the desktop.
- Select *Settings* and choose *Printers*.
- Highlight the *LQ-850* driver (or other appropriate driver) and click *File*, then *Properties*.
- Go to *Details* and *Setup*.
- To configure the paper, go to *Custom* and click on it (you'll have options to change paper sizes).
- Once paper size has been made, click *OK* to keep the setting.

Symptom 4.33: You intermittently lose data when serial printing at 9600 baud. This kind of fault is often related to the printer's particular configuration.

■ *Check the flow control.* If you're using a nonbuffered serial interface board and XON/XOFF (software flow control) is enabled, the XOFF signal may not reach the printer in time to delay data transmission—this would result in an overflow and loss of data. If you can use a DTR (hardware flow control) setting, change XON/XOFF to DTR.

■ *Check the baud rate.* If you must use XON/XOFF, try decreasing the baud rate in order to loosen the timing constraints on your XON/XOFF signal.

■ *Upgrade the printer's serial module.* If your printer supports serial upgrades, try a 32-KB buffered serial interface card. The buffered serial interface has built-in flag reset timing that sets aside additional buffer space to "catch" the data overflow. The specific flag reset timing feature settings are selectable through DIP switches on the serial interface card.

Symptom 4.34: There is difficulty with the printer's automatic "top of form" function. When you turn the printer on, the paper feeds through about one and a half pages (then stops). You hit the printer's Load/Eject button, but it feeds more paper instead of ejecting it backwards. This is almost always because the printer's paper feed system is set up improperly. Examine the printer's front panel to see if other paper bin (i.e., Bin 1 or Bin 2) lights are on. If so, turn the printer OFF and manually eject the continuous feed paper. Reinstall the paper on the printer's tractor-feed unit. Move the paper release lever to select *front push and front push/pull tractor* mode, or *rear push and rear push/pull tractor* mode. Turn the printer back ON—the printer should initialize properly and neither one of the Bin lights should be on. This should resolve the problem.

Symptom 4.35: You get strange symbols, incorrect fonts, or other odd characters when trying to print a document. Those symbols are often ESC codes used to operate the printer, and when you see them in print, it means that the computer is not "talking" to the printer properly.

- *Check the driver.* Check to be sure that the printer driver you have selected in your software matches the printer's compatible emulation. For example, using an IBM ProPrinter driver will not work if your impact printer will only support an Epson LQ driver—using the ProPrinter driver will cause bad characters.

- *Clear embedded commands.* If you have embedded any printer commands in your software, check to be sure that you entered them correctly, or disable/remove them outright.

Symptom 4.36: Ink smears on the paper when you print narrow columns. This kind of problem is typical of Oki Microline 390/391 printers, and is generally caused by excessive print head travel from the centering position. You'll need to tweak the printer's centering position to deal with this problem. For the Microline 390/391, enter the printer's menu mode and set the *Centering Position* to MODE 1. For the wide-carriage Oki ML391T, try setting the *Centering Position* to MODE 2.

Symptom 4.37: You notice that continuous-form paper "sticks" to the printer's paper separator. First make sure that the paper isn't wet or otherwise fouled. If the paper is fresh, chances are that the problem is due to static electricity. In extremely dry environments (especially in the winter) static charges can cause the paper to "cling." Try moving the paper guides together so that the paper rests on the guides rather than on the separator.

Symptom 4.38: When printing word processor files, the text doesn't print according to the printer characteristics set on the printer's control panel. This can affect things like font types, font sizes, margins, and so on. The printing application (i.e., the word processor) is often responsible for this. Before sending a file to the printer, many word processors send either an *initialization string* or a *soft reset* (i.e., an *I-Prime* signal) to the printer. An initialization string contains codes that override the panel and menu settings. You'll need to reconfigure your printer to ignore the reset code— enter the printer's menu mode and change the setting for *Reset Inhibit* to *Yes*. A *soft reset* signal will automatically override any front panel settings you have made. You'll need to reconfigure your printer to ignore the *soft reset*—enter the menu mode and change the setting for *soft reset* (i.e., *I-Prime*) to *Invalid*.

Symptom 4.39: The first line of print starts too far down the page, and you cannot use the printer's control panel to adjust the top-of-form. For example, with an Oki ML590/591, you can't get the paper any higher using the SHIFT-LF/ Micro Feed Down keys. The setting for the *Top of Form* will be restricted if you have the printer's *Form Tear-Off* feature engaged while you set the *Top of Form*. Enter the menu mode and change the setting for *Form Tear-Off* to OFF. Then exit the menu and set the *Top of Form*. When the *Top of Form* is set, enter the menu mode again and change the *Form Tear-Off* setting back to your original configuration.

Ink-jet Printer Troubleshooting

The ink-jet dot-matrix printer (or simply, ink-jet printer) is now embraced as one of the most popular printers for home and small-office printing (Figure 4.3). An ink reservoir feeds a series of microfine nozzles cast into a plastic cartridge. The cartridge may sport 50 nozzles or more depending on the sophistica-

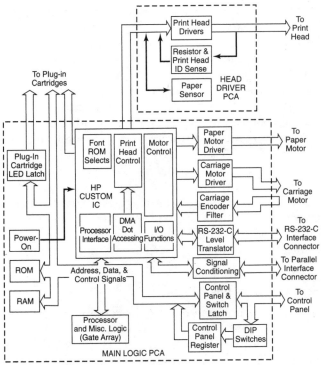

Figure 4.3 Block diagram of an ink-jet printer (*Courtesy of Hewlett-Packard Co.*)

tion of the particular printer and cartridge. The print head cartridge is mounted on a *carriage* that is carried back and forth along a *rail* by a *belt* that is driven by a *motor*. The print head is connected to the *electronic control unit* through a long, flat, flexible cable, called the *print head cable*.

The operation of an ink-jet printer is remarkably similar to that of an impact printer (only the print head is different). When the host computer sends a character to be printed, a series of vertical dot patterns representing that character (in its selected font and size) are recalled from the printer's permanent memory. The ECU sends each dot pattern in turn through a series of print nozzle *driver circuits*. It is the driver circuits that amplify digital logic signals from main logic into the fast, high-energy pulses needed to fire minute droplets of ink from each nozzle. As a pulse reaches the nozzle, it creates an intense surge of heat that literally creates a bubble. The bubble pops, launching a droplet. The nozzle cools in a fraction of a second and is ready for another pulse.

As a rule, ink-jet printers tend to be light and economical devices that enjoy a long, reliable working life. However, there are many situations where problems can occur. Trouble usually strikes in the ink head, paper transport, carriage transport, or electronic control unit (ECU). This part of the chapter offers a comprehensive selection of symptoms and solutions that can help you deal with ink-jet failures.

Head clog problems

An ink-jet print head is little more than a reservoir of liquid ink that feeds a series of tubes. These tubes simply lead to the open air. If the ink cartridge remains idle for a long period of time, the ink has a tendency to dry out over time as the ink's solvent evaporates. This results in a "clogged" nozzle. Depending on the severity of the clog, problems may range from misdirected droplets (deflected by a partial clog), to missing lines in the print, to complete head clogs where there is no printing at all. There are several ways to clear clogged print cartridges.

■ *Purge the ink cartridge*. Virtually all ink-jet printers support a *purge* function (a.k.a. the Purge key on the printer's control panel), which simply fires the nozzles continuously. In many cases, this is enough to "blow out" the clog and resume normal operation.

■ *Clean the ink cartridge*. If you cannot clear the clog after several purge cycles (or there is a lot of ink residue on the cartridge), try removing the ink cartridge and cleaning the nozzles manually using a fabric swab and fresh isopropyl alcohol.

■ *Replace the ink cartridge.* If the cartridge still refuses to operate, the clog may simply be too severe. Replace the ink cartridge outright.

Electrical contact problems

Another common issue that plagues ink-jet printers is the electrical contacts that connect the ink cartridge to the carriage. When you remove the ink cartridge, you can see these contacts as an array of gold-colored contacts. Over time, normal oxidization can interfere with these connections, and cause nozzle misfires. You should clean these contacts whenever you replace the ink cartridge, or when you notice that one or more nozzles fail to fire (resulting in white "lines" in the print). You can clean the contacts using a fabric swab lightly dipped in fresh isopropyl alcohol. Be sure to power-down the printer before cleaning, and allow the contacts to dry thoroughly before reinstalling the ink cartridge.

> **NOTE**: The *Basic Printer Maintenance* video covers ink-jet cleaning and maintenance in detail. You can obtain this 40-minute video show from Dynamic Learning Systems, using the order form at the back of the book.

Understanding ink-jet papers

Your *paper* plays an important role in the overall quality of ink-jet printing. The paper must accept ink, prevent color running, minimize absorption into the page fibers, and dry quickly (with a minimum amount of wrinkling). Although most of today's ink-jet printers will operate with a wide range of papers, your print quality will depend on the paper you choose. Selecting the "right" paper for the job will allow you to get the very best results from your ink-jet printer. Modern ink-jet driver software will actually optimize the amount of ink laid down on a page (depending on the paper type you select) to provide you the most vivid, photorealistic output imaginable. A selection of special coatings help prevent bleeding and oversaturation to give you sharper, more vivid results while using less ink.

General paper characteristics.   Paper is defined using several important characteristics: weight, opacity, brightness, and acidity. You should understand what each of these characteristics means:

- *Basis weight* (or simply, *weight*) is the weight per ream of a given paper—you typically see a number followed by pounds (such as 20-lb bond). The bigger the number, the heavier the paper (and usually the higher the quality). The thickness on some paper is measured in mils.

- *Opacity* is the ability to "see through" the paper. The higher the number, the more opaque the paper. For example, *100 percent opacity* means you cannot see through the paper at all. *Low opacity* means you can see your hand easily when placed behind the paper. Depending on your application, you may not want text or graphics to show through the other side, so you'd want high-opacity paper.

- *ISO brightness* (or simply, *brightness*) is a measure of diffuse light reflectance. The higher the value, the brighter the paper. It's easier to read graphics or text on brighter paper, and colors look best against a bright white background.

- *Acidity* (pH level) tells you how acidic or how alkaline a paper is. A pH value *above* 7 is alkaline, *at* 7 is neutral, and *below* 7 is acidic. A pH level of 7 or greater fits into the category of "acid free." Most papers break down over time, but low acidity helps to slow this process. For archival prints, an acid-free paper is the best choice.

Paper applications. Now that you know a few things about paper's characteristics, it's time to compare some of their applications below. This will allow you to best match the particular paper to your task at hand:

- *Plain paper.* For inexpensive, low-resolution everyday printing, most modern ink-jet printers work well with common office paper (i.e., 25 percent cotton bond paper, and 100 percent recycled paper that complies with DIN 19 309). Papers that work well with water-based inks will typically provide the best overall performance. Plain paper usually offers high acidity, low brightness, low opacity, and medium weight.

- *Multipurpose paper.* This everyday paper is normally coated for quick ink drying and minimum wrinkle, though it can often be used in laser printers, copiers, and plain paper fax machines. It is ideal for low-resolution memos, drafts, and most office printing. Multipurpose paper usually offers moderate acidity, low brightness, low-to-medium opacity, and low-to-medium weight.

- *Bright white paper.* This is bright paper intended for everyday color printing. It is coated to hold ink without bleeding at medium-to-high resolutions, and is opaque enough to print on both sides of the paper. It is ideal for newsletters, flyers, color presentations, and reports. Bright white paper normally offers low acidity, low opacity, and medium weight.

- *Premium ink-jet paper.* This coated paper is intended for serious, high-resolution business printing. Its bright white matte finish provides good results with most inks. It is ideal for cover sheets, letterheads, and reports containing graphs and charts—but is not an optimum choice for color printing or photos. Premium ink-jet paper offers moderate-to-low acidity, high brightness, low opacity, and medium-to-heavy weight.

- *Premium ink-jet heavyweight paper.* Coated on both sides for high-resolution printing, this high-quality paper provides sharp, vivid two-sided color printing that supports images such as photos. Brilliant colors will not show through to the opposite side. It is ideal for certificates, posters, report covers, calendars, and brochures. This paper offers low acidity, medium-to-high brightness, very low opacity, and heavy weight.

- *Photo paper / Premium photo paper.* This glossy, photo-weight paper is intended for general purpose high-resolution color photo printing. Ink dries quickly because of the coating. It is ideal for framed pictures, sales materials, land photo reprints, and enlargements. Photo paper offers low acidity, high brightness, low opacity, and heavy weight.

- *Deluxe photo paper.* This glossy, photo-weight paper is usually intended to take advantage of your printer's "image enhancement" features to ensure excellent skin tones and true-to-life landscape colors at the printer's highest resolutions. It is ideal for baby pictures, family photos, and nature photos. Deluxe photo paper offers low acidity, high brightness, low opacity, and heavy weight.

- *Premium ink-jet transparency film.* For everyday transparency printing needs, this transparency film provides crisp text and bright colors. It is ideal for overhead presentations and report covers.

- *Premium ink-jet rapid-dry transparency film.* Use this transparency film when you need to print transparencies in a hurry. It uses a quick-drying coating so the ink will dry faster than other transparencies.

Paper jams. Ink-jet printers almost always employ friction-feed paper transport systems to carry single sheets of paper, transparencies, envelopes, card stock, and other media through the printer. The problem with friction-feed systems is that they are *extremely* sensitive to factors such as age, wear, media type (and quality), and even environmental conditions (such as humidity). Foreign objects in the printer such as paper fragments or other debris can also obstruct the paper path and cause problems. When dealing with paper jams and other feed problems, refer to Table 4.1 for a set of handy guidelines.

TABLE 4.1   Ink-jet Paper Feed Issues

Problem	The printer does not pull paper from the tray properly
Probable Cause:	The paper tray is out of paper.
Solution:	Load paper in the tray and try printing again.
Probable Cause:	The paper width adjuster or paper length adjuster is not properly set.
Solution:	Make sure the paper width adjustment is against the left side of the paper stack, but is not blocking the stack. Push in the paper length adjustment to make sure the paper is fully seated in the printer. Make sure not to push too hard (causing the paper to buckle).
Probable Cause:	The paper tray is too full.
Solution:	Load no more than 100–150 sheets of 20-lb paper in the paper tray (150–250 sheets in an "accessory" paper tray).
Probable Cause:	The paper is out of specification.
Solution:	Verify that the media meets the specifications for your printer. If the media is out of specification, replace the media in the paper tray.
Probable Cause:	The "accessory" paper tray is not properly installed in the printer.
Solution:	Remove and reinstall the "accessory" paper tray as specified in your printer's documentation.
Probable Cause:	Different paper types, sizes, or weights are loaded at the same time.
Solution:	Reload with fresh paper using only one type, size, or weight.

Probable Cause:	The paper is improperly loaded in the tray.
Solution:	Remove the paper stack from the paper tray, make sure the stack is even and does not contain wrinkled, curled, or damaged paper, then reload the paper ensuring the paper sits snugly against the right side of the printer and that the paper width adjustment is snug against the paper.
Problem	The printer does not deposit paper in the output tray
Probable Cause:	The output tray is too full.
Solution:	Remove the paper from the output tray and try printing again.
Probable Cause:	The "accessory" paper tray is not installed correctly.
Solution:	Remove and reinstall the "accessory" paper tray as specified in your printer's documentation.
Probable Cause:	A *Pause* mode is active for the selected media type.
Solution:	A *Pause* mode allows media to have a longer drying time when using special media types such as transparencies or deluxe photo paper. Use the *Resume* button on the printer to drop the paused page into the output tray and continue printing, or change the printer settings for the paper type or print quality (disable the *Pause* mode).
Problem	Paper does not properly eject from the printer
Probable Cause:	The computer was turned off while the printer was printing.
Solution:	Turn off the printer. Now turn on the computer first, and then turn on the printer. The last page should eject.
Probable Cause:	The printer did not receive a `form feed` command.
Solution:	If the software does not send a `form feed`, `page eject`, or `reset` command at the end of a print job, press the *Resume* or *Form Feed* button on the printer to initiate a manual form feed.
Problem	Paper does not fully eject from the printer (printer lights may blink)
Probable Cause:	Paper is jammed in the printer, paper tray, or "accessory" paper tray.

Solution:	Turn the printer off and back on to see if the printer can clear the jam. If not, turn the printer off and remove all the paper from the paper tray and output tray, then open the printer. Carefully pull the jammed paper out of the printer. After all the jammed paper is removed, close the printer, turn it on, and try printing again.

Problem	The printer feeds paper in two or more sheets

Probable Cause:	The paper is stuck together.
Solution:	Remove, restack, and flex the paper, then reload it. Also verify that the paper meets the media specifications for your printer—if not, use fresh media that meets your printer's specifications.
Probable Cause:	There is too much paper is in the paper tray at one time.
Solution:	Remove some of the paper from the paper tray.
Probable Cause:	Different paper types, sizes, or weights are loaded at the same time.
Solution:	Remove the paper and reload with fresh media using only one type, size, and weight.
Probable Cause:	The paper in the in tray is bent (bowed).
Solution:	Remove the paper and reload it. Push the paper length and width adjustments toward the paper until they stop, but do not bend the paper.

Problem	Envelopes do not feed properly from the paper tray

Probable Cause:	The envelopes are improperly loaded.
Solution:	If using the paper tray to load several envelopes, push the paper length and width adjustments toward the envelopes until they stop. Make sure *not* to bend the envelopes.
Probable Cause:	The envelopes are bent or damaged.
Solution:	Do not use envelopes with bent or curled corners.
Probable Cause:	There are too many or too few envelopes loaded in the paper tray.
Solution:	Use more or fewer envelopes in the paper tray.
Probable Cause:	The envelope is too small.
Solution:	If using a single envelope slot to load a small envelope, the envelope may not be long enough to reach the paper feed rollers. Try using a longer envelope.

Problem	Cards do not feed properly from the paper tray
Probable Cause:	The cards are improperly loaded in the paper tray.
Solution:	Slide the paper length and width adjustments to their outermost positions and take the cards out of the paper tray, then reload the cards and readjust the paper length and width adjustments to fit snugly against the cards' edges (being careful not to bend the cards).
Probable Cause:	An unsupported type of card is loaded into the paper tray.
Solution:	Verify that the cards meet the media specifications for your particular printer. If not, replace the cards with stock that is suitable for the printer.

Color printing performance tips

No matter how sophisticated a color ink-jet printer may be, it still forms images on a "line-by-line" basis. This type of moving head printing presents some inherent speed limitations, but there are some steps that you can take to improve ink-jet printing performance and quality:

- *Check the printer driver.* Printer drivers have a profound effect on printer performance, and their interaction with other daisy-chained parallel port devices. See that you're using the very latest printer driver. In most cases, you can download the latest driver directly from the printer manufacturer's Web site.

- *Check the printer selection.* Make sure that the printer you've selected as the current (or default) system printer is the one that you actually have connected to the computer. If you select a *similar* make and model, you may get the printer to work, but the driver may be subtly different, and this may reduce the printer's performance (or even disable key printer features).

■ *Check the LPT mode.* Modern printers often use high performance parallel port modes such as ECP or EPP. Check the parallel port configuration in your CMOS Setup and *Device Manager*, and see that they're set for the best possible communication mode (usually ECP). If the port is configured for an older mode like *compatibility* or *bidirectional*, the PC is not communicating with the printer as fast as possible.

■ *Check the paper selection.* When specifying a paper, try choosing the *plain paper* option. You can use a specially coated ink-jet paper, but you can also load a standard 25 percent cotton bond paper (such as regular photocopier paper). Avoid the use of thin papers that can slip or pull in the printer's paper handling mechanism. Also avoid thick papers or papers that are heavily textured since these will tend to drink in ink. Always install a small amount of fresh paper when troubleshooting color problems.

■ *Check the print cartridge.* Print quality is also influenced by the age and condition of the color cartridge itself. Most ink cartridges have an expiration date, and should be replaced when the expiration date is reached. Whenever exploring color problems, you should always install a relatively fresh ink cartridge.

■ *Check the print settings.* Print speed is also influenced by the particular selections made about the print characteristics. Try reducing the time-intensive features involved in color printing:

Print Quality: *Standard* (not *Fine*)
Color Model: *Color* (not *Photo*)
Color Selection: *Fast Color*

■ *Try disabling the Windows print support.* For Windows 3.1x, you can disable the Print Manager. Go to *Main, Control Panel, Printers*, and disable *Use Print Manager*. Under Windows 95/98, you can disable the Print Spooler. Go to the printer properties dialog. From *Detail* choose *Spool Settings*, and enable the *Print directly to printer* option. Remember to save your changes and restart the computer if prompted to do so.

■ *Do not print monochrome images as color.* If you're printing a monochrome (or gray scale) document, make sure that the printer's driver is set for *Monochrome.* Printing a monochrome image in *color* mode will demand color inks, and a great deal more processing power.

■ *Do not judge color quality from old prints.* Inks can fade or shift hues over time when paper is exposed to direct sunlight, when paper quality is poor, and when temperature and humidity levels are not appropriate. Always examine a fresh print made at the time of testing.

Color matching tips

Often, the image colors displayed on a monitor don't precisely match the color output of an ink-jet printer. This can make for some perplexing problems when specific colors (i.e., flesh tones) are required. This part of the chapter outlines some guidelines that can help you achieve the best color matching:

■ *Start with a printer self-test.* The first step in any color matching effort is to run a printer self-test. A self-test will tell you if the printer is generating colors properly. If not (i.e., the color ink cartridge is exhaust-ed), you will not get proper color matching. Check and clean/replace the color ink cartridge as necessary.

■ *Check with the printer driver.* In many cases, the printer driver (or printer color applet) will offer a color matching option. Open the color printer's prop-erties dialog and see that any *color matching* option is enabled. For Windows 95/98:

1. Click *Start, Settings,* then click on *Printers.*
2. Right-click on your printer.

3. Click on the *Properties* option.

4. Click on the *Graphics* tab.

5. Click to check the *Image Color Matching* option (or similar color-matching feature).

■ *Check the amount of light in the work area.* Glare and other ambient light artifacts can adversely affect your perception of the colors on a monitor. When you compare the printed output to the monitor's image, it just won't look right. Try darkening the work area, or adjust the monitor's brightness and contrast to a more appropriate level.

■ *Check the video driver.* Many color printer drivers take their color information directly from the video driver. This usually assumes a good interaction between the video driver and color printer driver. When color matching proves difficult, updating to the latest version of video driver can sometimes correct the problem.

■ *Check the printer driver.* If problems continue, take another look at the color printer's driver. Check to see if there is a patch or upgrade designed to enhance color matching.

Ink cartridge symptoms

NOTE: Use the PRINTERS utility to generate standard printer test patterns. You can obtain PRINTERS from Dynamic Learning Systems, using the order form at the back of the book.

Symptom 4.40: The print quality is poor (dots appear faded or indistinct). There are many factors that affect the formation of dots on a printed surface including paper, the ink cartridge, and the printer's driver circuits (in the ECU).

■ *Check the paper.* The quality and type of paper used in an ink-jet system will profoundly affect the print quality. Make sure that the paper is well suited for use in an ink-jet printer. Porous papers such as ordinary xerography-grade paper tend to absorb ink quickly and run the ink through the fibers—the result is typically a dull, faded appearance. This can also happen if the paper has an unusual or chemically coated surface (such as transparencies).

- *Clean or replace the ink cartridge.* Suspect the print head next. In many cases, light or poorly formed dots can occur as the disposable print cartridge nears exhaustion. The print head may also be dirty—accumulations of dust or debris can eventually block the print head nozzles. Although a typical ink-jet printer routinely cleans a print head, an old or worn cleaning surface may no longer provide sufficient cleaning. If the cleaning pad is worn or missing, it should be replaced. If the problem persists, try a new print head (an ink cartridge can typically be replaced in a matter of seconds).

- *Replace the print head drivers/ECU.* If problems continue, there is probably a fault in the printer's driver circuitry. Ink-jet printers often use three separate PC boards: the *logic board* (ECU), the *driver board*, and the *power supply*. Chances are that one or more elements in the head driver circuit or power supply have become defective. Before replacing anything, check the power supply outputs. If any of the outputs are low or missing, replace the power supply. If all power outputs are correct, the fault is probably in the driver board, so try a new driver board. In some ink-jet printer designs, the power supply, driver circuits, and main logic are all assembled on the same PC board. In that case, simply replace the entire ECU outright.

Symptom 4.41: You notice that the printout is faded, or the colors appear dull.   Otherwise, the image itself appears properly printed. This is usually traced to a paper selection issue, or inadequate printer setup.

■ *Check the printer configuration.* Always start by checking your printer driver settings. If an *economy* or *fast* quality setting is selected, the printer will always skimp on the color ink in order to get the fastest printing, and most life from the ink cartridge(s). Select the *normal* or *best* quality print settings.

■ *Check the paper.* Another possible problem is the paper selection. Many coarse papers will "drink in" the ink, leaving the image dull or faded. Specially coated papers and transparencies are also frequently prone to dull or faded images. Insert the recommended paper type for your printer, or be sure that the *paper type* selected for your printer matches the paper that you've installed.

■ *Clean/purge the ink cartridge(s).* The color ink cartridge itself may be low or clogged. Perform a standard ink cartridge cleaning procedure. In actual practice, the procedure may vary a bit from printer to printer, but many current printers often automate the process, such as the HP DeskJet 600 or 800 series below:

1. Open the *HP DeskJet Utilities* folder or program group.
2. Double-click the *HP DeskJet Toolbox* icon.
3. Click the *Printer Services* tab.
4. Click the *Clean the print cartridges* button.
5. Follow through the instructions.

Symptom 4.42: Print has one or more missing dots that resemble "white" lines. This also takes place during a self-test. It seems as if one or more of the print head's nozzles will not fire. In most cases, this is a problem with the ink cartridge.

- *Clean and replace the print head.* If a nozzle has clogged or jammed from accumulations of dust or debris, it can shut down the nozzle. Make sure that the print head is clean. Normally, ink-jet printers wipe the print head every certain number of passes. However, you can remove thes cartridge and clean it as described earlier. Also clean the print head's electrical contacts to ensure a good connection. Replace the cartridge and try the printer again. If the problem persists, try another print head.

- *Replace the print head drivers/ECU.* If a new print head does not resolve the problem, the fault lies almost certainly with the print head driver board. If a driver circuit fails, the corresponding nozzle will not fire. Try another drive board. If the driver circuitry is integrated into a single ECU board, replace the entire ECU.

Symptom 4.43: Print head moves back and forth but does not print, or prints only intermittently. This also takes place during a self-test, and suggests a serious problem with the printer.

- *Check the print head.* The ink-jet head may simply be out of ink. Try a new ink-jet head with a fresh ink supply.

- *Check the print head cable.* If problems continue, check the ribbon cable between the driver circuit and print head. Intermittent connections in the print head or print head cable can lead to highly erratic head operation. A complete cable break can shut down the print head entirely, especially if the break occurs in a common (ground) conductor. Turn off and unplug the printer, then use your multimeter to check continuity across each cable conductor. You may have to disconnect the cable at one end to prevent false readings. Replace any print head cable that appears defective.

- *Check the power supply.* There may be a problem with the print head driver supply voltage(s). Use your multimeter to check each output from the power supply. If you find that one or more power supply voltage(s) are low or erratic, you can attempt to troubleshoot the supply, or replace the supply outright.

- *Replace the print head drivers/ECU.* When power supply outputs measure correctly, the fault is probably located in the print head driver board. Replace the driver board. Keep in mind that when the power supply, driver circuits, and main logic are integrated on the same board, the entire ECU will have to be replaced.

Symptom 4.44: The color printer will not initialize after installing or reseating an ink cartridge. The power light may blink continuously, or you hear three or more beeps. The ink cartridge may not move, or may remain in the middle of the carriage.

- *Reinstall the ink cartridge.* In virtually every case, the ink cartridge is not seated properly in its carriage holder, and is not making the necessary electrical connections. Simply remove and reinstall the ink cartridge.

- *Clean the electrical contacts.* If the problem persists, the electrical contacts on the back of the cartridge are not mating properly with the contacts on the carriage. Try gently wiping the electrical contacts with a soft dry cloth (or a cotton swab with a little isopropyl alcohol), then try reseating the ink cartridge.

Symptom 4.45: You replace an ink cartridge, but the cartridge refuses to print. In most cases, you forgot to remove the small piece of colored tape (usually orange or blue) that covers the ink nozzles. Remove the ink cartridge, remove the protective tape, reinstall the cartridge carefully, then retry the printer.

Symptom 4.46: When a new ink cartridge is installed, the printer begins performing continuous cleaning cycles. This is not always a problem, especially with today's more sophisticated color ink-jet printers. The very first time an ink cartridge is installed in the printer, it may take as much as 7 to 9 minutes to charge the ink system and initialize the printer. While the ink is charging, lights on the printer's panel will usually flash. *Never* turn off the printer while the ink system is charging. When installing replacement ink cartridges, a printer may take up to 4 minutes to charge the ink. If the charging time is significantly longer, try another fresh ink cartridge.

> **NOTE**: If you turn off the printer during the initial ink charging cycle because you thought it was taking too long, just power the printer back on and allow the printer to perform the complete charge of its ink delivery system.

Color-related symptoms

Symptom 4.47: The color printer is not holding its internal calibration settings after power is turned off or unplugged. In virtually all cases, sophisticated color printers (i.e., an Epson Stylus Color 850Ne) must be turned off by its own *Power* button, *not* by an external power switch such as a power strip. Some small amount of power is required to maintain the printer's internal calibration settings. If power is simply cut off to the printer, those settings are lost, and the printer must be recalibrated each time it is powered on.

Symptom 4.48: The placement of colors is incorrect on the print. You should first check for proper design and placement of the graphics that you're trying to print. If the colors are off in the image, they'll be off in the final printout. Use the *zoom* or *print preview* feature of your particular software program to check for gaps in the placement of graphics on the page. If the original image is correct, the most common cause of incorrect color placement is misalignment of the print cartridges. You may need to align print cartridges whenever you remove one for cleaning or replacement. Many printers provide a utility for alignment. For example, you could use the procedure below to align cartridges in HP DeskJet 600 and 800 series printers:

- Open the *HP DeskJet Utilities* folder or program group.
- Double-click the *HP DeskJet Toolbox* icon.
- Click the *Printer Services* tab.
- Click the *Align the print cartridges* button.
- Follow through the instructions.

Symptom 4.49: The printed image does not match the image on the monitor. First verify that the proper ink cartridge is securely installed, and check the printer's properties dialog (usually the *Graphics* tab) to see that any *color matching* feature is enabled. If you're attempting to print a photo-quality image, you may need to install a photo-cartridge in the printer, select a photo-related mode such as *SuperPhoto* in the printer's properties, or use a specially coated photo-quality paper.

Symptom 4.50: One or more colors are missing in a print-out. In virtually all cases, the ink cartridge is clogged, or is out of ink. Clean the cartridge, or purge the ink cartridge using the instructions for your specific printer. For a Canon BJ series printer, power the printer off, then hold the power button down until the printer powers up and beeps two times. If the problem persists, replace the ink cartridge with a fresh one.

Symptom 4.51: Colors appear to be bleeding into each other. This type of problem is caused by *too much* ink being applied to the page, usually due to an improper paper selection. Check your print setting and try a *draft* or *economy* setting rather than a *fine* or *normal* quality print setting. Also make sure that the paper you're using in the printer matches the paper selection in the printer's properties. For example, transparencies often require more ink than ordinary paper. If your paper setting is set for *transparency*, but there is ordinary paper in the printer, chances are that there will be too much ink delivered to the page, and bleeding will result.

Symptom 4.52: You notice visible "banding" in the ink-jet's print. *Banding* may be caused by a number of very different reasons. You'll need to examine each possibility closely.

■ *Check the paper*. Incompatible or improperly coated paper can cause banding due to the way the ink is absorbed into the paper. Try fresh ink-jet paper recommended by the printer manufacturer (i.e., HP Deluxe Photo Paper).

■ *Check the paper thickness lever/settings*. If you're using paper, make sure the paper thickness lever is in the normal position for ink-jet paper and *not* in the envelope position. Refer to your printer's documentation for paper thickness settings.

■ *Check your video driver*. Some video drivers may cause a conflict in memory between the printer driver and video memory. This is often the cause of strange printing problems such as heavy banding and missing characters. Try using the default Windows video driver provided by Microsoft, or check to see if the video card manufacturer has an updated video driver available.

■ *Check your printer driver*. Make sure you are using

the correct printer driver for your particular ink-jet model. Also make sure you have selected the correct print settings for the type of paper and resolution in the driver setup. Try reducing ink demands by using a *draft* or *quick print* mode.

■ *Clean/purge the ink cartridge*. Press the *Purge* button (sometimes called a *Cleaning* button) and run one or two cleaning cycles to clear any clogs in the ink cartridge.

■ *Replace the ink cartridge*. If purging does not clear the problem, try another fresh ink cartridge.

Symptom 4.53: Colors appear to streak or smear. This kind of behavior is often due to residual ink buildup, or a paper issue. Fortunately, this is a simple kind of problem to solve.

■ *Clean/purge the ink cartridge*. Check the nozzle plate area around the print cartridge. A buildup of residual ink and debris (dust, carpet fibers, and so on) around the nozzle plate will act like a brush— smearing the colors into one another before there's a chance to dry. The area around the print cartridge nozzles needs to be cleaned. You can clean the ink cartridge manually or automatically (through the printer software). For example, to run the cleaning procedure for an HP DeskJet 600 or 800 series printer:

1. Open the *HP DeskJet Utilities* folder or program group.
2. Double-click the *HP DeskJet Toolbox* icon.
3. Click the *Printer Services* tab.
4. Click the *Clean the print cartridges* button.
5. Follow through the instructions.

■ *Reduce your ink consumption*. Examine the page for wrinkling. Noticeable wrinkles usually mean that too much ink is being delivered to the page. Try setting the print mode to *fast* or *economy* in order to use a little less ink.

■ *Try specialized ink-jet paper.* You might also try using a different paper (i.e., a specially coated ink-jet paper) that is formulated to accept and dry ink quickly.

■ *Allow for more drying time.* Some types of print jobs (such as transparencies) need additional time to dry. Avoid handling printouts until the ink has had an adequate time to dry.

Symptom 4.54: Ink is not filling the text or graphics completely. This type of symptom usually means that there is not enough ink being delivered to the page.

■ *Check the paper selection.* Start by checking the paper type setting for your printer properties. Some paper types (i.e., transparencies) will require much more ink than other types of paper. If you do not apply sufficient ink, there will be visible gaps in the color. See that your paper type setting matches the paper installed in the printer.

■ *Check for empty or clogged ink cartridges.* As the ink cartridge nears exhaustion, there may be gaps in certain colors. Try cleaning the ink cartridge. If cleaning does not help, the cartridge is probably exhausted, and you should try a fresh ink cartridge.

■ *Clean the electrical contacts.* If there is adequate ink in the cartridge, try cleaning the electrical contacts between the cartridge and carriage. Over time, deposits can form between these contacts and cause signal problems—the nozzle(s) won't fire. Gently clean the contacts with a cotton swab and isopropyl alcohol.

Symptom 4.55: The colors on the page are completely different from the intended colors. When colors are *completely* wrong (for example, when green prints as blue or yellow), the color cartridge might have run out of one or more colors of ink. The best way to check this is to perform a cleaning procedure. If the color returns, a particular set of color nozzles may have been clogged. If the problem persists, a color may be exhausted, so try a fresh ink cartridge. If colors are printing in shades of gray, the *Print In Grayscale* option is probably selected in your printer settings dialog box. For color printing, clear the *Print In Grayscale* checkbox on the printer properties *Setup* tab.

Symptom 4.56: The printed colors appear incorrect. There are many issues that can affect the overall color quality of the printed image. Take a look at the "Color matching tips" listed earlier in this section, then cover the following steps:

- *Check the printer driver.* Verify that you are using the very latest manufacturer-specific driver for your particular printer and operating system. If you're already using the latest driver, try a generic Microsoft driver (i.e., one provided with Windows 98).

- *Check the paper installation.* See that the printable (coated) side of the paper is face up, and check that the type of paper being used is appropriate for your application. For example, you wouldn't use plain paper for printing high-resolution color photos.

- *Check the "media type."* In order to deliver the proper amount of ink to a page, verify that the *media type* setting in the printer driver is set properly. For example, if the driver is set for *transparency* and there is *plain paper* loaded in the printer, the printer will deliver far too much ink.

- *Check the ink settings.* If your printer driver allows for general ink settings like *economy* or *draft*, the print may be too light on some papers if those settings are used. Again, verify that the driver settings are appropriate for the paper you are using and the task at hand. The color settings in your particular application software may also need adjustment.

■ *Check the paper thickness setting.* Try changing the position of the paper thickness lever, especially if the ink is smearing or otherwise excessive.

■ *Clean/purge the ink cartridge.* The print head nozzles may be clogged. Use the *Purge* button on the printer (or the printer's diagnostic utility under Windows) to invoke a thorough print head cleaning.

■ *Try another ink cartridge.* If purging the print head doesn't resolve the problem, try a new ink cartridge (see that the "white label" on the cartridge is in place).

Mechanical symptoms

Symptom 4.57: The paper advance does not function, or functions only intermittently. All other functions check properly. Obstructions and roller damage can be a serious problem with friction feed paper transports common to ink-jet printers, but you must also consider mechanical and electronic problems. Be sure to check the paper feed issues in Table 4.1 before proceeding.

■ *Check the paper path and mechanics.* Begin by observing the paper advance drive train assembly. Check any pulleys or gears to ensure that all parts are meshed evenly and are able to move freely. You can watch this by turning the platen knob located outside of the printer. If there is no manual platen, you can run a *form feed*. Remove any foreign objects or obstructions that may be jamming the drive train (but *never* try to force a drive train that does not turn freely). Realign any parts that appear to be slipping or misaligned. Replace any damaged mechanical parts or assemblies.

- *Check the motor connections.* Turn off and unplug the printer, then check the cables to your paper advance motor. Try reinstalling the paper advance motor connector at the ECU (where the motor driver circuits are located).

- *Check the motor voltage.* Next, check the paper advance motor voltage by inspecting the +24 volt output from the power supply. If the motor voltage is low or absent, troubleshoot or replace the power supply as required.

- *Replace the ECU.* If the paper advance motor voltage is present, the problem is likely in the motor driver circuits on the ECU. Try replacing the ECU outright.

- *Replace the motor.* If problems still persist, the paper transport motor may be defective. Try replacing the paper transport motor—remember that this may require a substantial amount of mechanical disassembly and reassembly.

Symptom 4.58: Paper slips or walks around the friction-fed transport. Friction-feed is an ideal system for "single sheet" printers, but friction depends on factors such as paper weight, coatings, and roller conditions.

- *Check your paper.* Friction-feed paper transports are designed to work with only certain types of paper—brands within a certain range of thickness and weight. Very fine (light bond) paper or very heavy (card stock) paper will probably not advance properly. Slick or other unusual coatings can also upset a friction-feed system. Check the specifications for your particular printer to find its optimum paper type. If you find that you are using an unusual type of paper, try the printer using standard ink-jet paper.

- *Check the paper path.* Inspect your paper path for any debris or obstructions that may be catching part of the paper sheet. A crumpled corner of paper jammed in the paper path or caught in the feed guide can easily interfere with subsequent sheets. Turn off and unplug the printer, and remove all obstructions (be *very* careful not to nick any of the rollers). A straightened paper clip can often get into spaces that your fingers and tools will not. Use thin needle-nose pliers to put a small hook in the wire's end for grabbing and pulling the obstruction. *Do not disassemble the rollers unless absolutely necessary.*

- *Clean the rollers.* Advance the paper feed knob manually (if possible) and take careful note of each roller condition. An even, consistent paper feed depends on firm roller pressure applied evenly across its entire length. Rollers that are very dirty, or old and dry, may no longer be applying force evenly. Clean your rollers with light glass cleaner. Do *not* use rubber rejuvenating compounds on those rollers since almost no rollers are made from rubber today—rejuvenating compound can damage the rollers.

- *Replace the rollers.* If the rollers are old or damaged beyond cleaning, your best solution is to replace the entire paper feed/transport assembly.

Symptom 4.59: The carriage advance does not function properly (if at all). The printer relies on motors to move the print head. Problems with the carriage advance can typically be traced to motor-related or electronic motor control faults.

- *Check for mechanical damage.* Inspect the printer carefully for any signs of mechanical damage or obstructions (i.e., a stripped gear or broken carriage belt). Clear any obstructions of paper fragments or other foreign matter from the carriage mechanics. Replace any damaged mechanical parts or sub-assemblies.

- *Check the motor connections.* Turn off and unplug the printer, then check the cables to your carriage advance motor. Try reinstalling the motor connector at the ECU (where the motor driver circuits are located).

- *Check the motor voltage.* Next, check the motor voltage by inspecting the +24 volt output from the power supply. If the motor voltage is low or absent, troubleshoot or replace the power supply.

- *Replace the ECU.* If the motor voltage is present, the problem is likely in the carriage motor driver circuits on the ECU. Try replacing the ECU outright.

- *Replace the motor.* If problems still persist, the carriage motor may be defective. Try replacing the particular motor—remember that this may require a substantial amount of mechanical disassembly and reassembly.

Symptom 4.60: Carriage does not find its home position. This may result in a frozen initialization or erratic print spacing, and is usually caused by carriage sensor switch problems. As with paper sensors, the carriage sensing element can be mechanical or optical.

- *Reinstall the ink cartridge.* In some printer models, if the cartridge/carriage will not return to the home position, then the cartridge may need to be reseated. The contacts may also need to be wiped with a soft dry cloth (or a cotton swab and isopropyl alcohol).

- *Check and adjust the paper switch (mechanical).* If the *home sensor* is a mechanical switch, place your multimeter across its contacts and try actuating the switch by hand. You should see a voltage reading switch between a logic 1 and logic 0 as the switch is actuated. If voltage is present but the switch does not respond (or responds only intermittently), replace the defective switch. If it does respond, check its contact with the carriage to be sure that it actuates when the carriage is in its home position. You may have to adjust the switch position to achieve a better contact.

■ *Check the paper switch (optical).* An optical *home sensor* can be checked in much the same manner. Place your multimeter across the phototransistor output and try to actuate the sensor by hand by blocking the optical gap with a piece of paper or cardboard. You should see the output voltage shift between a logic 0 and logic 1 as the sensor is actuated. If the phototransistor does not respond, check for dust or debris that may be blocking the light path. If excitation voltage is present but the phototransistor does not respond, replace the defective optoisolator.

■ *Replace the ECU.* If the problem persists, chances are that you've encountered a serious fault in the printer's main logic circuit that interprets carriage home sensor signals. Replace the electronic control unit (ECU) outright.

Symptom 4.61: Carriage moves erratically or inconsistently. You notice a number of errors in print spacing across the page. This is generally due to a problem with the carriage motor, the carriage positioning sensor, or the ECU that interprets the carriage position signals.

■ *Check for mechanical damage.* Inspect the printer carefully for any signs of mechanical damage or obstructions (i.e., a loose or broken carriage belt). Clear any obstructions of paper fragments or other foreign matter from the carriage mechanics. Replace any damaged mechanical parts or subassemblies.

■ *Check the motor connections.* Turn off and unplug the printer, then check the cables to your carriage motor.

Try reinstalling the carriage motor connector at the ECU (where the motor driver circuits are located).

- *Check the motor voltage.* Next, check the carriage motor voltage by inspecting the +24 volt output from the power supply. If the motor voltage is low or absent, troubleshoot or replace the power supply as required.

- *Replace the ECU.* If the carriage motor voltage is present, the problem is likely in the motor driver circuits on the ECU. Try replacing the ECU outright.

- *Replace the motor.* If problems still persist, the carriage motor may be defective. Try replacing the carriage motor—remember that this may require a substantial amount of mechanical disassembly and reassembly.

   NOTE: Excessive or inappropriate lubrication along the carriage rail can sometimes cause carriage positioning problems.

Symptom 4.62: The ink-jet printer has trouble with vertical alignment. You see this in the print as misaligned vertical lines. This is a problem with the alignment of the printer's ink cartridges, and you'll need to correct this issue by calibrating the print heads. Calibration is accomplished using a calibration utility included with the printer's software (or available for download directly from the manufacturer's Web site). For example, the Epson Stylus 800+ driver CALIBRAT.EXE program can be used to align all monochrome Stylus printers. This particular utility runs in DOS, so exit Windows to the DOS mode or open a DOS window to run it. To run the utility, switch to the directory where the utility is stored, type CALIBRAT and press <Enter>. Although your calibration sequence may differ, it will probably follow a pattern similar to the following steps:

- Select your printer model from the list of suitable printers.

- Select the option to print a calibration pattern, then `<Tab>` over to highlight *Calibrate* and press `<Enter>`.

- A calibration pattern will then print. Look carefully at the calibration pattern and select an *Offset Value* that corresponds to the row of vertical lines that most closely aligns.

- Type in the appropriate *Offset Value* number and press `<Enter>`.

- A confirmation pattern will print using the *Offset Value* selected—if the lines are straight, press `<Enter>`. If not, `<Tab>` over to *Re-Calibrate* and select another *Offset Value*.

- Once the calibration procedure is complete, turn the printer off to save the alignment settings.

  NOTE: If the printer is powered off by unplugging it or turning it off with a power strip, the settings may not be saved. Always power the printer down with its own power switch.

  NOTE: Many calibration programs assume the printer is attached to LPT1. If LPT2 or any other port is the default port, connect the printer to LPT1 to calibrate. After saving the calibration, connect the printer back to the preferred port for printing.

Application or setup symptoms

Symptom 4.63: Printer does not print under computer control.   Operation appears correct in self-test mode. Before you attempt to disassemble the printer, take a moment to check its *online* status. There is almost always an indicator on the control panel that is lit when the printer is selected. If the printer is not selected (online), then it will not receive information from the computer—even if everything is working correctly.

- *Put the printer "online."* A printer can be offline for several reasons. Paper may have run out, in which case you will often have to reselect the printer explicitly after paper is replenished. Even the simplest printers offer a variety of options that are selectable through the keyboard (i.e., font style, character pitch, line width, etc.). However, you must often go offline in order to manipulate those functions, then reselect the printer when done. You may have selected a function incorrectly, or forgotten to reselect the printer after changing modes.

- *Check the printer driver or printing software.* Consider the importance of software compatibility. If you are using a "canned" software package, make sure that its printer driver settings are configured properly for your particular printer. If you are working through Windows, make sure that the proper Windows driver is selected.

- *Check the communication interface cable.* The printer cable may have become loose or unattached at either the printer or computer end. If this is a new or untested cable, make sure that it is wired correctly for your particular interface (i.e., serial or parallel). An interface cable that is prone to bending or flexing may have developed a faulty connection, so disconnect the cable at both ends and use your multimeter to check cable continuity. If this is a new, homemade cable assembly, double check its construction against your printer and computer interface diagrams. Try a different (known-good) cable.

- *Check the switch settings (if any).* Double-check the printer's DIP switch settings or setup configuration. DIP switches are often included in the printer to select certain optional functions such as serial communication format, character sets, default character pitch, or automatic line feed. If you are installing a new printer, or you have changed the switches to alter an operating mode, it may be a faulty or invalid condition. DIP switches also tend to become unreliable after many switch cycles. If you suspect an intermittent DIP switch, rock it back and forth several times, then retest the printer.

- *Replace the ECU*. If the problem persists, there may be a problem with the printer's communication module. Try replacing the ECU board outright.

Symptom 4.64: The printer prints only ½ or ¾ of the page.
Chances are that your PC is not using the correct parallel port mode for the printer. For example, Compaq PCs often experience parallel port compatibility problems with Canon ink-jet printers. There are generally three resolutions for this kind of problem. First, you can try setting the PC's parallel port to ECP:

- Boot Windows 95 and right-click on the *My Computer* icon.
- Select *Properties* and select the *Device Manager* tab.
- Double-click on *Ports (COM & LPT)*.
- Double-click on *ECP Printer port (LPT1)*. If your configuration is already *Printer Port*, this correction does not apply.
- Select the *Driver* tab, choose *Change Driver*, then select *Show all devices*.
- Under *Models*, select *Printer* port, then click *OK*.
- Click *OK* again.
- Shut down Windows 95 and reboot.

Next, you should check that the LPT port is using the correct resource settings:

- Boot Windows 95 and right-click on the *My Computer* icon.
- Select *Properties* and select the *Device Manager* tab.

- Double-click on *Ports (COM & LPT)*.

- Double-click *LPT*, then select the *Resources* tab.

- Deselect *Automatic Settings*.

- Change the *Basic Configuration*; find the configuration that meets the following conditions:

  1. Input/Output Range 0378-037?
  2. Input/Output Range 0778-077?
  3. Interrupt Request (IRQ) 07
  4. NO DMA

- Select *OK*.

- Shut down Windows 95 and reboot.

If odd characters such as "[K" are printed at top of page (but the rest of the page is correct), you may need to update your drivers:

- Boot Windows 95 and right-click on the *My Computer* icon.

- Select *Properties* and select the *Device Manager* tab.

- Double-click on *Ports (COM & LPT)*.

- Double-click *LPT*, then select the *Driver* tab.

- Look at the *File Revision* line, LPT.VXD v4.00.950— replace LPT.VXD v4.00.950 with LPT.VXD v4.00.503 (the LPT.VXD file is located in the Windows\System directory).

- Confirm that your port is set to *Standard Bidirectional* in the CMOS Setup.

Symptom 4.65: Only about ¾ of a page is printing with a Toshiba notebook. This is generally known as a *partial page* error. There are several possible reasons for this kind of problem depending on what type of computer the printer is attached to.

- *Check the parallel port mode*. Toshiba notebook PCs

are known to cause this kind of problem with certain ink-jet printers when the parallel port isn't configured properly. Try setting the printer port to a *Standard Bidirectional* mode rather than an *ECP* or *EPP* mode. For most standard computers, you'd adjust the parallel port mode through the system's CMOS Setup. However, for a Toshiba notebook, you can access the HWSETUP (or TSETUP) module under the Toshiba Utilities entry on the *Program* menu. Select *Hardware Options*, then select *Parallel/Printer*, and finally select *Standard Bidirectional*. Save your changes and reboot the PC.

- *Update the LPT device driver.* If this still does not resolve the partial printout problem, then you should replace the LPT.VXD file that is currently installed in the \windows\system subdirectory with a different (usually later) version of the same file. Check the technical support Web site for your particular printer manufacturer—when the LPT.VXD file is a known problem, you can often download a suitable version from there. The new LPT.VXD will have to be placed in the \windows\system subdirectory (replacing the same file already present in that location). Once you update the file, reboot the computer. If the problem disappears, you may be able to set the parallel port mode back to ECP for better performance.

- *Upgrade the BIOS.* If the problem still persists, your PC may need a BIOS upgrade to better support the printer port's operating modes. Check with the PC (or motherboard) maker to see if a BIOS upgrade is available.

Symptom 4.66: Only about ¾ of a page is printing with a Compaq Presario. This is generally known as a *partial page* error. There are several possible reasons for this kind of problem depending on what type of computer the printer is attached to.

■ *Check the parallel port mode*. Compaq Presario PCs are known to cause this kind of problem with certain ink-jet printers when the parallel port isn't configured properly. Try setting the printer port to *ECP* mode rather than *bidirectional* or *EPP* mode. For most standard computers (including Compaqs), you'd adjust the parallel port mode through the system's CMOS Setup. However, for a Compaq Presario, you must also adjust the port settings through the *Device Manager*:

1. Right-click on the *My Computer* icon and select *Properties*.
2. Select the *Device Manager* tab.
3. Double-click on *Ports (COM & LPT)*.
4. Double-click on *ECP Printer port (LPT1)*.
5. Select *Driver* tab and select *Change Driver*.
6. Select *Show all devices*.
7. Under *Models*, select *Printer port*, then click *OK*.
8. Click *OK* again, then shut down Windows 95 and reboot.

■ *Check the parallel port configuration*. It's also possible that the resources assigned to the Compaq's parallel port may not be adequate. Check the resource settings:

1. Right-click on *My Computer* and select *Properties*.
2. Select the *Device Manager* tab and double-click *Ports (COM & LPT)*.
3. Double-click *LPT* and select the *Resources* tab.
4. Deselect *Automatic Settings*.
5. Change the *Basic Configuration*; find the configuration that meets the following conditions:

   Input/Output Range 0378-037?
   Input/Output Range 0778-077?
   Interrupt Request (IRQ) 07
   NO DMA

6. Select *OK*, then shut down Windows 95 and reboot.

- *Update the LPT device driver*. If this still does not resolve the partial printout problem, then you should replace the LPT.VXD file that is currently installed in the `\windows\system` subdirectory with a different (usually later) version of the same file. Check the technical support Web site for Compaq or your particular printer manufacturer—when the LPT.VXD file is a known problem, you can often download a suitable version from there. The new LPT.VXD will have to be placed in the `\windows\system` subdirectory (replacing the same file already present in that location). Once you update the file, reboot the computer. If you do need to change the .VXD file, you may need to change the LPT port mode to *bidirectional* in the CMOS Setup and *Device Manager*.

- *Upgrade the BIOS*. If the problem still persists, your PC may need a BIOS upgrade to better support the printer port's operating modes. Check with the Compaq Web site to see if a BIOS upgrade is available.

Symptom 4.67: You encounter *Out of memory* errors when attempting to print.   There are a number of very real possibilities that can result in memory errors.

- *Check the printer selection*. Make sure that your current printer is configured as the default printer. You may need to change the printer selection through the printing application.

- *Free system resources*. Try closing down all unneeded or background programs.

- *Simplify the image*. Higher resolution means that more data must be sent to the printer, so try reducing the printer's resolution (i.e., from 720 × 360 to 360 × 360), or try the printer in "draft" mode.

- *Add memory to the printer*. If you require a certain printing resolution, it may be necessary for you to consider adding memory to the printer (if the printer can accommodate it).

■ *Simplify the print job.* If you're printing a multi-page document (especially a complex document), try printing only one or two pages at a time.

■ *Check drive space for .TMP files.* Also make sure that there is plenty of free hard drive space on the drive containing your /Temp directory—complex images may require 50 MB or more of free hard drive space for temporary printing files.

■ *Reduce the video resolution.* As a last resort, you might also try reducing your desktop video resolution to 640 × 480.

Symptom 4.68: The printer does not work when daisy-chained from another parallel port device. This often happens with parallel port scanners, tape drives, Zip drives, and other popular parallel port devices. You may also see this as random "gibberish" printed on the page when a port is shared with more than one parallel port device.

■ *Check the printer alone.* Most older ink-jet printers have a bidirectional communication feature. This feature does *not* share the parallel port, and causes intermittent problems with some parallel port devices. If this is the case, you may need to remove the other nonprinter devices and use the printer exclusively on the parallel port.

■ *Check the parallel port mode.* If the printer (and other parallel port devices) are compliant with advanced parallel port modes (such as *ECP* or *EPP* modes), make sure that the LPT port is configured for ECP or EPP operation in the host computer's CMOS Setup.

■ *Try the latest drivers.* It may also be necessary for you to download and install the latest LPT port drivers for your version of Windows.

Symptom 4.69: When starting Windows 95/98, a small amount of "gibberish" text is sent to the printer. You may also receive one of the following errors: *Unable to write data to the printer*, or *There was an error writing to LPT1*.

- *Check the printer status and connections.* Always check first to see that the printer is on (online), and that it is properly connected to the computer using a suitable cable. Also see that the printer is the *only* parallel port device attached to the LPT port.

- *Check for other parallel device drivers.* These kinds of errors are known to occur when other virtual device drivers are loaded for daisy-chained parallel port devices. For example, the DRVWPPQT.VXD file will cause this problem when it's loaded for a parallel port tape drive. During the drive detection process, a string of text is sent through the parallel port to be interpreted by tape devices. Many sophisticated printers interpret this string as printable text. To prevent this driver from being loaded, turn off and disconnect the printer. Click *Start*, point to *Find*, and then click *Files or Folders*. In the named box, type drvwppqt.vxd, and then click *Find Now*. Rename all instances of the file by changing the file name extension (i.e., change drvwppqt.vxd to drvwppqt.old). You must change the extension to prevent the driver from being loaded. Now reboot your system, then plug in the printer and turn it on.

  NOTE: Once the other parallel port drive and its offending driver(s) have been removed, you should now be able to set the LPT port mode to ECP in BOTH the BIOS and Device Manager in order to achieve peak communication performance.

Symptom 4.70: Text appears "jagged" along its edges. In many cases, it's the choice of font style or paper rather than a printer issue.

- *Try using TrueType fonts.* Some software programs offer custom "bitmapped" fonts that have jagged edges when enlarged or printed. By using TrueType fonts in your image, you can be confident that the fonts should appear smooth. Bitmapped fonts are notorious for this kind of "jaggy" appearance.

- *Check the paper.* Paper selections can have this kind of effect. Paper that is heavily textured or does not accept ink well can cause graphics and text to print poorly, resulting in uneven "jagged" edges (though this may not appear consistent across the entire page). Try a smoother paper, or a paper type recommended for your particular printer.

Symptom 4.71: The printer isn't feeding paper. This is a common problem with single-sheet paper feed printers such as the Epson Stylus Color family, and is usually due to jammed or improperly loaded paper. Turn the printer on and press the *Load/Eject* button to see if paper loads. If not, make sure the paper isn't curled or creased. The paper should also be fresh, and not over-loaded. Check that the paper isn't jammed in the printer. If the *Paper Out* light is on solid, reload the paper (taking care that the paper edge guide is adjusted to fit the paper's width), and then press the *Load/Eject* button again to see if the paper will load. If the *Paper Out* light is flashing, turn the printer off, reload the paper, turn the printer back on, and try pressing *Load/Eject* again to see if that clears the problem. If the printer still won't load paper, turn off the printer and make sure that there are no foreign objects (such as packing materials) in the paper path.

Symptom 4.72: After installing a new printer in Windows 95/98 you cannot run ScanDisk. This is a known problem with some current printer drivers (such as for the Epson Stylus Photo EX), and is almost always caused by interference from the printer's monitoring software running in the System Tray (such as Epson's "Status

Monitor 2"). You'll need to right-click on that monitoring software and disable it before running ScanDisk.

Symptom 4.73: The page's margins appear incorrect.
The two primary causes for this type of trouble are improper software setup and incorrect paper loading.

■ *Check the paper loading.* If the margins are off at an angle (i.e., the print appears skewed), the paper may be loaded incorrectly. Make sure that the left and right edge guides are flush against both sides of the paper, and verify that the paper is not "walking" in the paper transport.

■ *Check the printing application.* If the margins appear even, make sure the margins are set correctly in your software application (margins are not adjustable via the printer driver). Verify that you are not trying to print outside of the printable area of the page for your given paper size (see that the correct paper size is selected in the printer driver settings).

Symptom 4.74: You cannot clear the printer's memory.
This often occurs if you do not halt the print job from the PC first. Make sure that you cancel the print job from the computer *before* you try to clear the printer's memory. The printer should no longer be printing. After canceling the print job from the computer, turn the printer off, wait a few seconds (perhaps a minute), and then turn the printer on again.

Symptom 4.75: The printer's control panel locks up after printing from Windows. You'll probably find that the buttons on the panel do not respond unless you disconnect the parallel printer cable from the back of the printer. This often occurs because of the PC's parallel port—some computers send an initialize/reset signal during the boot process. If the printer cable picks up any noise during this process, the printer's initialization process line will not complete its reset cycle and cause the control panel to lock. Try booting the computer to Windows *first*, then turn the printer on and try printing again. A defective cable can also cause this type of problem, so try another cable (make sure you're using a fully shielded "Centronics"-type cable less than 6 feet long).

Symptom 4.76: The printer's *status monitor* doesn't indicate the ink levels in Windows 95/98. In most cases, a *status monitor* allows you to check the level of ink in the printer (as well as control the way your software warns you about printer issues). From your printing application (i.e., Excel), choose *Print* from the *File* menu (or click the *Print* button in the main tool bar) to see the printer settings dialog box. Click the *Utility* button to get the *Utility* menu, then select the *status monitor* entry. The software checks the amount of ink remaining in the printer and displays the "status monitor" window. If you want to change printer messages and warning conditions, click the *Configuration* button. Choose the options you want and click *OK* to save the settings.

Symptom 4.77: When trying to print, you get a *Printer Driver Busy* error. The error often indicates that another software application is also using the printer. The print job does not appear in the print spooler and must be resent. This is almost always due to a print spooling problem. Normally, the print spooler enables multiple print jobs to be sent to the printer at one time—while one job is printing, other jobs will accumulate in the print spooler and wait for their turn to print. If a printer is configured to *Print directly to the printer* or its *Spool data format* is configured as .RAW, print spooling for that printer is effectively disabled. This means multiple print jobs will not accumulate, and each print job *must* be allowed to finish before attempting to send another. To correct this issue, ensure that the Windows print spooler is enabled and that the *Spool data format* is set to .EMF in Windows 95/98/NT:

- Select *Start*, *Settings*, and *Printers*.

- Right-click your printer icon and choose *Properties*, *Details*, then *Spool Settings*.

- Select the options *Spool print jobs so program finishes printing faster* and *Start printing after first page is spooled*.

- Change *Spool data format* from .RAW to .EMF.

- If your printer has trouble with IEEE-1284 print modes (i.e., *ECP* or *EPP* modes), select the option *Enable bidirectional support for this printer*.

- Choose *OK* to close the *Spool Settings* window, then click *OK* to close the *Printer Properties* window.

If the problem persists, it usually means that your printing application is bypassing the Windows print spooler. If this happens, only *one* print job at a time may be sent to the printer. Once a print job finishes printing, another print job may be started.

Symptom 4.78: You get a *file in use* error when attempting to install a printer driver.   In most cases, you'll see an error such as *One of the files required for this printer is in use by another program. Quit all programs, and then click Retry. To quit the Add Printer wizard, click Cancel.* Choosing *Retry* will generally return the same error message, and choosing *Cancel* will abort the driver installation. This is a known issue with printers like the HP 2000C (i.e., the HPRC1607.DLL file). To work around this issue, you'll need to shut down all applications and restart Windows, then try installing the driver software again (if there are already icons in the *Printer* window for your failed installations, remove those icons before attempting to reinstall the drivers).

Symptom 4.79: When installing/using a printer connected to the passthrough port of a Zip drive, the Zip drive disappears. After restarting the system, the Zip drive's icon in *My Computer* and in Windows Explorer may be missing. In many cases, other devices (such as a parallel port Zip drive) attached to the same port as the printer can interfere with bidirectional communication. Disconnect any device connected between the computer and the printer, connect the printer directly, then reload the printer driver. As a workaround, allow the printer driver to fail the communication check and reconfigure the port manually:

- Reload the printer driver and select *File* as the port assignment.

- An error message may indicate that the communications test failed. Select *Skip* when the message appears, then continue the installation.

- After the printer driver installation has completed, change the port assignment from *File* to *LPT1*.

- Click *Start*, select *Settings*, and then click *Printers*.

- Right-click the icon of the printer to be modified. Select *Properties* and choose the *Details* tab.

- Under *Print to the following port*, select *LPT1*, then select *OK*.

- Now try printing again.

   NOTE: As a long-term fix, an additional parallel port should be added for the tape or Zip-type drive, or contact the manufacturer of the parallel port drive for other configuration suggestions.

Symptom 4.80: When installing/using a printer connected to the passthrough port of a Zip drive, the printer picks up a piece of paper and stops. The power light (or other indicator) may blink. In many cases, other devices (such as a parallel port Zip drive) attached to the same port as the printer can interfere with bidirectional communication. The drivers used for the other parallel port drives may also interfere with communication. For the Zip drive, try removing the *Iomega* icons from your Startup folder. You can test the Zip files for problems by preventing them from loading:

- Restart Windows 95/98.

- Press and hold the <Ctrl> key when the Windows logo appears, and continue to hold it down until Windows has fully booted—this will prevent any items in the Startup folder from loading.

- If the password dialog appears, type in the password, press and hold the <Ctrl> key on the keyboard, and press <Enter>.

If you notice that the printer runs properly when the Zip tools are disabled, remove them from the Startup folder (you can also use this process for other utilities in the Startup group):

- Right-click *Start*, select *Programs*, and Startup folders.

- Drag and drop all of the *Iomega* icons onto the Windows 95/98 desktop.

- After all the *Iomega* icons have been removed from the Startup folder, close all the open folders and restart the computer.

Symptom 4.81: When installing/using a printer connected to the passthrough port of a Zip drive, the printer cannot communicate with the printer. When you attempt to use the software utilities included with your printer, *general protection faults* (GPFs) may result. For example, if the *Printer Services* tab is selected in an HP printer's Toolbox, a GPF error message will occur stating *HP_TBX0_ caused a General Protection Fault in module MMSYSTEM.DLL* (the exact filename will depend on the printer and its driver). These kinds of errors are usually caused by changes made to the SYSTEM.INI file once the Zip drive is installed. Changing the altered line(s) back to their default settings should stop the GPFs from occurring, but it may disable some functionality of the Zip drive:

- Click *Start*, and select *Run*.

- On the *Open* line type SYSEDIT and then select *OK*. Double-click the title bar that reads C:\ WINDOWS\SYSTEM.INI to bring that window to the front and maximize it.

- Under the [boot] section, locate the line:

  DRIVERS=MMSYSTEM.DLL POWER.DRV PRINT PRO

- Move the cursor in front of the *Print Pro* reference and insert a semicolon. The line should now read:

  DRIVERS=MMSYSTEM.DLL POWER.DRV ;PRINT PRO

- Select *File* and *Save* to save your changes, then exit SYSEDIT and restart Windows for your changes to take effect.

  NOTE: This process affects the functionality of a *Zip drive*. Other parallel port drives (such as tape drives) may require other alterations to SYSTEM.INI or other .INI files.

Symptom 4.82: Your printer's *economy* print setting is grayed out. This is usually a problem with the design of the printer driver or support software that will not support *economy* printing with particular media types. In most cases, simply changing the media type to *plain paper* will reenable the *economy* print mode. Check with the printer manufacturer for updated drivers and support software which will allow *economy* printing on all media types.

  NOTE: In some cases, "economy" printing is intentionally disabled on the more expensive media types like transparencies or heavy gloss photo stock—this prevents "economy" printing from producing too-light an image and effectively wasting the sheet(s).

Symptom 4.83: There are printer communication errors when a parallel port scanner is also installed. In many cases, parallel port devices attached to the same port as the printer can interfere with bidirectional communication. The drivers used for the other parallel port drives may also interfere with communication. For example, during installation the printer driver will not find bidirectional communication if a scanner has already been installed on the parallel port. Also, if a scanner is installed after the printer driver has loaded successfully (with full bidirectional communication), a *printer not responding* or *lost communication with the printer* message may appear when you attempt to print.

- *Disable the scanner's cover sensor.* This kind of problem often happens with scanners that use cover switches to invoke the scanner software wizard (such as *ScanWizard*, used with Mustek parallel port scanners) when the scanner cover is opened. If you don't want to disable the cover sensor software completely, check the scanner software or properties for a checkbox that allows you to turn off the *cover driven* sensor feature. For the Mustek scanner, right-click the *Direct Scan* icon on the Taskbar, then uncheck *Cover Driven* to turn off the cover sensor feature.

- *Disable the scanner's background utilities.* Chances are that the scanner has one or more utilities loaded into the Startup folder. If you're having trouble printing or loading the printer driver, close the scanner's background drivers in the *Close Program* window. Press <Ctrl>+<Alt>+<Del> to bring up the *Close Program* dialog. Highlight the scanner's software, then select *End Task*. Now try installing the printer driver, or print a document. The scanner software will be disabled until Windows is restarted. If you need to disable the scanner software on a more permanent basis, remove the scanner software from the `Startup` folder.

- *Remove the scanner.* If all else fails, remove the scanner software and drivers, disconnect the scanner, and attach the printer directly to the parallel port.

Laser Printer Troubleshooting

The laser printer is considered to be the single most popular printer type for high-resolution professional printing applications in environments such as offices (Figure 4.4). Traditionally available only for black-and-white (B&W) printing, some high-end laser printers now offer color capabilities for photorealistic imaging and professional color documents. To make a laser printer work, a modulated laser beam scans across the length of a rotating charged drum. The drum is discharged wherever the beam strikes it, and these discharged areas pick up toner power as the drum rotates near a toner reservoir. The latent toner image is then transferred to the paper, and fixed to the page using high-temperature rollers. This process is generally known as *electrophotographic* (or EP) printing.

The use of electrophotographic printing offers some unique advantages for a printer. Since the laser beam can be controlled with extreme precision, laser printers tend to offer very high resolutions. The print also tends to be very consistent across the entire page since the page is formed in its entirety rather than by discrete passes of a print head—you don't see "pass marks" or variations in printing intensity as you look down the page. This trait has made laser printers the preferred printer for business and professional documents. EP printing also tends to be quite fast, and many high-end printers can supply as many as 30 pages per minute. It is also possible to provide large

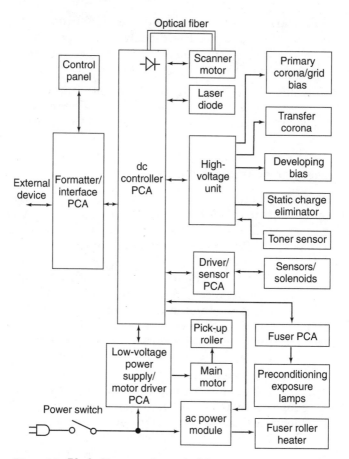

Figure 4.4 Block diagram of a typical laser printer. (*Courtesy of Hewlett-Packard Co.*)

quantities of dry toner, so a laser printer can supply thousands of pages before more toner is needed (compared to a few dozen full-color pages from an ink-jet printer before the ink cartridges need replacement).

Unfortunately, laser printers are expensive and heavy devices that require regular service. They don't just "sling ink" like impact or ink-jet printers. Their complex use of laser light, high-voltage, static electricity, toner, mechanical transports, heat, and pressure—all under the control of a complex ECU—leave a great deal of room for printing problems. This part of the chapter outlines a comprehensive selection of symptoms and solutions that can help you isolate and correct a wide selection of laser printer failures.

> **NOTE**: The *Basic Printer Maintenance* video covers laser cleaning and maintenance in detail. You can obtain this 40-minute video show from Dynamic Learning Systems, using the order form at the back of the book.

> **IMPORTANT NOTE**: *SHOCK WARNING*—Be sure to unplug the printer and allow ample time for the power supply (or supplies) to discharge before attempting to open the enclosure. High-voltage supplies are especially dangerous, and can result in a nasty shock if not allowed to discharge.

> **IMPORTANT NOTE**: *BURN WARNING*—Fusing assemblies in EP printers also reach over 200°F during normal operation. Even when opening the EP printer for routine maintenance, allow ample time for the fuser to cool (at least 10 minutes) before reaching inside.

EP cartridge tips

As you might imagine, the precision components in an EP cartridge are sensitive and delicate. The photosensitive drum and toner supply are particularly sensitive to light and environmental conditions, so it is important to follow several handling and storage guidelines:

- *Keep light away from the drum.* The photosensitive drum is coated with an organic material that is *extremely* sensitive to light. Although a metal shroud covers the drum when the cartridge is exposed, light may still penetrate the shroud and cause exposure (also known as *fogging*).

Deactivating the printer for a time will often eliminate mild fogging. *Do not remove the shroud in open light unless absolutely necessary, and then only for short periods.* This will certainly fog the drum. A seriously fogged cartridge may have to be placed in a dark area for several days. *Never* expose the drum to direct sunlight—direct sunlight can permanently damage the drum's coating.

■ *Avoid extremes of temperature and humidity.* Temperatures exceeding 40°C can permanently damage an EP cartridge. Extreme humidity is just about as dangerous. Do not allow the cartridge to become exposed to ammonia vapors or other organic solvent vapors—they break down the drum's photosensitive coating very quickly. Finally, keep a cartridge secure and level. Never allow it to be dropped or abused in any way.

■ *Redistribute toner regularly.* As the toner supply diminishes, it may be necessary to redistribute remaining toner so that it reaches the toner roller. Since toner is available along the entire cartridge, it must be redistributed by rocking the cartridge back and forth along its long axis. If you tip a cartridge upright, remaining toner will fall to one end and cause uneven distribution.

Printer memory troubleshooting tips

Laser printers use RAM to store the tremendous amount of image data used to form the intricate text and graphics that we associate with laser printing. Most modern laser printers will support anywhere from 4 to 100 MB of onboard RAM, often more. If you work with high-end printers at all, chances are that you'll be installing more RAM in the printer. In some cases, the additional single inline memory modules (SIMMs) are not recognized or acknowledged by the printer after installation.

The amount of RAM recognized by the printer is almost always reported on the printer's PCL self-test page. Refer to the printer's manual and run a self-test, then review the self-test page to determine the exact amount of RAM detected. If the detected memory is less than the amount of RAM installed, use the following checklist to help isolate the problem:

> **NOTE**: Always be sure to keep the printer turned off and unplugged, and use an antistatic wrist strap when installing memory. Failure to do so may damage the SIMM(s) and cause memory problems.

- Try resetting the printer, then perform a new self-test to see if the RAM is recognized.

- Try switching the printer off, waiting 15 to 30 seconds, then switching the printer on again. Perform a new self-test to see if the RAM is recognized.

- Concerning memory specifications, make sure that the memory you've installed in the printer is the same type and speed specified in the printer's documentation. If not, the printer may not recognize the new RAM. Install the proper RAM device(s) and try again.

- Concerning memory manufacturer, some printer memory is proprietary, and this usually requires that memory devices be purchased directly from the printer's manufacturer. Although this is rare today, double-check the memory specifications in the printer's documentation.

- Remove and reinstall the SIMM(s). Each SIMM should be firmly and evenly seated in its SIMM sockets. Distinct "clicks" should be heard as each SIMM is clipped into its socket.

- Try installing the SIMM(s) in a different bank. If another bank works properly, the previous bank may need cleaning, or the printer may require repair.

- Finally, remove the additional SIMMs and see that the original SIMMs are still working properly (and that you have the same amount of RAM you started with). If this is the case, your new RAM may be defective. Try other SIMM(s).

Paper jam troubleshooting tips

Of all the problems that occur with laser printers, paper feed problems (*paper jams*) are some of the most common. Jams are caused by a variety of potential problems ranging from poor media quality to serious mechanical problems within the printer. This part of the chapter examines the typical causes, messages, locations, and corrective measures for paper feed problems. Paper jams occur when the media (i.e., paper, envelopes, labels, transparencies, and so on) is obstructed at some point along the paper path. Table 4.2 outlines the most common symptoms and solu-

TABLE 4.2   Laser Paper Feed Issues

Problem	The media frequently jams in the printer
Probable Cause:	The media is not appropriate for your particular printer.
Solution:	Select different media that is suitable for your particular printer.
Probable Cause:	The media is old, wet, or otherwise in poor condition.
Solution:	Use fresh media in the printer.
Probable Cause:	The "media type" is set incorrectly.
Solution:	Select the correct "media type" through the printer's control panel and driver.
Probable Cause:	You are using media that has already passed through a printer or a copier.
Solution:	Use fresh media—do not refeed media that has already been printed.
Probable Cause:	The paper tray is overloaded (or loaded incorrectly).
Solution:	Remove any excess media from the paper tray, and press the media down under the tabs in the paper tray.

Problem	The media frequently jams in the printer
Probable Cause:	The media guides are not adjusted correctly.
Solution:	Adjust the media guides so that they are firmly against the media (but not bending the media).
Probable Cause:	You're printing on very heavy media.
Solution:	Try switching to a different paper path (use an alternate output bin if possible).
Probable Cause:	Sheets of media are binding or sticking together.
Solution:	Remove the remaining media, rotate it 180 degrees or flip it over, and then set it back in the paper tray (do not use the print media if they continue to stick together).
Probable Cause:	You're trying to remove pages from an output bin before the printer has finished.
Solution:	Do not remove pages from the output bins until the printer is finished printing.
Probable Cause:	Frequent jams at the fuser might suggest an incorrectly installed fusing unit.
Solution:	Check the fuser for obstructions, and try to reinstall the fusing unit.
Probable Cause:	Frequent jams at the transfer area might suggest an incorrectly installed transfer unit.
Solution:	Check the transfer unit for obstructions, and try to reinstall the transfer unit.
Probable Cause:	Frequent jams at the output bin might suggest an improperly installed bin.
Solution:	Check the output bin for obstructions, and try to reinstall the output bin. Make sure that the printer is on a level surface.
Probable Cause:	The printer's consumables are wearing out.
Solution:	Check the printer's control panel for messages prompting you to replace consumables (i.e., toner or EP engine), or print a configuration page to check the condition of your consumables.

Problem	The printer feeds multiple sheets
Probable Cause:	The media is not appropriate for your particular printer.
Solution:	Select different media that is suitable for your particular printer.
Probable Cause:	The paper tray is overloaded (or loaded incorrectly).
Solution:	Remove any excess media from the paper tray, and press the media down under the tabs in the paper tray.

Problem	The printer feeds multiple sheets

Probable Cause:	Sheets of media are binding or sticking together.
Solution:	Remove the remaining media, rotate it 180 degrees or flip it over, and then set it back in the paper tray (do not use the print media if they continue to stick together).
Probable Cause:	There is more than one type of media (i.e., paper and transparencies) in the paper tray.
Solution:	Remove all media except the current type that you want to print on.

Problem	The printer feeds the incorrect media type (or size)

Probable Cause:	The correct media type/size is not selected in your printing application.
Solution:	Select the correct media size in your printing application.
Probable Cause:	The media type(s) for each paper tray are not configured correctly in the printer's control panel.
Solution:	Verify that the correct media is installed in the printer, and reconfigure the media type for the paper tray in your printer's control panel.

Problem	The printer fails to feed media automatically

Probable Cause:	*Manual Feed (Tray 1)* is not selected in the printer driver.
Solution:	Select the correct media source at the printer and/or in the printing application.
Probable Cause:	The input tray is empty.
Solution:	Load the paper tray with appropriate media.
Probable Cause:	Media is still in the paper path after removing the previous media jam.
Solution:	Open the printer doors and remove any media from the paper path. Check the fuser area carefully for any jams.

Problem	The printer fails to feed media from tray 1

Probable Cause:	*Manual Feed (Tray 1)* is not selected in the printer driver.
Solution:	Select the correct media source at the printer and/or in the printing application.

Problem	The printer fails to feed media from tray 1
Probable Cause:	The expected media size in the printing application does not match the media detected in the paper tray. The printer will sense the difference in size and stop printing to prevent damage to the printer.
Solution:	Remove any remaining media from the paper tray. Verify the size expected by your application and the size of the media match. Adjust the media-width guides so they are firmly against the edges of the media. Try printing again.
Probable Cause	The wrong paper tray is selected as the media source from the printer driver or application.
Solution:	Configure the correct media type and size for tray 1 in the printer control panel. For example, if *TRAY 1 MODE=CASSETTE* is selected on the printer control panel, make sure that you select tray 1 as the source in the printer driver or application.
Probable Cause:	The media may not be properly installed in the paper tray.
Solution:	Verify that the media are being inserted far enough into tray 1. Reinsert the media into tray 1 until the media is tight against the printer, and slide the media-width guides until they touch both sides of the media (without bending the media).
Probable Cause:	Media is still in the paper path after removing the previous media jam.
Solution:	Open the printer doors and remove any media from the paper path. Check the fuser area carefully for any jams.

Problem	The printer fails to feed media from trays 2 or 3
Probable Cause:	The media type selected from the printing application has not been configured for the particular paper tray.
Solution:	Configure the media type for the input tray in the printer control panel.
Probable Cause:	Multiple trays may be configured for the same media type/size.
Solution:	If trays 2 and 3 are configured for the same media type and size, the printer will feed only from a specific paper tray if that input tray is selected in your printing application.

Problem	The printer fails to feed media from trays 2 or 3
Probable Cause:	Media is still in the paper path after removing the previous media jam.
Solution:	Open the printer doors and remove any media from the paper path. Check the fuser area carefully for any jams.
Problem	The printer fails to feed media from tray 4
Probable Cause:	The media is not appropriate for your particular printer.
Solution:	Select different media that is suitable for your particular printer.
Probable Cause:	The media guides may not be set correctly.
Solution:	Remove the media and verify that the media guides in the front, back, and left of the paper tray are configured to the correct media size.
Probable Cause:	The media type selected from the printing application has not been configured for the particular paper tray.
Solution:	Configure the media type for the input tray in the printer control panel.
Probable Cause:	The paper tray is overloaded (or loaded incorrectly).
Solution:	Remove any excess media from the paper tray, and press the media down under the tabs in the paper tray.
Probable Cause:	If tray 4 uses a power extension, the power cord may not be firmly plugged into the printer, tray 4, and the power receptacle.
Solution:	Remove and reconnect the power cord.
Probable Cause:	The paper rollers might need to be cleaned.
Solution:	Open the tray door, pinch together the release levers on the end of the rollers, and slide the rollers off their spindles. Clean the rollers with a hand wipe. Reinstall the rollers by holding the roller by the levers and sliding the rollers onto the spindle until the rollers click into place. You may also choose to replace the tray assembly.
Problem	Transparencies or glossy paper will not feed properly
Probable Cause:	The media is not appropriate for your particular printer.
Solution:	Select different media that is suitable for your particular printer.

Problem	Transparencies or glossy paper will not feed properly

Probable Cause:	The media type selected from the printing application has not been configured for the particular paper tray.
Solution:	Configure the media type for the input tray in the printer control panel.
Probable Cause:	The paper tray is overloaded (or loaded incorrectly).
Solution:	Remove any excess media from the paper tray, and press the media down under the tabs in the paper tray.
Probable Cause:	The media may not be properly installed in the paper tray.
Solution:	Verify that the media are being inserted far enough into the tray 1. Reinsert the media into tray 1 until the media is tight against the printer, and slide the media-width guides until they touch both sides of the media (without bending the media).
Probable Cause:	The media type(s) for each paper tray are not configured correctly in the printer's control panel.
Solution:	Verify that the correct media is installed in the printer, and reconfigure the media type for the paper tray in your printer's control panel.
Probable Cause:	There is only one sheet loaded in the paper tray.
Solution:	Load more than one sheet in the paper tray.

Problem	Envelopes jam or do not feed properly

Probable Cause:	The envelopes are not appropriate for your particular printer.
Solution:	Select different envelopes that are suitable for your particular printer.
Probable Cause:	Your printer may print envelopes only from the first paper tray.
Solution:	If the envelopes are in another input tray, remove the envelopes and place them in tray 1.
Probable Cause:	The paper tray may not be configured properly for envelopes.
Solution:	Verify tray 1 is configured for *cassette* mode, and the media type and size are correctly configured in the printer control panel.
Probable Cause:	The envelopes may be inserted upside-down.

Problem	Envelopes jam or do not feed properly

Solution:	Envelopes can often be printed only on the front (smooth) side. If the envelopes are loaded upside-down in tray 1, remove the envelopes and place them flap down on tray 1 with the return address area (short edge of the envelope) toward the printer.
Probable Cause:	The envelopes may not be properly installed in the paper tray.
Solution:	Verify that the envelopes are being inserted far enough into the tray 1. Reinsert the envelopes into tray 1 until they are tight against the printer, and slide the media-width guides until they touch both sides of the envelopes (without bending them).

Problem	Media does not eject to the correct output bin

Probable Cause:	The desired input bin is not selected.
Solution:	Verify that the correct output bin is selected in the printer driver.
Probable Cause:	The media is not appropriate for your desired output bin.
Solution:	Use fresh media that is appropriate for your particular output bin.
Probable Cause:	A multibin box isn't configured properly.
Solution:	Verify that the multibin box has been installed on the printer and in the printer driver. Also verify that you're printing in the multibin box mode (which will affect the print job's destination).

Problem:	Ejected pages are curled or wrinkled

Probable Cause:	The media is not appropriate for your particular printer.
Solution:	Select different media that is suitable for your particular printer.
Probable Cause:	The current media is damaged, wet, or in otherwise poor condition.
Solution:	Remove the damaged media from the paper tray, and then replace it with fresh, undamaged media.
Probable Cause:	There is excessive humidity in the printing environment.
Solution:	You are operating the printer in excessively humid conditions. Make sure the printer is operating within the environmental specifications, or keep the media in a lower humidity environment until you're ready to print.

Problem:	Ejected pages are curled or wrinkled
Probable Cause:	There is excessive toner in the image(s).
Solution:	If you are printing heavy, solid-fill areas, the amount of toner used on the page can cause excessive curl. Try printing different halftone patterns (a lighter shade of the same color), a lighter color, or a lighter pattern.
Probable Cause:	The curl may be caused by the design of the printer's paper path.
Solution:	Change the paper path by printing from a different paper tray to a different output bin.
Probable Cause:	The media has a poorly cut edge.
Solution:	Remove any remaining media, rotate it 180 degrees (or flip it over), and then set it back in the paper tray.

tions for paper feed problems in a laser printer. There are many possible causes for paper jams, but most causes can be corrected with a minimum of fuss:

- *Incorrect media installation.* The media (i.e., paper, labels, or envelopes) is installed incorrectly, and this is causing repeated jams due to poor feeding from the tray. Verify that the media is correctly installed, and see that the paper tray holding the media is seated evenly and completely.

- *Reusing printed media.* You are reloading media (i.e., paper) that has already passed through a printer or copier. Try using fresh media, or reposition the pre-printed media so that there is less curl at the pickup rollers. If this helps, avoid reusing media that has been printed or copied on your particular printer.

- *Excess media in the tray.* Feeding problems can occur if there is too much media (i.e., paper) in the tray—the tray is overloaded. Remove any excess media from the input tray, and be sure to press down the media in the tray so that it all fits below the metal tabs.

- *Media guide obstructions.* The paper should be seated straight in the tray. Make sure that the input-tray guides are positioned properly for the media being used (i.e., envelopes) and adjust the guides so that they hold the media firmly in place. The guides should not be so tight that they bend or restrict the media.

- *Media type mismatch.* The media being used is not appropriate for your particular printer. For example, paper that is too thick, too thin, or chemically coated may have trouble feeding through the printer. Check the printer manual to locate the correct media requirements.

- *Media sticking or binding.* The stack of media (i.e., labels) is binding on itself. This can be caused by poor-quality media, foreign matter or stains in the media, excess static cling, and so on. Remove the media, flex it, rotate it 180 degrees (or flip it over). Reload the media into the input tray and try again. If problems persist, try fresh media or a different media type. Media that is dirty, dusty, stained, or wet (humid) should be replaced.

- *Media size mismatch.* The media size specified in the printing software does not match the input tray's configuration. Verify that the media size selected in your software application or printer driver matches the media size specified in the printer control panel for the tray you are printing from.

- *Replaceable parts are exhausted.* A printer's "consumable" item(s) have reached the end of their useful life (i.e., transfer belt), and the wear in that item is causing paper-feed issues. Check the printer's control panel for messages prompting you to replace consumable items, or print a configuration page to verify the remaining life of vital consumable items.

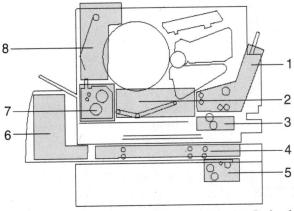

Figure 4.5   Paper jam locations. (*Courtesy of Hewlett-Packard Co.*)

Typical jam locations and errors.   Laser printers use a series of paper sensors to track the progress of paper through the mechanism. When media remains in one place for too long, a *jam* error is generated. The error is also reported on the printer's control panel for easy reference. You can see the major jam areas located in the HP LaserJet diagram of Figure 4.5, and their descriptions are as follows:

1. Input tray 1 area
2. Transfer belt area
3. Input tray 2 area
4. Front duplex drawer area
5. Tray 3 (500-sheet paper feeder) area
6. Rear duplex cover area
7. Fuser area
8. Rear paper path area

The most common jam errors that you'll see are listed below:

- *13.XX PAPER JAM—CHECK ALL REAR DOORS.* This error generally means that the media is jammed in the rear paper path or rear duplexing area. Open the upper rear door or rear duplex cover (if installed) and remove any jammed media.

- *13.XX PAPER JAM—CHECK MIDDLE FRONT DRAWER.* The media is jammed in the transfer belt area. Open the middle front drawer (or open the printer's main cover) and remove any jammed media.

- *13.XX PAPER JAM—CHECK FRONT DUPLEX DRAWER.* Media is jammed in the front paper path or front duplexing area. Open the front cover or front duplex drawer (if installed) and remove any jammed media.

- *13.1 JAM: OPEN MIDDLE DRAWER—CHECK IN REAR OF DRAWER.* A jam has occurred inside the middle front drawer area, and is probably located in the fuser area. Open the middle front drawer (or open the printer's main cover) and carefully inspect for any media. Also inspect the fusing area—you may need to access the fusing area through a rear door to remove any jammed media.

  NOTE: Not all printers use the same jam error messages. Simpler printers (i.e., those without duplexing capability) may use fewer, less-specific messages.

Tips for avoiding jams

- Try flexing, fanning, and inverting the media in the tray.

- Do not print on torn, worn, coated, or irregular media.

- Do not print on previously printed media.

- Verify that the media you're using is within the specifications supported by your particular printer.

- Verify that input trays are not overloaded.

- Paper that has absorbed moisture can easily cause paper feed problems. If the printer is used in a humid area, suspect damp paper as a cause of recurring paper feed and print quality problems. Try fresh paper, and move the printer to a drier area.

- Keep the printer clean. Toner and paper dust in the paper path inhibit free movement of media through the printer and block the paper sensors.

- Verify that your media is correctly loaded in the input trays, and that all length and width paper guides are correctly set.

- Periodically check the condition of the pickup rollers and feed roller(s). Worn separation pads on the multipurpose tray will cause page multifeeds. Bent separation tabs also cause misfeeds and page multifeeds.

- Defective paper tray switches can cause paper jams by indicating the wrong size paper to the formatter.

- Verify that the input tray is configured for the type of media loaded. For example, when Tray 1 is in *CASSETTE* mode, verify that the tray is properly configured for the size of media being loaded.

- If the jam rips or tears, remove all portions of the jammed sheet—this helps to avoid subsequent jams. Also inspect other areas of the printer to verify that all the jammed media has been removed.

- Scraps of paper left in the paper path can cause intermittent paper jams. Always check that the paper path is clear when cleaning the printer and when clearing paper jams. Also, remove the fuser and carefully check it for jammed paper.

> **NOTE**: Use the PRINTERS utility to generate standard printer test patterns and "stress-test" the paper feed system. You can obtain PRINTERS from Dynamic Learning Systems, using the order form at the back of the book.

Repetitive defect troubleshooting guidelines

A *repetitive defect* is a problem (i.e., lines, smudges, spots, and so on) that appears at *regular* intervals down the length of a printed page. Repetitive defects are usually indicative of an issue with one or more rollers in the printer. Since each roller has a different circumference, you can often determine the cause of a repetitive defect by simply measuring the distance between them. Simply note the location of the defect (on the page *front* or page *back*), measure the distance between defects, then compare the distance to the roller measurements shown in Table 4.3.

TABLE 4.3   Index of Repetitive Defects

Distance	Probable Cause	Suggested Action
HP LaserJet, LaserJet Plus, and LaserJet 500 Plus Printers		
$7\frac{3}{8}''$ (187 mm)	EP Drum	Replace EP engine
$5\frac{1}{8}''$ (130 mm)	Upper Fusing Roller	Replace cleaning pad, clean fusing roller, replace fusing unit
$2\frac{7}{8}''$ (73 mm)	Lower Fusing Roller	Clean fusing roller, replace fusing unit
$2\frac{2}{3}''$ (68 mm)	Developing Roller	Replace EP engine and/or toner cartridge
HP LaserJet II, IID, III, and IIID Printers		
$3\frac{3}{4}''$ (95 mm)	EP Drum	Replace EP engine
$2''$ (51 mm)	Developing Roller	Replace EP engine and/or toner cartridge
$3\frac{1}{8}''$ (79 mm)	Upper Fusing Roller	Replace cleaning pad, clean fusing roller, replace fusing unit
$2\frac{1}{2}''$ (64 mm)	Lower Fusing Roller	Clean fusing roller, replace fusing unit
$1\frac{1}{2}''$ (38 mm)	Upper Registration	Clean registration rollers, replace registration unit
$1\frac{3}{4}''$ (44 mm)	Lower Registration	Clean registration rollers, replace registration unit

Distance	Probable Cause	Suggested Action
	HP LaserJet II, IID, III, and IIID Printers	
$\frac{1}{2}''$ (13 mm)	Transfer Roller	Clean transfer roller and paper path
	HP LaserJet IIP, IIP Plus, and IIIP Printers	
$3\frac{3}{4}''$ (95 mm)	EP Drum	Replace EP engine
$1\frac{1}{2}''$ (38 mm)	Primary Charging	Replace EP engine
$2''$ (51 mm)	Developing Roller	Replace EP engine and/or toner cartridge
$1\frac{7}{8}''$ (48 mm)	Input Feed Roller	Clean the feed roller, replace the paper feed unit
$2''$ (51 mm)	Transfer Roller	Clean transfer roller and paper path
$2\frac{1}{2}''$ (64 mm)	Upper Fusing Roller	Replace cleaning pad, clean fusing roller, replace fusing unit
$2\frac{1}{8}''$ (54 mm)	Lower Fusing Roller	Clean fusing roller, replace fusing unit
	HP LaserJet IIISi, 4SI, and 4SI MX Printers	
$3\frac{3}{4}''$ (95 mm)	EP Drum	Replace EP engine
$2''$ (51 mm)	Developing Roller	Replace EP engine and/or toner cartridge
$1\frac{1}{2}''$ (38 mm)	Primary Charging	Replace EP engine
$3\frac{3}{4}''$ (95 mm)	Fuser Rollers	Replace cleaning pad, clean fusing roller, replace fusing unit
$1\frac{3}{4}''$ (44 mm)	Upper Registration	Clean the registration roller, replace the paper feed unit
$2\frac{1}{2}''$ (64 mm)	Transfer Roller	Clean transfer roller and paper path
	HP LaserJet 4, 4M Printers	
3.75″ (95 mm)	EP Drum	Replace EP engine
$2''$ (51 mm)	Developing Roller	Replace EP engine and/or toner cartridge
$1\frac{1}{2}''$ (38 mm)	Primary Charging	Replace EP engine
$2\frac{1}{2}''$ (64 mm)	Fuser Rollers	Replace cleaning pad, clean fusing roller, replace fusing unit

Distance	Probable Cause	Suggested Action

HP LaserJet 4, 4M Printers

$2\frac{1}{8}''$ (54 mm)	Transfer Roller	Clean transfer roller and paper path

HP LaserJet 4L, 4ML, 4P, and 4MP Printers

$3''$ (76 mm)	EP Drum	Replace EP engine
$1\frac{1}{2}''$ (38 mm)	Developing Roller	Replace EP engine and/or toner cartridge
$1\frac{1}{2}''$ (38 mm)	Primary Charging	Replace EP engine
$1\frac{1}{8}''$ (48 mm)	Lower Fusing Roller	Clean fusing roller, replace fusing unit
$3''$ (76 mm)	Upper Fusing Roller	Replace cleaning pad, clean fusing roller, replace fusing unit
$1\frac{3}{4}''$ (44 mm)	Transfer Roller	Clean transfer roller and paper path
$1\frac{1}{2}''$ (38 mm)	Face Down Delivery	Clean the roller
$4\frac{3}{4}''$ (121 mm)	Feed Roller	Clean the feed roller, replace the paper feed unit

HP LaserJet 4V and 4MV Printers

$3\frac{3}{4}''$ (95 mm)	EP Drum	Replace EP engine
$2''$ (51 mm)	Developing Roller	Replace EP engine and/or toner cartridge
$1\frac{1}{2}''$ (38 mm)	Primary Charging	Replace EP engine
$2\frac{3}{8}''$ (60 mm)	Transfer Roller	Clean transfer roller and paper path

HP LaserJet 4 Plus, 4M Plus, 5, 5M, and 5N Printers

$3\frac{3}{4}''$ (95 mm)	EP Drum	Replace EP engine
$2''$ (51 mm)	Developing Roller	Replace EP engine and/or toner cartridge
$1\frac{1}{2}''$ (38 mm)	Primary Charging	Replace EP engine
$3\frac{1}{8}''$ (79 mm)	Fuser Rollers	Replace cleaning pad, clean fusing roller, replace fusing unit
$2\frac{1}{8}''$ (54 mm)	Transfer Roller	Clean transfer roller and paper path

HP LaserJet 5P, 5MP, 6P, and 6MP Printers

$3''$ (76 mm)	EP Drum	Replace EP engine

Distance	Probable Cause	Suggested Action
HP LaserJet 5P, 5MP, 6P, and 6MP Printers		
1″ (25 mm)	Developing Roller	Replace EP engine and/or toner cartridge
$1\frac{1}{2}$″ (38 mm)	Primary Charging	Replace EP engine
3″ (76 mm)	Upper Fusing Roller	Replace cleaning pad, clean fusing roller, replace fusing unit
$1\frac{3}{4}$″ (44 mm)	Transfer Roller	Clean transfer roller and paper path
$1\frac{1}{2}$″ (38 mm)	Face Down Delivery	Clean the roller
$1\frac{7}{8}$″ (48 mm)	Lower Fusing Roller	Clean fusing roller, replace fusing unit
$4\frac{11}{16}$″ (119 mm)	Registration Roller	Clean the registration roller, replace the paper feed unit
HP LaserJet 5SI/5SIMX Printers and HP LaserJet 5SI Copier		
3.71″ (94 mm)	EP Drum	Replace EP engine
$2\frac{1}{8}$″ (54 mm)	Developing Roller	Replace EP engine and/or toner cartridge
$1\frac{3}{4}$″ (44 mm)	Primary Charging	Replace EP engine
3.71″ (94 mm)	Lower Fusing Roller	Clean fusing roller, replace fusing unit
4.92″ (125 mm)	Upper Fusing Roller	Replace cleaning pad, clean fusing roller, replace fusing unit
2.30″ (58 mm)	Transfer Roller	Clean transfer roller and paper path
HP LaserJet 5L, 5L/FS, 5LXTRA, 6L, 6L/SE, and 6L/XI Printers		
$3\frac{3}{4}$″ (95 mm)	EP Drum	Replace EP engine
$1\frac{1}{4}$″ (32 mm)	Developing Roller	Replace EP engine and/or toner cartridge
$1\frac{1}{2}$″ (38 mm)	Primary Charging	Replace EP engine
$1\frac{3}{4}$″ (44 mm)	Face Down Delivery	Clean the roller
1.9″ (48 mm)	Transfer Roller	Clean transfer roller and paper path
$2\frac{1}{2}$″ (64 mm)	Lower Fusing Roller	Clean fusing roller, replace fusing unit
3″ (76 mm)	Upper Fusing Roller	Replace cleaning pad, clean fusing roller, replace fusing unit

Distance	Probable Cause	Suggested Action
	HP LaserJet 1100 and 1100A Printers	
3″ (76 mm)	EP Drum	Replace EP engine
1¼″ (32 mm)	Developing Roller	Replace EP engine and/or toner cartridge
1½″ (38 mm)	Primary Charging	Replace EP engine
1.48″ (38 mm)	Face Down Delivery	Clean the roller
1.8″ (46 mm)	Transfer Roller	Clean transfer roller and paper path
2½″ (64 mm)	Lower Fusing Roller	Clean fusing roller, replace fusing unit
3″ (76 mm)	Upper Fusing Roller	Replace cleaning pad, clean fusing roller, replace fusing unit
	HP LaserJet 4000 series Printers	
3.71″ (94 mm)	EP Drum	Replace EP engine
2″ (51 mm)	Developing Roller	Replace EP engine and/or toner cartridge
1½″ (38 mm)	Primary Charging	Replace EP engine
2½″ (64 mm)	Lower Fusing Roller	Clean fusing roller, replace fusing unit
2.93″ (74 mm)	Upper Fusing Roller	Replace cleaning pad, clean fusing roller, replace fusing unit
1.87″ (48 mm)	Transfer Roller	Clean transfer roller and paper path

NOTE: This part of the chapter presents the standard repetitive defect chart for Hewlett-Packard printers, but you can easily apply this information to your own laser printers.

■ *Check the paper*. The cut and finish of a paper may also appear as a repetitive defect. Reverse your paper in the tray, or replace the media with a standard paper type (i.e., 20-lb bond xerography-grade paper) and see if the repetitive defect continues. Factors such as moisture, weight, and chemical concentration in the paper may produce repetitive-looking lines or spots.

- *Don't ignore routine maintenance.* In many cases, repetitive defects can occur because of neglected maintenance—dirty rollers may produce marks or lines on the page. Before you assume a serious fault, always perform routine maintenance and clean the printer's rollers carefully.

- *Check the cleaning pad.* Some printer types (i.e., the HP LaserJet, LaserJet Plus, and LaserJet 500 Plus, as well as the LaserJet II, IID, III, and IIID series) use a replaceable cleaning pad to wipe residual toner from the fusing roller. If the cleaning pad is old or worn, residual toner may be transferred as the fusing roller makes additional passes, appearing similar to a repetitive defect.

   NOTE: Always allow at least 15 minutes for the fusing system to cool before attempting to check or replace the cleaning pad.

Controller (logic) symptoms

Most EP printers use an ECU consisting of two parts: a main board and a mechanical controller. The *main board* provides the core logic for the printer—CPU, memory, an interface for the control panel, the communication circuits, and other processing elements. The *mechanical controller* provides an interface between the pure logic and the electromechanical components of the printer. For example, a mechanical controller holds the driver circuitry controlling the printer's motors and solenoids. Some printers integrate these functions onto a single PC board, whereas other printer designs employ two separate boards. Although controller circuitry is generally quite reliable, it does fail from time to time, so it is important that you recognize the signs of trouble.

Symptom 4.84: Fusing temperature control is malfunctioning. You find the fusing temperature never climbs, or climbs out of control. This may affect print quality or initialization for EP printers.

> **WARNING:** *Always allow at least 15 minutes for the fusing system to cool before working in the fusing system.*

- *Check and replace the thermistor.* Unplug the printer and disconnect the temperature control thermistor at its connector. Use your multimeter to measure its resistance. A short or open circuit reading may indicate a faulty thermistor, so replace any suspect part. If you get some resistance reading, warm the thermistor with your fingers and see whether the reading changes (even a little bit). A reading that does not change at all suggests a faulty thermistor. *Never touch a hot thermistor with your fingers!*

- *Chances are that the thermistor is intact.* If this is the case, the temperature sensing/control circuitry on your mechanical controller board has probably failed. You can try replacing the mechanical controller board outright.

Symptom 4.85: The printer's LCD shows a *CPU* error. Some printer designs may show this error as a series of blinking LEDs, or a sequence of beeps. The CPU is the heart of your printer's logical operation. When you first start the laser printer the CPU and its associated core logic is tested (much like the BIOS of a computer will execute a self-test). If the CPU fails to pass all of its test requirements, an error will be generated. As you might imagine, a CPU failure is catastrophic; that is, the printer simply will not work without it.

- *Try restarting the printer.* Turn off the printer for a few minutes, then try powering it up again to see if the error clears.

- *Check the main controller.* Turn off and unplug the printer, then examine each of the connectors on the main controller. Each connector should be installed properly and completely.

■ *Replace the CPU if possible.* If problems persist, you will have to replace the CPU. Replacing the CPU can be either cheap or expensive, depending on how it is mounted. If the CPU is socket-mounted on the main controller, you can often just remove the old CPU and plug in a new one.

■ *Replace the main controller.* If the CPU is soldered to the main controller board, you will have to desolder and resolder the CPU (if you have the proper surface-mount soldering tools), or replace the entire main controller board.

Symptom 4.86: The printer's LCD shows a *ROM Checksum* error. Your particular printer may also use an error code (i.e., *ERROR 11*) to represent the condition. As in a computer, all of the printer's onboard instructions and programming are held in a ROM on the main controller board. It is the ROM that provides the internal instructions and data (the *firmware*) needed by the CPU for processing. When the printer starts, a checksum test is run on the ROM to verify the integrity of its contents. If the resulting checksum does not match the checksum reference number stored in the ROM, an error is generated.

■ *Try restarting the printer.* Turn off the printer for a few minutes, then try powering it up again to see if the error clears.

■ *Check/reseat any font or option cartridge.* Turn off the printer and check to see that any supplemental font or option cartridges are installed properly—you may try removing the cartridge(s) to find if the problem disappears. If so, you may have a defective font or option cartridge.

■ *Check/replace the printer's firmware ROM.* If there are no option cartridges, check to see that the ROM

IC is installed securely. If the problem persists, you must replace the ROM IC. In many cases, ROM ICs are socket-mounted devices since they must be programmed outside of the logic board's assembly process. When this is the case, you may be able to replace the ROM IC directly.

■ *Replace the main controller.* If the ROM IC is soldered to the main logic board (or a replacement ROM IC is simply not available), you will have to replace the entire main logic board outright.

Symptom 4.87: The printer's LCD shows a *RAM R/W* error, a *Memory* error, or other memory defect. Your particular printer may also use an error number (i.e., *ERROR 12* or *ERROR 30*) to represent the condition. Dynamic RAM (or DRAM) serves as the workspace for an EP printer. Unfortunately, trouble in any part of the DRAM can adversely affect the image, especially PostScript images. Memory is tested when the printer is first initialized. Like PCs, the more memory that is installed, the longer it takes the printer to initialize. A typical test involves writing a known byte to each address, then reading those bytes back. If the read byte matches the written byte, the address is considered good; otherwise, a RAM error is reported.

■ *Check/replace the memory modules.* You can easily isolate the fault to a bad memory module or the standard (resident) memory. Turn off and unplug the printer, then remove any expansion memory modules that may be installed (you may have to set jumpers or DIP switches to tell the printer that memory has been removed). If the problem disappears, one or more of your expansion memory modules has failed. Try reinstalling one module at a time until the problem recurs—the last module to be installed when the error surfaced is the faulty module.

■ *Replace the main controller.* If the problem persists when memory modules are removed, you can be confident that the fault is in your resident memory. Although memory modules often take the form of SIMMs or other plug-in modules, resident RAM is typically hard-soldered to the printer's main controller board. You may have no choice but to replace the main controller board outright.

Symptom 4.88: Your printer's LCD shows a *Memory Overflow* error. Your particular printer may also use an error code (i.e., *ERROR 20*) to represent the condition. When data are sent from the computer to the printer, part of that data consists of *user information* such as soft-fonts and macro commands. If the amount of user information exceeds the amount of RAM set aside for it, a *Memory Overflow* (or similar) error will be generated. Try powering the printer off for several minutes, then restart the printer and see if the error clears. While this error is not directly related to the image size or complexity, complex images typically carry a larger overhead of user information—so you may find that "simplifying" the image can sometimes clear the problem even though the image itself is not really at fault. Generally speaking, you can eliminate this error by adding memory, or reducing the amount of data that must be transferred to the printer (such as reducing the image's resolution or size—these are often functions of the application doing the printing).

Symptom 4.89: Your printer's LCD shows a *Print Overrun* error. Your particular printer may also use an error code (i.e., *ERROR 21*) to represent the condition. Unlike a *memory overflow* error, *print overrun* problems almost *always* indicate that the page to be printed is too complicated for the printer—there is just not enough memory to hold all of the data required to form the image. To overcome this type of problem, try simplifying the image (i.e., use fewer fonts or try using solid shading instead of dithering). You may also try making the printed area smaller. For example, instead of printing an image at 8″ × 8″, try printing it at 5″ × 5″. The smaller image requires less raw data. The ideal way to correct this problem over the long term is to add memory to the printer.

Symptom 4.90: The printer reports an *I/O Protocol* error. Your particular printer may also use an error code (i.e., *ERROR 22*) to represent the condition. This is a communication fault. Protocol errors among parallel port devices are rare since parallel port operation is very well defined with hardware-based handshaking designed right into the signal layout. The most common protocol problems arise with serial communication—there are many variables in the serial data frame that must be matched between the printer and computer, and even the slightest error can cause problems.

- *Check the connection.* Start by checking the connections between the computer and printer. See that the communication link is parallel-to-parallel or serial-to-serial. Also try a new, high-quality cable (serial or parallel as appropriate) between the printer and computer. Also see that the printer port is active and configured properly at the computer end.

- *Replace the main controller (parallel).* When parallel communication is being used, a protocol error suggests a failure in the *communication interface IC*. You can try replacing the communication controller IC itself, or replace the main controller board entirely.

- *Check the serial configuration.* When serial communication is being used, you should examine any DIP switches or jumpers inside the printer. Check to see that the communication speed and framing bits are all set as expected, then see that the corresponding

COM port in the PC is configured to use the same data frame.

■ *Replace the main controller (serial).* If problems persist (even when the serial communication link is configured properly), suspect trouble in the communication interface IC. You can try replacing the communication controller IC itself, or replace the main controller board entirely.

Symptom 4.91: The image is composed of "garbage" and disassociated symbols. Your printer may also generate a *Parity/Framing* error, or use an error code (i.e., *ERROR 40*) to represent the condition. This error indicates that there is a problem with serial data framing. Serial data must be *framed* with the proper number of start, data, parity, and stop bits. These bits must be set the same way at the printer *and* the computer's COM port. If either end of the communication link is set improperly, data passed from the computer to the printer will be misinterpreted (resulting in a highly distorted printout).

■ *Check the serial configuration.* Examine the printer first and note any DIP switch, jumper, or control panel settings that affect the serial data frame. Next, check the COM port settings at the computer—the COM port's start, data, parity, and stop bit configuration should all match the printer's settings. If not, adjust either the COM port parameters or the printer DIP switch settings so that both ends of the communication link are set the same way.

■ *Replace the main controller.* If problems persist, there may be a fault in the printer's communication IC. You may try replacing the IC, or you may replace the main controller board entirely.

Symptom 4.92: The image appears "stitched." *Stitching* is an image distortion where points in the image

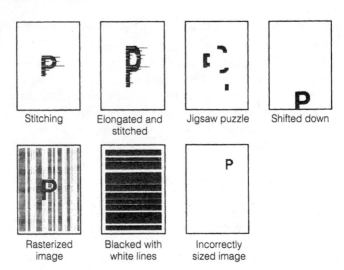

Figure 4.6 Recognizing controller board faults.

appear to have been "pulled" in the horizontal direction (typically to the right). Figure 4.6 illustrates the stitching effect, along with some manifestations of other controller errors. Images are formed by scanning a laser beam repetitively across the drum. Pixels are formed by turning the laser beam on and off while scanning (a function performed by the laser printer's mechanical controller board). If there is an intermittent fault in the mechanical controller logic, beam modulation may fail during one or more scanning passes, resulting in random "pulls" in the image.

- *Check the laser/scanner wiring.* Start by checking all of the cables between the laser/scanner assembly and the mechanical controller card. Loose wiring may result in intermittent laser fire. Turn off and unplug the printer, then try removing and reinstalling each of the connectors. Check any other wiring on the mechanical controller as well.

- *Replace the mechanical controller (or ECU).* If problems persist, chances are *very* good that the mechanical controller has failed. You may attempt to troubleshoot the mechanical controller, but it is often more efficient to simply replace the mechanical controller board outright. If the mechanical controller functions have been integrated into one ECU, replace the entire ECU board.

- *Replace the laser/scanner.* If a new mechanical controller fails to resolve the problem, replace the laser/scanner assembly.

Symptom 4.93: The image appears elongated and "stitched." This is a variation of Symptom 4.92—not only is the laser beam misfiring intermittently, but the image is being "stretched" along the page (Figure 4.6). Under most circumstances, there has been a logic failure on the mechanical controller. Before you attempt work on the controller, however, try reseating each of the connectors on the mechanical controller (be sure to turn off and unplug the printer *before* fiddling with any connectors). If problems persist, there is a serious fault in the printer's ECU. You may attempt to troubleshoot the ECU, but this type of fault can be very difficult to track down. As a result, it is often better to try replacing the mechanical controller board first. If that fails to correct the problem, try a new main logic board. If your particular printer design integrates all of the logic and controlling circuitry on a single ECU board, replace that board outright.

Symptom 4.94: Portions of the image are disassociated like a "jigsaw puzzle." Of all the controller failures, this is perhaps one of the most perplexing. You may note that some elements of the printed image are just fine, but other (larger) areas of print seem jumbled around (Figure 4.6). Even worse, the problem is often intermittent, so some printed pages may appear just fine. Under most circumstances, there has been a logic failure on the main controller board. Before you attempt work on the main controller, however, try reseating each of the connectors on the main controller and mechanical controller boards (be sure to turn off and unplug the printer *before* working with any connectors). If problems persist, there is a serious fault in the printer's ECU. You may attempt to troubleshoot the ECU, but this type of "jigsaw puzzle" operation can be very difficult to track down. As a result, it is often better to try replacing the main controller board first. If that fails to correct the problem, try a new mechanical controller board. If your particular printer design integrates all of the logic and controlling circuitry on a single ECU board, replace that board outright.

Symptom 4.95: The image appears to be shifted down very significantly. You can see this type of problem illustrated in Figure 4.6. At first glance, you might be tempted to think that this is a registration problem (which cannot be ruled out just yet), but it is also possible that a fault on the mechanical controller board is passing the page through far too soon before the developed image is aligned. Chances are that the pickup and registration mechanics are working correctly; otherwise, the page would likely lose its top margin or appear smudged. When the top margin is excessive, suspect a logic fault. Specifically, you should suspect that a logic error is firing the registration system *too soon* after a printing cycle starts. You should address this type of problem by troubleshooting or replacing the mechanical controller board outright. If the mechanical controller circuitry is integrated into a single ECU, replace the entire ECU board outright.

Symptom 4.96: The image appears "rasterized" with no intelligible information. A *rasterized* image is a complete distortion—there is rarely any discernible information in the printed page. Instead, the image is composed of broken horizontal lines such as in Figure 4.6. The trick with this type of fault is that it's *not* always easy to determine the problem's origin. Turn off and unplug the printer. Open the printer and check each cable and wiring harness at the controller board(s) and laser/scanning assembly. Try reseating each of the connectors. If the problem persists, the fault is almost certainly in the main controller board. You may be able to troubleshoot the ECU, but this type of logical troubleshooting can be extremely challenging and time consuming. It is usually easier to just replace the main controller board and retest the printer. If a new controller board fails to correct the problem, you should troubleshoot or replace the mechanical controller board. When the main controller is integrated into a single ECU, replace the ECU board outright.

Symptom 4.97: The image is blacked out with white horizontal lines. This type of problem creates a page that is blacked out except for a series of white horizontal bars (Figure 4.6), and will typically eradicate any discernible image on the page.

■ *Check all printer wiring.* Connector problems can readily cause this type of problem, so start your examination there. Turn off and unplug the printer, then check the wiring harnesses and reseat each connector on the main controller and mechanical controller boards. Be extremely careful to replace each connector carefully, and avoid bending any of the connector pins.

■ *Replace the main controller (or ECU).* If the problem continues, the fault is likely to be in the main controller board. You may be able to troubleshoot the ECU, but this type of "circuit-level" troubleshooting can be extremely challenging and time consuming—especially with these symptoms—so it is often easier to just replace the main controller board and retest the printer. If a new controller board fails to correct the problem, you should troubleshoot or replace the mechanical controller board.

Symptom 4.98: The image is incorrectly sized along the vertical axis.   Ideally, an image should be sized according the size of whatever paper tray is installed. When the image size is significantly smaller than expected (Figure 4.6), you should first check to see that the proper paper tray is installed, and that the printing application is set to use the correct paper size (especially under Windows).

- *Check paper tray sensors.* If the page setup is configured properly, you should examine the paper tray sensors inside the printer. Replace any defective tray sensor microswitches.

- *Check the printer wiring.* If problems persist, you should also inspect any wiring harnesses and connectors at the mechanical controller. Loose or defective wiring can cause erroneous page sizing.

- *Replace the mechanical controller (or ECU).* Next, you should suspect a logical problem in the mechanical controller board. You may attempt to troubleshoot the mechanical controller if you wish, or you may simply choose to replace the mechanical controller outright. If that should fail to resolve the problem, try a new main controller board.

Symptom 4.99: The printer's duplex unit is not showing up on the Configuration Page under *installed options.*   Also, when the front duplex drawer is opened, the printer's display shows an error such as *Close Front Duplex Drawer*. You find that these symptoms are not corrected by cycling the printer's power (i.e., turning it on and off), or by performing a cold reboot of the host PC. This is a common problem with high-end printers such as the HP Color LaserJet 4500 family, and is

generally due to a lack of printer memory. Some printers (such as the HP Color LaserJet 4500 series)
require a minimum of 40 MB of RAM in order to recognize the duplex unit, and to duplex some print jobs.
However, to print the internal duplex print test, at
least 64 MB of RAM must be installed. Due to the size
of the printer's internal duplex test file, the duplex
test page selection will not be available from the
printer's control panel until this additional memory is
installed.

**Symptom 4.100: You encounter a *79 Service Error* mes-
sage on the printer.** This type of problem normally
designates an electronic problem in the printer (see
Appendix A). Errors of this type can be caused by
either hardware or software faults. Try clearing the
error by turning off the printer, allowing it to cool,
then turning the printer back on. If the error persists,
check for a hardware failure.

■ *Disconnect the printer*. Turn the printer off and disconnect it from the PC or network. If the error message stops after disconnecting from the PC or network, and reappears once it is reconnected, verify
  that the print queue on the PC or print server has
  been cleared of all pending jobs.

■ *Simplify the printer*. Remove any accessories that
  have been installed on the printer (i.e., MIO cards,
  font cartridges, RAM SIMMs, ROM modules, and so
  on). If normal operation returns once an accessory
  has been removed, *that* accessory may be the cause
  of the problem.

■ *Cold reset the printer*. Power the printer on while
  holding down the *Online* button. Remember that a
  cold reset may cause a JetDirect card to lose its configuration.

■ *Replace the main controller (or ECU)*. If the problem persists, try replacing the printer's main con-

troller card. If the main controller features are integrated into a single ECU, replace the ECU board
outright.

Check the printing environment. Many *79 Error* conditions are caused by software problems. Try the following tips to help isolate potential software issues:

- Print from a different application.

- Print different documents within the same application.

- Change the graphics mode in the printer *Properties*
dialog.

- Change the resolution setting in the printer
Properties dialog.

- Select a PostScript driver instead of PCL (or vice
versa).

- Select a Microsoft generic PCL driver rather than
the manufacturer's PCL driver.

- Use a different font (if possible).

- Adjust the margin settings (if possible).

**Symptom 4.101: You encounter an *Error 53, Error 61*, or
Invalid SIMM Speed error.** You typically see this kind of
problem after installing PostScript SIMM(s) in the
laser printer. Verify that the PostScript SIMM product
number is correct for your particular laser printer.
Some printers (such as HP LaserJet models) are *very*
sensitive to SIMM types, and may malfunction if the
incorrect SIMM is installed. If you find that an incorrect SIMM type has been installed, you should remove
the SIMM in order to clear the error, then replace the
SIMM with the correct model. For HP LaserJet printers, you'd check the SIMM part numbers against the
list below:

- C2013A   HP LaserJet 4Si/4Si MX printer

- C2049A   HP LaserJet 4P/4MP printer

- C2080A   HP LaserJet 4/4M printer

- C3112A   HP Color LaserJet printer

- C3129A ABA   HP LaserJet 4 Plus/4M Plus printer

- C3159A   HP LaserJet 4V/4MV printer

- C3169A   HP LaserJet 5Si/5SiMX printer

- C3494D   HP LaserJet IIISi ROM version printer

- C3494E   HP LaserJet IIISi SIMM version printer

- C3918A   HP LaserJet 5/5N/5M printer

- C3963A   HP Color LaserJet 5/5M printer

Registration symptoms

The *registration process* involves picking up a sheet of
paper and positioning it for use. As a result, any problems in the paper tray, pickup roller, separation pad,
registration rollers, or the related drive train can
result in any one of the following problems.
Registration problems are really quite common—especially in older printers—where age and wear can
affect the rollers, gears, and critical mechanical spacing. In simple cases, you may be able to correct a registration problem with careful cleaning and a bit of
readjustment. For most situations, however, you will
need to replace a defective mechanical assembly, or a
failing electromechanical device (such as a clutch).

**Symptom 4.102: The print contains lines of print—usually
in the lower half of the page—that appear smudged.** You
can see a simple example of the problem in Figure 4.7.
This symptom is almost always the result of a problem with your registration rollers. Uneven wear can
allow the registration rollers to grip the page firmly at
one point, then loosely at another point. When the
grip tightens up, the page jerks forward just a fraction, but just enough to smudge (or blur) the print at

Figure 4.7   Recognizing pickup/registration faults.

that point. Turn off and unplug the printer, then expose the registration assembly and examine it closely. Look for any accumulations of debris or obstructions that may force the registration rollers apart at different points. Remove any obstructions and try cleaning the registration rollers. Examine the registration drive train and look for any gears that may be damaged or obstructed. Clean the drive train and replace any damaged gears. If the problem persists, you should consider replacing the registration assembly.

Symptom 4.103: There is no apparent top margin.   The image may run off the top of the page as in Figure 4.7. In just about every case, there is a fault in the pickup assembly. As a consequence, the page is not being passed to the registration assembly in time to be aligned with the leading edge of the drum image, so the image appears cut off at the page top.

- *Check the paper tray*. Make sure that the *lift mechanism* is not jammed or otherwise interfering with paper leaving the tray. If you're not sure, try a different paper tray.

- *Check the paper supply*. Consider your paper itself—unusually light or specially coated papers may simply not be picked up properly. Try a standard 20-lb bond xerography-grade paper. If problems persist at this point, chances are that your pickup assembly is failing.

- *Clean the pickup assembly*. Turn off and unplug the printer, then examine your pickup system closely. Check for any accumulations of debris or obstructions that may interfere with the pickup sequence. Remove any obstructions, then clean the pickup roller and separation pad.

- *Check/replace the pickup drive train and clutch*. Any jammed or damaged gears should be replaced. If the solenoid clutch is sticking or failing, you should replace the solenoid clutch or clutch PC board. If that fails to resolve the problem, you will have little alternative but to replace the entire pickup assembly and separation pad.

Symptom 4.104: There is pronounced smudging at the top of the image (generally near the top margin). This symptom almost always suggests that the registration assembly is failing, or has not been installed correctly (Figure 4.7). Turn off and unplug the printer, then expose the registration system. Carefully inspect the system to see that the rollers and drive drain are installed properly. Try reinstalling the registration assembly. If problems persist, try a new registration assembly.

Symptom 4.105: There is too much margin space on top of the image. When there is excessive margin space at the top of the image, it generally indicates that the paper has been picked up and started to the drum too soon—paper is traveling through the printer *before* the drum image is ready (Figure 4.7). This fault is usually related to the registration roller clutch. The registration rollers are supposed to hold the page until the drum image is aligned properly. This means that the registration rollers must be engaged or disengaged as required, typically through a clutch mechanism. If the clutch is jammed in the *engaged* position, the registration rollers will always run (passing each new page through immediately). Turn off and unplug the printer, then examine your registration clutch closely. If the clutch is jammed, try to free it and clean surrounding mechanics to remove any accumulations of debris or foreign objects. If the clutch fails to reengage or remains jammed again, replace the registration clutch entirely, or replace the clutch solenoid PC board.

Symptom 4.106: The image is "skewed" (not square with the page). *Skew* occurs when the page is passed through the printer at an angle rather than straight (Figure 4.7). Typically, paper *must* enter the printer straight because of the paper tray, so the page must shift due to a mechanical problem. In actual practice, however, a loose or bent paper guide tab can often shift the paper as it enters the printer.

■ *Check/replace the paper tray*. Start your examination by checking the paper tray, specifically the paper cassette guide tab. If the tab is loose or bent, replace it or try a new paper tray.

■ *Check the paper supply*. If the paper tray is intact, consider the paper itself—unusually light or specially coated papers can skew in the pickup and registration mechanics. If you are using an unusual paper, try some standard 20-lb xerography-grade paper.

■ *Check / replace the pickup and registration systems.*
If the problem continues, turn off and unplug the
printer, then examine the pickup and registration
mechanics. Check for obstructions, or any accumulations of foreign matter that might interfere with
the paper path and cause the page to skew. If there
is nothing conclusive, try replacing the pickup
assembly and separation pad, then the registration
assembly (in that order).

Laser/scanner symptoms

A laser beam must be *modulated* (turned on and off
corresponding to the presence or absence of a dot) and
scanned across the conditioned drum. Both modulation and scanning must take place at a fairly high
rate in order to form an image—up to 30 pages per
minute and more in some high-end models. However,
the process of writing with a laser beam is not so simple a task as you see in Figure 4.8.

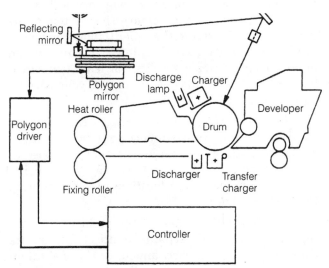

Figure 4.8 Writing with a laser beam. (*Courtesy of Tandy
Corporation*)

Changes in laser output power (often due to age), variations in polygon motor speed (also due to age and wear), and the accumulation of dust and debris on the polygon mirror and other optical components will all have an adverse impact on the final image. Faults can even creep into the laser sensor and affect beam detection and alignment. EP printer designers responded to the problems associated with these delicate assemblies by placing all of the laser, control, and scanning components into a single *laser/scanner* assembly. Today, the laser/scanner is an easily replaceable module—and that is how you should treat it.

Symptom 4.107: Right-hand text appears missing or distorted. Figure 4.9 illustrates a typical example. In many cases, this is simply a manifestation of low toner in your EP/toner cartridge.

■ *Check/redistribute the toner*. If any area of the development roller receives insufficient toner, it will result in very light or missing image areas. Turn off and unplug the printer, remove the EP/toner cartridge, and redistribute the toner (follow your manufacturer's recommendations). If you see an improvement in image quality—at least temporarily—replace the EP/toner cartridge at your earliest opportunity.

■ *Check the laser/scanner mounting*. Examine the shock mountings that support your laser/scanner assembly. If the laser/scanner assembly is loose or not mounted correctly, scan lines may not be delivered to the proper drum locations. Try remounting the laser/scanner assembly.

■ *Replace the laser/scanner*. If the problem persists, replace the writing mechanism entirely. If you are using a laser writing mechanism, pay special attention to the installation and alignment of the laser beam sensor.

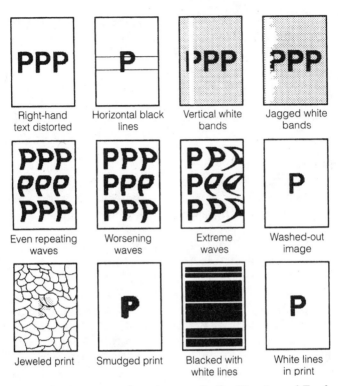

Figure 4.9 Recognizing laser/scanner faults. (*Courtesy of Tandy Corporation*)

Symptom 4.108: You encounter horizontal black lines spaced randomly through the print. Remember that black areas are the result of light striking the drum. If your printer uses a laser/scanner assembly, a defective or improperly seated beam detector could send false scan timing signals to the main logic (Figure 4.9). The laser would then make its scan line while main logic waits to send its data. At the beginning of each scan cycle, the laser beam strikes a detector. The detector carries laser light through an optical fiber to a circuit that converts light into an electronic logic signal that is compatible with the mechanical controller's logic. Circuitry interprets this *Beam Detect Signal* and knows the polygon mirror is properly aligned to begin a new scan. The mechanical controller then modulates the laser beam on and off corresponding to the presence or absence of dots in the scan line.

Positioning and alignment are critical here. If the beam detector is misaligned or loose, the printer's motor vibrations may cause the detector to occasionally miss the beam. Printer circuitry responds to this by activating the laser full duty in an effort to synchronize itself again. Reseat the laser/scanner assembly, or try reseating the beam detector and optical fiber. If the problem persists, try replacing the beam detector and cable, or replace the laser/scanner unit outright.

Symptom 4.109: Your printer's LCD reports a *polygon motor synchronization* error.   The printer may also display an error code (i.e., *ERROR 31*) to represent the condition. The polygon mirror is the heart of the laser scanning system. The motor's speed must be absolutely steady. If the motor fails to rotate, or fails to synchronize at a constant rate within a few seconds of power-up, scanning will fail. In early EP printers, the polygon motor and mirror were implemented as discrete devices. In today's EP printers, however, the laser, scanner motor, and polygon mirror are all integrated into a replaceable laser/scanner assembly. When a scanner error is reported, you should first shut down the entire printer, let it rest for several minutes, then turn it back on to see if the error clears. If the fault persists, your best course is simply to replace the laser/scanner assembly entirely.

Symptom 4.110: There are one or more vertical white bands in the image.   At first glance, this symptom may appear to be a problem with the transfer corona (Figure 4.9). However, you will notice that the white band(s) appearing here are thick and well defined (and cleaning the transfer corona will have no effect). A hard white band such as this suggests that the laser beam (or LED light) is being blocked. This is not as uncommon as you might imagine. Dust, foreign matter, and debris can accumulate on the focusing lens and obstruct the light path. It is also possible that there is a chip or scratch in the lens.

- *Check the transfer corona.* Turn off and unplug the printer. Start your examination by checking and cleaning the transfer corona—the trouble is probably *not* here, but perform a quick check just to eliminate that possibility. If the transfer corona should prove dirty, certainly retest the printer.

- *Check dust from the optics.* If the problem persists, expose the *beam-to-drum mirror* and focusing lens, and examine both closely. Look for dust, dirt, toner, paper fragments, or any other foreign matter that may have accumulated on the optics. If you find foreign matter, you should not just blow it out with compressed air—it will make a mess, and the dust will eventually resettle somewhere else. Take the nozzle of a vacuum cleaner and hold it in proximity of the optical area, then blow the optics clean with a canister of compressed air. This way, the foreign matter loosened by the compressed air will be vacuumed away rather than resettle in the printer. The key idea to remember here is: *Do not touch the optics!*

- *Clean stains from the optics.* For stains or stubborn debris, clean the afflicted optics *gently* with a high-quality lens cleaner fluid and wipes from any photography store. *Be very careful not to dislodge the "beam-to-drum" mirror or lens from its mounting.* Never blow on a lens or mirror yourself—breath vapor and particles can condense and dry on a lens to cause even more problems in the future. Allow any cleaner residue to dry completely before reassembling and retesting the printer.

- *Check/replace the laser/scanner.* If the problem should persist, suspect a problem with the laser/scanner assembly. There may be some foreign matter on the laser aperture that blocks the scanned beam as it leaves the scanner. Check the laser/scanner's beam aperture and clean away any foreign matter. If the material is inside the laser/scanner assembly, it should be replaced.

Symptom 4.111: There is a white jagged band in the image. This symptom is similar in nature to the previous symptom—foreign matter is interfering with the laser beam path. The major difference is that instead of a solid white band, you see a random jagged white band (Figure 4.9). A major difference, however, is that the obstruction is *random* (drifting in and out of the laser path unpredictably). This suggests that you are dealing with a "loose" obstruction such as a paper fragment that is able to move freely.

■ *Check the transfer corona.* Turn off and unplug the printer, then check for obstructions around the transfer corona. Although the transfer corona itself is probably not fouled, a paper fragment stuck on the monofilament line can flutter back and forth resulting in the same jagged appearance.

■ *Check the laser/scanner assembly.* Examine the optical path for any loose material that can obstruct the laser beam. Be particularly concerned with paper fragments or peeling labels. Fortunately, such obstructions are relatively easy to spot and remove. When removing an obstruction, be careful to avoid scratching or moving any of the optical components.

■ *Replace the laser/scanner assembly.* If the problem persists, you may have an obstruction inside of the laser/scanner assembly, so it should be replaced.

Symptom 4.112: There are repetitive waves in the image. You can see a simple example of this fault in Figure 4.9. All of the image elements are printed, but there is a regular "wave" in the image. This kind of distortion is typically referred to as *scanner modulation*, where scanner speed oscillates up and down just a bit during the scanning process. In virtually all cases, the fault lies in your laser/scanner assembly. Turn off and unplug the printer, then try reseating the cables and wiring harnesses connected to the laser/scanner unit. Try the printer again. If problems persist, replace the laser/scanner assembly.

Symptom 4.113: There are worsening waves in the image. This type of problem is a variation of the *scanner modulation* fault shown in the previous symptom. In this case, however, the modulation is relatively mild on the left side of the page, and gradually increases in magnitude toward the right side. These *worsening waves* can take several forms as shown in Figure 4.9, but typical manifestations can be heavy or light. Regardless of the modulation intensity, *all* of these symptoms can often be traced to a connector problem at the laser/scanner assembly. Turn off and unplug the printer, then carefully reseat each connector and wiring harness between the laser/scanner unit and the mechanical controller board. If problems persist, replace the laser/scanner assembly.

Symptom 4.114: The image appears washed out—there is little or no intelligible information in the image. Typically, you will see random dots appearing over the page, but there are not enough dots to form a coherent image. Now, you may recall that light images may suggest a problem with the high-voltage power supply or the transfer system, but in many such circumstances, some hint of an image is visible. You may also suspect the toner supply, but toner that is too low to form an image will almost always register a *low toner* error. Still, a quick check is always advisable. Remove the EP cartridge and try redistributing the toner, then try darkening the print density wheel setting. If the image improves, check the EP/toner cartridge and suspect the HVPS; otherwise, you should suspect a failure at the laser/scanner unit itself. Although solid-state lasers tend to run for long periods with little real degradation in power, an aging laser diode may produce enough energy to satisfy the laser sensor, but not nearly enough to discharge the EP drum. Try replacing the laser/scanner assembly.

Symptom 4.115: The print appears "jeweled." You can see this kind or print in Figure 4.9. This is caused when the laser beam is totally unable to synchronize with the printer—the laser sensor is failing to detect the beam. In many cases, the fiber-optic cable carrying the laser signal has been detached or broken. When the optical cable is a stand-alone component, it is a relatively easy matter to replace the cable and sensor. If the cable and sensor are integrated into the laser/scanner assembly, your best course is to reseat the cables and wiring harnesses between the laser/scanner and the mechanical controller board. If problems persist, replace the laser/scanner assembly outright.

Symptom 4.116: You see regular "smudging" in the print. When dirt, dust, and other foreign matter accumulate on the "beam-to-drum" mirror or compensating lens, they tend to block laser light at those points, resulting in vertical white bars or lines down the image. However, mild accumulations of dust or debris that may not be heavy enough to block laser light may be enough to "scatter" some of the light. This *scattered light* spreads like shrapnel, resulting in unwanted exposures (Figure 4.9). Since each point of exposure becomes dark, this often manifests itself as a "dirty" or "smudged" appearance in the print. Your best course is to clean the printer's optical deck. Turn off and unplug the printer, then expose the optical area. Place the nozzle from your vacuum cleaner in the immediate area, and blow away any dust and debris with a can of pho-

tography-grade compressed air. *Do not attempt to vacuum inside of the printer!* Just let it remove any air-
borne contaminants dislodged by the compressed air.

**Symptom 4.117: The print is blacked out with white hori-
zontal lines.** In order to modulate the laser beam to
form dots, the data must be synchronized with the position of the laser beam. This synchronization is accomplished by the *beam detector*, which is typically located
in the contemporary laser/scanner assembly. If the
detector fails to detect the laser beam, it will fire full-
duty in an attempt to reestablish synchronization.
When the beam fires, it will produce a black line across
the page (Figure 4.9). Multiple subsequent black lines
will effectively "black-out" the image. The white gaps
occur if the beam is sensed, or if a time-out/retry period
has elapsed. In most cases, the beam sensor in the
laser/scanner assembly has failed or become intermittent. Turn off and unplug the printer, then try reseating each of the cables from the laser/scanner. If the
problem persists, your best course is simply to replace
the laser/scanner assembly entirely.

**Symptom 4.118: The image forms correctly except for ran-
dom white gaps that appear horizontally across the page.**
This is another manifestation of trouble in the laser
beam detection process. A kink in the fiber-optic cable
can result in intermittent losses of laser power. In
older printers with a discrete fiber-optic cable, it was
a simple matter to replace the cable outright. Now
that beam detection is accomplished in the laser/scan-
ner assembly itself, your best course is simply to
replace the unit outright.

**Drive and transmission
symptoms**

With so much emphasis placed on the key electronic
and mechanical subassemblies of an EP printer, it can

be easy to forget that each of those mechanical assemblies is coupled together with a comprehensive drive train of motors, gears, and (sometimes) pulleys. A failure—even an intermittent one—at any point in the drive or transmission will have some serious consequences in the printed image. Figure 4.10 outlines the printer's mechanical system.

The *mechanical controller* (sometimes referred to as the *DC Controller*) starts the main motor. Once the main motor starts, a gear train will operate the *EP drum*, the *transfer* (or *feed*) *roller(s)*, and the *fusing*

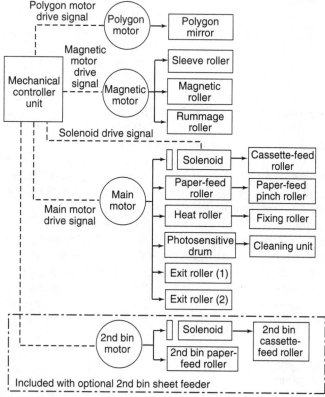

Figure 4.10   An EP mechanical system. (*Courtesy of Tandy Corporation*)

rollers. In some designs, the main motor will also operate a set of exit rollers that direct the page to an output tray. Of course, there must also be a provision to pick up and register each page, but those assemblies cannot run "full-duty"—instead, they must be switched on and off at the proper time. To accomplish this timing, a solenoid-driven *clutch* (marked *Solenoid*) is added to the pickup roller and registration roller assemblies. For the system in Figure 4.10, a separate motor (marked *Magnetic motor*) is used to drive the printer's development system.

Symptom 4.119: There are gaps and overlaps in the print. Figure 4.11 shows you an example of this symptom. The problem here is almost always due to a slipping gear or failing drive motor. Unfortunately, this is not so simple a problem to spot—gear assemblies are generally quite fine, and an intermittent gear movement can easily go unnoticed. Start with a careful inspection of the gear train. Make sure that all gears are attached and meshed securely (it is not uncommon for older gear assemblies to loosen with wear). Also check that the main motor is mounted securely and meshed properly with other gears. Be especially careful to check for obstructions or foreign matter that may be lodged in the gear train. Finally, you will need to check each gear for broken teeth—a time-consuming and tedious process, but preferable to dismantling the entire drive

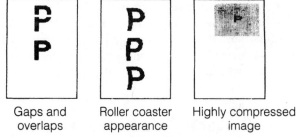

| Gaps and
overlaps | Roller coaster
appearance | Highly compressed
image |

Figure 4.11 Recognizing drive or transmission problems.

train. A high-intensity pen light will help to highlight broken gear teeth. Replace any gears that may be damaged. If the problem persists and the drive train is flawless, try replacing the main motor assembly.

Symptom 4.120: The print has a "roller-coaster" appearance. This type of roller-coaster distortion is typically the result of a fault in the gear train (Figure 4.11). Start with a careful inspection of the gear train. Make sure that all gears are attached and meshed securely (it is not uncommon for older gear assemblies to loosen with wear). Also check that the main motor is mounted securely and meshed properly with other gears. Be especially careful to check for obstructions or foreign matter that may be lodged in the gear train. Finally, you will need to check each gear for broken teeth—a time-consuming and tedious process, but preferable to dismantling the entire drive train. A high-intensity pen light will help to highlight broken gear teeth. Replace any gears that may be damaged.

Symptom 4.121: The image is highly compressed in the vertical axis. A highly compressed image can indicate a failing main motor—especially when the amount of "compression" varies randomly from page to page (Figure 4.11). Since the main motor is responsible for driving the entire system, a fault can interrupt the page transport. Check the main motor to see that it is mounted securely to the frame and meshed properly with other gears. Also check the connector and wiring harness at the main motor and mechanical controller board to be sure that everything is attached properly. If problems persist, try replacing the main motor. If that fails to correct the problem, replace the mechanical controller board.

HVPS symptoms

High voltage is the key to the electrophotographic process. Huge electrical charges must be established in order to condition the EP drum, develop a latent image, and transfer that image to a page. A high-voltage power supply (HVPS) for the classical "SX-type" engine develops −6000, +6000, and −600 volts. The newer "CX-type" engine requires far less voltage (−1000, +1000, and −400 volts). Still, high voltages impose some important demands on the power supply and its associated wiring. First, high-voltage supplies require *precise* component values that are rated for high-voltage operation. Whereas ordinary circuits might easily tolerate a "close" component value, HV supplies demand *direct replacements*. The other factor to consider is the wiring. Most commercial wire is insulated to only 600 volts or so—higher voltages can jump the inexpensive commercial insulation and arc or short-circuit, even electrocute you. So HVPS wiring harnesses and connectors are specially designed to operate safely at high voltages.

As a technician, these factors present some special problems. Replacement components are expensive and often difficult to find. Installing those components can be tedious and time-consuming. And even when things are working perfectly, you cannot measure the outputs directly without specialized test leads and equipment. When all of this is taken into account, it is almost always preferable to replace a suspect HVPS outright rather than attempt to troubleshoot it.

Symptom 4.122: Your printer's LCD displays a *high-voltage* error.   The printer may also use an error code (i.e., *ERROR 35*) to represent the condition. This indicates that one or more outputs from the HVPS are low or absent. The preferred technique is to replace the HVPS outright. Before replacing an HVPS, turn off and unplug the printer, and allow at least 15 minutes for charges in the HVPS to dissipate. When replacing the HVPS, be very careful to route any wiring *away* from logic circuitry, and pay close attention when installing new connectors. It is also important that you bolt the new HVPS securely into place—this ensures proper grounding.

Symptom 4.123: The image is visible, but the printout is darkened. You can see this type of symptom in Figure 4.12. In order for an image to be developed, the EP drum must be discharged. This can also happen if the primary corona fails to place a conditioning charge on the drum. At first, you might suspect that the −6000 volt source (or −1000 volt source for a "CX" engine) is low, but in actual practice, this type of symptom is typically the result of bad HVPS grounding. Turn off and unplug the printer, then allow at least 15 minutes for the fuser to cool and HVPS to discharge. Open the printer and inspect the mounting bolts holding the HVPS in place. Chances are that you'll find one or more grounding screws loose. Gently tighten each of the mounting/grounding hardware (you don't want to strip any of the mounting holes). Secure the printer and retest. If the problems persist, you may wish to try another supply.

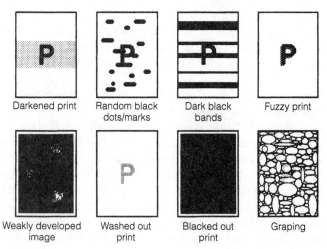

| Darkened print | Random black dots/marks | Dark black bands | Fuzzy print |

| Weakly developed image | Washed out print | Blacked out print | Graping |

Figure 4.12 Recognizing HVPS problems.

Symptom 4.124: There are random black splotches in the image. Generally, the image will appear, but it will contain a series of small black marks spaced randomly throughout the page (Figure 4.12). This type of image problem suggests that the HVPS is arcing internally (and is probably very close to failure). Turn off and unplug the printer, then allow at least 15 minutes for charges in the HVPS to dissipate. Check the high-voltage connectors and high-voltage wiring harness to the EP engine. Try reseating the connectors to check for failing contacts. If problems persist, replace the HVPS outright.

Symptom 4.125: There is "graping" in the image. The *graping effect* places small, dark, oval-shaped marks on the page, usually along one side of the page (Figure 4.12). Graping is often due to a short-circuit in the primary corona high-voltage (HV) connector—*this means your high-voltage is arcing out.* Turn off and unplug the printer, then allow at least 15 minutes for any charges in the HVPS to dissipate. Inspect the primary corona wiring, and check for any shorts along the corona, or along the high-voltage lead from the HVPS. Try reseating the HV connectors and wiring. If problems persist, replace the primary corona HV lead (if possible); otherwise, replace the HVPS.

Symptom 4.126: The image appears, but it contains heavy black bands. You can see an example of this in Figure 4.12. If the HVPS ground is loose, the image can be darkened, but if the HVPS ground is simply intermittent, portions of the image may be exposed just fine. As the grounding cuts out, however, primary voltage fails, and the lack of conditioning voltage causes a black band to form. When the ground kicks in again, the image formation resumes, and so on. Turn off and unplug the printer, and allow at least 15 minutes for the fuser to cool and the HVPS to discharge. Gently tighten or reseat each of the grounding screws holding the HVPS in place (being careful not to strip the threaded holes). Also check the high-voltage (HV) wiring harness to see that it is not crimped or shorted by other assemblies. If problems persist, replace the HVPS.

Symptom 4.127: The image appears fuzzy—letters and graphics appear "smudged" or "out of focus." This type of problem suggests a fault in the ac bias voltage (Figure 4.12). Toner is heavily attracted to the exposed EP drum. When toner jumps to the exposed drum, some toner lands in nonexposed areas near the exposed points. By using an ac developer bias, the developer voltage varies up and down. As developer voltage increases, more toner is passed to the exposed drum areas. As developer voltage decreases, toner is pulled back from the nonexposed drum areas. This action improves image contrast while cleaning up any "collateral" toner that may have landed improperly. If the ac element of your developer voltage fails, that contrast-enhancing feature will go away, resulting in fuzzy print. Since developer voltage is generated in the HVPS, try replacing the HVPS outright.

Symptom 4.128: There are weakly developed areas in the image. The image appears, but various areas of the image are unusually light (Figure 4.12). This can often be attributed to moisture in the paper. Try a supply of fresh, dry paper in the paper cassette. Also make sure that the paper does not have a specialized coating. If the problem persists, you should suspect that the HVPS is weak and nearing failure. For a symptom such as this, your best course is usually just to replace the HVPS outright. Be sure to turn off and unplug the printer, and allow at least 15 minutes for the HVPS to discharge *before* attempting a replacement.

Symptom 4.129: The image appears washed out. This type of symptom can often be the result of several causes (Figure 4.12). Before proceeding, check the print density control and try increasing the density setting. If problems continue, check your paper supply. Specialty or chemically coated papers may not transfer very well. If the problem continues, you should suspect that the transfer voltage is weak or absent, or the primary grid voltage (SX-type engines) may be failing. In either case, you should replace the HVPS. Be sure to turn off and unplug the printer, and allow at least 15 minutes for the HVPS to discharge *before* attempting replacement.

Symptom 4.130: The page is blacked out. This symptom suggests that the primary corona voltage has failed (Figure 4.12). Without a conditioning charge, the EP drum will remain completely discharged—this will attract full toner that will result in a black page. Before attempting to replace the HVPS, check the primary corona to see that it is still intact, and check the wiring between the primary corona and the HVPS. If the primary corona is damaged, replace the EP/toner cartridge and engine; otherwise, replace the HVPS. Be sure to turn off and unplug the printer, and allow at least 15 minutes for the HVPS to discharge *before* attempting replacement.

Fusing symptoms

The fusing assembly is another focal point for many printer problems. In order to "fix" toner to the page surface, a combination of heat and pressure is applied with a set of fusing rollers. The upper roller provides heat while the lower roller provides pressure. In order for the fusing assembly to work properly, there are several factors that must be in place. First, the heating roller must reach and maintain a constant temperature—that temperature must be consistent across the roller's surface. Second, pressure must be constant all the way across the two rollers, so the two rollers

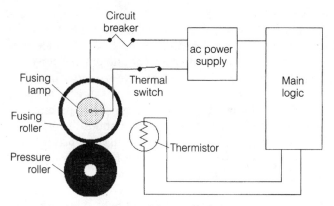

Figure 4.13   A basic diagram of the fusing system.

must be aligned properly. Third, not all melted toner will stick to the page; some will adhere to the heating roller. So there must be some provision for cleaning the heating roller. Finally, there must be a reliable method for protecting the printer from overheating.

The basic fusing unit design shown in Figure 4.13 addresses these concerns. Heat is generated by a bar heater or a long quartz lamp mounted inside of the upper fusing roller. Power to operate the heater is provided from the printer's dc power supply (typically 24 volts). A separate thermistor in the roller changes resistance versus temperature, so it acts as a temperature detector. The thermistor's resistance is measured by a circuit on the mechanical controller board that, in turn, modulates the power feeding the heater. This process "closes the loop" to achieve a stable operating temperature. If a failure should occur that allows the heater to run continuously, a thermal fuse will open and cut off voltage to the heater above a given limit. Although Figure 4.13 does not show it, the upper and lower fusing rollers are held together with torsion springs—the springs keep both rollers together with the right amount of compression, and can adjust for slight variations in paper weight and system wear.

Toner that sticks to the upper fusing roller can transfer off the roller elsewhere on the page—resulting in a "speckled" appearance—so the upper roller is coated with Teflon to reduce sticking, and a *cleaning pad* rubs any toner off the roller. You will find that temperature, alignment, and cleaning problems are some of the most frequent fusing troubles.

Symptom 4.131: The printer's LCD indicates a *Heater* error or other type of fusing temperature malfunction. Your particular printer may use an error number (i.e., *ERROR 32*) to represent the condition. Three conditions will generate a fusing malfunction error: (1) fusing roller temperature falls below about 140°C, (2) fusing roller temperature climbs above 230°C, or (3) fusing roller temperature does not reach 165°C in 90 seconds after the printer is powered up (your particular printer may utilize slightly different temperature and timing parameters).

> **NOTE**: A fusing error will often remain with a printer for 10 minutes or so after it is powered down, so be sure to allow plenty of time for the system to cool before examining the fusing system.

■ *Check the fuser connections/power*. Examine the installation of your fusing assembly and see that all wiring and connectors are tight and seated properly. The quartz heater power supply is often equipped with a fuse or circuit breaker that protects the printer (this is *not* the thermal switch shown in Figure 4.13). If this fuse or circuit breaker is open, replace the fuse or reset your circuit breaker, then retest the printer. Remember to clear the error, or allow enough time for the error to clear by itself.

■ *Replace the fuser or DC power supply*. If the fuse or breaker trips again during retest, you have a serious short circuit in your fusing assembly or power supply. You can attempt to isolate the short circuit, or simply replace your suspected assemblies—fusing assembly first, then the dc power supply.

■ *Check/replace the thermistor.* Turn off and unplug the printer, allow it to cool, and check your temperature sensing *thermistor* by measuring its resistance with a multimeter. At room temperature, the thermistor should read about 1 Kohm (depending on the particular thermistor). If the printer has been at running temperature, thermistor resistance may be much lower. If the thermistor appears open or shorted, replace it with an exact replacement part and retest the printer.

■ *Check/replace the thermal switch.* A *thermal switch* (sometimes called a *thermoprotector*) is added in series with the fusing lamp. If a thermistor or main logic failure should allow temperature to climb out of control, the thermal switch will open and break the circuit once it senses temperatures over its preset threshold. This protects the printer from severe damage—*and possibly a fire hazard.* Unplug the printer, disconnect the thermal switch from the fusing lamp circuit, and measure its continuity with a multimeter. The switch should normally be closed. If you find an open switch, it should be replaced.

■ *Check/replace the quartz lamp.* Check the quartz lamp next by measuring continuity across the bulb itself. If you read an open circuit, replace the quartz lamp (or the entire fusing assembly). Be sure to secure any disconnected wires.

■ *Replace the mechanical controller (or ECU).* If the printer *still* does not reach its desired temperature, or continuously opens the thermal switch, troubleshoot your thermistor signal conditioning circuit and the fusing lamp control signal from the mechanical controller, or replace the mechanical controller board entirely. If the mechanical controller is integrated into a single ECU, replace the entire ECU board.

Symptom 4.132: Print appears smeared or fused improperly. If fusing temperature or roller pressure is too low during the fusing operation, toner may remain in its powder form. Resulting images can be smeared or smudged with a touch. You can run the PRINTERS fusing test to check fusing quality by running a series of continuous prints. Place the first and last printout on a firm surface and rub both surfaces with your fingertips. No smearing should occur.

- *Check the fusing unit.* If your fusing level varies between pages (one page may smear while another may not), clean the thermistor temperature sensor and repeat this test (remember to wait 10 minutes or so before working on the fusing assembly). If fusing performance does not improve, *replace* the thermistor and troubleshoot its signal conditioning circuit at the mechanical controller. If smearing persists, replace the entire fusing assembly and cleaning pad.

- *Check/clear the paper path.* A foreign object in the paper path can rub against a toner powder image and smudge it before fusing. Check the paper path and remove any debris or paper fragments that may be interfering with the image.

- *Check/replace the static discharge comb.* This *comb* discharges the paper once toner has been attracted away from the EP drum, and helps paper to clear the drum without being attracted to it. An even charge is needed to discharge paper evenly; otherwise, some portions of the page may retain a local charge. As paper moves toward the fusing assembly, remaining charge forces may shift some toner resulting in an image that does not smear to the touch, but has a smeared or pulled appearance. Examine the static discharge comb once the printer is unplugged and discharged. If any of its teeth are bent or missing, replace the comb.

- *Check/replace the cleaning pad*. A *cleaning pad* rubs against the fusing roller to wipe away any accumulations of toner particles or dust. If this cleaning pad is worn out or missing, contamination on the fusing roller can be transferred to the page, resulting in smeared print. Check your cleaning pad in the fusing assembly. Worn out or missing pads should be replaced immediately.

- *Check the drive train*. Inspect your paper transport for any gears that show signs of damage or excessive wear. Slipping gears could allow the EP drum and paper to move at different speeds. This can easily cause portions of an image to appear smudged—such areas would appear bolder or darker than other portions of the image. Replace any gears that you find to be defective.

- *Replace the toner cartridge/engine*. If you do not find any defective drive train components, try replacing the toner cartridge and/or the EP engine assembly.

Symptom 4.133: There are narrow horizontal bands of smudged print.   Figure 4.14 shows you an example of this problem. Although smudging usually suggests a fusing problem, its occurrence in relatively narrow bands actually points to a problem with the paper feed—the registration or transfer rollers are not moving *evenly*, so they are jerking the paper. When the paper jerks, the toner immediately being transferred from the EP drum becomes smudged.

- *Check your paper*. Make sure that your paper is a type recommended for the printer. Unusually light or specially coated papers may slip periodically, resulting in a slight jerking motion. Try a standard 20-lb xerography-grade paper.

- *Check the registration assembly*. Either your rollers are worn (allowing loose contact at some point in

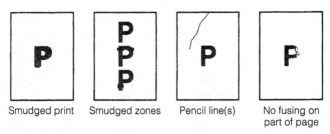

Smudged print	Smudged zones	Pencil line(s)	No fusing on part of page

Figure 4.14 Recognizing fusing system faults.

their rotation), the rollers are obstructed (effectively jamming the paper at some point in their rotation), or there is a fault in the drive train. Unfortunately, observing the paper path while the printer is running will rarely reveal subtle mechanical defects, so turn off and unplug the printer, then inspect your registration rollers for signs of wear or accumulations of foreign matter. If the registration rollers appear damaged or worn, replace the registration assembly. If there is a buildup of foreign matter, carefully clean the registration rollers.

- *Check the drive train.* If the problem persists, inspect the mechanical drive train carefully. Check each gear to see that they are meshed properly, and see if there are any broken gear teeth (a small, high-intensity pen light will make this inspection easier). Replace any gears that are worn or damaged. If there are obstructions in the gear train, clean them away carefully with a cotton swab lightly dampened in isopropyl alcohol.

- *Replace the toner cartridge/engine.* If this still fails to correct the problem, the fault is probably in the EP engine mechanics. Try replacing the toner cartridge and/or the EP engine assembly.

Symptom 4.134: There are wide horizontal areas of smudged print. You can see this type of symptom in Figure 4.14. Although this problem may sound quite similar to the previous symptom, the fault is almost always in the fusing assembly. Excessive pressure from the lower fusing roller squeezes the page so tightly that paper doesn't pass smoothly, and the print is smudged—typically across a wide area. Turn off and unplug the printer, and allow 15 minutes or so for the fusing assembly to cool. Inspect the fusing assembly carefully. If there are torsion springs holding the upper and lower fusing rollers together, you can probably reduce the tension to relieve some of the pressure. You may have to work in small increments to get the best results. Also check the lower fusing roller itself—if the roller is worn or damaged, it should be replaced. As an alternative, you can replace the entire fusing assembly outright.

Symptom 4.135: There are dark creases in the print. These are visible creases (also referred to as *pencil lines*) in the page itself, not just in the printed image (Figure 4.14). In virtually all cases, pencil lines are the result of a bloated lower fusing roller. The way in which it applies pressure on the page causes a crease in the page. First, check your paper supply. Light bond or specially coated papers may be especially susceptible to this kind of problem. Try a standard 20-lb xerography-grade paper. If the problem persists, you will need to inspect the fusing assembly. Turn off and unplug the printer, and allow 15 minutes for the fusing system to cool before opening the printer. Check the lower fusing roller for signs of bloating, excessive wear, or other damage. Try replacing the lower fusing roller; otherwise, you should replace the entire fusing assembly.

Symptom 4.136: There is little or no fusing on one side of the image. However, the other half is fused properly (Figure 4.14). This problem occurs when there is a gap in the fusing rollers. Even if the upper fusing roller is producing the correct amount of heat, it will not fuse toner without pressure from the lower fusing roller.

Gaps are often caused from physical damage to the fusing assembly, or an accumulation of foreign matter that forces the rollers apart. Turn off and unplug the printer, then wait about 15 minutes for the fusing assembly to cool. Inspect the rollers carefully. You can expect to find your problem on the side that does not fuse. For example, if the right side of the page is not fusing, the problem is likely on the right side of the fusing rollers. Check for mechanical alignment of the rollers. You may be able to restore operation by adjusting torsion spring tension. If problems continue, you should replace the entire fusing assembly.

Symptom 4.137: You encounter a *50.x Error* message on the printer. This error represents a common fusing error. The fuser is not reaching or maintaining its required temperature, and the printer will refuse to print. Try resetting the printer before attempting to replace the entire fusing unit.

- *Power down the printer*. Turn the printer off and allow 15 to 20 minutes for the system to cool and discharge.

- *Remove power devices*. If the printer is powered through a UPS or battery backup system, try plugging the printer directly into an ac outlet. You might also try another working ac circuit.

- *Cold reset the printer*. Power the printer ON while holding down the *Online* button. Remember that a "cold reset" may cause a JetDirect card to lose its configuration.

- *Check the PostScript configuration*. On some laser printers, it may be necessary for you to verify that there is only one PostScript chip installed on the printer.

- *Replace the fusing unit*. If the problem persists, one or more components of the fusing unit may have failed. Replace the entire fusing unit outright.

Corona (charge roller) symptoms

There are two high-voltage charge areas in the EP printer: the primary area and the transfer area. Classical "SX-type" engines use corona wires, so the primary area will use a *primary corona*, and the transfer area will use a *transfer corona*. The newer "CX-type" engines replace the corona wires with charge rollers, so the primary area will use a *primary charge roller*, and the transfer area will use a *transfer charge roller*. Although these areas very rarely fail, there are a suite of problems that plague the coronas. This part of the chapter shows you some of the more pervasive faults.

Symptom 4.138: Pages are completely blacked out, and may appear blotched with an undefined border. You can see an example of this problem in Figure 4.15. In many cases, the borders of the blacked out image are uneven.

■ *Check the primary corona or charge roller*. Turn off and unplug the printer, remove the EP cartridge, and examine its primary corona. Remember that a primary corona/charge roller applies an even charge across a drum surface. This charge readily repels toner, except at those points exposed to light by the writing mechanism that discharge those points and *attract* toner. A failure in the primary corona will prevent charge development on the drum. As a result, the entire drum surface will tend to attract toner (even if your writing mechanism works perfectly). This creates a totally black image. If you find a broken or fouled corona wire, clean the wire or replace the EP engine as appropriate.

■ *Check the laser/scanner assembly*. If your blacked out page shows print with sharp, clearly defined borders, your writing mechanism may be running out of control. In this case, the primary corona is probably working just fine, but a writing mechanism that is

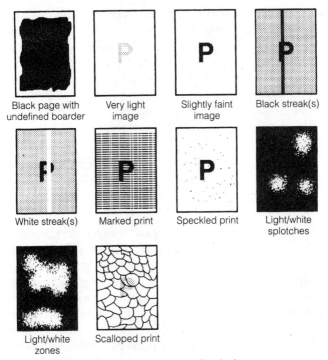

Black page with undefined boarder

Very light image

Slightly faint image

Black streak(s)

White streak(s)

Marked print

Speckled print

Light/white splotches

Light/white zones

Scalloped print

Figure 4.15 Recognizing corona/charge roller faults.

always on will effectively expose the entire drum and discharge whatever charge was applied by the primary corona. The net result of attracting toner would be the same, but whatever image is formed would probably appear crisper, more deliberate. Try replacing the laser/scanner mechanism.

■ *Replace the mechanical controller (or ECU).* If the problem persists, replace the mechanical controller board. If the mechanical controller is integrated into a single ECU board, replace the ECU outright.

Symptom 4.139: Print is very faint. You notice that the image is extremely light, even when the image density adjustment is turned up (Figure 4.15).

- *Check/replace the toner cartridge.* Turn off and unplug the printer, remove the EP cartridge, and try redistributing toner in the cartridge. Keep in mind that toner is largely organic—as such, it has only a *limited* shelf and useful life. If redistribution temporarily or partially improves the image, or if the EP cartridge has been in service for more than six months, replace the EP cartridge.

- *Check the paper.* If you are using a paper with a moisture content, finish, or conductivity that is not acceptable to your particular printer, image formation may not take place properly. Try a standard 20-lb xerography-grade paper.

- *Check your transfer corona or transfer charge roller.* The transfer corona applies a charge to paper that pulls toner off the drum. A weak transfer corona or charge roller may not apply enough charge to attract all the toner in a drum image. This can result in very faint images. Turn off and unplug the printer, allow ample time for the high-voltage power supply to discharge completely, then inspect all wiring and connections at the transfer corona. If the monofilament line encircling the transfer corona is damaged, replace the transfer corona assembly, or attempt to rethread the monofilament line. If faint images persist, repair or replace the high-voltage power supply assembly.

- *Check/replace the EP engine.* Finally, check the drum ground contacts to be sure that they are secure. Dirty or damaged ground contacts will not readily allow exposed drum areas to discharge. As a result, very little toner will be attracted and only faint images will result. If the problem persists, replace the EP engine.

Symptom 4.140: Print is just slightly faint. Print that is only *slightly* faint does not necessarily suggest a serious problem. There are several simple checks that can narrow down the problem (Figure 4.15).

- *Check the print density control dial.* Turn the dial to a lower setting to increase contrast (or whatever darker setting there is for your particular printer).

- *Check your paper supply next.* Unusual or specially coated paper may cause fused toner images to appear faint. If you are unsure about the paper currently in the printer, insert a good-quality, standard-weight xerographic paper and test the printer again.

- *Check your toner level.* Unplug the printer, remove the toner cartridge, and redistribute toner. Follow all manufacturer's recommendations when it comes to redistributing toner. The toner supply may just be slightly low at the developing roller. If this fixes the problem, it may be time to install fresh toner.

- *Check the transfer corona / roller.* Dust particles in the air are attracted to the transfer corona and accumulate there. This eventually causes a layer of debris to form on the wire. This cuts down on transfer corona effectiveness and reduces the charge to your paper. Less toner is pulled from the drum, so the resulting image appears fainter. Turn off and unplug the printer, allow ample time for the high-voltage power supply to discharge, then gently clean the transfer corona with a clean cotton swab or corona cleaning tool (be very careful *not* to break the monofilament line wrapped about the transfer corona assembly). If this line does break, the transfer corona assembly will have to be rewrapped or replaced.

- *Check the EP engine sensitivity.* Unplug your printer and examine the EP cartridge sensitivity switch settings. These microswitches are actuated by molded tabs attached to your EP cartridge. This tab configuration represents the relative sensitivity of the drum. Main controller logic uses this code to set the power level of its writing mechanism to ensure optimum print quality. These switches also tell main logic whether an EP engine is installed at all. If one of these tabs is broken, or if a switch has failed, the drum may not be receiving enough light energy to achieve proper contrast. Check your sensitivity switches, or try another EP engine.

■ *Replace the HVPS.* If the problem persists, your high-voltage power supply is probably failing. Replace your high-voltage power supply.

Symptom 4.141: There are one or more vertical black streaks in the print.   Black streaks may range from narrow lines to wide bands, depending on the severity of the problem (Figure 4.15). In most cases, this fault is due to foreign matter accumulating on the primary corona. Foreign matter will prevent charges from forming on the drum. In turn, this will invariably attract toner that creates black streaks. Typically, the edges of these streaks are fuzzy and ill-defined. Your best course is simply to clean the primary corona— most printers enclose a cleaning tool for just this purpose. The process takes no more than a minute. If the problem should persist, replace the EP engine.

Symptom 4.142: There are one or more vertical white streaks in the print.   Either toner is not reaching the drum during the development process, or it's not being transferred to the page (Figure 4.15).

■ *Check your toner level.* Toner may be distributed unevenly along the cartridge's length. Turn off and unplug the printer, remove the toner cartridge, and redistribute the toner (follow your manufacturer's recommendations when handling the toner cartridge). If this improves your print quality (at least temporarily), replace the nearly exhausted toner cartridge.

■ *Check the transfer corona / roller.* Examine your transfer corona for areas of blockage or extreme contamination. Such faults would prevent the transfer corona from generating an even charge along its length—corrosion acts as an insulator, which reduces the corona's electric field. Uncharged page areas will not attract toner from the drum, so those page areas will remain white. Clean the transfer corona *very* carefully with a clean cotton swab. If your printer comes with a corona cleaning tool, use that instead. When cleaning, be sure to avoid the monofilament line wrapped around the transfer corona assembly. If the line breaks, it will have to be rewrapped, or the entire transfer corona assembly will have to be replaced.

■ *Check / clean the laser optics.* Check the optical assembly for any accumulation of dust or debris that could block out sections of light. Since EP drums are only scanned as fine horizontal lines, it would take little more than a fragment of debris to block light through a focusing lens. Gently blow off any dust or debris with a can of high-quality, optical-grade compressed air available from any photography store. For stains or stubborn debris, clean the afflicted lens *gently* with a high-quality lens cleaner and wipes from any photography store. *Be very careful not to dislodge the lens from its mounting and never blow on a lens or laser / scanner aperture yourself*—breath vapor and particles can condense and dry on a lens to cause even more problems in the future.

Symptom 4.143: The print appears "scalloped." You can see an example of the *scalloping effect* in Figure 4.15, characterized by a unique and unmistakable appearance, and almost always an indication that the primary corona has broken. The image that forms is then expressly the result of random discharge from the drum's erase lamps. In many cases, the failure of a primary corona will simply blacken the page. In some circumstances, however, the erase lamps will leave a latent image which will be developed into the scalloped pattern. You should immediately suspect a failure in the primary corona. Your best course is simply to replace the primary corona by exchanging the EP engine.

Symptom 4.144: The print contains columns of horizontal "tick" marks. An image appears as expected, but it is marked vertical swatches of small horizontal ticks (Figure 4.15). Experience has demonstrated that this type of symptom is frequently due to a short-circuited transfer corona. Turn off and unplug the printer, then allow at least 15 minutes for the printer to cool and the HVPS to discharge. Inspect the transfer corona carefully, as well as any wiring at the corona. Gently clear away any foreign material (especially conductive material) from the transfer area, and try the printer again. If the problem persists, try replacing the transfer corona assembly.

Symptom 4.145: Print appears speckled. In almost all cases, speckled print is the result of a fault in your primary corona grid (Figure 4.15). A *grid* is essentially a fine wire mesh between the primary corona and drum surface. A constant voltage applied across the grid serves to regulate the charge applied to the drum to establish a more consistent charge distribution. Grid failure will allow much higher charge levels to be applied unevenly. A higher conditioning charge may not be discharged sufficiently by the writing mechanism—toner may not be attracted to the drum even though the writing is working as expected. This results in a very light image (almost absent except for some light speckles across the page). Since the primary grid assembly is usually part of the EP engine, replace the EP engine (and toner cartridge if necessary) and retest the printer. If speckled print persists, you should suspect a fault in the HVPS.

> **NOTE**: Since the newer "CX" type EP engines do not use coronas or grids, you'll mainly find this kind of symptom in laser printers using the older "SX" type engines.

Symptom 4.146: There are light/white splotches in the image. When you see a symptom such as this (Figure 4.15), your first suspicion should be moisture in the paper supply, a common occurrence in humid summer months. When the paper becomes damp (even just from the air's humidity), charges do not distribute properly across the page. As a result, paper will not charge in the damp areas, so toner is not attracted from the drum. Damp areas then remain very light or white. Paper that is unusually treated or chemically coated can have similar problems. In virtually all cases, a supply of fresh, dry, 20-lb xerography-grade paper should correct the problem. To correct the problem over the long term, consider adding a dehumidifier or air conditioner in the work area to keep paper dry.

Symptom 4.147: There are light/white zones spread through the image. At first glance, you may think that this symptom is similar to the previous one. In practice, however, random white zones in the printed page are much larger and more distinct than simple light splotches—in effect, the white areas have just disappeared. This symptom is indigenous to the newer "CX"-type EP engine, which uses charge rollers rather than coronas. In most cases, you will find that the transfer charge roller has failed or is missing. Even without a working transfer corona, the CX engine can transfer portions of the latent image to the page, but you can see from Figure 4.15 that the transfer is very unstable. Check and replace the transfer charge roller, or replace the EP engine outright.

Other laser printer symptoms

This chapter has focused on problems that plague key areas of an EP printer. However, there are some symptoms that cannot easily be associated with one particular area of focus within the printer. As a consequence, these problems can be particularly difficult to track down and correct. This part of the chapter illustrates some of the printer's miscellaneous problems.

Symptom 4.148: Your printer never leaves its warm-up mode.

You see a continuous *WARMING UP* status code. EP printers must perform two important tasks during initialization. First, a self-test is performed to check the printer's logic circuits and electromechanical components. This usually takes no more than 10 seconds from the time power is first applied. Second, its fusing rollers must warm up to a working temperature. Fusing temperature is typically acceptable within 90 seconds from a cold start. At that point, the printer will establish communication with the host computer and stand by to accept data, so its *WARMING UP* code should change to an *ON-LINE* or *READY* code.

- *Check the printer's communication.* When the printer fails to go online, it may be the result of a faulty communication interface, or a control panel problem. Turn the printer off, disconnect its communication cable, and restore power. If the printer finally becomes ready *without* its communication cable, check the cable itself and its connection at the computer. You may have plugged a parallel printer into the computer's serial port, or vice versa. There may be a faulty communication interface in your host computer.

- *Check the control panel*. If the printer still fails to become ready, unplug the printer and check that the control panel cables or interconnecting wiring is attached properly. Check the control panel to see that it is operating correctly.

- *Check or replace the interface/formatter (or main controller)*. Also check the control panel *interface circuit* (a.k.a. the *interface/formatter*). Repair or replace your faulty control panel or interface/formatter circuit. Depending on the complexity of your particular printer, the interface/formatter may be a separate printed circuit plugged into the main logic board, or its functions may be incorporated right into the main logic board itself.

Symptom 4.149: You receive a *PAPER OUT* message. When the printer generates a *PAPER OUT* message, it means that either paper is exhausted, or the paper tray has been removed. When a paper tray is inserted, a series of metal or plastic tabs make contact with a set of microswitches. The presence or absence of tabs will form a code that is unique to that particular paper size. Microswitches are activated by the presence or tabs. Main logic interprets this paper type code, and knows automatically what kind of media (paper, envelopes, etc.) that it is working with. This allows the printer to automatically scale the image according to paper size.

The presence of paper is detected by a mechanical sensing lever. When paper is available, a lever rests on the paper. A metal or plastic shaft links this lever to a thin plastic flag. While paper is available, this flag is clear of the "paper out" sensor. If the tray becomes empty, this lever falls through a slot in the tray which rotates its flag into the *paper out* sensor. This indicates that paper is exhausted. The *paper out* sensor is usually mounted on an auxiliary PC board (known as the *paper control* board), and its signal is typically interpreted by the mechanical controller board.

- *Check the paper tray*. Remove the paper tray. Be sure that there is paper in the tray, and that any ID tabs are intact (especially if you have just recently dropped the tray). Reinsert the filled paper tray carefully and completely. If the *PAPER OUT* message continues, then there is either a problem with your paper ID microswitches, paper sensing lever, or the "paper out" optoisolator.

- *Check the paper ID switches*. You can check the paper ID microswitches by removing the paper tray and actuating the paper sensing lever by hand (so the printer thinks that paper is available). Actuate each switch in turn using the eraser of pencil. Actuate one switch at a time and observe the printer's display—the *PAPER OUT* error should go away whenever at least one microswitch is pressed. If the error remains when a switch is pressed, that switch is probably defective. Replace any defective switch.

- *Replace the main controller (or ECU)*. If the paper ID switches work electrically, but the printer does not register them, troubleshoot or replace the main controller board.

- *Check the "paper out" lever and sensor*. When paper is available, the "paper out" lever should move its plastic flag clear of the sensor. When paper is empty, the lever should place its flag into the optoisolator slot (this logic may be reversed depending on the particular logic of the printer). This check confirms that the paper sensing arm works properly. If you see the lever mechanism jammed or bent, repair or replace the mechanism. Check the "paper out" optoisolator, and replace the sensor if it appears defective.

- *Replace the mechanical controller (or ECU)*. If the

sensors appear operational, replace the mechanical controller board.

Symptom 4.150: You see a *PRINTER OPEN* message. Printers can be opened in order to perform routine cleaning and EP cartridge replacement. The cover(s) used to access your printer are usually interlocked with the laser/scanner and high voltage power supply (HVPS) to prevent possible injury from laser light or high-voltages while the printer is opened.

■ *Check the printer cover(s).* Make sure that covers are all shut securely (try opening and reclosing each cover). Inspect any actuating levers or pushrods carefully under each cover. Replace any bent, broken, or missing mechanical levers. Unplug the printer and observe how each interlock is actuated (it may be necessary to disassemble other covers to observe interlock operation). Adjust the pushrods or switch positions if necessary to ensure firm contact.

■ *Check the interlock switch(es).* Turn off and unplug the printer, then use your multimeter to measure continuity across any questionable interlock switches. Actuate the switch by hand to be sure that it works properly. Replace any defective interlock switch, reattach all connectors and interconnecting wiring, and retest the printer.

■ *Replace the mechanical controller (or ECU).* If the interlock mechanisms are behaving as expected but a *PRINTER OPEN* message remains, replace the mechanical controller outright. If the mechanical controller is integrated into a single ECU, replace the ECU board.

Symptom 4.151: You see a *NO EP CARTRIDGE* message. An electrophotographic engine assembly uses several tabs (called *sensitivity tabs*) to register its presence, as well as inform the printer about the drum's relative sensitivity level. The ECU regulates the output power of its laser/scanner mechanism based on these tab arrangements (i.e., high-power, medium-power, low-power, or no-power—NO Cartridge). Sensitivity tabs are used to actuate microswitches located on a secondary PC board. The sequence of switch contacts forms a *sensitivity* code that is interpreted by the mechanical controller.

■ *Check the EP engine.* Make sure that the EP engine is in place and seated properly. Check to be sure that at least one sensitivity tab is actuating a sensor switch. If there are no tabs on the EP engine, replace it with a new or correct-model EP engine having at least one tab. Retest the printer.

■ *Check the sensitivity switches.* If the *NO EP CARTRIDGE* error persists, check all sensitivity switches in the printer. Turn off and unplug the printer, then use your multimeter to measure continuity across each sensitivity switch. Actuate each switch by hand and see that each one works properly. Replace any microswitch that appears defective or intermittent.

■ *Replace the mechanical controller (or ECU).* If the sensitivity switches are working properly, troubleshoot or replace the mechanical controller board or replace it outright.

Symptom 4.152: You encounter an error such as *54.2 Carousel Error* when installing color toner cartridges. This is a very common problem during initial printer setup, or when replacing exhausted toner. In almost all cases, the problem is caused by incorrect installation of one or more toner cartridges. Inserting a cartridge too vigorously can damage the shutter mechanism. Cartridges should be installed using light pressure to ease them into position. Verify that the arrows on the toner cartridge and the printer match when inserting the cartridges. Misalignment during insertion can damage the toner cartridge. Use the following steps to check and reseat the cartridge(s):

- Turn the printer off and open its main access door.

- Locate the toner access door and open it.

- Manually rotate the carousel until it is possible to unlock a toner cartridge and remove it.

- Locate the carousel release lever inside the toner cartridge compartment, then reach into the toner cartridge compartment and release the carousel so that it may be rotated freely.

- Rotate the carousel to the next toner cartridge.

- Unlock the cartridge and remove it.

- Repeat this process until all the cartridges are removed.

- Make sure the shutter on each cartridge is fully functional and not broken. The pivot arm that connects the shutter to the cartridge can become disengaged. If this happens, snap the arm back in place. If you find a cartridge with a broken shutter, the cartridge will have to be replaced.

- When all cartridges appear to be in working order, power on the printer and follow the prompts to reinsert the toner cartridges.

Symptom 4.153: You see a *TONER LOW* message constantly, or the error never appears. A toner sensor is located within the EP/toner cartridge itself. Functionally, the sensor is little more than an antenna receiving a signal from the high-voltage ac developer bias. When toner is plentiful, much of the electromagnetic field generated by the presence of high-voltage ac is blocked. As a result, the toner sensor generates only a small signal. Main logic would interpret this low signal as a satisfactory toner supply. As toner volume decreases, more high-voltage energy is picked up by the toner sensor, in turn developing a higher voltage signal. When toner is *too* low, the signal becomes strong enough to trigger a *TONER LOW* warning.

■ *Check the EP/toner cartridge*. Turn off and unplug the printer, then gently shake the cartridge to redistribute the toner supply, or insert a fresh EP/toner cartridge (refer to the user's manual for your particular printer to find the recommended procedure for redistributing toner). Retest the printer.

■ *Replace the mechanical controller (or ECU)*. If the problem persists, there may be a fault in the mechanical controller board's detection circuit. Replace the mechanical controller outright.

Symptom 4.154: Your printer's LCD displays a *fan motor* error or similar fault.   The printer may also use an error code (i.e., *ERROR 34*) to represent the condition. The typical EP printer uses two fans: a high-voltage cooling fan, and an ozone venting fan. In most cases, the ozone venting fan runs offline and is not detected by the printer. The power supply cooling fan, however, is vital for the supply's reliability—if the cooling fan fails, the power supply will quickly overheat and fail. To prevent this from happening, the fan's operation is often monitored. If the fan quits, an error will be produced. In most cases, the fan is simply defective and should be replaced. Check the voltage available at the fan. If fan voltage is available (but the fan does not spin), the fan is defective and should be replaced. If fan voltage is missing, you will need to work back into the printer to find where fan power was lost—check any loose wiring or connectors. In a few cases, the mechanical controller (or ECU) is defective and should be replaced.

Symptom 4.155: There is ghosting in the image.   The expected image prints normally, but upon inspection,

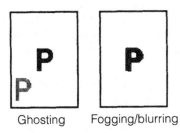

Ghosting   Fogging/blurring

Figure 4.16 Recognizing miscellaneous faults.

you can see faint traces of previous image portions as shown in Figure 4.16. This is a case of poor house-keeping—ordinarily, a cleaning blade should scrape away any residual toner remaining on the EP drum prior to erasing and conditioning. If the cleaning blade is worn out, or the scrap toner reservoir is full, cleaning may not take place as expected, and resid-ual toner will remain on the EP drum for one or more subsequent rotations. If the residual toner comes off on another rotation, it will often appear as the "ghost" of a previous image. Unfortunately, the only way to really correct this problem is to replace the toner cartridge, or the entire EP engine. Cleaning blades are hardly replaceable parts, and if the scrap toner bin is full, there is no way to recycle the toner back into the reservoir. Turn off and unplug the printer, replace the EP engine, and try the printer again.

Symptom 4.156: The print appears fogged or blurred. This may appear somewhat like smudging in previous symptoms, but where smudging was generally limited in other symptoms, it occurs throughout the page here (Figure 4.16). This is a situation where you should examine the paper transfer guide—the passage between the static discharge comb (the transfer area) and the fusing assembly. Most transfer guides are coated with Teflon or similar material to reduce static. Over time and use, the antistatic coating can wear off revealing the static-prone plastic below the coating. If the plastic of the transfer guide causes a static charge, it may be strong enough to "drag" the toner image just slightly, resulting in a blurred of fogged image. If you find wear in the transfer guide, replace the transfer guide assembly.

Symptom 4.157: Nothing happens when power is turned on. You should hear the printer respond as soon as power is turned on. You should see a power indicator on the control panel (alphanumeric displays will typically read *self-test*). You should also hear and feel the printer's cooling fan(s) in operation.

- *Check the AC power.* If the printer remains dead, there is probably trouble with the ac power. Check the ac line cord for proper connection with the printer and wall outlet. Try the printer in a known-good ac outlet. Also check the printer's main ac fuse. When the ac and fuse check properly, there is probably a problem with the printer's power supply.

- *Check/replace the DC power supply.* If the printer's fan(s) and power indicator operate, you can be confident that the printer is receiving power. If the control panel remains blank, there may be a problem with the dc power supply. You may troubleshoot or replace the dc power supply at your discretion.

- *Replace the ECU and control panel.* When the power supply checks properly, the trouble is likely somewhere in the ECU or control panel assembly itself. Remove power from the printer and check the control panel cable. If there are no indicators at all on the control panel, replace the control panel cable. If problems remain, try replacing the ECU. When only one or a few indicators appear on the control panel, try replacing the control panel cable. If problems remain, replace the control panel.

Symptom 4.158: The color laser printer prints only on letter, A4, and executive size media. You find that you cannot print on legal, tabloid (11″ × 17″), or A3 sizes of media. This kind of limit is common for HP Color LaserJet printers (i.e., the 5/5M). The limitations for printing multiple colors on media sizes larger than letter, A4, or executive size paper is due to the circumference of the print drum. Since the entire image must be placed on the drum *before* transferring it to the media, the drum size restricts the size of the image which can be formatted on the drum. There is no workaround for this problem except to reformat the image to an acceptable media size.

Symptom 4.159: The printed text is garbled when using "enhanced" printing under PCL XL or PCL6. This kind of error normally occurs when the printer misses (or misinterprets) part or all of the document's PCL header code. Check the printer cable and verify that it's correct for your printer, and under 6′ in length. Cancel the print job, then try sending it again. If the same error occurs, clear the print job again and resend it using the Standard (PCL) printer driver rather than the PCL XL driver.

> **NOTE**: If PCL code was added to a PCL XL (a.k.a. *enhanced*) print job, the result will be garbled text since PCL code and PCL XL code are *not* compatible with each other.

Symptom 4.160: Toner from a document sticks to the clear plastic surface of a binder. When a document is placed into a plastic binder, toner particles from documents that come directly into contact with the surface of the binder will adhere to the binder covers. The plastic (vinyl) that the binder is manufactured from contains "plasticizers" to aid in flexibility. These substances are volatile and tend to evaporate and migrate over time. They also act as a solvent when in contact with toner on a document. The toner particles are softened and become sticky. When the document comes into contact with the binder cover, a portion of the soft toner particles tend to stick to it. Simply place a blank sheet of paper between the printed page and the cover of the binder. This will drastically reduce or eliminate toner adhesion because it allows air space between the document and the binder cover, dispersing the "plasticizers" before they are allowed to come into contact with the document.

Symptom 4.161: Print is terribly garbled. PJL commands may appear on the page, PostScript commands may appear instead of the document, the text may be distorted or garbled, or you may find that printer time-outs are occurring. In most cases, the problem is due to an incorrect LPT.VXD file (v4.00.950). An updated LPT.VXD (v 4.00.503) file is on the Windows 95 installation CD-ROM that corrects this problem.

> **NOTE**: Before proceeding, determine whether the printer can print a test page correctly, then print directly from a DOS prompt outside of Windows 95. If *both* the test page and the DOS printout are correct, proceed with a fix within Windows 95. If the test prints are incorrect, troubleshoot as a hardware or communications issue.

Check the Windows 95 setting. If both the DOS printout and the demo page print correctly, try changing the following settings in Windows 95 before proceeding with the solution in the rest of this document:

- Click *Start*, select *Settings*, and then click *Printers*.

- Highlight the printer you want to use. Click *File* and select *Properties*.

- Select the *Details* tab and select the *Spool Settings* button.

- Verify that the *Spool Data Format* is set to *RAW* and select *OK*.

- Select the *Port Settings* button and "deselect" both *Spool MS-DOS print jobs* and *Check Port State before printing*, then select *OK*.

- Close the *Printers* dialog and try printing again.

Identify the LPT.VXD file. To identify the current version of the LPT.VXD file in use on the system, perform the following steps:

- Click *Start*, select *Find*, then click *Files or Folders*.

- In the *Named* entry, type `lpt.vxd`.

- Select *Find Now*.

- Once the file is located, right-click the filename and select *Properties*.

- Select the *Version* tab and write down the version number.

Install the updated LPT.VXD file. To install the updated file, follow the procedures below:

- Select *Start*, *Programs*, and then *Windows Explorer*. Near the top of this window, select *View* and *Options*. Select *Show All Files*, then click *OK*.

- On the left side of this window, click the "+" sign next to the C: drive—this will show any folders under the C: drive.

- Find the `Windows` folder under the C: drive and click the "+" next to it. Find the `System` folder and double-click it. On the right side of this window under *Contents of System*, find the LPT.VXD file and highlight it. At the top of the window, select *File* and then *Rename*, then rename the file to LPT.OLD.

- Next, insert the Windows 95 installation CD, then select your CD-ROM drive on the left side of this screen (usually the D: drive).

- Click the "+" sign to the left of the CD-ROM drive— this will show the folders beneath it.

- Scroll down until you come to the folder entitled *Drivers* and click the "+" sign.

- This will show the folders in this path. Scroll down until you come to `Printer` folder and click the "+" sign near it—this will show even more folders.

   NOTE: If you're using the Windows 95 OSR2 installation CD, the path to the LPT.VXD file will be `Drivers\Printr\LPT`.

- Scroll down until you come to the `LPT` folder and double-click it—this will bring up all the LPT files on the right under *Contents of LPT*. Find the LPT.VXD file and highlight it. At the top of this window, click *Edit* and then *Copy*.

- On the left side of this window, once again click the "+" sign next to the C: drive—this will bring up folders on the C: drive.

- Find the `Windows\System` folder once again and double-click it. At the top of this window, select *File* and then *Paste*. This will paste a copy of the LPT.VXD file from the CD-ROM to your `\Windows\System` directory.

- Close Windows Explorer, exit Windows 95, and reboot the system.

   NOTE: The LPT.VXD file is not located on the Windows 95 installation diskettes. If you are using diskettes, you must download the latest LPT.VXD file from Microsoft's Web site—the file can be located by searching on LPT.VXD and selecting the appropriate Service Pack.

Check the printer port configuration.   If the new LPT.VXD file does not solve the problem, check to see if the PC is configured for an ECP printer port (go to *Printers*, *Properties*, and *Details*; check the line *Print to the following port*). If it is an ECP port, reconfigure the port to *standard* or *bidirectional*.

Symptom 4.162: An extra page with a "diamond" in the upper left corner is printed after every print job. This is a known issue with PostScript printers like the HP Color LaserJet 8500 family, and is caused when the printer mistakes the end-of-job character (a "diamond" symbol) as an ASCII character, and then attempts to print it. You can usually correct this type of problem by changing the printer's "personality" setting from the printer's control panel. For the HP 8500 family:

- Press either side of the *Menu* key until *Configuration Menu* is displayed.

- Press the right end of the *Item* key until *PERSONALITY = AUTO*.

- Press the right end of the *Value* key until *PERSONALITY = PS*.

- Press the *Select* key to save the setting.

- Press *Go* to return the printer to a *READY* state.

Symptom 4.163: An error appears on the printer's control panel when trying to print an Adobe Acrobat (.PDF) document. You may see errors such as *49 FF02* or other numerical errors. This kind of trouble is most common with HP Color LaserJet printers (such as the HP 4500 family), and is almost always caused by an inappropriate PostScript driver. You should switch to another driver (i.e., a PCL 6 driver), or adjust the PostScript driver to Level 1 in the PostScript options dialog. You might also try downloading and installing the latest PostScript driver for the printer.

Symptom 4.164: You receive an error message such as *Control Panel cannot perform the current operation because <filename> is not a valid printer driver file.* This almost always happens when an HP LaserJet printer is installed when an Okidata printer (i.e., the OL600e) had been previously installed on the system. The

Okidata software will not allow any other printer to be installed off of the Windows (or Windows for Workgroups diskettes). Also, once the Okidata software is installed, it will not allow any other devices to access the parallel port, including some laser printers. You must remove all traces of the previous printer's software and support utilities. In some cases, you may even need to edit the Registry to remove traces of the printer software.

Symptom 4.165: You find that images containing gradients of color (and/or pattern fills) print incorrectly or very slowly.   This may happen with particular applications and drivers (i.e., Publisher 97 using a PCL level 5 or 6 printer driver), and is almost always due to the printer's configuration under that application. There are several workarounds depending on the type of printer (or emulation) that you're faced with:

HP LaserJet 5L and 6L PCL driver

- In the printing application, select *File* and *Printer Setup*.

- Select *Properties*.

- Select *Print Quality* and *Manual Settings*.

- Select *Settings* and locate the *Graphics Mode* area.

- Select *Raster* and locate the *Text Mode* area.

- Select *True Type as Graphics*.

- Click *OK* and select *OK* again to close the *Print Quality* window, then try printing again.

  NOTE: As an alternative, load the host-based driver and try printing the document again.

HP LaserJet 6P/6MP printers

- In the printing application select *File* and *Printer Setup*.

- Select *Properties*.

- Select *Print Quality* and locate the *Graphics Mode* area.

- Select *Raster* and locate the *Text Mode* area.

- Select *True Type as Graphics*.

- Click *OK* and select *OK* again to close the *Print Quality* window, then try printing again.

Tips for other printers

- If your printer is capable of understanding PostScript, try printing with a Microsoft or HP PostScript driver.

- Paste the object as a picture from *within* the printing application.

- Try the Microsoft DeskJet 500 driver in Windows 95 (margins and text will need to be adjusted).

- Remove any items with color gradients or pattern fills from the document.

Application-related symptoms

Symptom 4.166: When printing through Microsoft Word, much of the italic fonts print with the tops and bottoms clipped. This is a printer driver problem that often occurs with Word 7 and printers and some Hewlett-Packard printers (such as the LaserJet 5 and 5M). You may see this kind of problem especially when printing multiple copies of a document. In most cases, updating to the very latest printer driver will correct this kind of problem, but you can usually work around this problem by changing the printer driver as shown below:

- Close the application (i.e., MS Word).

- In the printer driver, select the desired number of copies.

- Set another PCL driver (i.e., CLJ 5/5M) as the default driver.

- Close the *Print* dialog.

- Reopen the printing application.

- Open the desired document, click *File*, then select *Print*.

- In the *Print* dialog, the copies should automatically show up as the number selected in the driver.

- Print the document normally.

Symptom 4.167: Paper tray selections do not take effect.
You find that paper source and other settings made under an application's *File, Page Setup* dialog do *not* take effect when you attempt to print. This occurs because the printing application (i.e., Microsoft Word) does not take precedence over the settings made in the printer's PCL driver *Properties* dialog. Tray and other printer selections *must* be made in the printer's *Properties* dialog in order for them to take effect in Windows 95/98 (or under the Document Defaults section in Windows NT 4.0). Exit the application, open the printer's *Properties* dialog, and make your selections there. Reboot Windows 95/98 if necessary, then reopen your document and try printing again.

Symptom 4.168: You cannot print objects under Access 7.0.
You may see an error message such as *Microsoft Access cannot print object...Please make sure that your default printer is selected*. This often occurs with printers such as the HP LaserJet 5 family because the printer driver doesn't spool data properly from Access 7.0. You can try updating the printer driver, or using a similar (emulation) driver. In the meantime, you can work around the problem by switching the printer spooling mode.

- Click *Start*, select *Settings*, and then click *Printers*.

- Highlight the icon for your current printer.

- Choose *File* and select *Properties*.

- Choose the *Details* tab, then click the *Spool Settings* button.

- Change *Spool Data Format* to *RAW*.

- Try printing from Access 7.0 again.

  NOTE: If the printer's host-based driver is installed when the error message is encountered, deinstall the printer's host-based driver (using the *Add / Remove Programs* wizard) and install the printer's PCL driver (and change Graphics Mode to *HP-GL / 2*). After installing the PCL driver, follow the steps outlined earlier.

Symptom 4.169: After installing a new DOS printer driver, existing documents do not format or print correctly. You often find this type of problem with documents in DOS applications such as WordPerfect 5.1—existing documents (those created *before* acquiring the new printer driver) are no longer formatted or printed correctly. Sometimes only one line per page prints (though you may see many other formatting changes). This happens because the wrong printer driver has been installed, or the wrong printer has been selected in the DOS application. You may need to indicate whether you want your old documents formatted for the current printer driver. For example with WordPerfect 5.1:

- From a blank document, press <Shift>+<F1>.

- Choose *Initial Settings*.

- Choose *Format retrieved documents for current printer driver*.

- Choose *Yes*.

- Press <F7> back to the blank document.

- Retrieve a document—in the lower left corner of the screen, the words *Formatting current document for default printer* will appear.

■ Try printing again.

Symptom 4.170: The printer defaults to *Manual Feed* when printing envelopes. You may notice this in particular printing applications such as WordPerfect for Windows (versions 6.1, 7.0, and 8.0). This happens even when the printer driver is set to the desired tray. This happens when the default paper source selection for envelopes is set to *Manual Feed* in the printing application. The setting must be changed within the application itself. For WordPerfect, use either of the following methods.

Method 1

■ Select the *Format* menu.

■ Choose *Page* and then select *Page Size*, *Paper Size*, or *Page Setup*.

■ In the *Page Size*, *Paper Size*, or *Page Setup* dialog, select *Envelope #10* Landscape (or other applicable envelope size), then choose *Edit*.

■ Change the *Paper Source*, *Paper Location*, or *Source* from *Manual Feed* to the desired tray selection, then choose *OK*.

■ Close the *Page Size*, *Paper Size*, or *Page Setup* dialog.

Method 2

■ Select the *Format* menu, then choose *Envelope*.

■ In the *Envelope* window, select *Create New Definition*.

■ In the *New Page Size* or *Create Envelope Definition* dialog, locate the *Paper Source*, *Source*, or *Paper Location* area and change the setting from *Manual Feed* to the desired tray setting.

■ In the *Page Definition*, *Paper Name*, or *Name* area, enter the title under which the new paper definition will be saved, then select *OK*.

■ Enter the envelope address information and choose *Print Envelope*.

Symptom 4.171: You cannot print *Speaker Notes* correctly from Freelance 3.0. When printing *Speaker Notes* from this application at 600 dpi, the text only appears to go halfway across the page, and then wraps to the next line as if a margin had been set. This occurs in any graphics mode. You should download and install the latest printer driver (or try an "emulation" driver). As a workaround, set the resolution to 300 dpi to resolve this problem.

Symptom 4.172: The *envelope tool* doesn't print envelopes correctly. This most often occurs under older DOS versions of Microsoft Word (i.e., version 5.1) on printers without a *center feed*. You'll need to create a custom envelope setting under the printing application. For example (using Microsoft Word), use one of the ready-made envelope templates under Word. Create the envelope using margin settings in *Page Setup*. Select *left feed* from within the Word envelope tool. Try printing again.

Symptom 4.173: Excel cell size grows or shrinks depending on where it's printed on the page. The text will stay as you selected, but the information may be "#"ed out because the string can no longer fit in the appropriate cell. This problem occurs because the normal style font for a worksheet is usually set to MS Sans Serif. This is actually an unprintable font that is mapped to an appropriate internal printer font (which may be different for each printer). For example, when printing to the HP LaserJet III printer, this font is mapped to the internal font (Univers). If printing to the HP LaserJet IIISi printer, this font is mapped to the internal font (Univers Cond). If printing to the HP LaserJet 4 printer, this font is mapped to an internal TrueType font (Arial).

To prevent this problem, change the normal style font from MS Sans Serif to a font that is universal to all printers (a good choice is Arial because it is internal to Windows and can be downloaded to a printer if it is not already built into the printer). To change the normal style font:

- Select *Format* menu.
- Select *Style* option.
- Press the *Define* button.
- Press the *Font* button.
- Change the font to *Arial*, for example, and then click *OK* to go back to the main window.

A

Laser Printer Error Codes and Messages

Laser Printer Panel/ Error Messages

The first resource available for laser printer troubleshooting is the laser printer itself—even basic laser printers sport LCD displays that can report printer status and error conditions. By understanding this myriad of printer messages, you can often move *directly* to the problem area. This appendix outlines a comprehensive suite of alphabetized printer messages, warnings, and errors that you can use to help explain the often cryptic nature of these messages.

> **NOTE**: Entries marked with "*" are often found in color laser printers, whereas entries marked with "**" are frequently found in network laser printers.

20.0 INSUFFICIENT MEMORY (20.00.00) More data have been received from the computer than will fit in the printer's internal memory. When this occurs, only the data that fit in the printer's internal memory are printed. If this error occurs frequently (or if large complex print jobs are often sent to the printer), add more memory to the printer.

22.x EIO <n> BUFFER OVERFLOW (22.00.01)** The EIO buffer has overflowed during a busy state. This might happen if several complex jobs are sent simultaneously via the network and are larger than the overflow will allow. If <n> is 1, the problem occurred with the bottom EIO slot; if <n> is 2, the problem occurred with the top EIO slot. The current data in the print buffer will be lost. You may be able to correct this type of error by reducing the printer's workload, simplifying the pages to be printed, or adding memory to the printer.

22.x PARALLEL I/O BUFFER OVERFLOW (22.00.01) This error indicates that the parallel port buffer has overflowed. This might happen if several complex jobs are sent simultaneously via the parallel port and are larger than the overflow will allow. The current data in the print buffer will be lost. Try reducing the printer's workload.

40.0 <n> EIO ERROR (40.00.00)** An EIO accessory connection has been abnormally broken while transferring data from the computer to the printer (1 is the bottom EIO slot; 2 is the top EIO slot). Print an EIO configuration page to verify that the EIO accessories are installed properly. Check that all cables are connected to the EIO ports, and that the EIO accessory is seated properly. Turn the printer off and on to reset it (all data in the print buffer will be lost). If the printer is on a network, you might try printing to another network printer to verify the network is working properly.

41.2 PRINTER ERROR (41.00.02) This error indicates that a *beam detect laser scanner* error has occurred on the previous page. The page will reprint and continue, though the printed page may appear badly distorted. Remove any paper jams from inside the printer, then try turning the printer off and on to reset it. If the problem persists, the laser scanner/sensor may be damaged, or the printer's laser control circuits may be failing.

41.3 UNEXPECTED PAPER SIZE: LOAD TRAY 1 <width> <length> (41.00.03) Tray 1 is configured for a specific media size, but the printer detects a different size being fed from the tray. For example, the printer was expecting a letter-sized page, but detected that an 11″ × 17″ page was fed instead. Verify that the correct size paper (width and length) is loaded in tray 1, and see that the paper guides are set correctly. If the problem persists, the tray may be damaged, or the printer's paper sensor switches/system may require service.

41.5 UNEXPECTED PAPER TYPE: LOAD TRAY <x> <type> <size> (41.00.05)

The printer was expecting one type of media to be fed from an input tray, but a different type was fed. For example, the printer was expecting transparencies, but plain paper was fed. Open the printer and remove any paper jams. Verify that the correct media is loaded in the input tray and the printer control panel is configured correctly.

49.xxxx ERROR: CYCLE POWER** (49.xxxx)

This error indicates that a software or data communications error has occurred (or that corrupt data were sent to the printer). This can be caused during times of high network traffic or incomplete/out-of-bounds print data. This error can also occur because of defective EIO devices. Verify that all printer cables are connected properly. Turn the printer off and on to reset it. Remove all EIO cards and reinstall them to ensure they are seated correctly. If you're using a parallel port connection, verify that the cable is fully IEEE-1284 compliant.

50.x FUSER ERROR: CYCLE POWER (50.00.01, 50.00.02, 50.00.03, 50.00.04, 50.00.06)

This error indicates that a low temperature error has occurred in the fuser. Verify that the fuser assembly is completely seated inside the printer. Turn the printer off and on to reset the printer. Check the printer for any paper jams. If the problem persists, the printer may require service to replace the defective fuser assembly or fix defective fusing temperature control circuits.

51.x LASER ERROR: CYCLE POWER (51.00.01)

This error indicates that a laser malfunction has occurred. Turn the printer off and on to reset it. If the condition persists, the printer may require service to replace the laser or fix defective laser control circuits.

52.0 SCANNER ERROR: CYCLE POWER (52.00.00)

The laser's scanner motor is not turning properly to sweep the laser beam across the drum. Turn the printer off and on to reset it. If the condition persists, the printer may require service to replace the defective scanner motor/assembly, or to fix defective scanner control circuits.

53.x y.zz ERROR DIMM SLOT <n> (53.x y.zz)   This is a *serious* problem that indicates a memory error has occurred during the configuration and validation of DIMM memory. Use Table A.1 to decode the meanings of each error entry.

TABLE A.1   Traditional "Error 53" Definitions

x	Hardware type	y	Hardware device	zz	Error message	n	EIO slot
0	ROM	0	Onboard ROM/RAM	00	Unsupported memory	1	bottom
1	RAM	1	DIMM slot 1	01	Unrecognized memory	2	top
2	Font DIMM	2	DIMM slot 2	02	Unsupported memory size		
		3	DIMM slot 3	03	Failed RAM test		
		4	DIMM slot 4	04	Exceeded max. RAM size		
		5	DIMM slot 5	05	Exceeded max. ROM size		
		6	DIMM slot 6	06	Invalid DIMM speed (check DRAM)		
		7	DIMM slot 7	07	DIMM reporting bad checksums		
		8	DIMM slot 8	10	DIMM address error		
				11	PDC XROM out of bounds		
				12	Couldn't make temporary mapping		
				13	Invalid RAM type		
				14	DIMM not paired properly		
				15	Bad firmware upgrade (DIMM checksum)		
				16	More than 1 set of firmware upgrade DIMMs		
				17	Not enough DRAM to run		

Verify that the printer's DIMM board is installed correctly, and that each DIMM is configured correctly. DRAM DIMMs may need to be installed in synchronous pairs in adjacent slots (with the same size and speed in both slots). Turn the printer off and on to reset it. Remove and replace the DIMM that caused the error. If the problem persists, the printer may require additional service in its CPU/memory addressing circuitry.

54.1 TEMPERATURE SENSOR ERROR: CYCLE POWER

(54.00.01) This error indicates that the temperature/humidity sensor in the printer has malfunctioned (for example, the temperature/humidity sensor in an HP 8500 series printer is located below tray 2). Turn the printer off and on to reset it. If the condition persists, the printer may require service to replace the defective sensor, or fix the sensor's control circuit.

54.2 CAROUSEL ERROR: CYCLE POWER* (54.00.02)

This error indicates that the color toner carousel is not working correctly. This is often caused by an obstruction in the carousel path (such as a loose shutter or disengaged toner cartridge). Make sure that the carousel path is clear, and all cartridges are secure. Turn the printer off and on to reset it.

54.3 DENSITY SENSOR ERROR: CYCLE POWER*

(54.00.03) This error indicates a *density sensor* error, or that the printer is not receiving data back from the density sensor. Turn the printer off and on to reset it. Clean the density sensor (using the brush located next to the sensor) to remove all toner particles from the sensor face. To prevent scratches on the sensor, do not use any paper products (such as tissue or paper towels) to clean the sensor. If the condition persists, the printer may require service to replace the defective sensor, or fix the sensor's control circuitry.

54.4 WASTE TONER SENSOR ERROR: CYCLE POWER

(54.00.04) The waste toner sensor has failed. Printing cannot continue. Turn the printer off and on to reset it. If the condition persists, the printer may require service to replace the defective sensor, or fix the sensor's control circuitry.

55.x PRINTER ERROR: CYCLE POWER (55.00.01) This

problem indicates a printer command error. Commands cannot be exchanged between the printer and its controller. Turn the printer off and on to reset it; otherwise, you may need to replace the printer's communication controller.

56.1 ERROR: CYCLE POWER (56.01.01) This problem indicates an input feed error (such as requesting to feed transparencies through a duplexer), or the input tray is not installed. If the input tray you are trying to print from is not installed, install the input tray securely. Turn the printer off and on to reset it, then ensure that you have configured an acceptable input path.

56.2 ERROR CYCLE POWER (56.00.02) This problem indicates an illegal output error (for example, a multibin mailbox is not installed, but it was selected as the output destination, or there are transparencies in the duplexer). Open the printer and remove any jammed media from the paper path. Verify that the media type is set properly in the printer control panel. Turn the printer off and on to reset it, then ensure that you have configured an acceptable output path.

57.x FAN FAILURE (57.00.01; 57.00.02; 57.00.03) One of the printer's cooling fans failed or is obstructed (where <x> is the fan number). Turn the printer off and on to reset it. If the error persists, clear/replace the defective fan immediately. *Turn the printer off and do not operate the printer without adequate cooling—it can be seriously damaged.*

58.1 ERROR: CYCLE POWER (58.00.01) This error indicates that a paper diverter inside the printer is out of position, causing an error feeding media from tray 1. Open the printer and check for a paper jam or misfed media. Turn the printer off and on to reset it.

59.x MOTOR ERROR: CYCLE POWER (59.00.0x) This problem indicates that the printer's main drive train motor (M4) is not working properly (where <x> lists the nature of the motor problem: 0 is a general error, 1 is a startup error, and 2 is a rotation error). Turn the printer off and on to reset the printer. If the condition persists, the printer may require service to replace the defective motor/drive train, or to fix the motor's control circuits.

62.x SERVICE: CYCLE POWER (62.00.0x) This error indicates a serious problem with the printer's internal memory (where <x> is the general location of the error: 0 is the internal ROM or RAM, and 1–8 represents DIMM slots 1 through 8). Turn the printer off and on to reset it. If the condition persists, the printer may require replacement memory or other service.

63.0 SERVICE: CYCLE POWER (63.00.00) This error indicates that the internal RAM memory test failed. Turn the printer off and on to reset it. If the condition persists, isolate and replace the defective printer RAM.

64.0 PRINTER ERROR: CYCLE POWER (64.00.00) This indicates a scan buffer error, which means the data controlling the on/off firing of the laser beam are being corrupted. Turn the printer off and on to reset it. If the problem persists, the printer's laser control circuits may require service.

65.0 PRINTER ERROR: CYCLE POWER (65.00.00) This error indicates a DRAM controller error, which is probably corrupting the contents of your printer's RAM. Turn the printer off and on to reset it. If the condition persists, the printer's CPU board/DRAM controller may require replacement.

66.x0.yy C-LINK COMM ERROR: CHECK CABLES AND CYCLE POWER This indicates a communication error between the high-capacity (i.e., 2000-sheet feeder or a multibin mailbox) input unit and the printer. The term <x> denotes the device number in the link, whereas <yy> designates the error code from the optional device. Verify that the power cables are connected, then turn the printer off and on to reset it.

66.11.0x INPUT DEVICE FAILURE: CHECK CABLES AND CYCLE POWER (66.11.01, 66.11.02, 66.11.03) This problem indicates an error with a high-capacity input unit (i.e., 2000-sheet feeder). Verify that the power cables are connected. Turn the printer off and on to reset it. Check that there are no objects, paper, or other obstructions stored in the left side of the tray.

66.22.xx OUTPUT DEVICE FAILURE: CHECK CABLES AND CYCLE POWER (66.22.08, 66.22.09, 66.22.XX) This problem indicates an error with a high-capacity output unit (i.e., a multibin mailbox). Verify that the power cables are connected. Turn the printer off and on to reset it. Check for jams in the output (multibin mailbox) area.

67.x ERROR: POWER CYCLE (67.00.0x) This indicates an electronic controller error (where <x> designates the nature of the error: 1 is a controller board error, 2 is a controller board IC malfunction, and 3 is an internal communication malfunction). Turn the printer off and on to reset it. If the condition persists, the printer may require service to replace the defective controller.

68.0 NVRAM ERROR SETTINGS CHANGED (68.00.00)

This message indicates that a recoverable error has been detected in the NVRAM (nonvolatile random-access memory). Values for some NVRAM settings were found to be illegal, and were set back to their default value. Turn the printer on and off to reset it. If the condition persists, the NVRAM may be damaged.

68.x NVRAM FULL SETTINGS LOST (68.00.01)   This error indicates that the NVRAM is full, and the printer is unable to write new data to the NVRAM. Verify the printer's control panel settings—one or more fields might have been reset to their factory defaults during error recovery. The next time the printer is cycled off and on, NVRAM will be cleared and all factory defaults will be restored.

79 SERVICE xxxx: CYCLE POWER (79.xxxx)   The printer's firmware has detected a hardware failure within the formatter. This failure can be caused by defective EIO devices and communication ports. The <xxxx> term designates the error: 01xx is an I/O ASIC register error, 02xx is a Video ASIC register error, and 03xx is an IDE ASIC register error. Turn the printer off and on to reset it. If the condition persists, the printer's formatter may require replacement.

[color] TONER LOW*   The printer's toner supply is running out. Replace toner cartridge when print quality deteriorates.

[color] CHG DRUM*   The printer's imaging drum is near the end of its life. Normal printing should continue, but replace the image drum cartridge as soon as possible (or when print quality deteriorates).

[color] FUSER*   The printer's fusing assembly is near end of its life. Normal printing should continue, but replace the fuser as soon as possible (or when print quality deteriorates).

[size] PAPER   The printer is requesting a specified size of paper in the tray. Insert the requested size of paper and continue.

[size] MANUAL REQUEST   The printer is requesting that a specified size of paper be loaded in the manual feed slot. Insert the requested size of paper in the manual feed slot and continue.

ACCESS DENIED MENUS LOCKED**   The user has attempted to select a menu value while the printer control panel lockout is enabled. See your system administrator for access to the printer's control panel.

ACTIVE   This is not an error. Normal data are being received, or are in process of being output. No direct intervention is required.

BAD DUPLEXER CONNECTION   The duplex printing accessory is not correctly installed. Check that the printer's duplex printing accessory power cord is plugged into the printer, and the power cord is plugged into the duplex unit. Turn the printer off and then on again. If the error continues, verify that the duplex printing accessory is correctly installed, or replace the duplexing unit.

BELT LIFE   The printer's transfer belt assembly is exhausted, and needs to be replaced as soon as possible.

BELT NOT INSTALLED   The printer's transfer belt unit is not installed correctly. Open the printer covers, and check/reinstall the transfer belt as necessary. The printer will not function until this error is corrected.

CALIBRATION EXECUTING*   The laser printer is executing an internal color calibration. This process should take approximately 90 seconds, and no direct intervention is required.

CANCELING JOB   The printer is canceling its current print job, and all incoming data for the current job will be discarded. No direct intervention is required.

CANNOT DUPLEX: CHECK REAR BIN   This message may alternate with **CANNOT DUPLEX: CHECK PAPER**. The printer cannot duplex because the rear output bin is open, or the media is not supported by the duplex printing accessory. Close the rear output bin, and verify that the media is properly supported by the duplex printing accessory.

CANNOT DUPLEX: CLOSE REAR BIN   The printer cannot duplex because the rear output bin is open. Close rear output bin door.

CHANGE DRUM   The imaging drum is near 90 percent of its working life. You should change the drum and reset the drum counter. On some printer models, if the drum counter is not reset when you replace the drum, the

CHANGE DRUM message will return with the next *Toner Low* condition.

CHECKING PRINTER The printer is performing an internal test. This process should take approximately 30 seconds. The message is displayed during the initiation of the engine test. When complete, the printer goes online. No direct intervention is required.

CHG DRUM [color]* One or more of the printer's image drums needs to be replaced as soon as possible.

CLEARING PAPER FROM PRINTER The printer has jammed (or was turned on while media was in the paper path). The printer is attempting to clear these pages, and no intervention should be required unless the paper cannot be cleared.

CLOSE FRONT DUPLEX DRAWER The duplex drawer is not completely closed. Close the duplex drawer.

CLOSE MIDDLE FRONT DRAWER The drawer that holds the intermediate transfer belt is open. Close the middle front drawer. If the message persists, the printer might require service to fix the sensor or transfer belt unit.

CLOSE TOP COVER The printer's main top cover is open. Close the top cover. If the message persists, the printer might require service to fix the sensor.

CLOSE UPPER FRONT DRAWER The upper front drawer (the drawer that holds the imaging drum) is open. Open the drawer and firmly push the drawer closed using one hand in the middle of the drawer. If the message persists, the printer might require service to fix the sensor or the imaging drum.

CLOSE UPPER REAR DRAWER The upper rear drawer is open. Close the upper rear drawer. If the message persists, the printer might require service to fix the sensor.

COLD RESET The *cold* reset power-up sequence has been selected. Most printer variables will reset to their factory default values.

CONTINUOUS PAGE: PRESS CANCEL JOB The printer Configuration Page is being printed continuously. Press <CANCEL JOB> to terminate continuous Configuration Page printing and return the printer to the READY state.

COVER   One or more of the printer's covers/doors are open. Close all covers/doors.

COVER OPEN   One or more of the printer's covers are open. Check and secure all the printer's covers.

CPYnn   This is not an error. When more than one copy of a document is being printed, this figure indicates the number of copies. No direct intervention is required.

DATA   Data remain in the printer's buffer. Press <ON-LINE> or <FORM FEED> to empty the buffer.

DATA PRESENT .xxx   This is not an error. There are data present at the printer, and <xxx> is the emulation mode used for the data.

DATA RECEIVED   This is not an error. The printer has received and processed data normally, and is waiting for a form feed. Load appropriate media (if necessary) to continue the print job.

DENSITY SENSOR OUT OF RANGE*   This message may alternate with **CLEAN DENSITY SENSOR**. A *density sensor out-of-range* error was detected during the printer's color calibration. The density sensor might be dirty, so inspect and clean the sensor carefully. Open the lower-front drawer and remove the cleaning brush mounted inside. Open the top-front drawer and remove the imaging drum using the blue handle. Use the cleaning brush to remove all dust and toner particles from the sensor. Replace the imaging drum and secure the printer. CAUTION: *To avoid scratching the sensor, do not clean it with any paper products.*

DIAGNOSTICS MODE   The printer's *extended diagnostics* power-up key sequence has been selected. No direct intervention is required while the printer completes its diagnostic mode.

DLL BUFF OVERFLOW   Data in the printer's DLL (font) buffer have overflowed. Press <RECOVER> to continue. To avoid this problem, decrease the number of DLL (Windows TrueType) fonts being downloaded to the printer, or install more printer memory.

DRUM CNT RESET   The printer's imaging drum counter is to be reset (usually after replacing the imaging drum). Press <ENTER> to reset drum counter, or press <MENU> to review the next category.

DRUM ERROR: REPLACE DRUM KIT   An error has been detected with a component of the print drum kit, which means the drum assembly has failed. Replace the drum kit as soon as possible.

DRUM LIFE LOW: REPLACE DRUM KIT   Approximately 80 percent of the drum's life has been utilized. Drum replacement will be required in the near future, so order a drum replacement package at your next convenient opportunity.

DRUM LIFE OUT: REPLACE DRUM KIT   The imaging drum has reached the end of its expected life, so you'll need to replace the print drum kit at your earliest opportunity. The printer may continue to run (and the image quality may still be acceptable) until the drum is replaced, but this message will continue to appear.

DRUM CLEANING   The printer is generating a drum cleaning page. No direct intervention is required.

DUPLEX FEED JAM 1   Paper jammed as it was being fed to the reverse roller in a duplex feeder. Open the duplex unit and clear the jam. Verify that the paper path is unobstructed.

DUPLEX FEED JAM 2   Paper jammed as it was being reversed in a duplex feeder. Open the duplex unit and clear the jam, then verify that the paper path is unobstructed.

DUPLEX FEED JAM 3   Paper jammed as it was being fed through a duplex feeder. Open the duplex unit and clear the jam, then verify that the paper path is unobstructed.

DUPLEX INPUT JAM   Paper jammed as it was being fed in from the paper tray. Remove the tray, open the duplex unit, and clear the jam.

DUPLEX OPEN JAM   The paper tray was opened as the paper was being fed through a duplex feeder. Close the paper tray, and verify that the paper path is unobstructed.

DUPLEXER ERROR: CHECK DUPLEXER   An error has occurred in the duplex printing accessory (the duplexer). Verify that the duplex printing accessory is correctly installed and plugged in.

EEPROM RESETTING   The EEPROM is resetting to its factory default values, and should return to "online" after the reset is complete.

EIO X INITIALIZING YYY This message is informational, and may alternate with **DO NOT POWER OFF**. The EIO (Extended I/O) device in slot "X" is initializing. The "YYY" value will increment every 10 seconds during this process. No direct intervention is required at this point.

EIO X NOT FUNCTIONAL The EIO (Extended I/O) slot specified by "X" does not have a card installed, or is not functional. If an EIO device is installed but not functional, the device should be checked and replaced if necessary.

ERROR <nn> An internal error has occurred in the printer, where <nn> is the type of error. Try cycling the printer off/on to clear the error. If the problem persists, the printer's main board may require replacement.

ERROR <nn> <aaaaaaaa> An error has occurred in the printer's controller where <nn> is the "exception code," and <aaaaaaaa> is the "error address." Cycle the printer off/on to recover from the fault. If the problem persists, the printer's controller may need to be replaced.

ERROR D6 [XXXXXXX]* The yellow image drum is not installed properly. Open the printer, check the yellow image drum, and reinstall as necessary.

ERROR D7 [XXXXXXX]* The magenta image drum is not installed properly. Open the printer, check the magenta image drum, and reinstall as necessary.

ERROR D8 [XXXXXXX]* The cyan image drum is not installed properly. Open the printer, check the cyan image drum, and reinstall as necessary.

ERROR D9 [XXXXXXX]* The black image drum is not installed properly. Open the printer, check the black image drum, and reinstall as necessary.

ERROR D0 [XXXXXXX] The printer's fusing unit is not installed correctly. Open the printer's covers, check the fusing unit, then replace or reinstall the fusing unit as necessary.

ERROR DF [XXXXXXX] The printer's transfer belt unit is not installed correctly. Open the printer's covers, check the transfer belt, then replace or reinstall the transfer belt assembly as necessary.

EVENT LOG EMPTY You selected the *SHOW EVENT LOG* option from the printer's *Information* menu, but the event log has no entries. This is not a problem.

FLUSHING JOB Data are being discarded as a result of command received.

FUSER LIFE The printer's fusing unit is exhausted, and needs to be replaced as soon as possible.

FUSER LIFE LOW: REPLACE KIT Approximately 95 percent of the fuser's life has been utilized. Fuser replacement will be required in the near future, so order a fuser replacement package at your next convenient opportunity.

FUSER LIFE OUT: REPLACE KIT The fuser has reached the end of its expected life, so you'll need to replace the fuser kit at your earliest opportunity. The printer may continue to run (and the image quality may still be acceptable) until the fuser is replaced, but this message will continue to appear.

HEX DUMP The printer is to dump its data in hexadecimal format. Press <ENTER> to start the hex dump of all received data, or select <MENU> for the next category. Cycle the printer's power off and on to clear the *hex dump* mode.

HOST I/F ERROR There is an error in the printer's optional serial interface. This error is displayed when a parity error, framing error, or overrun error is detected. Press <RECOVER> to release the error, then check the protocol between your host and printer. If the problem persists, the serial interface may require replacement.

INITIALIZING This is not an error. The message is displayed when the printer is initially turned on, and the printer's controller is being initialized.

INSTALL DRUM KIT The printer's imaging drum kit is not installed, or is installed incorrectly. Verify that the drum kit is correctly installed, or install another imaging drum kit.

INSTALL TRAY 2 The printer cannot print until media is loaded into Tray 2, so load the appropriate media for printing. Also, if the paper path for Tray 3 passes through Tray 2 (on a multitray printer), you may need to insert Tray 2 into the printer so that printing from Tray 3 can continue.

MACRO OVERFLOW Data in the printer's *Macro Buffer* have overflowed. Press <RECOVER> to continue. To avoid this error, decrease the macro size, or install more printer memory.

MEMORY FULL: STORED DATA LOST The printer has no available memory. As a result, the current job might not print correctly. Some downloaded fonts may have been deleted. Try printing simplified pages (i.e., lower the printing resolution). If this does not resolve the problem (or you require the higher resolution), add memory to the printer.

MEMORY SETTINGS CHANGED   The I/O buffering settings were changed by the printer because there is not enough memory available to use the previous settings. No direct intervention is required with this warning, but you should consider adding printer memory to prevent this warning from recurring.

MEMORY SHORTAGE: JOB CLEARED   The printer's available memory was insufficient to continue printing, and the remainder of the current print job was canceled. Add printer memory or simplify the print job to prevent this error from recurring.

MEMORY SHORTAGE: PAGE SIMPLIFIED   This is the type of error that might occur on current printers employing sophisticated adaptive data compression techniques to speed printing time. In this case, the printer's data compression had to resort to lossy compression in order to fit raster graphics into the available memory, and this has caused a data loss in the printer's raster output. Reduce the complexity/resolution of the page to improve the print quality. Adding printer memory will not correct this type of problem.

MENU RESET   The printer is to be reset as the result of a *RESET* selection through the maintenance menu. Press <ENTER> to reset menus 1 and 2 to their factory default settings, or press <MENU> to review the next category.

NO JOB TO CANCEL   This is not an error. The <CANCEL JOB> option was selected, but there is no active job or buffered data to cancel. The printer automatically returns to the READY state.

OFF LINE   This is not an error. The printer is offline and there are no error messages pending. Simply return the printer to the READY state.

OIL ROLLER LIFE   The fusing unit's oil roller needs to be replaced as soon as possible.

OIL ROLLER NOT INSTALLED   The oil roller is not installed correctly. Open the printer's top cover, check the oil roller, and reinstall it as necessary. The printer will not function until this error is corrected.

ON LINE This is not an error. The printer is ready to receive data. A second message line may alternate between messages such as *Emulation* and *PWR SAVE* if the fuser and fan are turned off by the printer's power-saving features.

OP MENU This is the printer's *Control Panel Enable/Disable* feature. Select *disable* to deactivate the printer's control panel—then its features can be controlled only through software. To reset, enter the maintenance menu, toggle *Enable/Disable*, then press <ENTER>.

PAGE BUF OVERFLOW The printer's page buffer is full, and extra data will be lost. Press <RECOVER> to continue. Try resending the job beginning with the page that did not print. You might also try reducing the complexity (i.e., resolution) of the page. If the problem persists, additional printer memory is required.

PAGE CANNOT PRINT NOW This message may alternate with **RETRY WHEN PRINTING STOPS**. An internal page has been requested while the printer is already printing an incoming job. Interrupting the current job to print the internal page would corrupt the current job's environment, and probably cause the job to finish printing incorrectly after the internal page is completed. As a result, internal pages are generally not permitted to interrupt current jobs, and can be printed only when the printer is idle. Retry the internal page after printer has completed its current job.

PAGE SIMPLIFIED This is the type of error that might occur on current printers employing sophisticated adaptive data compression techniques to speed printing time. In this case, the printer's data compression had to resort to lossy compression in order to fit raster graphics into the available memory, and this has caused a data loss in the printer's raster output. Reduce the complexity/resolution of the page to improve the print quality. Adding printer memory will not correct this type of problem.

PAGE TOO COMPLEX TO PRINT This message may alternate with **PRESS "XX" TO CONTINUE**. The page could not be printed because it is simply too complex for the printer. Accept the error to continue printing (with noticeably poor results on this page), then select <CANCEL> to terminate the entire job. Reduce the complexity of the page to allow it to print successfully. Note that adding memory will not correct this type of problem.

PAPER EXIT JAM Paper jammed as it was exiting the printer. Open the printer's exit cover and clear the jam.

PAPER EXIT JAM n Paper jammed at exit 1 or 2. Open the printer and clear the jam from the exit path.

PAPER FEED JAM Paper jammed somewhere between the input and the paper exit. Open the printer's cover(s), then locate and clear the jam. Be sure to remove all fragments of paper.

PAPER INPUT JAM Paper jammed as it was being fed in from the paper tray or other source. Remove the tray and clear the jam.

PAPER SIZE ERR The wrong size paper is in the tray. Check for paper in the tray, and check for too much paper. Ensure that the paper size expected by the printer matches the size that you are using. Open/Close the top cover to recover and continue.

PLEASE WAIT This is not an error. The printer is simply in the process of purging data so that it can go offline or into the menus.

POWERSAVE ON The printer is in its power-saving mode. This message is cleared (and the printer returned to normal mode) by pressing any key on the control panel, or by sending a print job to the printer.

PRESS "XX" TO PRINT This message may alternate with **PRESS SELECT TO CHANGE TONER**. The top cover was opened and closed when the printer was not in toner cartridge replacement mode. Press any key to resume printing, or press the proper key(s) to enter the printer's toner replacement menu.

PRINT CLEANING The printer is generating a "Cleaning Page." No direct intervention is required.

PRINT DEMO This is not an error. The printer is generating a test page.

PRINT FONTS This is not an error. The printer is generating a font sample page. No direct intervention is required while this page is printing.

PRINT MENU This is not an error. The printer is generating a menu page. No direct intervention is required while this page is printing.

PRINT OVERRUN   The page is simply too complicated to print—it contains too much data to be held in the printer. Press <RECOVER> to release the error, and try adding more memory to the printer.

PRINTER LANGUAGE NOT AVAILABLE   The printer received a request for a new language (a.k.a. "personality") that does not exist in the printer. There is no means of correcting this problem other than to select a language that the printer can use.

PRINTING   This is not an error—data are simply being received and printed.

PRINTING ACCESSORIES   This is not an error. The printer is listing its installed accessories, and will return to the READY state upon completion of this page. No direct intervention is required.

PRINTING CALIBRATION PAGE*   This is not an error. The calibration page is being generated (color laser printers may include color calibration data also). The printer will return to the READY state upon completion of this page. No direct intervention is required.

PRINTING COLOR GUIDE*   This is not an error. The printer's color test page is being generated. The printer will return to the READY state upon completion of this page.

PRINTING CONFIGURATION   This is not an error. The printer's configuration page is being printed. The printer will return to the READY state upon completion of this page. No direct intervention is required.

PRINTING FONT LIST   This is not an error. A typeface list for the printer's available languages (a.k.a. "personalities") is being printed. The printer will return to the READY state upon completion of these pages. No direct intervention is required.

PRINTING MENU MAP   This is not an error. The printer's menu map is being printed, and the printer will return to the READY state upon completion of this page. No direct intervention is required.

PRINTING REGISTRATION PG   This is not an error. The printer's registration test page is being generated, and the printer will return to the READY state upon completion of this page. No direct intervention is required.

PRINTING "XXXXXX" DEMO   This is not an error. The printer's first test page is being generated. The printer will return to the READY state upon completion of this page. No direct intervention is required.

PRINTING "XXXXXX" DEMO 2   This is not an error. The printer's second test page is being generated. The printer will return to the READY state upon completion of this page. No direct intervention is required.

PROCESSING JOB   This is not an error. The printer is simply processing the current job.

PROCESSING .xxx   This is not an error—data are simply being received and processed, where <xxx> is the emulation mode used for the data.

READY   This is not an error. The printer is online and ready to receive data, and no status or device attendance messages are pending.

REC BUFFER OVERFLOW   The printer's "receive buffer" is full, and extra data will be lost. Press <RECOVER> to continue. Be sure to check the printer's *flow control* settings, and check the cable configuration to see that the proper "handshaking" signals are in place.

REINSTALL TRANSFER BELT   This message occurs when an intermediate transfer belt is not installed properly in the printer, or if the home position marks (on the intermediate transfer belt) are not detected by a sensor. The intermediate transfer belt must be rotating before the sensor is able to detect the "home position" marks on the belt. Verify that the intermediate transfer belt is installed in the printer. If it is installed and seated properly, the printer might require service to fix the transfer belt drive train.

REMOVE PAPER TOP OUTPUT BIN   There is too much paper stacked up in the output bin. A sensor that detects the height of the output paper stack has determined that the output bin capacity has been reached. Remove the job from the top output bin and then press any necessary key(s) to continue.

RESET   The printer has been reset. Any data not yet printed are deleted from the buffer, and your printer initializes to its factory defaults (temporary DLL fonts are deleted).

RESET TO SAVE   Invoke the reset function to save data or DLLs in buffer. Press the <RESET> button to save changes and exit the menu.

RESETTING MEMORY   The printer is executing a memory reset. The printer returns to the READY state upon completion of this test.

RESETTING VALUES FINISHED*   The printer's color calibration density values have been reset to their default values.

RESTORING FACTORY SETTINGS   The printer is executing a *RESTORE FACTORY SETTINGS* or a *COLD RESET* function in order to clear potential problems or errors in its configuration. No direct intervention should be required here.

SELECT LANGUAGE   The printer's language (a.k.a. "personality") selection key sequence has been selected. The printer will prompt you to select a new control panel display language once it has completed its initialization process. Select new language when prompted.

SERVICE MODE   The printer's service mode key sequence has been selected. The printer will remain in its service mode until the appropriate key is pressed.

TNR SNS [color]*   A low toner color is detected. Make sure the specified image drum is installed. If it is, check that there are no obstructions, paper fragments, or other issues that are interfering with the toner sensors.

TONER CMYK LOW*   This message may alternate with **PRESS <SELECT> TO CHANGE TONER**. The specified color toner cartridge is low on toner. Printing will continue until a *TONER OUT* message appears. To change the toner cartridge now, press <SELECT> to enter the printer's toner replacement menu.

TONER CMYK OUT*   This message may alternate with **PRESS SELECT TO CHANGE TONER**. The specified toner cartridge is out of toner. If the *TONER OUT* setting in the *CONFIGURATION* menu is set to *OVERRIDE*, pressing any key will resume printing. Press <SELECT> (or another appropriate key) to enter the toner replacement menu. Press any other specified key(s) to resume printing *without* changing the cartridge.

TONER POSITION [COLOR] = [STATE]*   This informational message indicates the current state of a particular toner cartridge, and is normally displayed when the printer is in its toner replacement mode. If necessary, replace the specified toner cartridge.

TONER SNS   A fault has occurred in the toner sensor, or the imaging drum cartridge is not properly installed. Install/reinstall the image drum cartridge. If the problem persists, the printer may require service to replace the toner sensor, fix the toner sensor circuit, or replace the imaging drum assembly.

TRANSFER KIT LOW: REPLACE KIT   The transfer belt assembly is near the end of its expected life. Although printing can continue, the transfer belt should be replaced for optimum printer operation. Replace the transfer belt at your earliest opportunity.

TRANSFER KIT OUT: REPLACE KIT   The transfer belt assembly has reached the end of its expected life. Although the printer may continue to print until the transfer belt is replaced, this message will continue to appear. Replace the transfer belt as soon as possible.

TRAY n FEED JAM   Paper jammed while feeding inside printer from tray 1 or 2. Open the printer and clear the jam from the paper feed path.

TRAY n INPUT JAM   Paper jammed while being supplied from tray 1 or 2. Open the tray and clear the jam.

TRAY PAPER OUT   The printer has run out of paper. Add more paper, envelopes, or other media as required.

TRAY X EMPTY [TYPE] [SIZE]   The specified tray is empty, but the current printing job does not require this tray in order to complete the job. Load this tray with the appropriate media to avoid this message.

TRAY X LOAD [TYPE] [SIZE]   The specified media type and size must be loaded into the requested tray. Load the proper media into the requested tray.

TRAY X OPEN   The specified tray is not completely closed, probably because it was not inserted properly or completely. Close the specified tray.

TRAY X SIZE [SIZE]   Media has been loaded into Tray "X." The most recently configured size is typically displayed.

From here, you can usually scroll through and select other possible media sizes.

TRAY X TYPE [TYPE]   Media has been loaded into Tray "X." The most recently configured type is typically displayed. From here, you can usually scroll through and select other possible media types.

USER MNT   The printer is now in the *User Maintenance* mode, and you can access several different maintenance menu selections from here.

WARM(ING) UP   This is not an error. The fuser is warming up, and printing will continue when the fuser reaches its optimum working temperature.

WASTE TNR NF FULL   The waste toner box is almost full, and should be replaced soon. Be prepared to replace it when the *WASTE TONER FULL* message appears.

WASTE TONER BOX NOT INSTALLED   The waste toner box is not installed correctly. Open the printer covers, then check and reinstall the waste box as necessary (you may need to replace the entire imaging drum assembly). The printer will not function until this error is corrected.

WASTE TONER FULL   The waste toner box is full, and must be replaced immediately.

WASTE TONER FULL: REPLACE DRUM KIT   The *waste toner full* sensor detects a filled waste toner container. Replace the drum kit. If the message persists, the printer might require service to fix the waste toner sensor or image drum system.

Ink-Jet Printer
Dialog Codes
and Messages

Ink-Jet Printer
Dialog/Error Messages

The first resource available for ink-jet printer troubleshooting is the printer itself—even basic ink-jet printers sport LCD displays or Windows status dialogs that can report printer media and error conditions. By understanding this myriad of printer messages, you can often move *directly* to the problem area. This appendix outlines a comprehensive suite of alphabetized printer messages, warnings, and errors that you can use to help explain the often cryptic nature of ink-jet error messages.

> **NOTE**: The error messages discussed below assume a typical four-color ink-jet printer using black, cyan (blue), magenta (red), and yellow ink cartridges.

NOTE: The terms *print head* and *ink cartridge* are often used interchangeably, since the ink and nozzles are often integrated into one assembly. However, some printers distinguish between the two as separate devices where an "ink cartridge" is simply a reservoir of ink, and a "print head" provides the nozzles that fire ink.

BLACK INK CARTRIDGE EMPTY   The ink in the black ink cartridge has been used up and the cartridge is empty. The printer will not print until the empty cartridge is replaced.

BLACK INK CARTRIDGE EXPIRED   Inks used in an ink-jet printer have a long but finite storage life. When the ink in an ink cartridge has exceeded its expected life span, it can begin to deteriorate (and can eventually damage the printer). This error means the printer's black ink cartridge has expired and must be replaced. The printer will not print until the expired ink cartridge has been replaced.

BLACK INK CARTRIDGE EXPIRING SOON   The ink used in your ink-jet printer has a long but finite storage life. This error means the black ink cartridge in your printer is nearing its expiration date and will need to be replaced *soon*. Now is the time to purchase a new ink cartridge so that you'll have a replacement cartridge on hand when the ink cartridge expires. You may replace the cartridge now, or wait until it expires completely (see **BLACK INK CARTRIDGE EXPIRED**).

BLACK INK CARTRIDGE MISSING   The printer cannot detect the presence of a black ink cartridge. The cartridge is not installed, or the cartridge is not secured in the carriage. The printer will not print until this problem is corrected. If the black ink cartridge is missing, you'll need to install a new cartridge. If the black ink cartridge is installed, remove it. Align the ink cartridge correctly and reinsert the ink cartridge firmly and completely into the carriage holder. Also make sure that the ink cartridge is the correct type to use with your particular printer (i.e., an HP No.10 Black Ink Cartridge for an HP2000C). If the problem persists, the ink cartridge may be defective. Try replacing it with a new one.

BLACK INK LOW   The black ink level is low, and the cartridge will soon be empty. You can continue to print with the printer until the cartridge is empty. Now is the time to pur-

chase a new ink cartridge so that you will have a replacement cartridge on hand when the black ink cartridge is
empty. You may replace the cartridge now, or wait until it is
completely empty (see **BLACK INK CARTRIDGE
EMPTY**).

BLACK PRINT HEAD MISSING   The printer is unable to
detect the presence of a black print head. The printer will
not print until it can detect a print head (in each print head
slot for color printers). If one or more of the print heads are
missing, you'll need to install the correct print head in each
empty print head slot. If all four print heads are installed
(for color printers), the print head identified as "missing"
may have protective tape covering its electrical contacts
(preventing the printer from detecting the print head). This
is the most common cause of this problem. Check the copper
contact area on the print head and remove any tape you
find. If all the print heads are installed, remove and reseat
the print head that is marked as "missing." Reinsert the
suspect print head firmly and completely into the carriage
holder. Make sure that the print head is the correct type to
use with your particular printer (i.e., an HP No.10 Black
print head for an HP2000C). If the problem persists, the
print head's electrical contacts may be contaminated with
ink and debris. Try cleaning the print head contacts, or
replace the suspect print head outright.

BLACK PRINT HEAD SHOULD BE REPLACED SOON   The
black print head is nearing the end of its useful life, and will
need to be replaced in the very near future. You may begin
to notice a decrease in print quality. When the print head
reaches the end of its useful life, you will be notified by
another message. Now is the time to purchase a new print
head so that you'll have a replacement on hand when the
print head finally needs replacement. It is not necessary to
replace the print head at this time unless you have unacceptable print quality.

CYAN INK CARTRIDGE EMPTY   The ink in the cyan ink
cartridge has been used up and the cartridge is empty. The
printer will not print until the empty cartridge is replaced.

CYAN INK CARTRIDGE EXPIRED   Inks used in an ink-jet
printer have a long but finite storage life. When the ink in
an ink cartridge has exceeded its expected life span, it can
begin to deteriorate (and can eventually damage the

printer). This error means the printer's cyan ink cartridge has expired and must be replaced. The printer will not print until the expired ink cartridge has been replaced.

CYAN INK CARTRIDGE EXPIRING SOON The ink used in your ink-jet printer has a long but finite storage life. This error means the cyan ink cartridge in your printer is nearing its expiration date and will need to be replaced *soon*. Now is the time to purchase a new ink cartridge so that you'll have a replacement cartridge on hand when the ink cartridge expires. You may replace the cartridge now, or wait until it expires completely (see **CYAN INK CARTRIDGE EXPIRED**).

CYAN INK CARTRIDGE MISSING The printer cannot detect the presence of a cyan ink cartridge. The cartridge is not installed, or the cartridge is not secured in the carriage. The printer will not print until this problem is corrected. If the cyan ink cartridge is missing, you'll need to install a new cartridge. If the cyan ink cartridge is installed, remove it. Align the ink cartridge correctly and reinsert the ink cartridge firmly and completely into the carriage holder. Also make sure that the ink cartridge is the correct type to use with your particular printer (i.e., an HP No.10 Cyan Ink Cartridge for an HP2000C). If the problem persists, the ink cartridge may be defective. Try replacing it with a new one.

CYAN INK LOW The cyan ink level is low, and the cartridge will soon be empty. You can continue to print with the printer until the cartridge is empty. Now is the time to purchase a new ink cartridge so that you will have a replacement cartridge on hand when the cyan ink cartridge is empty. You may replace the cartridge now, or wait until it is completely empty (see **CYAN INK CARTRIDGE EMPTY**).

CYAN PRINT HEAD MISSING The printer is unable to detect the presence of a cyan print head. The printer will not print until it can detect a print head (in each print head slot for color printers). If one or more of the print heads are missing, you'll need to install the correct print head in each empty print head slot. If all four print heads are installed (for color printers), the print head identified as "missing" may have protective tape covering its electrical contacts (preventing the printer from detecting the print head). This is the most common cause of this problem. Check the copper contact area on the print head and remove any tape you find. If all the print heads are installed, remove and reseat the print head that is marked as "missing." Reinsert the suspect print head firmly and completely into the carriage holder. Make sure that the print head is the correct type to use with your particular printer (i.e., an HP No.10 Cyan print head for an HP2000C). If the problem persists, the print head's electrical contacts may be contaminated with ink and debris. Try cleaning the print head contacts, or replace the suspect print head outright.

CYAN PRINT HEAD SHOULD BE REPLACED SOON The cyan print head is nearing the end of its useful life, and will need to be replaced in the very near future. You may begin to notice a decrease in print quality. When the print head reaches the end of its useful life, you will be notified by another message. Now is the time to purchase a new print head so that you'll have a replacement on hand when the print head finally needs replacement. It is not necessary to replace the print head at this time unless you have unacceptable print quality.

INCOMPATIBLE BLACK INK CARTRIDGE The black ink cartridge in the printer is the wrong cartridge type for use in your particular printer. The printer will not print until the correct ink cartridge has been installed. Replace the installed black ink cartridge with an appropriate cartridge type.

INCOMPATIBLE BLACK PRINT HEAD The installed black print head is the wrong print head for use in this particular printer. The printer will not print until the correct print head has been installed. Replace the installed black print head with an appropriate print head.

INCOMPATIBLE CYAN INK CARTRIDGE The cyan ink cartridge in the printer is the wrong cartridge type for use in your particular printer. The printer will not print until the correct ink cartridge has been installed. Replace the installed cyan ink cartridge with an appropriate cartridge type.

INCOMPATIBLE CYAN PRINT HEAD The installed cyan print head is the wrong print head for use in this particular printer. The printer will not print until the correct print head has been installed. Replace the installed cyan print head with an appropriate print head.

INCOMPATIBLE MAGENTA INK CARTRIDGE The magenta ink cartridge in the printer is the wrong cartridge type for use in your particular printer. The printer will not print until the correct ink cartridge has been installed. Replace the installed magenta ink cartridge with an appropriate cartridge type.

INCOMPATIBLE MAGENTA PRINT HEAD   The installed magenta print head is the wrong print head for use in this particular printer. The printer will not print until the correct print head has been installed. Replace the installed magenta print head with an appropriate print head.

INCOMPATIBLE PRINT MANAGER   This Windows 3.1x error message will occur on a Windows 3.1 system if Windows 3.1 is reinstalled *after* the printer's driver software is installed. When the printer's driver is installed, it replaces the Windows 3.1 print manager with the Windows 3.1 print manager (which is compatible with the printer). When Windows 3.1 is reinstalled, the Windows 3.1 print manager is also reinstalled, but the printer isn't compatible with it. To correct this issue, reinstall the software that came with the printer.

INCOMPATIBLE YELLOW INK CARTRIDGE   The yellow ink cartridge in the printer is the wrong cartridge type for use in your particular printer. The printer will not print until the correct ink cartridge has been installed. Replace the installed yellow ink cartridge with an appropriate cartridge type.

INCOMPATIBLE YELLOW PRINT HEAD   The installed yellow print head is the wrong print head for use in this particular printer. The printer will not print until the correct print head has been installed. Replace the installed yellow print head with an appropriate print head.

INK BUILDUP WARNING   Ink may have gotten onto one or more of the print head electrical contacts. If this occurs, it can cause a number of problems with the print (such as misfiring nozzles). The printer will not print until this problem has been fixed. Clean the print head electrical contacts using a swab lightly dipped in isopropyl alcohol. Be sure to allow the contacts to dry thoroughly before reinstalling the print head(s) or ink cartridge(s).

INK CARTRIDGE INSTALLED (BLACK)   This is not an error. This message simply means that the printer has recognized the installation of a new black ink cartridge. The cartridge expiration and ink level should also be reset.

INK CARTRIDGE INSTALLED (CYAN)   This is not an error. This message simply means that the printer has recognized the installation of a new cyan ink cartridge. The cartridge expiration and ink level should also be reset.

INK CARTRIDGE INSTALLED (MAGENTA)   This is not an error. This message simply means that the printer has recognized the installation of a new magenta ink cartridge. The cartridge expiration and ink level should also be reset.

INK CARTRIDGE INSTALLED (YELLOW)   This is not an error. This message simply means that the printer has recognized the installation of a new yellow ink cartridge. The cartridge expiration and ink level should also be reset.

INK CARTRIDGES INSTALLED   This is not an error. This message simply means that four new ink cartridges (black, cyan, magenta, and yellow) have been successfully installed and recognized in the printer. The cartridges' expiration dates and ink levels should also be reset.

LOWER TRAY OUT   The printer's lower paper tray is out of paper. Load the appropriate paper (or other fresh media such as labels or transparencies) in the paper tray, then click *Resume* (or press the *Resume* button on the printer) to continue printing after you have loaded the paper.

LOWER TRAY OUT (NETWORK)   The network printer's lower paper tray is out of paper. Load the appropriate paper (or other fresh media such as labels or transparencies) in the paper tray, then click *Resume* (or press the *Resume* button on the printer) to continue printing after you have loaded the paper.

MAGENTA INK CARTRIDGE EMPTY   The ink in the magenta ink cartridge has been used up and the cartridge is empty. The printer will not print until the empty cartridge is replaced.

MAGENTA INK CARTRIDGE EXPIRED   Inks used in an ink-jet printer have a long but finite storage life. When the ink in an ink cartridge has exceeded its expected life span, it can begin to deteriorate (and can eventually damage the printer). This error means the printer's magenta ink cartridge has expired and must be replaced. The printer will not print until the expired ink cartridge has been replaced.

MAGENTA INK CARTRIDGE EXPIRING SOON   The ink used in your ink-jet printer has a long but finite storage life.

This error means the magenta ink cartridge in your printer is nearing its expiration date and will need to be replaced *soon*. Now is the time to purchase a new ink cartridge so that you'll have a replacement cartridge on hand when the ink cartridge expires. You may replace the cartridge now, or wait until it expires completely (see **MAGENTA INK CARTRIDGE EXPIRED**).

MAGENTA INK CARTRIDGE MISSING The printer cannot detect the presence of a magenta ink cartridge. The cartridge is not installed, or the cartridge is not secured in the carriage. The printer will not print until this problem is corrected. If the magenta ink cartridge is missing, you'll need to install a new cartridge. If the magenta ink cartridge is installed, remove it. Align the ink cartridge correctly and reinsert the ink cartridge firmly and completely into the carriage holder. Also make sure that the ink cartridge is the correct type to use with your particular printer (i.e., an HP No.10 Magenta Ink Cartridge for an HP2000C). If the problem persists, the ink cartridge may be defective. Try replacing it with a new one.

MAGENTA INK LOW The magenta ink level is low, and the cartridge will soon be empty. You can continue to print with the printer until the cartridge is empty. Now is the time to purchase a new ink cartridge so that you will have a replacement cartridge on hand when the magenta ink cartridge is empty. You may replace the cartridge now, or wait until it is completely empty (see **MAGENTA INK CARTRIDGE EMPTY**).

MAGENTA PRINT HEAD MISSING The printer is unable to detect the presence of a magenta print head. The printer will not print until it can detect a print head (in each print head slot for color printers). If one or more of the print heads are missing, you'll need to install the correct print head in each empty print head slot. If all four print heads are installed (for color printers), the print head identified as "missing" may have protective tape covering its electrical contacts (preventing the printer from detecting the print head). This is the most common cause of this problem. Check the copper contact area on the print head and remove any tape you find. If all the print heads are installed, remove and reseat the print head that is marked as "missing." Reinsert the suspect print head firmly and completely into the carriage holder. Make sure that the print head is the correct type to use with your particular printer (i.e., an HP No.10 Magenta print head for an HP2000C). If the problem persists, the print head's electrical contacts may be contaminated with ink and debris. Try cleaning the print head contacts, or replace the suspect print head outright.

MAGENTA PRINT HEAD SHOULD BE REPLACED SOON
The magenta print head is nearing the end of its useful life, and will need to be replaced in the very near future. You may begin to notice a decrease in print quality. When the print head reaches the end of its useful life, you will be notified by another message. Now is the time to purchase a new print head so that you'll have a replacement on hand when the print head finally needs replacement. It is not necessary to replace the print head at this time unless you have unacceptable print quality.

NEW INK CARTRIDGE SUCCESSFULLY INSTALLED (BLACK)   This is not an error. This message simply confirms that a new black ink cartridge has been successfully installed and recognized by the printer. Click *OK* to clear the message dialog box and continue.

NEW INK CARTRIDGE SUCCESSFULLY INSTALLED (CYAN)   This is not an error. This message simply confirms that a new cyan ink cartridge has been successfully installed and recognized by the printer. Click *OK* to clear the message dialog box and continue.

NEW INK CARTRIDGE SUCCESSFULLY INSTALLED (MAGENTA)   This is not an error. This message simply confirms that a new magenta ink cartridge has been successfully installed and recognized by the printer. Click *OK* to clear the message dialog box and continue.

NEW INK CARTRIDGE SUCCESSFULLY INSTALLED (YELLOW)   This is not an error. This message simply confirms that a new yellow ink cartridge has been successfully installed and recognized by the printer. Click *OK* to clear the message dialog box and continue.

OUT OF DISK SPACE   The printer software uses an area of the hard disk to temporarily store information while it is processing a document for printing (usually .TMP files). If your hard disk is nearly full, the printer may not have enough disk space to complete the print job. Features such as high printing resolution, "copies," two-sided printing, and "ordered" printing usually demand additional disk space. Start by freeing disk space of unnecessary files (do not remove files if you are unsure of their purpose, or you might eliminate files that a software program needs). Try printing only one page (or copy) at a time, or disable "ordered" or two-sided printing. If you have set up a RAM disk as your temporary directory, you probably have only 1 to 4 megabytes on your RAM disk. Turn off the RAM disk and try printing again. If problems persist, try reducing the printing resolution (or otherwise "simplify" the page).

PAPER JAM   Paper (or other media such as labels or transparencies) has jammed in the printer. The printer will not function until the jam has been cleared. Remove any paper from the supply tray and output tray. Remove all paper supply trays. Locate the media jammed inside the printer, and pull firmly on the jammed media to remove it. Make sure all scraps of media are removed from the paper path, and look for any other obstructions in the paper feed. Replace the paper tray(s) and try the printer again.

If this problem occurs frequently, make sure that no scraps of media remain in the printer from a previous jam. Verify that the media you are using is approved for use in the printer and is fresh (not wrinkled, crimped, or otherwise damaged)—media that is too thin, has a slick texture, or "stretches" easily can feed improperly through the printer. If the problem persists, the paper transport may be damaged and require service.

PAPER JAM (LOWER TRAY)   Paper (or other media such as labels or transparencies) has jammed in the printer's optional accessory ("lower") paper tray. The printer will not function until the jam has been cleared. Remove the optional accessory ("lower") paper tray and set it aside. Remove any paper from the paper feed slot. Remove the paper drawer from the optional Accessory Paper Tray. Remove the jammed media, and make sure that all scraps of paper or other media are removed from the paper path. Reload fresh media into the accessory paper tray, and reinstall the tray into the printer. Try printing again. If the problem persists, the paper transport may be damaged and require service.

PAPER SIZE ERROR   In the "printer properties" of your printing application, you specified a paper size that is too narrow, too wide, too short, or too long for the printer to handle. Click *Cancel* to exit the error dialog. In the *Custom Paper Size* dialog, enter new values for paper width and/or length (as a rule, paper must be between 3″ and 8.5″ wide, and 5″ to 14″ long). Click *OK* to exit the *Custom Paper Size* dialog.

PAPER TOO SHORT   The paper used to print the last page was too short to accommodate the page. Click *OK* to exit from the error dialog. Remove the media in the printer's paper tray and replace it with media long enough to accommodate the page to be printed. Try printing again.

PORT CONFIGURATION   There is a problem with the printer's bidirectional communication with the host computer. Make sure that the printer cable is attached properly, and verify that it is the suitable length and type for IEEE-1284 (ECP/EPP) printing. Check the port configuration in the printer's CMOS Setup and verify that it is in the correct mode (i.e., *bidirectional*, *ECP*, or *EPP*). If the port is in *EPP* mode, try *ECP*. If the port is in *ECP* mode, try *bidirectional*. If the port is in *bidirectional* mode, try ECP. Be sure to save your changes to the CMOS Setup before rebooting the computer.

PRINTER DRIVER BUSY   This message will appear under Windows 3.x when background printing is disabled, and a job is sent to the printer while it is processing another job. Disable your background printing by turning off the print spooling—this forces only one job to be processed at a time. Open the *Print* dialog and click the *Options* button. In the *Options* dialog, check the *Background Printing* checkbox. Click *OK* to return to the *Print* dialog, then click *OK* to print, or click *Close* to exit without printing (but saving the setting you changed).

PRINTER DRIVER PROBLEM   The printer driver cannot find files that it needs in order to support proper printing, and it cannot function without these files. Restart Windows—this may restore the lost or corrupted files in memory. If this error occurs again after Windows has been restarted, reinstall the printer software, or download and install the newest driver software to replace the old driver. If reinstalling the driver does not solve the problem, you must first try removing the existing driver software from the system by using the driver's "uninstaller" program (or the *Add/Remove Programs* wizard).

PRINTER ERROR   The computer is unable to establish two-way communication with the printer. Make sure that the printer is turned on, and see that a known-good printer cable is firmly connected to the printer and computer. In the printer's utility software (if any), select the *Services* or *Diagnostics* tab, and test printer communication through a *test page* or *communication test* (or similar) feature. Try the printer on another PC. If the printer continues to fail on other PCs, the printer's main controller board may need to be replaced.

PRINTER NOT RESPONDING   When the printer driver sends data to the printer, it is generally able to detect if the printer is accepting those data (even if there is only one-way communication from computer to printer). This type of error dialog is displayed if the driver software does *not* detect that the printer is accepting the data. The printer might be paused. Try pressing the printer's *Pause/Cancel Print* button or the *Resume* button to resume printing; otherwise, check the printer for any kind of paper jam. Make sure that a known-good printer cable is firmly connected to both the printer and computer.

PRINTER OUT OF PAPER   The paper tray is out of paper (or other media such as labels or transparencies). Load fresh media in the appropriate tray and try printing again (you may need to click *Resume* or press the *Resume* button on the printer to continue printing).

PRINTER OUT OF PAPER (NETWORK)   The network printer's paper tray is out of paper (or other media such as labels or transparencies). Load fresh media in the appropriate tray and try printing again (you may need to click *Resume* or press the *Resume* button on the printer to continue printing).

PRINTER PORT PROBLEM   The printer's driver software cannot access the I/O port to which the printer is connected (i.e., LPT1). Another program might be printing to the same printer port. Click *Cancel* and wait for the other software program to complete its printing, then try printing your document again. If you have another device (such as a tape backup unit or another computer system) attached to the same port, that device might be using the port. Click *Cancel* and wait until the other device has finished using the port, then try printing your document again. Make sure your printer is connected to the correct port. Open the `Printers` folder and select your printer, then select *Properties* on the *File* menu. Click the *Details* tab (Windows 95) or the *Ports* tab (Windows NT 4.0), and select the correct port from the *Printer Port* list. Now restart your computer and printer, and try the print job again. If the document still will not print, try reinstalling/updating the printer driver software that came with your printer.

PRINTER READY FOR MANUAL PAPER FEED This message indicates that the printer is waiting for you to click *Resume* (or press the *Resume* button on the printer) before it can pick up the next sheet of media. This occurs when you send a print job to the printer and select *Manual Feed* as the paper source. Make sure that an ample supply of fresh paper or other media is installed in the appropriate paper tray. Click *Resume* in the *Printer Ready for Manual Paper Feed* dialog (or press the *Resume* button on the printer) to print the first page. You will need to click *Resume* in the dialog (or press the *Resume* button on the printer) for each page of the document to be printed. After the printing job is finished, disable the *Manual Feed* option before starting any subsequent print jobs.

PRINTER READY FOR MANUAL PAPER FEED (NETWORK) This message indicates that the network printer is waiting for you to click *Resume* (or press the *Resume* button on the printer) before it can pick up the next sheet of media. This occurs when you send a print job to the network printer and select *Manual Feed* as the paper source. Make sure that an ample supply of fresh paper or other media is installed in the appropriate paper tray. Click *Resume* in the *Printer Ready for Manual Paper Feed* dialog (or press the *Resume* button on the printer) to print the first page. You will need to click *Resume* in the dialog (or press the *Resume* button on the printer) for each page of the document to be printed. After the printing job is finished, disable the *Manual Feed* option before starting any subsequent print jobs.

PRINTER TURNED OFF INCORRECTLY The last time the printer was powered off, power to the printer was interrupted externally (i.e., the power cord was unplugged, or a power strip was turned off) rather than by using the *Power* button. Interrupting power to the printer without first using the *Power* button can shorten the life of the print heads. Always power off the printer by using its *Power* button—

never disconnect the printer from its ac outlet first. If your print quality has deteriorated since the last time you used the printer, you might need to clean the print heads.

PRINT HEAD COVER OPEN   The protective cover around the print head(s) is open, and the printer will not function until the cover is secured. Open the ink cartridge door, lift the print head access cover, and remove the ink cartridge door and print head access cover assembly from the printer. Position the print head access cover over the printer. Rest the tabs on the back edge of the cover on either side of the tab on the back of the printer. Gently lower the print head access cover until it snaps into place, and then close the ink cartridge door. The *Print Head Access Cover Open* error dialog should disappear.

PRINT HEAD LATCH OPEN   The print head latch (which secures the print heads in position in the print head carriage) is not properly closed. The printer will not function until the print head latch is properly closed. Open the ink cartridge door, lift the print head access cover, and remove the ink cartridge door and print head access cover assembly from the printer.

If the print head latch is lying on top of the print heads, fold the latch forward over the ink cartridges until the hook on the latch engages the carriage lock, then fold the latch back until it lies flat on top of the print head area.

If the print head latch is lying on the ink cartridges, lift the front edge of the latch until the hook on the latch engages the carriage lock, then make sure the hook on the latch is secured inside the carriage lock. Fold the latch back until it lies flat on top of the print head area.

Position the print head access cover over the printer. Rest the mating tabs on the back edge of the cover on either side of the tab on the back of the printer. Lower the print head access cover until it snaps into place, and then close the ink cartridge door. The *Print Head Latch Not Properly Closed* dialog should disappear.

PRINT HEAD MOVEMENT OBSTRUCTED   Mechanical damage or some foreign object is obstructing the movement of the print head carriage. The printer cannot function until the obstruction is removed. Check under the print head access cover for a paper jam or other physical obstruction. Open the ink cartridge door and lift the print head access cover. Remove the ink cartridge door and print head access cover assembly. Visually check the inside of the printer for a paper jam or other obstruction. Clear the paper jam or remove any object that may be blocking the normal movement of the print head carriage.

REPLACE BLACK INK CARTRIDGE   The black ink cartridge has failed, and the printer will not function until the black ink cartridge has been replaced with another appropriate black ink cartridge. Once the cartridge is replaced, click *Cancel* to exit from the error message dialog.

REPLACE BLACK PRINT HEAD   The black print head has failed, and the printer will not function until the black print head has been replaced with another appropriate print head. Once the print head is replaced, click *Cancel* to exit from the error message dialog.

REPLACE CYAN INK CARTRIDGE   The cyan ink cartridge has failed, and the printer will not function until the cyan ink cartridge has been replaced with another appropriate cyan ink cartridge. Once the cartridge is replaced, click *Cancel* to exit from the error message dialog.

REPLACE CYAN PRINT HEAD   The cyan print head has failed, and the printer will not function until the cyan print head has been replaced with another appropriate print head. Once the print head is replaced, click *Cancel* to exit from the error message dialog.

REPLACE MAGENTA INK CARTRIDGE   The magenta ink cartridge has failed, and the printer will not function until the magenta ink cartridge has been replaced with another appropriate magenta ink cartridge. Once the cartridge is replaced, click *Cancel* to exit from the error message dialog.

REPLACE MAGENTA PRINT HEAD   The magenta print head has failed, and the printer will not function until the magenta print head has been replaced with another appropriate print head. Once the print head is replaced, click *Cancel* to exit from the error message dialog.

REPLACE YELLOW INK CARTRIDGE   The yellow ink cartridge has failed, and the printer will not function until the yellow ink cartridge has been replaced with another appropriate yellow ink cartridge. Once the cartridge is replaced, click *Cancel* to exit from the error message dialog.

REPLACE YELLOW PRINT HEAD   The yellow print head has failed, and the printer will not function until the yellow print head has been replaced with another appropriate print head. Once the print head is replaced, click *Cancel* to exit from the error message dialog.

SOFTWARE ERROR   One or more printer software files are missing or corrupt. Click *Cancel* to stop the print job and exit from the error message dialog, then reinstall the latest version of the printer driver software that came with the printer.

SPOOLING ERROR   This message indicates a problem with the print spooler. The print spooler manages multiple print jobs and puts all of the print jobs in a queue so that each is processed by the printer in turn. Turn off the print spooling. For Windows 95, click *Start*, select *Settings*, and click *Printers*. Right-click the printer and select *Properties*. In the printer's *Properties* dialog, click the *Details* tab, and then click *Spool Settings*. In the *Spool Settings* dialog, select *Print directly to the printer*, then click *OK*. After spooling is turned off, print jobs will be sent directly to the printer without spooling. This means that only one print job can be processed at a time. If you attempt to send another job while one is printing, the computer will display an error message and the job will not be accepted.

THE PRINTER IS PAUSED   The *Pause/Cancel* button has been pressed. Simply press *Resume* or press the *Pause/Cancel* button again to resume printing. Click *Cancel Print* to cancel the print job.

THE PRINTER IS PAUSED (NETWORK)   The network printer's *Pause/Cancel* button has been pressed. Simply press *Resume* or press the *Pause/Cancel* button again to resume printing on the network printer. Click *Cancel Print* to cancel the print job.

UNKNOWN INK CARTRIDGE (BLACK)   A black ink cartridge has been installed that is not recognized by the printer. The printer may not function until an acceptable ink cartridge is installed. Also, some ink-related functions (i.e., monitoring of the ink level) may not work correctly until a suitable cartridge is installed.

UNKNOWN INK CARTRIDGE (CYAN)   A cyan ink cartridge has been installed that is not recognized by the printer. The printer may not function until an acceptable ink cartridge is installed. Also, some ink-related functions (i.e., monitoring of the ink level) may not work correctly until a suitable cartridge is installed.

UNKNOWN INK CARTRIDGE (MAGENTA) A magenta ink cartridge has been installed that is not recognized by the printer. The printer may not function until an acceptable ink cartridge is installed. Also, some ink-related functions (i.e., monitoring of the ink level) may not work correctly until a suitable cartridge is installed.

UNKNOWN INK CARTRIDGE (YELLOW) A yellow ink cartridge has been installed that is not recognized by the printer. The printer may not function until an acceptable ink cartridge is installed. Also, some ink-related functions (i.e., monitoring of the ink level) may not work correctly until a suitable cartridge is installed.

UPPER TRAY OUT The printer's upper paper tray is out of paper. Load the appropriate paper (or other fresh media such as labels or transparencies) in the paper tray, then click *Resume* (or press the *Resume* button on the printer) to continue printing after you have loaded the paper.

UPPER TRAY OUT (NETWORK) The network printer's upper paper tray is out of paper. Load the appropriate paper (or other fresh media such as labels or transparencies) in the paper tray, then click *Resume* (or press the *Resume* button on the printer) to continue printing after you have loaded the paper.

YELLOW INK CARTRIDGE EMPTY The ink in the yellow ink cartridge has been used up and the cartridge is empty. The printer will not print until the empty cartridge is replaced.

YELLOW INK CARTRIDGE EXPIRED Inks used in an ink-jet printer have a long but finite storage life. When the ink in an ink cartridge has exceeded its expected life span, it can begin to deteriorate (and can eventually damage the printer). This error means the printer's yellow ink cartridge has expired and must be replaced. The printer will not print until the expired ink cartridge has been replaced.

YELLOW INK CARTRIDGE EXPIRING SOON The ink used in your ink jet printer has a long but finite storage life. This error means the yellow ink cartridge in your printer is nearing its expiration date and will need to be replaced *soon*. Now is the time to purchase a new ink cartridge so that you'll have a replacement cartridge on hand when the ink cartridge expires. You may replace the cartridge now, or wait until it expires completely (see **YELLOW INK CARTRIDGE EXPIRED**).

YELLOW INK CARTRIDGE MISSING The printer cannot detect the presence of a yellow ink cartridge. The cartridge is not installed, or the cartridge is not secured in the carriage. The printer will not print until this problem is corrected. If the yellow ink cartridge is missing, you'll need to install a new cartridge. If the yellow ink cartridge is installed, remove it. Align the ink cartridge correctly and reinsert the ink cartridge firmly and completely into the carriage holder. Also make sure that the ink cartridge is the correct type to use with your particular printer (i.e., an HP No.10 Yellow Ink Cartridge for an HP2000C). If the problem persists, the ink cartridge may be defective. Try replacing it with a new one.

YELLOW INK LOW The yellow ink level is low, and the cartridge will soon be empty. You can continue to print with the printer until the cartridge is empty. Now is the time to purchase a new ink cartridge so that you will have a replacement cartridge on hand when the yellow ink cartridge is empty. You may replace the cartridge now, or wait until it is completely empty (see **YELLOW INK CARTRIDGE EMPTY**).

YELLOW PRINT HEAD MISSING The printer is unable to detect the presence of a yellow print head. The printer will not print until it can detect a print head (in each print head slot for color printers). If one or more of the print heads is missing, you'll need to install the correct print head in each empty print head slot. If all four print heads are installed (for color printers), the print head identified as "missing" may have protective tape covering its electrical contacts (preventing the printer from detecting the print head). This is the most common cause of this problem. Check the copper contact area on the print head and remove any tape you find. If all the print heads are installed, remove and reseat the print head that is marked as "missing." Reinsert the suspect print head firmly and completely into the carriage holder. Make sure that the print head is the correct type to use with your particular printer (i.e., an HP No.10 Yellow print head for an HP2000C). If the problem persists, the print head's electrical contacts may be contaminated with ink and debris. Try cleaning the print head contacts, or replace the suspect print head outright.

YELLOW PRINT HEAD SHOULD BE REPLACED SOON The yellow print head is nearing the end of its useful life, and will need to be replaced in the very near future. You may begin to notice a decrease in print quality. When the print head reaches the end of its useful life, you will be notified by another message. Now is the time to purchase a new print head so that you'll have a replacement on hand when the print head finally needs replacement. It is not necessary to replace the print head at this time unless you have unacceptable print quality.

Printer
Manufacturers
Online

Alps Electric Inc.	*www.alpsusa.com*
Apple	*www.apple.com*
Brother	*www.brother.com*
C. Itoh	*www.citoh.com*
CalComp	*www.calcomp.com*
Canon	*www.usa.canon.com*
Casio	*www.casio-usa.com*
Citizen America	*www.citizen-america.com*
CoStar	*www.costar.com*
Dataproducts	*www.dataproducts.com*
Digital (DEC)	*www.digital.com*
Eastman Kodak	*www.kodak.com*
Epson	*www.epson.com*
Fargo	*www.fargo.com*
Fujitsu	*www.fujitsu.com*
Ganson Engineering	*www.ganson.com*

Genicom	www.genicom.com
Hewlett-Packard	www.hp.com
IBM	www.ibm.com
JetFax	www.jetfax.com
Konica	www.konica.com
Kyocera	www.kyocera.com
LaserMaster	www.lasermaster.com
Lexmark	www.lexmark.com
Mannesmann Tally	www.tally.com
Mita	www.mita.com
NEC	www.nec.com
Okidata	www.okidata.com
Olivetti	www.olivettipc.com
Panasonic	www.panasonic.com
Printronix	www.printronix.com
QMS	www.qms.com
Radio Shack	www.radioshack.com
Ricoh	www.ricoh.com
Samsung	www.sosimple.com
Seikosha	www.seikosha.com
ServiceWorks	www.serviceworks.com
Sharp	www.sharp-usa.com
Star Micronics	www.starmicronics.com
Sun Microsystems	www.sun.com
Talaris	www.talaris.com
Tandy Corporation	www.tandy.com
Tektronix	www.tektronix.com
Texas Instruments	www.ti.com
Toshiba	www.toshiba.com
Unisys	www.unisys.com
Verifone	www.verifone.com
Westrex International	www.westrex.com
Xante Corporation	www.xante.com
Xerox	www.xerox.com

Printer Glossary

10-Base-T An alternative term for "twisted-pair" network connections.

A3, A4, A5 paper Standard European paper sizes; A3 measures 297 × 420 mm, A4 measures 210 × 297 mm, and A5 measures 148 × 210 mm.

Adobe PostScript A page description language (PDL) developed by Adobe Systems Incorporated, and used on many high-end graphics-intensive laser printers.

Adobe Type 1 Font A font definition format for "outline fonts" developed by Adobe for use with PostScript printers. Type 1 fonts include a "hinting" technique that helps in the aesthetic reproduction of fonts at small sizes to overcome restrictions imposed by low-resolution printers.

Adobe Type 3 Font A font definition format for "outline fonts" developed by Adobe for use with PostScript printers. Type 3 fonts do not use the "hinting" technique employed by Type 1 fonts, but they are easier to reproduce.

Adobe Type Manager (ATM) A font management utility that converts Adobe Type 1 and Type 3 fonts to bitmaps for printing or display on a monitor. ATM is available as a Windows program to support the display of PostScript fonts by Windows programs, and is built-in to some other graphical user interfaces.

American Standard for Computer Information Interchange (ASCII) ASCII defines a number of character set codes that can be selected to represent different languages. ASCII encoding is used on most computers other than IBM mainframe and minicomputers that have their own character set encoding (EBCDIC).

AppleTalk A network protocol used by Apple Macintosh computers, normally used in conjunction with *LocalTalk*, Apple's proprietary network topology.

AUI A type of connector used in standard "thick" Ethernet installations to connect devices to the network. An AUI connector is a 15-pin D-type plug.

Average Monthly Print Volume (AMPV) A method of expressing the monthly volume of intended printer usage.

B4 paper A rarely used European paper size measuring 250×353 mm.

bitmap font A font in which each character is stored as an array of dots, the pattern of which forms a letter or symbol.

Bi-Tronics A fast bidirectional parallel communications interface developed by Hewlett-Packard, which is backward-compatible with the Centronics parallel interface.

BNC A bayonet-style coaxial connector normally used to connect devices to "thin" Ethernet networks.

built-in font See **resident font**.

bus and tag connection The connection scheme normally used to connect devices to the IBM 370 Channel interface on IBM mainframes.

cache RAM used as a temporary holding place to allow fast access to temporary data. In printers, cache memory primarily refers to the font cache, where bitmaps generated from outline fonts are kept ready for use.

cartridge A generic term that may refer to a ROM cartridge, font cartridge, emulation cartridge, toner cartridge, toner/developer cartridge, or print cartridge.

Centronics A parallel communications interface designed by the Centronics Corporation for use with printers, and adopted as the de facto standard for parallel communications between computers and printers.

channel interface   An abbreviation for the IBM 370 Channel interface used by IBM mainframes for the connection of peripherals.

character   An individual letter, number, or other symbol in a given font.

character attributes   A name applied to a font's typestyle, commonly used to refer to bold, italic, underline, and other typestyle qualifiers used with a typeface.

charge roller   A roller in a laser printer that imparts an electrostatic charge to an EP drum surface. Charge rollers are used in some small printers in place of coronas to reduce ozone emissions.

client/server   A generic term for a network topology where the network has two types of computers attached: those that access the network (clients), and those that provide facilities to network users (servers).

communication interface   A mechanism through which data may be transmitted or received by a computer, printer, or other computing device. Communications interfaces normally fall into three categories: serial, parallel, and network interfaces.

consumable   Any replaceable component of a printer, such as the toner, paper, ink cartridge, ribbon, and so on.

contour font   Another name for an *outline font*.

control panel   The panel on the front of a printer that allows you to configure a printer by selecting which emulation is used, which communications port to use, and so on. The control panel normally includes a status display that presents configuration menu options and printer operation status messages.

controller   A printer controller circuit—the dedicated "computer" in a printer that receives the image to be printed and operates the printer's mechanisms to produce the image.

corona   A wire in the printer mechanism that carries a very high voltage used to generate an electrostatic charge on a nearby surface (i.e., the EP drum or paper). There are two coronas in most "SX-type" printers. The high voltage carried by coronas will ionize the air surrounding the corona and generate ozone gas.

coverage   This normally refers to the amount of the paper that is covered with toner. A typical page of text will have a coverage of 4 to 5 percent, whereas a complex graphic may approach 90 percent coverage.

Customer Replaceable Unit (CRU)   Another term for a *consumable*.

Cyan, Magenta, Yellow, Black (CMYK)   A color encoding method frequently used on color printers, where a color other than black is defined by the proportions of cyan, magenta, and yellow required to reproduce the given color. Black is provided separately to ensure proper "blackness."

Dataproducts   A parallel communications interface designed by the Dataproducts Corporation for use with printers, and used by some minicomputers for parallel connection to printers. The Dataproducts interface is generally *not* compatible with ordinary Centronics interfaces.

developer   The mechanism and magnetic powder (toner) used to transfer toner from the toner cartridge onto the EP drum.

dot   A single point written by a laser (or a single point in a bitmap).

download   The process of transferring data from a computer to a printer.

downloaded font   A font that is stored in a computer, then sent to the printer over the communications interface as required. Normally, downloaded fonts are held in the printer's RAM, and are lost when the printer is switched off.

drum   The photosensitive cylinder that receives the latent image from the writing mechanism (also called an *EP drum*).

duplex   Double-sided; a sheet of paper on which *both* sides are printed.

edge enhancement   A generic term for the "edge-smoothing" technique that reduces the jagged appearance of angled lines on laser printers (i.e., HP's Resolution Enhancement Technology).

emulation A generic term for a "printer language"—most printers mimic or "emulate" the behavior of the market-leading models (such as HP or Epson printers) by copying their printer language.

engine A generic term for a laser printer's image formation system—the mechanism that "writes" a bitmap onto the EP drum, then transfers the latent image to paper.

escape code A special control character (number "27" decimal or "1Bh") used to set the printer into a special operating mode for changing print characteristics such as "bold" or "underline." Normally, the escape code is used to signify that what follows is a command rather than data.

escape sequence A sequence of characters that form a printer command preceded by the "escape code" and ended with a termination character.

Ethernet A popular physical connection scheme for connecting groups of computers together in a network. Ethernet can be used to form client/server or peer-to-peer networks.

"Eurolegal" paper A European paper size measuring 8.5″ × 13″. "Eurolegal" paper is supported by few laser printer manufacturers.

Extended Binary-Coded Decimal Interchange Code (EBCDIC) EBCDIC defines the character set encoding used by most IBM mainframes and minicomputers. The majority of non-IBM computers and personal computers use ASCII.

face-down An output tray configuration where pages are delivered with the readable side facing *down*. As each sheet is placed on top of the last, multipage documents delivered to a face-down tray are normally in the correct page order.

face-up An output tray configuration where pages are delivered with the readable side *up*. As each sheet is placed on top of the last, multipage documents delivered to a face-up tray are normally in *reverse* page order.

firmware Software that is stored in ROM chips. In printers, the firmware is normally the software permanently stored in the printer controller unit (CPU).

first print out time The time taken between the printer receiving data for the first page of a print job, and delivering the page to the output tray. Most printers do not start printing immediately (they need a few seconds in which to assimilate the data, set up the page formatting, and start the motors that drive the paper path).

flash memory A type of EPROM that can be erased and reprogrammed electronically, and is well suited for permanent storage of downloaded fonts and other printer characteristics.

font A collection of characters provided in a particular typeface, style, and character set. A "bitmap" font is normally also defined by size and orientation.

font cache An area of RAM in the printer that is used for the temporary storage of bitmap fonts that have either been downloaded from the PC or retrieved from a font cartridge.

font cartridge A ROM cartridge containing either bitmap or outline printer fonts.

fuser The mechanism in a laser printer that bonds toner to the paper. Most fusers use hot rollers and fuse the toner into the paper using heat and pressure (a few printer designs use radiant fusers that fuse using infrared heat alone).

fuser oil A temperature-resistant oil used on fuser rollers to prevent toner from adhering to the surface. On small printers, the fuser oil is normally contained in the fuser "cleaning pad."

grammes per square metre (gsm) The standard European measurement of paper weight.

Graphical Device Interface (GDI) A term normally used to refer to the software technique used by Windows to exchange information (which must be displayed or printed) between the Windows environment and applications.

gray scale A technique where shades of gray are simulated using patterns of black and white dots. Denser concentrations of dots result in darker shades of gray.

Hewlett-Packard Graphics Language (HPGL) A vector graphics language used by HP plotters, and commonly supported by CAD software. Some laser printers emulate HPGL to allow their use with CAD packages.

Hewlett-Packard Interface Bus (HP-IB) A parallel communications mechanism used primarily for the connection of scientific and engineering instruments and computers, but also provided on a few printers.

Hewlett-Packard Printer Control Language (HP PCL) The most popular and widely emulated "escape code" printer language. PCL is available in several variants (including PCL 3, 4, and 5).

host computer The PC to which the printer is attached.

images per minute (ipm) A measure of printer speed, where each sheet of paper has more than one image (as in duplex printing). This is also known as *impressions per minute*.

input tray Another term for *paper tray*.

Intellifont A font definition format for outline fonts developed by Compugraphic for use with laser printers. Intellifont outline fonts are used by HP PCL 5 printers and many PCL 5 emulations.

job separator A "cover sheet" produced by some workgroup printers before each print job to identify who sent the print job.

landscape Refers to the orientation of a page. A page is said to have "landscape" orientation when the image runs along the long edge of the paper.

ledger paper A standard North American paper size measuring 11″ × 17″.

legal paper A standard North American paper size measuring 8½″ × 14″.

letter paper A standard North American paper size measuring 8½″ × 11″.

Light Emitting Diode (LED) A solid-state electronic component that emits light.

Local Area Network (LAN) A method of interconnecting groups of computers, allowing them to share resources such as disk storage and printers.

LocalTalk The physical wiring and connection mechanism used in AppleTalk networks.

logo   A graphic image (such as a company logo or special symbol) that can be stored as a character in a special font for use with laser printers.

media   Anything that a laser printer can print on (i.e., paper, card stock, transparencies, and labels).

memory   Solid-state data storage space (typically RAM). The larger the amount of memory in a printer, the more data the printer can hold, and generally the more complex its images can be.

network interface   A mechanism that allows a printer to be connected directly to a LAN—normally in the form of a card that plugs into the printer controller—but is also available as an external box, called a *print server*.

network printer   A printer that is designed to connect to a network and be used by groups of users, a subclass of workgroup printers.

network protocol   The software mechanisms that pass data between computers (and between computers and printers) on a LAN.

network topology   The manner and design in which computers are connected to a network. The topology describes both the physical connection mechanism (such as Ethernet) and the network type (such as client/server).

office printer   A printer that is designed for general purpose office use, and may be used by an individual user or shared by a small group of users.

offset mechanism   A mechanism in the output tray of some workgroup and production printers that pushes alternate jobs sideways in the output stack, thereby separating one job from another.

outline font   A font in which each character is represented by sets of equations or vectors that define the outline of the character. An outline font cannot be printed "as is," but must first be scaled to the appropriate size and "filled" with dots to make a bitmap. Since outline fonts can be scaled, they may be used to create characters of any size, and may be rotated to any angle.

output tray   A shelf or tray on the outside of the printer that receives and collects the printed pages.

ozone   A unstable corrosive gas (O^3) produced by the ionization of air that occurs around corona wires.

ozone filter   A carbon filter (normally a mesh) that ozone gas oxidizes, thus reducing the ozone back to oxygen.

Page Description Language (PDL)   A programming language used to describe a page in terms of the text, graphics, and effects that may be applied to them.

pages per minute (ppm)   The standard measure of throughput (or speed) for a printer. PPM is an adequate measure for simplex (single-sided) printers, but the throughput measure for duplex printers is more appropriately expressed in images per minute (ipm).

paper feed   The part of a printer that feeds sheets of paper from a stack into the printing mechanism. Normally the paper feeder feeds from a paper tray, but some designs of paper feeder do not use a tray.

paper path   The path a sheet of paper takes as it moves through the printer from the paper feed to the output tray.

paper tray   A cassette that holds a particular size of paper and inserts into the paper feeder. Some cassettes are adjustable for several sizes of paper, and some paper feeders provide adjustable paper guides eliminating the need for a paper tray.

parallel interface   A parallel communication standard used to transfer data from a computer to a printer. Most parallel interfaces are 8 bits wide, and transfer one byte at a time. However, a few are 16 bits wide, transferring two bytes at a time.

peer-to-peer   A network topology in which all computers on the network are able to access each other's resources, as opposed to client/server networks where clients access common resources provided by servers.

personal printer   Generally, a small laser printer (typically producing 4 to 5 ppm), which is physically compact to fit easily on a desk, and inexpensive enough to justify ownership by an individual rather than a business.

port   An abbreviation of *communications port*, an alternate term for a communications interface.

portrait   Refers to the orientation of a page. A page is said to have "portrait" orientation when the image runs along the short edge of the paper.

print cartridge   A printer consumable that normally contains all the major replaceable elements in a laser printer such as toner and the EP drum.

print drum   The photosensitive drum that receives the latent image drawn by the writing mechanism, and transfers the latent image to the paper.

print job   Any group of pages that are to be printed together.

print server   A device used to connect a stand-alone printer to a LAN.

Printer Command Language (PCL)   Normally referring to the Hewlett-Packard Printer Command Language (HP PCL), but most manufacturers emulating HP PCL leave out the "HP."

printer controller   The "dedicated computer" in a printer that receives data to be printed from a computer (along with commands defining how the data should be formatted), and uses this data to create a bitmap describing the image on the paper.

printer driver   A software utility that (1) enables the application to determine the commands required by the printer to format data for printing, and (2) provides the application with information about the facilities provided by the printer.

printer font   Any font that is designed for use on a printer.

production printer   A large heavy-duty printer designed for almost continuous printing in a production environment, either for large quantities of small documents such as invoices and account statements, or for small quantities of large documents such as reports, short-run books, newsletters, and so on.

rasterization   The process of converting data and commands received from a computer into a bitmap containing an image to be printed.

Read-Only Memory (ROM)   A type of memory used in computers and printers that may be read but may not be written to. A ROM retains its contents indefinitely (even when power is off).

Red, Green, Blue (RGB)   A color encoding method normally used on computer displays in which each color to be displayed is described in the proportions of Red, Green, and Blue.

resident font   Any font that is built-in to a printer by the manufacturer as one of the standard features offered by that printer.

resolution   The number of individual dots a printer can print in a given area, normally expressed as dots per inch (dpi).

RJ45   A connector commonly used with twisted-pair networks—an RJ45 plug is very similar in appearance to a telephone plug.

ROM cartridge   A small case containing a printed circuit board on which several ROM chips are mounted, and which can be inserted into a special slot in a printer. The ROM chips are normally used to hold fonts or printer language emulations.

RS-232C   A common serial communication method supported by most IBM-compatible computers and printers.

RS-422   A serial communications method that offers higher performance than RS232C, but is not commonly used.

scalable font   A font that can be scaled to any size. This is also referred to as an *outline font*.

screen font   A font that is designed for display on a computer screen.

serial interface   A communication technique used to transfer data from a computer to a printer, one bit at a time. Serial communication is much slower than parallel communication, but may be used to transfer data over long distances and requires fewer wires. See RS-232C.

simplex   Single-sided printing where one side of a sheet of paper is printed on, and the other side is not.

soft font   Another term for *downloaded font*.

software driver   A generic term for a software utility used to interface hardware to the operating system.

speed   The throughput of a laser printer measured in pages per minute (ppm) or images per minute (ipm).

stacker   A paper output tray—normally a high-capacity output tray that incorporates a motorized elevator that lowers the height of the output paper stack to allow more paper to be added to the top of the stack.

status message   A message displayed on the printer's control panel to indicate its status, indicate an error condition, or highlight the need for more toner or paper.

throughput   The productivity of a printer, usually measured as pages per minute (ppm).

toner   A fine, colored powder (usually black) that is used to form an image on a sheet of paper.

toner cartridge   A cartridge or cassette that holds toner for easy loading into a printer.

TrueType   A font definition format for outline fonts used by Windows for the creation of screen fonts and downloaded fonts.

twisted pair   A low-cost connection method for creating Local Area Networks, often used to distribute connections from a multiple connection point (a "hub") on an Ethernet network.

Type 1 font   An abbreviation of "Adobe Type 1 font," generally used by other font suppliers when supplying fonts in Adobe Type 1 format.

Type 3 font   An abbreviation of "Adobe Type 3 font," generally used by other font suppliers when supplying fonts in Adobe Type 3 format.

typeface   The visual design of a set of characters or a font.

typestyle   A modifier used to vary the appearance of a typeface without changing its basic shape (i.e., such as **bold** or *italic*).

vector graphics   A method of describing lines and curves as mathematical equations (or "vectors"), which result in very precise printed graphics.

warm-up time   The time taken for a printer to achieve a "ready" status after powering it up. The warm-up time is normally dictated by the time taken to heat up the fuser to its operating temperature.

workgroup printer A medium-sized laser printer designed to handle the printing requirements of several users, normally attached to a LAN or multiuser computer.

Index

About the Author

Stephen J. Bigelow is the founder and president of Dynamic Learning Systems, a technical writing, research, and publishing company specializing in electronic and PC service topics. He is the author of more than 14 feature-length books for TAB/McGraw-Hill and over 100 major articles for mainstream electronics magazines such as *Popular Electronics, Electronics NOW, Circuit Cellar INK,* and *Electronic Service & Technology.* He is also host of the "DLS Video Lecture Series," and editor and publisher of *The PC Toolbox*—a premier PC service newsletter for computer enthusiasts and technicians. You can contact the author at:

Stephen J. Bigelow
Dynamic Learning Systems
PO Box 282
Jefferson, MA 01522-0282 USA
http://www.dispubls.com
sbigelow@cerfnet.com